W9-AEC-112

7.60 (Title II) ERS 9-66 (Sweeningen)

SCHOOL OF
ORIENTAL AND AFRICAN STUDIES
UNIVERSITY OF LONDON

Historical Writing on the Peoples of Asia

HISTORIANS OF SOUTH EAST ASIA

Edited by

D. G. E. HALL

Professor Emeritus of the
History of South East Asia
University of London

LONDON
OXFORD UNIVERSITY PRESS
NEW YORK   TORONTO

Oxford University Press, Amen House, London E.C.4

GLASGOW NEW YORK TORONTO MELBOURNE WELLINGTON
BOMBAY CALCUTTA MADRAS KARACHI LAHORE DACCA
CAPE TOWN SALISBURY NAIROBI IBADAN ACCRA
KUALA LUMPUR HONG KONG

First published 1961
Reprinted 1962 *and* 1963

SET IN GREAT BRITAIN BY
WESTERN PRINTING SERVICES LTD, BRISTOL
AND REPRINTED LITHOGRAPHICALLY BY
JARROLD AND SONS LTD, NORWICH

PREFACE

Between the years 1956 and 1958 the School of Oriental and African Studies, University of London, held a series of study conferences to survey and evaluate the course and character of historical writing on the peoples of Asia. The subject is large and to bring it down to manageable parts the method of analysis by region was adopted; and South Asia, South East Asia, the Near, Middle, and Far East were in turn examined. In historical depth the survey of each region extended from the period of the early empires and literatures, through the age of Western dominance and the freedom movements down to the present day. Writings in both Western and Asian literatures were analysed.

The conferences brought together the leading authorities in these studies from Asia and the West and had the effect of making them more keenly aware not only of the underlying assumptions, predilections and prejudices of past writers but also of their own standpoints as historians. These investigations, which are continuing, have an enhanced value because they are taking place at a time when historians are seeking to rewrite Asian history and the peoples of Asia and the West are adjusting their relationships.

In preparing for each conference the same methods were used. Seminar groups, including a judicious balance of mature scholars and younger historians in training from Asian and Western countries, were established to analyse in detail the papers which had been prepared according to an agreed, comprehensive plan by the prospective members of the forthcoming conference. The business of the conferences therefore consisted not in reading papers but in attempting to solve the problems thrown up by the seminars.

Believing that these conferences have made a contribution to 'the wellbeing of mankind' I wish to affirm my deep appreciation of the Rockefeller Foundation, which met the major part of the financial costs, and also of the farsightedness and support of its officers, who contributed substantially to the effectiveness of the work done.

In the view that the papers which were submitted to the conferences possess an intrinsic and comparative value the School of Oriental and African Studies has generously provided funds for their publication and, suitably edited and introduced, they will appear under the following editors:

Professor W. G. Beasley and Professor E. G. Pulleyblank: China and Japan.

Professor D. G. E. Hall: South East Asia.

Professor B. Lewis and Dr. P. M. Holt: the Near and Middle East.

Professor C. H. Philips: India, Pakistan, and Ceylon.

School of Oriental and   C. H. PHILIPS
African Studies

CONTENTS

INTRODUCTION

South East Asia is so far-flung, and contains so many peoples with their own historical traditions and literatures, that it was impossible to attempt an exhaustive survey of the whole field in the first Conference of its kind ever to be assembled. For notwithstanding the remarkable achievements that have been made, particularly during the present century, the gaps and deficiencies in the study of this field of history are too great, and the number of workers of adequate academic standing far too few, for adequate treatment of the subject. Thus in the present collection of papers nothing like enough attention is given either to the immense body of indigenous writings that is known to exist, or to the pioneer labours of scholars, both European and Asian, upon either the rich harvest of epigraphical remains so far yielded by our area, or the Chinese sources, which are of such vital importance to the elucidation of the problems of its earlier history.

Regarding the workers themselves the achievement of independence, particularly by Burma, Indonesia, and the states of the former French Indo-China, has naturally resulted in a marked decline in the recruitment of young European scholars to fill the places of the older generation which gained its inspiration and received its training in the service of one or other colonial power. A new generation of Asian scholars will one day take its place, but not for some time to come; for it has regretfully to be stated that at present far too few South East Asian scholars of academic distinction are at work in the field, notwithstanding the efforts that the new states are making to rewrite their own histories. For one thing the universities of South East Asia are nearly all of very recent foundation, the academic life of those in existence before World War II was completely disrupted by the Japanese occupation, and, with independence coming so soon afterwards, the main task of universities in the post-war period has been to provide the administrators, doctors, technicians, and teachers that are urgently needed by the new states. There have been no spare energies for research work, and little inducement for graduates of the highest intellectual equipment to undertake it, since other walks of life have offered greater attractions in the way of promotion, remuneration, and status. This helps also to explain the little progress so far made by the post-war states with their plans for producing new histories.

Nevertheless, even allowing for deficiencies and shortcomings, the extent of the field actually surveyed in this volume is enormous, both in scope and in depth, and the impression to be gained from the papers collected here is of a rich legacy of writings from the past, as well as of the strong vitality

of South East Asian historical studies today, notwithstanding the revolutionary political changes that have taken place in the area. For we must
not blind ourselves to the fact that the immense advances in both historical
knowledge and interpretation, described and analysed in the present
volume, are very largely the product of the West's contacts with South East
Asia. Through these contacts western scholars became interested in South
East Asian history, and South East Asians developed an awareness of their
own history that they had never before experienced. It was a complex
business. The western history teacher—usually through the medium of
western history—gave to his Asian pupils not so much a new notion of
history as indeed their first real notions of history. It is a significant fact
that none of the languages of South East Asia possessed a word capable of
expressing correctly the western concept of history. The western researcher
showed how to handle materials scientifically, and in his writings on South
East Asian history revealed much of it for the first time, rescuing from
oblivion much that would otherwise have been irretrievably lost.

Incidentally, the discoveries and writings of western scholars have contributed to the growth of the national sentiment which has been an outstanding feature of South East Asian history during the present century.
They have stimulated the nationalist's pride in the past of his people and
his desire for respect in the eyes of the West. On the other hand the treatment of national myths and legends by western scholars has often offended
nationalist susceptibilities, and provided weapons for those who claimed
that it was part of the technique of western colonialism to teach people to
despise their pre-colonial past. Naturally, therefore, the demand for political independence was accompanied by the efforts to rewrite history from
a nationalist angle to which reference has been made above.

Thus under the stimulus of nationalism the peoples of South East Asia
have become history-minded as never before. They have been reviving and
popularizing the study of their old writings, previously the exclusive prerogative of small coteries of court or monastic scholars. They have also
been striving to reassess their history during the time when they were under
western dominance. Some want to take away from it the sting which hurts
them. Others who have imbibed the best traditions of western scholarship
want to treat it as their own history and not as mainly the record of
European activities seen from a European angle.

What all this adds up to, therefore, is that there is now a more intense
and widespread interest in South East Asian history than ever before; more
intense among the peoples of the area because of their increasing consciousness of their own past; more widespread, because of the awakening
of the world to the fact that South East Asia is, for various reasons, one of
the world's most important areas. And though with the coming of independence to the old colonial territories some of the opportunities which

once existed for western researchers are no longer available, and, indeed, the number of French and Dutch scholars working in the particular fields in which in the past they have achieved such notable distinction seems to be dwindling, nevertheless the desire of the post-war South East Asian states to encourage their own scholars to take up the task, and the increasing signs that university history departments in many parts of the world, notably where English is used, are beginning to broaden the scope of their studies to include some South East Asian history, are matters of moment to all working in this field. For they pose many questions extremely difficult to answer, so difficult indeed that our conference was concerned rather to identify them than to attempt to answer them. Some could not be answered for lack of information, others because in the past there has been so little contact between scholars working upon different countries or periods, still others because of their newness: they have only recently begun to stir in the minds of historical students. But the mere asking of questions is at this stage of great significance, for they are questions with which every individual student or writer must wrestle, and whether or not he can find a satisfactory answer, upon his effort in trying to come to terms with them the future development of South East Asian historiography must inevitably depend. To many participants in the preliminary seminar discussions, as well as in those of the conference, the identification of the questions with which South East Asian historical scholarship is faced was one of the most fruitful and satisfying results of our meetings.

South East Asian historiography had never before been surveyed as a whole by a conference. Hence one very important object of our gathering was to take stock, and the contributors of papers tended to be as much concerned with the provision of bibliographical information as with the discussion of tendencies, outlooks, and values. For it must be borne in mind that not only are the peoples of our area very ignorant of each other's history, but European scholars themselves—particularly the Dutch—have tended to concentrate upon their own national responsibilities, the French upon Indo-China, the Dutch upon Indonesia, the Americans until recently upon the Philippines, and the British upon Burmese or Malay history. It is only in quite recent times that some effort to break down these walls of isolation and ignorance has been made. One of the biggest factors in the situation has always been the language barrier. The indigenous writings of South East Asia were written in the vernacular languages, i.e. Burmese, Mon, Thai, Malay, Khmer, Javanese, Balinese, Buginese, and Vietnamese, to name only the more important. And, to add a further complication, the modern writings about the area are in a variety of European languages, chiefly Portuguese, Spanish, Dutch, French, and English. Thus the linguistic equipment required for the study of the historical literature relating to only one subdivision of our area, is formidable. Moreover, through the 'colonial' relationship, which grew up between the various indigenous peoples and their western rulers, the European-educated ones would normally be able to use only the particular European language in which they had received their education in addition to their own vernacular, together with (in most, but not all, cases) a relevant classical language, e.g. Sanskrit, Pali, Chinese, or Arabic. Hence, at the conference, by pooling information and ideas provided by history specialists of each region, our hope was that a modest step would be taken towards spreading a common awareness of the whole range of South East Asian historical studies.

In opening the discussion on the older indigenous writings Professor C. C. Berg stressed the need for a comparative study of the ideas of history in the earlier indigenous literatures, and posed a number of fundamental questions. Excluding Vietnamese writings, he divided the historiographies under review into two groups, 'though not very sharply': those pertaining to the area of Indian civilization and those reflecting the influence of Islam. In this connection, he thought, Java should be regarded as a part of the Indian area, since its historiography, though reflecting in a way its conversion to Islam, retained its pre-Muslim character. In the first group, he thought, the cases of the Mons and Javanese appeared to be similar since the theme of their historiographers was to explain the divine qualities and functions of the king by establishing the line of his descent and his identity with some heavenly ruler. He wondered whether the Mon picture of the past represented facts, or, as in the Javanese case, 'optatives'. The Burmese Chronicles, on U Tin Ohn's showing, differed from the Javanese in that their compilers seemed to have had a critical attitude: they made extensive use of libraries and archives, and discussed the results of this investigation. It was noteworthy, he suggested, that the Burmese annals had been adopted by Mon historiographers after the expiration of the *rājāwan* tradition, dealt with by Mr. Shorto, and that the transplantation did not seem to have changed the Mon substratum.

The relation between the historical writings of Java and those of Macassar provided in his opinion another telling example of the need for comparative study. Once more in this case there was the difference between a functional, pseudo-historical literary activity and the recording of facts, but at the same time, he suggested, the possibility that Macassar 'learnt historiography' from Java. For instance, *palontara*, the word for annalist in Macassar, was of Javanese origin. And the fact that between 1512 and 1515 Tomé Pires was able to gather information about Javanese history at Malacca is evidence that the contents of Javanese books of history were discussed outside Java. It might well be that having learnt about the *Nāgarakrtāgama* and the *Pararaton* the Macassarese desired to imitate 'this element of a superior culture'. On the other hand it was noteworthy that they never learnt the Javanese art of chronology. Their own system of dating was cyclic before 1500, and was replaced by a rectilinear system as a result of their learning first Muslim and, later, European chronology from foreigners visiting Macassar. On this last point of international contacts he strongly supported Sir Richard Winstedt's view that the Malay chronicles reflected them to a greater extent than any of the other historical literatures of South East Asia; indeed, the *Sĕjarah Mĕlayu* was unique in that it emanated from a commercial society and was written by a man of mixed origin. Thus, together with the later *Misa Mĕlayu* and the still later *Salasilah Mĕlayu dan Bugis*, it pictured other aspects of life than the Javanese *Babad Tanah Jawi* and was more realistic.

Professor Berg ended his survey by asking two general questions. In the first place why was it that historiography began to play a part in different areas of South East Asia at about the same time? 'I see', he commented, 'one possible answer, namely that it is one of the repercussions of the great change in India, which was caused by the penetration of Islam, and which may have made the peoples of South East Asia more culture-conscious and, therefore, may have paved the way for interest in the past. But I do not pretend to know the answer to my question.'

In the second place he asked why did some communities in South East Asia have ideas of history and not others? This question had already been raised in a seminar discussion on Vietnamese historical writings in which attention was drawn to the contrast between writings of the Javanese type and the Vietnamese imperial annals, which showed strong Chinese influence. How far, it was asked, did China's historical traditions spread beyond her own borders. Was, for instance, the careful chronological treatment of events in the Burmese chronicles a sign of Chinese influence? Against this it was pointed out that in Nanchao, a country much more under Chinese influence than Burma, Chinese traditions of historical writing had apparently failed to make any impression, and the conclusion was reached that despite strong Chinese cultural influence on South East Asia in some respects, certain elements of Chinese civilization, being ingrained in the Chinese character, were not suitable for export, and their historical traditions might have been in this category. The Vietnamese, it must be remembered, were in a special category, for before attaining independence in 939, they had been for over a thousand years under Chinese domination, and not only was their early culture strongly influenced by China, but from the time of the Emperor Wu Ti (140–87 B.C.) onwards they had been subjected to intense Chinese cultural pressure.

The South East Asia section of the Conference submitted Professor Berg's challenging exposition of the unhistorical nature of the old Javanese chronicles to close scrutiny.

On one point, namely the importance of indigenous chronicles in general, the members of the section expressed unanimous agreement, and the attitude of mind which, in simple terms, condemned chronicles as un-reliable and upheld inscriptions as reliable, came in for strong criticism. What, it was asked, did we expect of historiography? If, indeed, as Pro-fessor Berg suggested, not much historiography in a European sense was to be found in older Indonesian literature, what is found was of no less value, particularly for the student of cultural history. If we wanted to learn what man did, how and why he acted as he did, and what sort of a person he was, the materials for this kind of study, though far from abundant, were adequate. The number of students working on them, however, was far from adequate, and appeared to be rapidly diminishing.

In the discussion on modern historical writing by indigenous scholars the idea was mooted that a development pattern might be discerned. Thus from the writing of annals and court-histories, which, for example, was in full swing in Burma until well after the middle of the nineteenth century, the next step was to the production of idealized histories for use in the nationalist struggle, with a further progression to the present concerted efforts in each of the newly independent countries to rewrite their his-tories. The later stages in this process, it was contended, were the inevitable product of the European impact, for not only the scientific approach, but nationalist history writing also, was a European importation. Indeed, the mere fact of writing 'history', it was argued, implied positive European influence, even when the 'history' itself represented a reaction against an alleged Europe-centric approach.

The question which attracted most discussion was that of the attitude of indigenous writers towards the colonial period. In Indonesia in par-ticular, it was claimed, the colonial period, which was far longer there than in any other part of South East Asia, was regarded as a 'dark age', chiefly useful for providing propaganda points for the nationalist movement. Several, however, thought that a change of attitude was beginning to show itself, in that Indonesians were being taught to think of the colonial period as an 'international' period, in which their history had to be studied against the background of international developments. The Indonesian member of the conference said it was important to see this period as a time when new values were transferred from the West and integrated with Asian traditions. Hence, in dealing with it the co-operation of European and indigenous historians was now recognized to be essential, and, as he put it, indigenous writers need not be concerned only with the oppression, nor western writers embarrassed by a sense of guilt, when writing about the colonial period.

On the subject of Western writings about ancient and medieval South East Asia, very warm tribute was paid to the outstanding contributions to knowledge made by the French and the Dutch in particular, and also by the great body of 'amateurs' belonging to all the colonial powers, who, though engaged in full-time administrative, educational, or commercial occupations, had devoted their spare time to the discovery, preservation, and interpretation of the antiquities of the countries in which they had served. Nevertheless, while fully conscious of the fine achievements of Westerners in this field, and of the great service they had thereby performed to the peoples of South East Asia, the members of the discussion group were concerned to examine the weak spots in the Western approach.

The culminating point of the discussion was reached when the question was posed whether it was possible to write a real history of South East Asia before the coming of the European. The difficulties were recognized to be enormous. Many peoples, for instance, had left no historical material of any sort, while of the available material not all was amenable to scientific treatment. Obviously, however, it was of the highest importance to investigate the available material, which was vast, but the question arose: would the result justify the application of the term 'history'? There appeared to be a feeling that we could not hope to write the sort of history that had been written about ancient Greece and Rome, though we could obviously learn a good deal about the past of South East Asia and its peoples. Several speakers, on the other hand, thought that this was taking too gloomy a view. For instance, in reply to one speaker who contended that we knew practically nothing of the economic life of the peoples of this period, it was pointed out that the inscriptions were a very rich source of historical materials, especially on economic affairs, but that as yet they had been inadequately explored. Research into them, however, was extremely difficult, both because of the terminology found in them and because our knowledge of the older languages used in them was far from adequate. Again it was asked whether the difference in the knowledge of the past of early Europe and of early South East Asia was as great as had been suggested, or whether the real trouble lay in the shortage of scholars in the field. Obviously an enormous amount of work remained to be done before a satisfactory answer could be given to the question, and for this reason the historical works so far produced on the subject must be regarded rather as interim reports challenging further investigation.

In considering the writings of Western historians questions of bias naturally assumed big proportions. There was on the one hand the general question of Europe-centricity, which has occasioned so much agonized reappraisal since World War II, and the special question of the bias in the writings of those belonging to particular groups labelled 'imperialists' (e.g. British, Dutch, Portuguese, Spanish, French), 'anti-colonialists' (e.g. Americans), and 'neutrals' (e.g. Danes), or classified according to religion as Protestants or Catholics, with the former consisting mainly of traders and seamen and the latter of missionaries and fighting men. Dr. Hugh Tinker, in introducing the discussion on the European interpretation of colonial history confined himself to a survey of the second question. He pointed out that almost as soon as colonial rule was established an 'imperialist' school of writing arose, fostered by officials and other empire-builders. Almost equally early an 'anti-imperialist' school arose, typified by the Manchester men, the French Radicals and anti-clericals, the Dutch humanitarians, etc. He claimed that these two forces were woven into colonial historical writing, with imperialism in the ascendant in the late nineteenth century, overtaken thereafter by anti-colonialism. With this latter school were associated radical politicians, disillusioned officials, and humanitarians. The American evolution, he declared, was in reverse: it was overwhelmingly anti-colonial up to 1900, thereafter moving to a new evaluation, which emerged *circa* 1950. The Christian missionaries, he noted, were always accused of writing propaganda, but clearly all the classes of writers he had mentioned had their bias and their logs to roll.

He then asked whether any dispassionate, uncommitted school of colonial history had arisen in the universities of the West. In the Netherlands, he said, South East Asian studies had been closely linked with training for the Netherlands East Indies administration. At Oxford and Cambridge the links had been less systematic, but there were close associations with the Indian Civil Service and the Colonial Service, and similar conditions prevailed in France. The United States had produced virtually no academic studies on Asian colonial history before 1900 except for some marginal missionary inquiry. The result was that South East Asian colonial history consisted very largely in studies of colonial administration. There was little work in the fields of social and economic history and in the history of ideas. In looking for a colonial history *genre* he suggested that the Portuguese provided something of the kind in the form of a national epic of Asian dominance, but was it merely an extension of the crusading epics? The other European writers failed to develop new concepts of history, though the Dutch had built up a solid corpus of knowledge through research. He summed up by declaring that colonial history remained either a study of administration (usually constructive and enlightened) by and for administrators, or a study of colonial repression by and for those in revolt. These were basic differences, which continued to divide East and West today.

The discussion concerned itself largely with the bias resulting from centrical approaches, and particularly with the criticism of Europe-centricity levelled by students today against writers of the pre-World War II generation. It was generally conceded that this was a result of the revolutionary political changes that had taken place during and after World War II, which had caused Western students of South East Asian history to see the subject in a new light and in a different perspective. At the same time, however, members of the discussion group were concerned to point out that Europe-centricity was only one facet of the problem. For instance, a large body of modern Indian writings dealing with Indian influence upon the development of South-East Asian civilization showed a clearly India-centric approach to the subject. It was also claimed that the deplorable limitation of the denotation of the epithet 'colonialism' to the domination over Asian and African peoples by certain Western powers was an indication of a further kind of centrical approach. And in any case, if the matter was to be seen in its proper proportions, one must not lose sight of the fact that the interest in the scientific study of the history of the peoples of South East Asia had its source in Europe, and hence all writings, whether by European or indigenous writers, tended to have an implicit Europe-centricity.

Finally the question that arose in everybody's mind was: what did all this awareness of centrical approaches and colonial-mindedness in past writers amount to? Did it indicate a 'new enlightenment' in the present approach of Western scholars to the study of South East Asian history? There certainly did seem to be many signs of a new outlook. One discerned them in the attempts to look at South East Asia as an entity and its history from a South East Asian centre rather than from outside; in the search for an appropriate nomenclature and a periodization free from colonial implications; in an urge to break away from the Procrustean bed of political and administrative history and give more attention to social and economic history; in a recognition of the claims of the minority peoples without written traditions, and, strikingly, in Professor Berg's approach to old Javanese historical writings. Could it be defined or explained? This was another question which the conference posed without answering.

One is, however, tempted to ask whether part of the explanation is that while in the past Western historiography was produced exclusively for Western readers, nowadays writers of South East Asian history are becoming aware for the first time of their potential Asian, and, in particular, South East Asian readers. This would mean that an attempt is now being made to arrive at a real world-history sense of values.

What did the conference achieve? In the first place the valuable series of papers collected together in this volume and their detailed discussion at weekly meetings of the South East Asia History Seminar during the two terms preceding the main gathering. The stocktaking represented by all this activity resulted among other things in a sober recognition of needs, and in particular the urgent need felt by scholars in South East Asian countries for better access to information. One strongly felt need was for ways and means of overcoming language barriers, and in this connection two desiderata were specially mentioned: the translation into English of important historical works in other languages along the lines of the new series of Selected Studies on Indonesia by Dutch Scholars now being produced by W. F. Wertheim's committee,[1] and the provision of English editions of older indigenous historical texts of South East Asia. The practical difficulties involved in the latter were recognized to be vast, but with specialists in so many of the languages of the area available in the Department of South East Asia at the School there seemed to be a unique opportunity for doing something of this sort, which might ultimately open the door for much more comparative study than is at present possible.

Another need equally strongly felt was for effective measures to be taken to collect and organize research materials in the different countries of South East Asia, involving such things as the microfilming of manuscripts, the photographing of rare books, and a host of other operations, all costing more money than the newly-independent states were prepared to spend upon such things. In the same connection members of the conference deplored the fact that in all these countries archaeological survey work, so vitally important to the historian, was languishing—if indeed, that is a strong enough word to describe the situation—through inadequate provision of funds and the failure to recruit and train indigenous scholars capable of succeeding their European predecessors.

And lastly, the conference as an international gathering provided a welcome opportunity for contacts, not only between workers in the South East Asian field, but also between them and workers in the fields of South Asia and the Far East.

The discussions were remarkable for the degree of understanding and goodwill between Eastern and Western scholars; there was the feeling of being fellow-workers in a joint enterprise, and the efforts made to arrive at a common sense of values must surely have their effect upon future writings.

Editor's note. In view of the variety of systems of romanization of the languages of the area in current use, it has been impossible to prescribe a common system for the purposes of this volume. Papers 16, 17, and 23 are translations of the originals as submitted by their authors.

[1] Published for the Royal Tropical Institute, Amsterdam, by W. van Hoeve Ltd. (The Hague and Bandung).

PART I

INDIGENOUS WRITINGS

1. JAVANESE HISTORIOGRAPHY—A SYNOPSIS OF ITS EVOLUTION

C. C. BERG

Professor of Indonesian Linguistics, University of Leiden

1. The great majority of the Indonesian speech communities do not know —or did not know at least until their recent contact with Western civilization—what historiography is, their notions of the past being a product of imagination and entirely unchronological. Apart from the influence of Europe, the larger speech communities have been literate since the early centuries of our era. Within this smaller group some have developed a kind of literature which might be called historiographical; in each different case the term 'historiography' may have a different meaning, however.

As far as the Javanese are concerned, the question arises whether their historiography is autochthonous or not, and in the latter case whether the Javanese have got acquainted with the historiography of some other nation(s) or only borrowed elements of culture which enabled them to develop a historiography of their own. It must be borne in mind that the Javanese had contacts with the Chinese and the Indians, both history-writing nations, though to different extents. Too little is known of the history of Javanese civilization to allow of an answer, for the time being. So much is sure that the Javanese acquired their knowledge of the alphabet from the Hindus and that their ancient documents give evidence of their familiarity with Indian chronology and elements of Sanskrit literature, including the main epics (*Mahābhārata* and *Rāmāyaṇa*) and some purāṇas, as early as the first millennium A.D.

It is not certain whether the Javanese did or did not learn the art of writing allegorical poems from the Hindus. On the one hand we must realize that the close similarity in literary traditions allows of supposing so, or at least of supposing that the Javanese had heard of Sanskrit poems dealing with classical subjects, but actually referring to a situation experienced by the author himself. On the other hand it is a truism that allegorical expression is a normal by-product of human language, whereas familiarity with epic stories—whether they are foreign or autochthonous —induces the habit of comparing one's acquaintances with generally known 'prototypes', as is clearly seen in modern Java where comparing people with characters of the *wayang* repertoire is a normal phenomenon. The same holds good for verbal or literary magic: the Javanese must have known the many Indian stories about the tremendous effect of priestly words upon the course of events and may have applied the theory implied within their own sphere, but on the other hand exaggerated belief in the power of speech is so universally human that we need not think of Indian influence especially to explain the practice of verbal magic amongst the Javanese.

Some of the specific features of Javanese historiography—to be discussed in the following sections—are retraceable to a Javanese origin. The study of the available materials has been limited so far, however, and one-sided at that. Any conclusion is liable to considerable change, therefore. As to the present writer, his own research has rendered him more or less familiar with materials older than A.D. 1700. Even though we may be aware that the insufficiency of preliminary studies renders our theoretical formulations somewhat premature, we may have need of a tentative theory which will give direction to our primary researches, viz., the study of the documents. It is as a contribution to such operative theory that the present suggestion is offered.

2. In Java two different systems of chronology were in vogue, viz. the indigenous system of concurrent weeks of different lengths and larger cycles of repeating combinations, and the Indian system based on the solar year. The indigenous system was and is used for everyday occurrences and in divination. On special occasions the Javanese described the moment in terms of hebdomad days, lunar months, and solar years, counting the latter in the Çāka era (=A.D. −78), though in our tenth century a Sanjaya era was used (cf. HJG 191), at least for some time. In 1633, Agung intro-duced the Muslim calendar of twelve lunar months, but not the Hegira era. Today the Gregorian calendar is known and even practised wherever schools are found. Early Javanese inscriptions record the days of pentad and hexad weeks alongside the corresponding date in the Indian calendar, together with a lot of astrological notations; in recent centuries, too, com-bining calendars has remained a normal practice.

It is noteworthy that Aji Saka, i.e. 'the Çāka king', is still well-known in Java, but as the inventor of the Javanese alphabet and the apostle of civilization, and that Sanskrit *çākakāla*, modern Javanese *sĕngkala*, has survived, but neither in connection with Aji Saka, nor in its original meaning, 'Çāka era'. For, when one takes into account the relative posi-tions of the rival systems of chronology and the evolution of the terms 'Çāka king' and *çākakāla*, the thought suggests itself that the larger Javanese community had no use for two chronological systems, so that when the Javanese system held its own, the *çākakāla* developed into something differ-ent, viz., a witty amusement of the clergy. In early Java *çākakāla* often meant 'chronogram', i.e. a series of words with specific cipher values com-bined into a sentence which describes the event of the year, whose number is suggested by the separate words, and sometimes a poem in which a chronogram holds the key-position; modern *sĕngkala* has only the first meaning. The game-aspect of these chronograms was often preponderant, for on the one hand the truth of the number of the year was often second in importance to the opportunity to launch a witty formula, and on the other hand stories were often reduced to formulae so as to suggest the year in which the events described could have occurred. When, for instance, Nādajña (in stanza 14 of the Simpang inscription) chose 1289 as the year of erection of the statue of Akṣobhya/Kṛtanagara at Wurare, the fact that *bhawacakra*, 'change of aspect', $=12+11=1211$ Ç$=1289$ A.D., was a handsome chronogram must have been the main object of his consideration. And when Prapanca in 1365 added Sanganusapati or Sang Anusapati to the list of kings of Singasari, he made him ascend the throne (Nag. 40, 5 iuncto 41, 1) in 1149 Ç$=$A.D. 1227, because 'king' $=1$, *pati*$=1$, *nusa*$=4$, and *sanga*$=9$.

The importance of this amusement factor should not be underestimated. The Javanese have perfectly mastered the Indian technique of dating, but year figures were not relevant to them as long as they lacked the historical mind and did not practise historiography. They seem to have dated their early inscriptions because that's how it *should* be, according to tradition, and perhaps also to increase the strength of the spell around royal decrees. When one has no urgent reason to deviate from the truth why should one prevaricate? So many inscription dates are probably reliable because they were so unimportant, from a general point of view. Then, when the habit of playing chronograms became an element of culture (before the socialization of historiography) and when this habit furthered the easy manipulation of year numbers, the discipline of dating went astray and historiograph was seriously handicapped in its evolution. We find quite a lot of unreliable dates in Javanese documents—I am inclined to think, gradually increasing in percentage in the later texts though we cannot be sure of this before all dates have been verified.

There is no general rule for the evaluation of dates in Javanese documents, to judge from the cases whose background we think we know. Dates may be correct. Dates may have been calculated, with more or less ability, or puzzled out in a divinatory way. Dates may be a mere product of fantasy and then serve the author to mask his ignorance or simply to show off. Dates may have been deliberately falsified or invented. Dates may have been added to increase the magical effect of a text, or to evoke the impression of authenticity. Dates may be wrong, because of ignorance or error. For all these different cases examples with evidence are available. The European scholar is conditioned by his training in a scientific milieu to overestimate the reliability of precise dates in Javanese documents; a large-scale study of dates may help him to overcome his reluctance to doubt the integrity of the official records as well as to learn that the Javanese horizon was relatively narrow.

3. Another source of misunderstanding is the optative character of many Javanese texts. We have to realize that magic did, and love of historical truth did not, play a part in early Javanese social life, and that early Javanese texts are more likely, therefore, to reflect a magician's mind than a historian's interest in the past. Verbal magic is a priest's endeavour to replace, through the power of his words, the reality of sense experience by a situation which corresponds to the meaning of his text. Such a text is an optative by nature, whether or not formal criteria enable the reader[1] to distinguish it from a statement or a story. As far as the magician's contemporary compatriots were concerned, their sense experience helped them, of course, to discriminate. Those, however, who have or had neither sense experience nor formal criteria to rely upon, are or were liable to confuse optatives and statements, or optatives and stories in such cases when the optative is couched in the form of an allegory.

H. Kern, for instance, believed the first part of the Erlangga Hymn, the Sanskrit text of the Calcutta inscription, to be a statement (VG 7, 85 ff.), and subsequent authors have followed in his path. The text in question mentions king Erlangga's ancestors, rather vaguely, but then vagueness need not be proof of forgery. However, more recent specimens of court literature provide us with two parallel cases: Rājasanagara's genealogy in the *Nāgarakrtāgama* and Agung's genealogy in the *Babad Tanah Jawi*; the latter is admittedly fantastic and the former is a fabrication, if the story of Krtanagara's daughters is a myth, as I think it is. At any rate, the case of Agung's genealogy makes us mistrust the reliability of the text of the Erlangga Hymn. The unspoken argument of Kern's supporters seems to be that the hymn is a respectable document, in Sanskrit and carved on stone. However, the Simpang inscription (BKI 78, 426 ff.) is in Sanskrit and carved on stone as well and yet it suggests an intrinsically improbable situation, viz., that Nādajña who was the Buddhist high priest in Majapahit as late as 1359 had erected a previously erected statue of Aksobhya/Krtanagara in 1289; 1289 is too early for Nādajña to officiate as a high priest and for Krtanagara (who died in 1292) to be deified. A lot of additional arguments lead to the conclusion that Erlangga's genealogy is a fake and that Erlangga, therefore, was a usurper whose claim to the throne was justified by his priest(s) through verbal magic which provided him with royal ancestors indispensable to a king.

Why should a Javanese priest practise magic to make people believe what they had believed before and what they would believe without his magic as well? It is reasonable to assume that whenever verbal magic is practised the situation which is suggested by the priest is the opposite of what people knew, that is to say, as far as the predicative parts of the text are concerned, not with respect to the subject, though it may be difficult

[1] Or hearer.

for us to find out which parts are predicative. Thus Erlangga was probably said to be Sindok's descendant because he was not. Jayabhaya, the royal patron of the poem *Bhāratayuddha* (1157), was said to be as pure as the full moon because he was a sinner. The *Nāgarakrtāgama* emphasizes Rājasanagara's descent from Angrok through one of the daughters of Krtanagara, because Angrok had never been heard of in Majapahit before 1359, and Krtanagara's daughters were known to be fictitious. In the same way Agung was said to be the heir of the Majapahit empire because he had no legal right to be a king. In Agung's case our knowledge of Maja- pahit documents has prevented us from accepting the poet's story off-hand. In the other cases such corrective documents fail us.

In my opinion it is not a matter of pure chance that better information is not available in the cases of Erlangga, Jayabhaya, and Krtanagara. For a priest who wants to replace an observed reality by a product of his imagination, writing an efficacious text is only one thing, theoretically the essential thing, perhaps, but practically not shock-proof. So the additional thing to be done is to destroy the documents containing such information as might jeopardize the effect of his magic. It appears from details of the *Babad Tanah Jawi* that the author of this work had a copy of the *Pararaton* in his collection of manuscripts, but when the European interest in Javan- ese literature awoke, Central Java was void of early Javanese literature, which was said to have been lost during the—imaginary—war between Majapahit and the Muslim coastal lords. Moreover, not a single sixteenth- century inscription has ever been found. We know early Javanese litera- ture because it has survived in Bali which was out of Agung's reach and where Javanese literature was *hors de concours*. Djajadiningrat's suggestion (BSB 304) that proselytes are anti-traditionalists and that Islām meant denial of the old belief is incompatible with the dominatingly traditional character of Javanese literature posterior to Mataram's official conversion to Islām in 1633, whereas the absence of early literature is in complete accordance with our functional interpretation of the Babad Tanah Jawi. A survey of the whole set of Javanese historical documents exposes similar and as interesting lacunae elsewhere; we have no Krtanagara inscriptions later than 1269 and no literature older than the *Arjunawiwāha* (probably ±1040), though the technical perfection of the latter poem suggests a long period of previous training. It seems to me that the interpretation of some outstanding documents as instruments of verbal magic explains the peculiar distribution pattern of our source materials, and the unavoidable conclu- sion is, therefore, that what we are reconstructing from those sources is necessarily that picture of the past that some ancient priests have wanted us to believe in: even if we see through their designs, we still only have such sources at our disposal as they thought fit to leave, with some rare excep- tions.

One might raise the objection that we do have a lot of inscriptions of the tenth century, and affirmative of the genealogy of the Erlangga Hymn at that. Indeed. But these inscriptions, ascribed to 'king' Sindok, are so flat as to their contents and so uniform in their details that even Krom was puzzled, though he had no doubt as to the historicity of Sindok's kingship. I am afraid that forging antedated inscriptions which are corroborative of a state myth is the more or less necessary counterpart of the destruction of unwelcome documents and that, therefore, the absence of pre-Erlangga literature and the wealth of Sindok inscriptions are two aspects of one problem. Though we may say that forgery is an art which makes high demands upon the forger's intelligence and that exaggeration is apt to betray him, the difficulty in making an indictment on these grounds is that the arguments depend on the theory they are to prove. In my opinion the charters of 1296 (INI 1, 33 ff.) and 1305 (TBG 76, 373 ff.) have been made after 1331 because they emphasize the importance of the daughters of Krtanagara, but others may say the daughters of Krtanagara to have been real personages who played a role in early Majapahit history.

The crucial question then, in our reconstruction of Javanese history as well as in our study of Javanese historiography, is a problem of general evaluation, now that the interpretation of the individual documents has laid bare the Javanese assertions. In order to be able to evaluate we must understand the mentality of the Javanese priests as revealed in the totality and the inner structure of their books. It is not sufficient for a student of Javanese history to read a text and to pick out only such details as seem to be useful materials for his reconstruction. The main question is again and again: why did the man write his book, and why did he write it thus? This question leads us to the subject of the following sections.

4. The Angrok story which in the course of the fifteenth century developed into the *Pararaton* (ed. Brandes, VBG 49/1; enlarged ed. by Krom, VBG 62) was written in prose and more open to change and expansion, therefore, than a well-structured poem. It came into existence in the eleventh century when Erlangga's subjects had to believe in Sindok, founder of the dynasty and the god Çiwa in human shape at that. As nobody knew Sindok, fantasy had free play, beyond those restrictions imposed by his being Çiwa. *Si* being a personal article in Javanese, the name was liable to being corrupted into *Ndok* of which form *Ngrok* and *Angrok* were variants; *Ndok* became the name of Angrok's mother. As a founder of a dynasty, according to the ancient Javanese, is functionally divine and historically first a non-king, but later a king, the outlines of the first part of the myth were typical, i.e. the same as we find elsewhere: the 'heat' of royalty, descended from the Fire-God Brahmā, passed through Ndok's womb and developed into a luminous child who killed Ndok's

husband in the first days of her pregnancy and who was therefore thrown away after his birth. In accordance with his ambiguous position (non-king/king) the youngster Angrok is alternately liked and disliked, protected and prosecuted, poor and full of miraculous power, until at last he becomes king of Tumapĕl (Singasari). After becoming king Angrok is married to Ḍĕḍĕs and Umang in whom we recognize Durgā and Umā (Çiwa's malign and benign power respectively. Ḍĕḍĕs's peculiar quality—probably adopted from Nḍok—is a luminous vulva which guarantees her husband command of the world. Each wife has three sons and one daughter whose names are correlative; the name of the eldest children represent their mother's quality, 'Danger of the Flaming Womb' and 'Fortune of Victory Well-established' respectively, whereas Ḍĕḍĕs's grandson is called *Rangga-Wuni* which seems to mean 'vulva flower' or 'vulva heat'.

To judge from details of the Rangga-Wuni story the original Rangga-Wuni may have been identical with Erlangga, but the story is too complicated to allow of one solution. In the thirteenth century, however, he was identified with Wiṣnuwardhana of Singasari. If the latter was a usurper, the identification is remarkable, but not queer, supposing that the adapter did not belong to the upper circles; for a man of lower rank who had heard about allegorical poems the popular Angrok story may quite well have been a prototype. Though the details of the reinterpretation escape us, the fact of the reinterpretation itself is evident. Another important detail is that Wiṣnuwardhana's famous son Krtanagara, who maintained relations with Malayu and Campā in the years of the expansion of the Mongol empire over South East Asia, in his turn was mentioned in the Angrok story. In a milieu not accustomed to historiography the result could only be that in the course of the years Krtanagara became known as the great-grandson of Angrok.

In 1292, Krtanagara was murdered by a man whom we know as Jaya-Katong, king of Kĕḍiri. A few months later the Mongols invaded Java and killed Jaya-Katong. A certain Wijaya, who had co-operated with the Mongols against Jaya-Katong, saw his way to seize the power after their departure and took up his residence in Majapahit. His adventures in the turbulent days of the invasion could not be told without mentioning Krtanagara's death. However, in the last years of the thirteenth century Krtanagara was no longer a famous king, but a fallen scarecrow to pick on, and Wijaya had completely taken his place. It appears that a second adapter has reconstructed the existing text of his days from the Majapahit point of view, because in the *Pararaton* text which we now have at our disposal the real great-grandson of Angrok and Ḍĕḍĕs is Wijaya, whereas Krtanagara, the overthrown one, is now said to have been the great-grandson of Ḍĕḍĕs and Tunggul-Amĕtung, the man whom Angrok had put aside. That this version is an adaptation of an existing story appears from many details, for instance from the corruption of the flaming womb story, as Tunggul-Amĕtung in the final version has a child with Ḍĕḍĕs and nevertheless dies without obtaining command of the world.

Majapahit had remained a centre of power for at least 150 years and probably even considerably longer. To readers of the fifteenth century the Angrok story could but suggest that Singasari and Majapahit had sprung from the same ancestress; Singasari, the first dynasty, had sprung from an improper marriage and had been no more than Majapahit's forerunner, whereas Majapahit, the permanent dynasty, had sprung from the proper marriage and was, therefore, successful, after going through a short period of incubation. When the author of the *Babad Tanah Jawi* in the seventeenth century chose Majapahit to be Mataram's prototype, he saw no other way to attain his end than to repeat the story of Singasari and Majapahit in new terms, maintaining, however, the feature of the improper against the proper marriage. Small wonder, therefore, that the 'dynasty' of the Dutch in Batavia, once having become Mataram's rival, was also 'explained' in the Babad literature by means of the flaming womb and the improper marriage stories.

5. In the same way as Angrok had been made Wiṣnuwardhana's prototype in the thirteenth century, Krtanagara was made Rājasanagara's prototype and ancestor in 1331, when Gajah-Mada decided to take up the line of Krtanagara's foreign policy, though in a more aggressive style. In accordance with this new political programme Wiṣnuwardhana was mentioned in inscriptions of this time as Tribhuwana's great-grandfather. The magical rites to establish the new order seem to have been very elaborate and to have lasted for twenty years at the end of which period the great Krtanagara temple at Singasari was consecrated. One of the texts which played a part in these rites is the Simpang inscription mentioned above.

In 1359, however, Prapanca who was the son of the man who had arranged the installation of Krtanagara, found a copy of the Angrok story in the monastery of Darbaru. It is interesting to state that even this Buddhist high priest and son of a Buddhist high priest believed Angrok to be Wiṣnuwardhana's grandfather, though Angrok had never been heard of in Majapahit. The error is pardonable, because Wiṣnuwardhana was not really king Rājasanagara's great-great-grandfather and the Angrok story was not the type of allegory Prapanca was accustomed to; moreover, the bearers of Singasari tradition probably had been massacred in 1292. It appears from the *Nāgarakrtāgama* that Prapanca had some knowledge of early inscriptions, but if he was acquainted with the practice of destroying old and fabricating new inscriptions, the absence of Angrok inscriptions is not likely to have stirred his doubts as to Angrok's historicity. So he must have thought his father to have been wrong in 1331. I suppose that this is the reason why he wrote his *Nāgarakrtāgama* in 1365, because this poem is clearly a synthetic myth in that it combines the essential elements of Nādajña's myth and the Angrok story, though Prapanca dropped elements of the latter in favour of the previous state myth. In this way the official list of kings of 1331 was enlarged with a Rājasa, founder of the dynasty, in whom we recognize Angrok, and his son Anusapati or Sanganusapati. Nag. 40 ff. gives a complete list of the kings of Singasari and Majapahit in which each king is chronologically fixed by means of chronograms consisting of Sanskrit words without sentence value; the latter detail might be interpreted as suggestive of the factual exactness of the chronograms.

6. If we accept that each new element of culture develops from an entity which was essentially different, but formally similar to it, we may regard the case of the *Nāgarakrtāgama* as the starting-point of Javanese historiography. The *Nāgarakrtāgama* was not written in order to transfer knowledge about the past, but in order to combine contradictory myths into a new one and to help Majapahit to establish a new basis for its ritual activities. Nevertheless, this poem was the first case of high-class literature exclusively dealing with what seemed to be actual situations and including a list of Javanese kings; in contrast to the Erlangga Hymn and the Simpang inscription it was written in Javanese and circulatable. It is reasonable to suppose that Prapanca's motive, re-establishment of certainty and order in the ritual sphere, lost much of its importance in the course of the following decades; that to the same extent the tendency increased to believe that the high priest Prapanca himself had been interested in the Javanese past; and that, therefore, interest in the Javanese past became as fashionable as familiarity with Sanskrit literature. At any rate, it is in the fifteenth century that we encounter an abnormal interest in stories about the past. These stories (Rangga-Lawe, Kidung Sunda, Panji) were more or less fantastic, as historiography was no discipline as yet, but they must have stimulated the evolution of historical consciousness and the awareness of chronological order in community life. This does not mean, however, that the new fashion had supplanted the earlier practice of verbal magic; wayang literature and wayang performances have remained functional, and so have other elements of literature.

7. Agung's court poet for one, the author of the *Babad Tanah Jawi* (1626), was not interested in history, but in the old tradition of the high priests. It appears from his book that he wanted Agung to be king of Java and heir of the kings of Majapahit who had been sole rulers of the island and overlords of 'the other islands' (*nusántara*). Agung's prototype was 'the king' of Majapahit, but as the poet was acquainted with both the *Pararaton* and the *Nāgarakrtāgama*, he combined his allegory with a *list* of the 'preceding' kings, and hence was forced to add the real story of Singasari and Majapahit to the metaphorical one. The poet was certainly not able

to discriminate between facts and fiction in connection with the story of Majapahit he knew; no king of Majapahit has ever been ruler of the entire island, but as the kings of Majapahit were *said* to have been sole rulers, in the court poet's eyes this quality was essential to any real king. In my opinion, therefore, the myth of Greater Majapahit is at the bottom of Agung's policy and the real cause of Agung's war against Batavia which ended in catastrophe.

When Agung was defeated by the Dutch in 162-89 Mataram was, from a priestly point of view, in the same position as Majapahit had been after Prapanca's discovery of the Angrok myth: something seemed to be wrong with the state myth in force. So a few years later the *Babad Tanah Jawi* was published once more, in a considerably reconstructed form which maintained, however, the essential elements of the first text. In the second text the Dutch had to become the obedient servants of the king, as the poem was an optative; in order to normalize their presence in Java the poet incorporated their 'dynasty' into his picture of the past by making the Dutch kings descendants of Angrok or Krtanagara whom he moved to this end to Western Java where they reigned in Pĕjajaran instead of Singasari. A second important innovation was the introduction of Islām as a power in Eastern Java to counterbalance the Dutch in Western Java; in this way the myth of Majapahit's fall after a war against the Muslims came into existence. And finally, as the poet did not distinguish between 'historical' ancestors and the divine objects of ancestor worship, he re-dressed the balance which was lost in 1629 by extending the number of Agung's predecessors; seven being the normal number of the members of a dynasty, the list had consisted of twenty-one members in the first edition (Singasari, Majapahit, Singasari/Dĕmak) but was now enlarged unto forty-nine members, including the heroes of the *Mahābhārata*.

8. It appears from the preceding section that the element of culture induced by Prapanca's *Nāgarakrtāgama* was no more than pseudo-historiography. In autochthonous evolution pseudo-historiography is, of course, the indispensable condition for the development of historiography, as science essentially is a process of clearing myths of products of mere fantasy.[2] But the odds were against Mataram achieving the second part of the process, as in the history of mankind only Greece succeeded in crossing the line between myth and science by its own strength. This means that Javanese documents are generally unreliable and often even fantastic, though individual exceptions are possible, as man's language, too, is dualistic, symbolic as well as pseudo-symbolic. Of course prevarication is no more common in the everyday life of the Javanese than of other peoples, and accurate reports may, therefore, have found their way to the *Babad Tanah Jawi* (cf. Brandes, TBG 32, 371). But in opposition to Drewes

[2] I use the word 'myth' in the technical sense of any unit of socially established belief.

(D 19, 244 ff.) I should only then call such reports characteristic of Javanese historiography if they would have induced a more or less general need of more or less objective reports of events.

As the author of the *Babad Tanah Jawi* followed the *Pararaton* in that he gave his book its overt structure, his text allowed of supplements as well as adaptations to later viewpoints. For the time being we do not know how this has worked out. The Dutch East India Company had become an entirely new factor in Javanese history as early as the second half of the seventeenth century, and a stabilizing factor at that, as it kept the kingdom of Mataram alive against opponents who would otherwise have founded new dynasties. The stabilizing effect of the Company's influence engendered an entirely new development which might be called 'multiplication of the *Babad Tanah Jawi*'. I am inclined to think that this was a symptom of frustration and confusion rather than a symptom of enthusiasm, and to regard Ranggawarsita's attempt to rewrite the history of Java along new lines, in the nineteenth century, in this light. After him nobody tried to take up again the task of court poet so that the Javanese call Ranggawarsita the last *pujangga*.

This, however, is no more than a provisional observation. A study of the *Babad Tanah Jawi* by a competent author who has taken into account the different aspects of its evolution is lacking, so that this synopsis must necessarily be incomplete.

ABBREVIATIONS

BKI—*Bijdragen tot de Taal-, Land- en Volkenkunde (van Nederlandsch-Indië)* (The Hague).

BSB—H. Djajadiningrat, *Critische Beschouwing van de Sadjarah Banten* (The Bantĕn chronicle critically discussed), (Haarlem, 1913).

HJG—N. J. Krom, *Hindoe-Javaansche Geschiedenis* (Hindu-Javanese History) (The Hague, 1926), second edition, 1931. (The second edition is quoted.)

INI—*Inscripties van Nederlandsch-Indië* (published by Koninklijk Bataviaasch Genootschap van Kunsten en Wetenschappen, Batavia).

Nag—*Nāgarakṛtāgama*, 1919 edition, annotated by Krom (The Hague).

TBG—*Tijdschrift voor Indische Taal-, Land- en Volkenkunde* (published by (Koninklijk) Bataviaasch Genootschap van Kunsten en Wetenschappen, Batavia).

VBG—*Verhandelingen van het* (Koninklijk) (Bataviaasch Genootschap van Kunsten en Wetenschappen, Batavia).

VG—H. Kern, *Verspreide Geschriften* (Collected Works) (The Hague, 1913 ff.).

2. MALAY CHRONICLES FROM SUMATRA AND MALAYA

SIR RICHARD WINSTEDT, K.B.E., C.M.G., F.B.A.

Formerly Reader in Malay in the University of London

Apart from a few inscriptions dating from the seventh to the fourteenth century A.D., there has survived no Malay written in other than Perso-Arabic script and there are no records of the language free from Arabic loan-words. Marco Polo found Islam already established at Perlak in Sumatra in 1292, and when Ibn Batuta visited Pasai in 1385 it was the state religion. The oldest Jawi or Malay written in Perso-Arabic script occurs on a stone from Trengganu, bearing the date 1326 or 1386, and recording in a mixture of Malay Sanskrit and Arabic the Muslim penalties for sexual and other offences to be enforced by a Raja Mandulika; the spelling, omitting vowel points already, with a few exceptions, inserts vowels on the principles found in all Malay writing until recently. These facts go to determine the age of extant Malay chronicles and digests of law, which were all compiled after Malays had had time to learn and employ many Arabic loan-words in literature and conversation.

The oldest of their chronicles is a history of Pasai written between 1350 and before 1524 when the state was annexed by Acheh. It is important for its influence on the Malaccan *Sĕjarah Mĕlayu*, best of all Malay histories, and so for its influence on all later Malay annals. This influence may be seen in the ascription of episodes from the *Ramayana*, *Mahabharata*, and *Katha Sarit Sagara* to historical personages and incidents; in the adoption of similar folklore to explain place-names; in long ethical exhortations put into the mouths of dying rulers and in semi-mythical accounts of the Malay conversion to Islam. More generally, like most Malay histories till modern times, it is a chronicle of court intrigues and the wars of rulers, whose dates have to be solved by researches from their tombstones. It is silent on constitutional and economic history, but is unconsciously valuable in suggesting close relations between Pasai and southern India; and in the name of one of the rulers, Merah Silu, there appears to survive a Sinhalese form of Chuli or Chula.

Next in date comes the *Sĕjarah Mĕlayu* or 'Malay Annals' written mostly at the end of the fifteenth or beginning of the sixteenth century, by an anonymous and probably half-caste author, to whom Sanskrit, Tamil, and Persian words, Javanese literature and Arabic texts are all familiar. He professes a smattering of Chinese, Siamese, and Portuguese. He is a conscious artist whose story of Malacca's warriors asking their Sultan for the romance of Hanafiah to read the night before the Portuguese attack looks reminiscent of Krishna reciting the *Bhagavad-Gita* to Arjuna before the battle between the Pandavas and Kauravas began. The annalist has also an intimate knowledge of Muslim romances and makes Malay princes write letters to their adversaries before engaging in war, as Alexander does in the Malay *Hikayat Iskandar*, from which as well as from the Pasai chronicle long passages are borrowed. The annalist is also well enough acquainted with Sufism to throw light on its esoteric mysticism. But with all his culture he still leaves us to discover the dates of his Malaccan kings from tombstones and Chinese records. Writing half a century or more later he may not have known that Iskander Shah, the founder of Malacca, was identical with Permaisura, last ruler of Singapore, or as a Muslim he may not have troubled to recall the Hindu title. Often he ignores facts which like his contemporaries he considered too well known to require mention. For example the now obsolete term Mandulika for a provincial governor, is mentioned once only and nowhere explained, though it occurs in contemporary Malacca laws and in Tomé Pires, and still survives as a meaningless honorific for a few chiefs. Certainly the anonymous annalist essays historical method, beginning his narrative with the Chula raids on Malaya, though folklore deceived him into making Tilattama, a nymph of Indra's heaven, the founder of Singapore instead of a prince, who, a Dravidian scholar tells me, was most likely the third son of Rajendra Chola I, namely Vira Rajendra *alias* Nita Uttama, a Buddhist, who conquered the island in 1068 A.D. and is said then to have given it its modern name. Equally fantastic are chapters on early relations between Malacca's royal house and the rulers of Palembang and Majapahit. Not, of course, that even the folklore of the 'Malay Annals' is to be dismissed as worthless. Till lately there seemed no meaning or value in their story of how the first ruler of Minangkabau won his throne by slaying a serpent, Saktimuna (that harassed farms) with a weapon called in the *Sějarah Mělayu* 'a knife from lake Mandakini' on the Ganges and in Sumatran folklore 'Mountain-hewer'. But now our knowledge that Malay Hindu rulers were often incarnations of Indra enables us to correct this myth with that thunder-god, who in the Rigveda clove a serpent alias a mountain to release water for the fields.

The author of the 'Malay Annals' is not only a medieval scholar but also proves the value of some historians being literary artists. His artistry has left us a vivid picture of a port thronged with Indian traders, Hindu and Muslim as well as settlers from China, Java, and Sumatra. There are lifelike vignettes of Tamil archers, Pathan horsemen, bibulous mahouts, and Indian missionaries self-important but cowardly in battle. There are wonderful portraits of the old chief who put gold-dust along skirting and panelling for his grandchildren to play with, of a Prime Minister too diplomatic to go abroad in a litter given him by his Sultan, of another who had a long pierglass and consulted his wife on the set of his hat. As Wilkinson has written, these Annals 'give us a lifelike picture of the times, reflect the mentality of the Malays and explain to us the working of Malacca government . . . They are the best record we have.'

There are many manuscripts and two versions of the *Sějarah Mělayu*. The later version, drastically edited in Johore in 1612, is a notable example of the way Malays will change words they do not understand and alter facts to please the ruler of their day. Only the older version, for example, retains Ma'abri (the Maabar of Marco Polo and Ibn Batuta), an Arab name for the Coromandel coast, as the centre from which Islam spread to the East Indies. And there is much alteration of facts to enhance the prestige of the family of Bendaharas or prime ministers, who succeeded the last Sultan of the old Malacca royal line in 1699. According to the earlier version, Sultan 'Ala'u'd-din Shah (ob. 1488 A.D.) was the son of a Javanese woman; according to the latter, her son was killed by a man who ran amuck and 'Ala'u'd-din was the son of a Bendahara lady. Neither version for some reason mentions that ruler's brother Sulaiman Shah, whose name occurs in d'Albuquerque and whose tomb is at Sayong on a tributary of the Johore river.

A century ago students took considerable interest in the *Hikayat Měrang Mahawangsa* or so-called 'Kedah Annals'. But critical scholarship has exposed it as a farrago of folk-tales, where the Prophet Solomon is called the master of Vishnu's Garuda and stories from the *Ramayana*, the *Katha Sarit Sagara* and the *Jataka* collection appear as authentic history. The discovery of the names of kings of Sri Vijaya and Kadaha has exploded its early genealogies, and even its siting of Langkasuke is disputed, though the frequent changing of the capitals of Perak and Johore should make critics cautious. The work is full of omissions, gross anachronisms and errors, and the lateness of its compilation is corroborated by the paucity and modernity of the manuscripts.

An interesting history is the *Misa Mělayu*, a contemporary account of Perak from about 1742 until 1778 written by a Raja Chulan. Much space is devoted to court ceremonies, marriages, and funerals; and a royal trip round the coast contains much incident set forth in unusually good verse. Casual details throw light on Perak's trade and politics. The writer mentions the sale of two cannons by the master of an English ketch in return for tin-ore, and talks also of royal trading with India in elephants. There are references to a lodge maintained by the Dutch on the estuary of the Perak river to enforce their monopoly of the purchase of tin and to the signing of a treaty with a Dutch commissioner, and there are allusions to the state's relations with Selangor and Kedah. Throwing much light on life in a Malay state two centuries ago, the *Misa Mělayu* eschews folklore and is one of the more realistic of Malay chronicles.

But by far the greatest Malay history after the 'Malay Annals' is the *Tuhfat al-Nafis* or 'Precious Gift' compiled in 1865 by a Raja 'Ali of Riau, who wrote also a *Salasilah Mělayu dan Bugis*, a work identical in style and containing some of the same material as his *magnum opus*. After recapitulating briefly previous accounts of the history of medieval Singapore and Malacca, the *Tuhfat* relates the story of Johore and Riau from the beginning down to 1865. It describes the main incidents in the relations between Malays, Bugis and Dutch, throws light on the history of the Peninsular states, gives an account of Major Farquhar's visits to Lingga and of the fetching of Raffles' Sultan to Singapore. It has the adventitious interest of giving the Malay viewpoint of events, of which there are Dutch and English records. There are still marks of traditional historiography in thirty pages of genealogies and in anecdotes like that of the death of a famous warrior Raja 'Ali under a hail of Dutch bullets, as he stood relying on a magic dagger in one hand and a Muslim treatise on Grace in the other. But Raja 'Ali lacks the psychological insight and graphic pen of his great predecessor, the author of the 'Malay Annals'. On the other hand his dates are many and accurate and his anecdotes have historical value. For example, he tells of one teacher of mysticism who earned 4,000 dollars at Riau and of another, a heterodox pantheist, who first of all had his head shaved as a punishment and later was executed for claiming to be the reincarnation of the warrior Raja Haji. One passage gives the price of gambir, rice, raw and woven silk in the heyday of Riau's prosperity and tells how there were six hundred rajas and eighty chiefs and merchants on the small island.

The writing of history was popular then at Riau, as in Perak, so that the *Tuhfat* can be compared with a *Sějarah Raja-Raja Riau* as well as with a *Hikayat Něgěri Johor* (1673–*c.* 1800). The last work is so far from the romantic exaggeration of early works that it records how after a Bugis attack on Malacca three or four men carrying yokes could not have removed the shoes and hats of the dead. Occasionally, even an unconsidered fragment will furnish some valuable detail, one such supplying a long-sought link in the royal Johore pedigree.

In the nineteenth century the Peninsula produced no purely historical work of signal merit, though the Autobiography of 'Abdullah, a man of mixed Tamil Arab and Malay blood, is famous for its anecdotes of Raffles, its account of the founding and growth of Singapore, and its descriptions of contemporary worthies, British and Asian down to 1846. As its latest translator has said, 'any analysis of his work must show up his frequent blunders of fact, his occasional deliberate distortion of the truth and his often hopelessly confused chronology. The great value of his work lies not in the dry records of a period well-served by the chronicler and annalist, but in the intimate pen-pictures he gives of the personages of his time.'

In short, 'Abdullah was the last notable exponent of the tradition of Malay historiography.

There are minor nineteenth-century histories of Johor, Perak, Kedah, Pahang, Trengganu, and Kelantan. Though containing details of value, none of them broke new ground in method. A prominent Malay writer has noted the *Tawarikh Mĕlayu*, produced by me in 1918 for the Malay schools 'as undoubtedly *the* book which, by popularising the Arabic word *tawarikh* first opened the eyes of the average Malay to the meaning of history as distinct from legend. Before it, all Malay history and biography had been styled *hikayat* or 'stories' and there had been no clear distinction in the Malay mind between fact and fiction.' The outcome of this new conception lies with the University of Malaya.

AUTHORITIES

JRASMB—*Journal of the Royal Asiatic Society, Malayan Branch.*

A. H. Hill, 'The Hikayat Abdullah', an annotated translation, JRASMB (1955), xxviii, pt. 3.

G. E. Morrison, 'The coming of Islam to the East Indies', JRASMB (1951), xxiv, pt. 1.

R. J. Wilkinson, 'The fall of Malacca', JRASMB (1935), xiii, pt. 2, 69.

R. O. Winstedt, 'Indra and Saktimuna', JRASMB (1950), xxiii, pt. 1, 150.

R. O. Winstedt, Bibliography to 'A History of Malay Literature', JRASMB (1939), xvii, pt. 3, 241.

C. C. Brown, 'Sejarah Melayu', a translation of Raffles MS. 18, JRASMB (1952), xxv, pts. 2 and 3.

R. O. Winstedt, 'The Malay Founder of Medieval Malacca', BSOAS (1948), xii, pts. 3 and 4.

R. O. Winstedt, 'Malay History from Chinese Sources', BSOAS (1949), xiii, pt. 1.

3. SOME ASPECTS OF MACASSAR-BUGINESE HISTORIOGRAPHY

J. NOORDUYN

Linguist in the service of the Netherlands and Indonesian Bible Societies

1. *Introduction*

Population and culture. The south-western peninsula of Celebes is inhabited by four Indonesian peoples which are closely related in culture: the Macassars in the south (over 700,000), the Buginese to the north of them (over 1½ million), the Luwurese still farther to the north, and the Mandarese in the north-west. Some characteristics they have in common are: all four of them are wholly islamized, use a non-European script originally derived from an Indian script, and occupy themselves largely with navigation, trade, and fishery. The interior, between the Luwurese and Mandarese territories, is inhabited by the South Toradjas, who, though in several respects also related, lack the above-mentioned characteristics. Except for the Luwurese, who formed a single large state, which expanded its influence far into the interior of Celebes, they were organized in several states of different size, as for instance Goa and Tallo' in the Macassar region, Bone, Wadjo', Soppeng, Sidenreng, and Tanete in the Buginese part and the seven Mandarese states. Within the borders of these larger states and subordinate to them smaller ones were situated, as for instance Pammana in Wadjo', and Timurung and Mampu in Bone.

Their political history, too, though for the greater part consisting of feuds, wars, treaties, and pacts between and against the various states, shows the coherence of these peoples. Although already in the Javanese *Nagarakrtagama* (1365) some place-names of these regions are mentioned, e.g. Bantayan, the modern Bantaeng (Bonthain on the maps), it was not until the sixteenth century that they entered into the light of history. In the first part of that century Portuguese merchants and priests for the first time came into contact with them, but they found that Moslem merchants from Malaya and Sumatra were already there. In the beginning of the next century Dutch and soon afterwards also English merchants came to Macassar, which, being the principal port of the rapidly expanding commercial state of Goa, was more and more becoming the centre of the whole region. In the years 1605 till 1607 Goa, together with its ally Tallo', officially adopted Islam and from 1608 till 1611 islamized the principal Buginese states by force, in this way establishing its hegemony over the peninsula for which during the sixteenth century it had contended in vain, especially with Bone. In 1667 Goa was subdued by the Dutch Company

(Treaty of Bungaya), with help from the Buginese, and thenceforward the Dutch held the peninsula under control, favouring Bone as their principal ally. In the eighteenth century several attempts by Goa to rise to power again were crushed, but in the nineteenth century it was the powerful position of Bone which compelled the Dutch to wage several 'Bone-wars' to maintain their position. The last of these, in 1905, established Dutch dominance until the outbreak of the Pacific war.

The languages of the four peoples, though closely related, differ rather considerably. Their literature, however, especially their historical literature, has much in common, and may consequently be treated together. The literature of the Buginese, the largest of the four peoples, is the most important as to volume, but one has to reckon with possible Macassar influences from the important state of Goa and foreign influences penetrating via Macassar.

Historical writing is still highly regarded by many groups belonging to these four peoples, but we have to confine ourselves here to Macassar and Buginese historiography, since about the other two next to nothing is known as yet. This does not mean that the former has been sufficiently investigated: actually, in both languages only one text has been published in transcription together with a translation, and only two major prose texts have been published in the Macassar-Buginese script without any translation. Thus, owing to the limited material available, no definitive or general conclusions can be reached as yet.

On the other hand certain results have been obtained thus far: in an article by Professor Cense, which gives a general picture of the various genres of Macassar and Buginese historiography with some details characteristic for each of these, in an article by R. A. Kern about a Buginese historical poem, and in an inquiry into historical writing of Wadjo' till the end of the eighteenth century. These are interesting enough to justify calling attention to this writing as a third kind of Indonesian historiography, ranking in importance with the Javanese and Malay historiographical traditions.

The beginnings of historical writing. Although many of the chronicles known to us are sometimes largely devoted to the sixteenth century, none of them can be said to have originated in that century: the chronicles of Tallo', Bone, and Goa, as well as the earliest chronicle of Wadjo', end with events from 1641, 1660, 1670, and 1650 respectively, and, we may assume, therefore, that their composition was later than those dates. On the other hand, the diary of Goa and Tallo' contains correct dates from the beginnings of Islam (1605) onwards. So at least some contemporaneous annotations must have been written down in the first part of the seventeenth century. And during the sixteenth century historical interest must have existed to some extent, if details regarding this time have been recorded from oral tradition at a later date. Written documents now lost, dating back to these years may have existed. The Indian origin of their script at least shows that these peoples knew the art of writing already before their adoption of Islam, otherwise they would have adopted the Arabic script along with Islam. The chronicle of Goa states that under the reign of Tumapa'risi'-kallonna ($\pm$1511–1547), the first more historical king of Goa, his minister and *shahbandar* Daeng Pamatte' 'made' the Macassar script. About the kings who reigned before this time this chronicle records nothing more than their names, because, as it says, at that time writings (*lontara'*) did not yet exist. The initial parts of most chronicles, in treating of these times (before $\pm$1500), do show more mythical and legendary traits, telling for instance about the first king of the dynasty, who descended from heaven: the *manurung*.

As the chronicle informs us, under the reign of Tunidjallo' (1565–90) official clerks, *palontara'*, were appointed in Goa, who may have been charged, *inter alia*, with noting down contemporaneous events.

For the time being, however, it is safest to assume that Macassar and Buginese historical writing dates from the seventeenth century.

2. *Sources*

Diaries. 'The keeping of diaries, still practised several decades ago, is a practice which, as far as I know, is nowhere in Indonesia so generally adhered to as among the Macassar and Buginese peoples, except among those groups of the population which are influenced by the Macassar-Buginese culture such as the Bima-people and the Malay at Macassar.' The importance of this statement by Cense lies in the fact that originally this practice of keeping diaries must either have been an invention of these peoples of Celebes themselves or an imitation of a non-Indonesian example, e.g. of a Portuguese custom, as Crawfurd suggests.[1] But apart from its origin its widespread acceptance also requires an explanation.

There are diaries kept officially at the court of ruling princes as well as diaries of private persons. The pages of the book to be used were subdivided beforehand with ink-lines so that dates and short notes could be readily filled in. Often pages were left blank, to be used for longer annotations. The official diaries contain annotations concerning state affairs, expeditions, treaties or birth, marriages, and deaths in the royal family, etc. The annotations of private diaries are often of less general importance, but can give a picture of all sorts of social relations and circumstances. A special category of annotations concerns supernatural events, such as the return to life of a dead person, and natural phenomena, such as solar and lunar eclipses, earthquakes, comets, etc. Probably these phenomena were considered to be portents. Prescriptions for neutralizing the unfavourable

[1] *History of the Indian Archipelago* (1820), ii, 382.

effects of portents, such as earthquakes, lunar eclipses and certain animals and birds entering into villages or houses, are to be found in Buginese manuscripts.

The notes are usually dated either according to the Christian as well as the Moslem calendar or according to the Christian calendar only. In the former case internal harmony of this double date is a sufficient guarantee for the authenticity of the information. The names of the European month are often in Portuguese. Some diaries from Bone are at present in the archives of the British Museum in London.

Texts of treaties and correspondence. The pages left empty in the diaries were sometimes used as a letter-book for correspondence which, often by means of envoys with verbal messages, was carried on between states, and they contain, *inter alia*, records of the negotiations eventually leading up to formal treaties.

The texts of numerous treaties, concluded in the course of time between the various states, have been handed down in writing either separately or in a chronologically arranged series. In Goa the *ulukanaya* '(the book of) the treaties', were officially kept by the chancellor of the state. Part of these old treaties, consisting mainly of concise formulas or metaphorical expressions, has been preserved. Most of the older treaties can only be dated approximately, by means of the names of the kings mentioned in them. The most important treaties were named after the place where they were concluded, sometimes also with symbolical names, e.g. 'Breaking steel at Unnji' ' or 'The cloths tied together at Topatjĕ'do' or 'Planting stones at Timurung'. Perhaps, and certainly in the last case, these names are reminiscences of symbolic acts performed at the conclusion of the treaties. In Goa from time to time pacts with vassals were renewed, on which occasion often their previous history was shortly retold.

Genealogies and lists of rulers. Genealogies of dynasties, either in the form of pedigrees or as enumerations of names of married persons and their offspring, generation by generation, sometimes contain short tales about the principal persons mentioned. Likewise, lists of rulers sometimes contain short notes about their reign.

3. *Chronicles*

Apart from separate tales about historical episodes, the above-mentioned historical writings were the main written sources for the authors of the chronicles of the various states. They are only partly historical sources in the strictest sense, because many of them are only known from the chronicles themselves, which are often no more than copies from copies, often rewritten by the copyists and rendering the distinction between fiction and authenticity very difficult.

The chronicles formed a literary genre, written in a simple prose-style their composition, style, and choice of words were to a great extent left to the taste of the author or the copyist. Moreover, they contain almost no dates. Chronological details are given in time-distances (years, months, or days), also in those chronicles whose authors had diaries at their disposal, e.g. those of Goa and of Tallo'.

As to their composition, most of them are not strictly chronological, but devote a chapter to each ruling prince of the dynasty concerned, and, as e.g. those of Goa and Tallo', enumerate successively his names and titles, his age at important stages of his career, his expeditions and conquests, the qualities of his character, and his wives and children. In this way there is not much room left for chronology nor for detailed descriptions. The chronicle of Bone is less 'systematically' rubricated and pays more attention to chronology and anecdotes. The chronicle of Tanete is still more anecdotical, it is also the longest one known, but it contains almost no chronological data, nearly always introducing a new subject with such words as 'After some time . . .'

The chronicles mentioned so far are probably more or less official versions, as no other redactions exist and not one of them has been continued in later times. The little chronicle of Timurung also tells part of the history of Bone, which it continues till ± 1800, but only because the kings of Bone were at the same time hereditary princes of Timurung.

The main historical writings from Wadjo' differ from the above mentioned chronicles in two respects, owing probably to the lack of a strong centralized government of a hereditary dynasty (the chief rulers were chosen). The rewriting and continuation of the chronicle of Wadjo' has gone on from the seventeenth century up to the present. There are four great chronicles: one from the seventeenth, two from the eighteenth century, and the last great compendium was completed shortly before the last war, next to several shorter ones from the eighteenth and nineteenth century. Secondly, these great chronicles on the whole are not compiled into chapters and sections but are chronological throughout. The extension of the chronicle does not only mean continuation of the story into later times, but also enlargements at the beginning and elsewhere. E.g., each time more details are told about the foundation of Wadjo' and even about the history previous to that, and the eighteenth century versions are interspersed with genealogical passages concerning the families of the three highest hereditary chiefs.

Something of the chronicler's method in using his sources can be seen from a comparison between a long text concerning the history of the notorious Arung Singkang of Wadjo' during the years 1735–42 and the corresponding passage of the chronicle. The writer shortens his material, but not by summarizing what he thinks of less importance, but by leaving it out completely, often without even indicating how long a period of time he passes over in silence. Writing tales in separate scenes only loosely knit together, as if sculpturing reliefs on temple walls, is a well-known Indonesian style of story-telling.

The chronicler never lets us know the reasons why he tells us one thing and passes over another, nor does he give his judgement nor, for that matter, any moral lessons.

But he sometimes does tell his reasons for writing history at all, at the beginning of his story, e.g.: 'because it is to be feared that the old princes would be forgotten by their posterity', or 'unacquaintedness with these things would bring about that we would think that there is no heaven above us or that foreigners would think that we are but common people'.

These sayings characterize the attitude of the chroniclers towards history. Although they are mainly concerned with the kings and princes and their exploits, they do not regard them (apart from the mythical first kings) as semi-gods endowed with superhuman powers, but as human beings who by birth and position are the leading forces in history. Sometimes they show a bias to give more credit to their own country than is justified, but on the whole they are only interested in facts. Especially when they write about their own time or about the recent past, their historical writings are quite reliable, as sometimes can be demonstrated from a comparison with the information in contemporary Dutch documents. Kern has shown this for the Buginese historical poem (*tolo*) treating of two Dutch expeditions against some Buginese states in the years 1824 and 1825, and written in 1842. An inquiry into the historical writings of Wadjo' has led us to the same conclusions for a large part of these writings, especially for the above-mentioned text about Arung Singkang. The modern historian concerned with the history of South Celebes (and of Indonesia in general) can by no means dispense with the historical literature, diaries, and chronicles in particular, which originated in this region itself.

4. *Origin*

One of the first conditions for a sound historiography is a reliable system of chronology. The Moslem calendar has been used as the main chronology since the country's islamization, although it was already known before that time. It is not the calendar commonly used in the Moslem world, and which reckons by cycles of thirty years, but one which knows cycles of eight years, and may differ from the former by one or two days. This system, however, has never yet been fully investigated.

There are indications that before the adoption of Islam the Christian calendar was officially used, probably adopted at some time from the Portuguese, since the names of the European months, used in the older Macassar and Buginese diaries, are clearly of Portuguese origin. Next to these there existed an old Buginese calendar, which had the considerable shortcoming of not numbering the years or indicating them in any way, but which reckoned by solar years.

Analysis of the chronicle of Goa brings to light that 1511, the year of the conquest of Malacca by the Portuguese, was the first synchronical date which could be established by the Macassars, and that it was used as the starting point for building up a chronology of Macassar history.

Presumably this question of chronology has been, next to the introduction of the art of writing, the main impulse in originating Macassar-Buginese historiography. Without a suitable breeding-ground, however, it would have had no success, as is shown by the example of Ambon's history-writer Ridjali, who, being a fugitive Moslem living at Macassar, around 1650 wrote a history of his native land at the instigation of Goa's Chancellor of the state, but who never had any followers.

Among the stimulating factors may have been an existing oral tradition such as e.g. the South Toradjas possess reckoning their history by generations, and pseudo-historical epopees such as the extensive pre-islamic Buginese mythical epic La Galigo which tells of gods and heroes in seven successive generations. All this, however, is still too little explored to hazard any conclusions.

There are no indications of influences from other Indonesian regions. The peculiar characteristics of Javanese historiography as presented by Berg, as well as the tales and words and expressions clearly borrowed from Java by which some Malay historiography shows its indebtedness to Javanese literature, are lacking in the Macassar-Buginese historical writings. On the other hand, the main characteristic of the latter, its objectivity and concern for facts, appears in other domains of this culture as well, as is shown by the annotations on maps for navigators, the precise data about weapons, houses, ships, etc., in notebooks, and the inventories drawn up by administrators of estates.

The historiography of South Celebes must, I think, mainly be regarded as an independent phenomenon.

Addendum

In response to questions asked at the Seminar Dr. Noorduyn sent the following notes on his paper:

Wajarese historical writing is of some importance because of its bulk and its character. Though mainly concerned with its own people (just like Malay and Javanese historiography) it also contains incidentally many data concerning Malaya, Java, and Bima. The chronicle of Tanete for example contains an elaborate description of the part the Buginese took in the expedition against Kartasura during the Chinese troubles in Java.

Some Buginese tracts deal with the eighteenth-century Buginese conquista-dores operating in Malaya. Winstedt's characterization of the historical writing by Raja Ali—himself of Buginese extraction—mutatis mutandis fits excellently with the best Buginese writings.

The oldest chronicles—judging from their individual unity of composi-tion and style—make the impression of having been written as entities. This appears clearest in the chronicles of Goa and Tallo', in which the author sometimes anticipates later happenings, and even once sends his readers from one chronicle to the other for the treatment of a certain point. On the other hand the work edited by Noorduyn has its final part borrowed from an existing treatise, which was perhaps adapted, whereas its middle part was written as a liaison.

Did prototypes of the eldest known chronicles exist? This point has not yet been studied.

About the eight-year cycle no sufficient data are as yet available.

The remaining historical writings deal with material partly older than the seventeenth century. A rough sketch of the sixteenth century could be drawn. Concerning literal tradition before 1605 for the moment no positive answer can be given.

BIBLIOGRAPHY

B. F. Matthes, *Makassaarsche Chrestomathie* ('s-Gravenhage, 1883), pp. 146-203 (the Chronicles of Goa and Tallo').

— *Boeginesche Chrestomathie I* (Makassar, 1864), pp. 465-98 (the chronicle of Bone).

— *Boegineesch heldendicht op Daeng Kale'boe* . . . met vertaling en aanteekeningen Makassar, 1858).

— *Boegineesch heldendicht op den eersten Bonischen veldtocht van* 1859, met vertaling en aanteekeningen (Makassar, 1862).

G. K. Niemann, *Geschiedenis van Tanette*, Boeginesche tekst met aantekeningen ('s-Gravenhage, 1883).

A. Ligtvoet, 'Transcriptie van het dagboek der vorten van Goa en Tello met vertaling en aanteekeningen, BKI (1880), pp. 1-259.

J. Noorduyn, *Een achttiende-eeuwse kroniek van Wadjo'*, Buginese historiografie ('s-Gravenhage, 1955).

— Een Boeginees geschriftje over Arung Singkand, BKI (1953), pp. 144-52.

A. A. Cense, 'Enige aantekeningen over Makassaars-Boeginese geschiedschrij-ving, BKI (1951), pp. 42-64.

R. A. Kern, 'Proeve van Boegineesche geschiedschrijving, BKI (1948), pp. 1-31.

———

BKI=*Bijdragen tot de taal-, land- en volkenkunde van het Koninklijk Instituut voor taal-, land- en volkenkunde* ('s-Gravenhage).

4. MUSLIM MYSTICS AND HISTORICAL WRITING

A. JOHNS

Senior Lecturer in Indonesian and Malayan Studies, Canberra University College

Indonesian history is bewilderingly complex, and most difficult to handle as a unit. This is particularly true of the period beginning with the seventeenth century, which for the sake of convenience may be taken as a starting point for the process which marked the gradual spread of effective European control over the commercial and political life of the area. A spread which van Leur complains has been anticipated and exaggerated by 'Colonial' historians, for, as he rather colourfully puts it: 'With the arrival of ships from Western Europe . . . the Indies are observed from the deck of the ship, the ramparts of the fortress, the high gallery of the trading house.'[1] Further on he complains that Stapel takes the history of the Dutch Company as the frame of reference for the history of Indonesia in the seventeenth century, and says: 'If so, one necessarily arrives at the epic of mariners and warriors. Indonesian history was not merely that and nothing more. The preponderance of the oriental element was at that time still too strong.'[2] He begins his essay on the study of Indonesian history with the challenging sentence: 'Whoever approaches the history of Indonesia enters into an unknown world.'[3]

One of the unifying themes of the history of Indonesia is the spread and development of Islamic religious life. An Islam at that which came orchestrated with various Indian and Persian accretions, and which was to grow mixed, to a greater or less extent with local practices, animist or Hindu. So that a historical study of Indonesian Islam thoroughly documented by texts, carefully related to the social and economic background is one of the fields of research which can throw light on the thought and life of Indonesians themselves.

Of the large number of MSS. of Sumatran origin the contents of which date from this period, an important proportion, whether in Arabic, translated from Arabic, or original Malay works are in mystical subjects written by representatives of various of the Islamic *tarīḳas*, some by native-born Sumatrans, others by foreigners. The number of MSS. show clearly that the followers of the *tarīḳas* formed an important element in this area of Indonesian society at that time.

These mystical writings are of value as historical material because they

[1] J. C. van Leur, *Indonesian Trade and Society* (The Hague, 1955), p. 261.
[2] op. cit., p. 265.   [3] Ibid., p. 147.

were written without any consciousness of the possible interest of posterity. They may properly be called 'traces' which are both a guide and a challenge. Although difficult to interpret they were, at least, not written to glorify any particular family or party, and so were not liable to the kind of revision of which the two versions of the *Sĕjarah Mĕlayu* are a good example. And if examined in the light of other elements of history already known or inferred, be they political, mercantile/economic, social or religious, they can illuminate some dark corners, and in some cases add a new dimension to our knowledge, bringing us a more acute awareness and appreciation of the social life behind data already known.

Since the documents are the product of an international religion they have a double interest. Not only do we get an inkling into some aspects of the social life of Indonesians and their religious mentality, but also an illustration of the effective movement of various currents in the Muslim world from one area to another. Thus at one point of investigation there is a phenomenon which has become an enthusiastic part of a certain area of a culture, and an international background against which to assess it. International because from certain aspects Islam can be considered as a mercantile religion. It rose in an international centre of trade—Mecca. In the Qur'ān in a *sūra* revealed at Medina there is evidence of the enthusiasm of the early Muslims for trade in the verse: 'Whenever they see an opportunity for trade or diversion, they flock towards it, and leave you (Muhammad) standing.'[4] And there is also the injunction: 'When prayer is ended then disperse through the land, and strive for the bounty of God.'[5] The early expansion of Islam was into areas of great commercial wealth such as Syria and Persia, from where it was gradually to gain control of and develop a trading system extending from the Mediterranean through Persia and India to South East Asia and China. A detailed analysis of the spread of Islam in Sumatra is an illustration of the process in miniature— from the north Sumatran ports down the pepper areas on the West coast, and up the rivers and estuaries on the East to the pepper and gold from the highlands. So that Schrieke remarks: 'The pepper at Jambi came from Minangkabau, which exported it via the rivers of Indragiri, Kampar, and Jambi. The "Emperor" of Minangkabau was lord of the pepper and the gold.'[6] And in another place he mentions that the West coast had the Achinese to thank for its conversion to Islam after the middle of the sixteenth century, at least in so far as it had not come from the East coast.[7] Without doubt, newly converted Muslims, especially if in a minority at first, would welcome a close relationship with their co-religionists; and association in trade, and a search for material for it, besides a desire for travel, would play their part.

[4] Qur. 61: 11.
[6] *Indonesian Sociological Studies* (The Hague, 1955), p. 55.
[5] Qur. 61: 10.
[7] Ibid., p. 52.

However the presence of mystical writings is of even more specific value as an illustration of a general tendency of the Muslim world after the capture of Baghdad by the Mongols in 1258, clearly reflected in Indonesia. On Gibb's analysis,[8] after the capture of the Caliphate the task of maintaining the unity of the Islamic community passed to the Sufis, a development rising from the close relationship between the Sufi Shaikh and his disciples, the Sufi missionary spirit, and the popular basis of the movement. The Sufi orders gradually became stable and disciplined foundations, and some of them spread over wide areas. This spread helped to counteract one consequence of the destruction of the Caliphate—the hardening of the division of Muslim lands into Arabic, Persian, and Turkish linguistic regions. For teachers and their disciples journeyed from one end of the Muslim world to the other, carrying ideas across language frontiers and fostering their parallel development. It is against a background such as this that the visits of the various Shaikhs, Makhdums, and Sunans from Arabia, India, and Java to Malacca which are mentioned in the *Sĕjarah Mĕlayu* and the *Babad Tanah Djawi* have an added meaning, and the travels of such Sumatran mystics as Hamzah Pansuri (d. ± 1600) and 'Abd al-Ra'ūf of Singkel (d. ± 1690) gain in significance.

The development of the Sufi orders was paralleled by the elaboration of a theoretical basis for their mysticism which took two principal forms—a neo-Plotinian monism more or less pantheistic which received its decisive formulation from ibn al 'Arabi and al-Jīlī, and a kind of Persian illuminationism formulated by Suhrawardi. The mystical writings we are discussing show the presence of three and perhaps four major international Sufi orders in Acheh in the first half of the seventeenth century, representing both types of speculative thought.

There was the Qadiriyya order, founded by 'Abd al-Qadir Jilani (d. 1166, although its rule was not promulgated until about half a century later). This order was founded in Baghdad. It had branches not only in Indonesia, but also as far afield as Yemen, Egypt, the Sudan, India, and Anatolia. There was the Nakshabandi order founded by Bahā al-Dīn (d. 1388). This was founded in Turkestan, but besides its Indonesian branches existed also in China, Kazan, Turkey, and India. Then there was the Shaṭṭariyya order founded by 'Abdullah Shaṭṭar (d. 1415 or 1428). At its fullest development this order was most widely spread in India and Indonesia, but in the first part of the seventeenth century its headquarters was at Mecca, where the Sumatran 'Abd-al-Ra'ūf studied under two of its *khalīfa*, Aḥmad Qushashi and Burhān al-Dīn Mullā Ibrahīm. From the latter he got an *ijāza* to found the order in Indonesia where it spread very rapidly, especially in Java. Snouck Hurgronje makes the tantalizing

[8] H. A. R. Gibb, 'An Interpretation of Islamic History II,' *Muslim World*, xlv (2 January 1955), pp. 130 *et seq.*

remark that at this time Mecca itself was under Indian influence,[9] but unfortunately does not offer any further information. The conceptual framework on which the teaching of these orders was based is of the ibn al-'Arabi emanationist type, interpreted at times pantheistically.

I know of no direct evidence for the existence of the Suhrawardi order, but there is no doubt that Persian influence was strong at Malacca when it was the centre of Indonesian trade—the division into chapters of the *Sĕjarah Mĕlayu* according to Van Ronkel reflects Persian influence, and according to him also the romances of Amir Hamzah and Muhammad Hanifiyya were translated directly from the Persian. There was also a popular *Hikayat Nur Muhammad* giving an exposition of the Suhrawardi light philosophy. There are also traces of it in various of the mystical writings in which Muhammad is represented as saying: 'The world was created from my light as I was created from that of Almighty God.' Hamzah in fact offers a synthesis of both schools of thought[10]. Indeed it is reasonably certain that Hamzah knew Persian. Kraemer offers the opinion that Hamzah was familiar with the Persian erotic mystical poetry,[11] and Hamzah himself writes that he uses Malay for the benefit of those who do not know Arabic or *Persian*.[12] Here then we see these mystical documents showing us something of the thought and ideals of the people themselves, and their diffusion throughout the Muslim world.

There is another aspect, in as much as they may give us a clue to the social life of the time, for the *tarīḳas* may have played some secular fraternal function. Gibb writes (speaking of the *tarīḳas* in general): 'At some stage, not yet definitely established, lay membership was integrated with the guild organisations of artisans and other professions, each guild being affiliated to a particular *tarīḳa*, and extended also to village and tribal areas.'[13] There is no direct evidence for this, but the notion that the representatives of these major *tarīḳas*, at a time when the *tarīḳas* were playing a predominant role in the life of Islam, existed on some secluded orbit of their own seems unlikely, although just what their relationship with society at large was remains conjectural. It seems safe to infer, however, that the expansion of trade and the changing economic conditions it brought about must have had social consequences, and that these social consequences were not unrelated to the life of the *tarīḳas*.

There is a further point. To say simply that Islam came with trade is to beg the question. It is not usual to think of sailors or merchants as bearers of a religion. If, however, we think of certain traders belonging to Sufi trade guilds, accompanied by their Shaikhs, there seems a more plausible basis for the spread of Islam. This puts the importance of the *tarīḳas* in a

---

[9] *The Achenese*, ii, 10.
[10] Doorenbos, *De Geschriften van Hamzah Pansoeri. Diss.* (Leiden, 1933), p. 142.
[11] Ibid., p. 3. [12] Ibid., p. 176. [13] Gibb, loc. cit., p. 131.

new light. The fact that there were *tarīḳas* in Indonesia has often been noted. As far as I know their paramount importance has not. At all events their interpretation of Islam was certainly suited to the background of the Indonesians, and it should not be going too far to say that the conversion of Indonesia to Islam was very largely the work of the *tarīḳas*—even though they are ungratefully spurned at the present day.[14]

It is useful to recall that the Shaṭṭariyya order had its headquarters at Mecca. Mecca was not, and is not only a centre for the pilgrimage, but a study centre as well. Snouck Hurgronje writes that after every pilgrimage groups of young men from every country stay there to devote themselves for several years to the study of Medieval Muslim scholasticism, and at length return to consolidate the international bonds of the religion.[15] He was writing in particular of pan-Islamism towards the end of the nineteenth century, but the process is as old as Islam itself. It is also important to remember that recognized stopping places on the way to Mecca from Indonesia, such as Surat, for example, were also trading centres.

There are some interesting examples in Malay writing of the way Islamic ideas travelled. As early as the reign of Sultan Manṣur of Malacca there was an interest, in court circles at least, in the classical problems of esoteric Islam. One of these was whether the damned and blessed were in Heaven and Hell for all eternity.[16] The esoteric answer is that they are now, for the sufferings of the damned are eventually to be turned to pleasure. This was a point which received its most popular expression in the *Insān al-Kāmil* of ʿAbd al-Karim al-Jīlī (d. 1417).[17] Sultan Mansur ascended the throne in 1459. It is fair to assume that the contents of the book and its author were well known (at least in Pasai) well before it is referred to in the *Sĕjarah Mĕlayu*, so that the possibility of the work being known in Indonesia within fifty years of its author's death is not unreasonable. The probabilities are that as soon as it gained any kind of currency in the Middle East, it found its way to Indonesia. Another interesting example is the mirror imagery used to express the relation of the many to the one formulated by ibn al-ʿArabi in the *Futuhāt al-Makiyya*. Al-Ranīrī uses it in his *Jawāhir alʿulūm fī kashf al-maʿlūm*.[18] ʿAbd al-Raʾūf uses it in

[14] Gibb, *Modern Trends in Islam* (Chicago, 1945), p. 25: '. . . the spread of Islam in the new territories to the East and South in Asia and Africa was largely the work of the Sufi brotherhoods . . . the brotherhoods were in many cases tolerant of traditional usages and habits of thought which ran contrary to the strict practice of Islamic unitarianism.'

[15] Snouck Hurgronje, *Verspreide Geschriften*, iii, 205.

[16] *Sĕjarah Mĕlayu*, ed. Winstedt, JMBRAS, xvi, pt. 3 (1938), p. 128.

[17] Encyclopaedia of Islam, s.v. *Insān al-Kāmil*.

[18] The account al-Ranīrī gives in a MS. at SOAS is as follows (I quote from memory): 'A thing that is one in point of its being does not become plural or manifold because it is seen in several places at once. If, for example, we take a man, or a lighted candle, and surround them with mirrors—some large, some small, some clear, some dull, some exact, some distorting, will they not appear in each of them with a different shape and form? But the man and the candle have not become several, nor have they changed—on the contrary they are as they were.'

his *Daḳā' iḳ al-Ḥurūf*,[19] and Burhān al-Dīn Mullā Ibrahīm gives an outline of it in a letter to 'Abd al-Ra'ūf, a MS. of which is in Leiden University Library.

A closer study of this mystical literature shows that the years between
1600 and 1670 were a period of change and reformulation in the conceptual framework used by the mystics. This development and adjustment
was not isolated, but parallel to similar adjustments in India. Hamzah
(d. 1600) follows fairly closely the emanation system worked out by al-Jīlī.
One of the characteristics of the system is that the number of emanations
in the series is not limited. The system formulated by an Indian writer
Faḍl Allāh (d. 1620) comprised a series of seven stages divided into two
groups, one of three, the other of four.[20] This was to become *the* Indonesian
system and is popular in the neo-metaphysical speculation in presentday
Indonesian and India/Pakistan Sufi circles. There is probably sufficient
MSS. material to get some idea of the stages of the transfer from one
system to the other. From this point on there seems to have been no change
in the thinking of the *tarīḳas* (the writings of the present day Nakshabandis
in Indonesia might have been taken word for word from the seventeenth
century), except in the multiplication of sub-divisions and the arrange-
ment of terms—a stop evident in other parts of the Muslim world. The
remarks Gibb makes in general apply as exactly to the situation of Sufi
thought in Indonesia as elsewhere: 'The intellectual consequences (of this
anti-rational speculation) were extremely grave. Instead of revitalizing
the inert matter of scholastic instruction in the madrassas, it drew intellectual energies off into subjective and anti-rational speculation, leaving
energies off into subjective and anti-rational speculation, leaving the
former more inert than ever and supplying no rigorous intellectual discipline in its place.'[21] The next important stage in the history of Sumatra
Islam does not come until the irruption of the Paderi/Wahhabi movement
in 1803, which is the watershed of the Islamic modernist movement in
Indonesia.

Another feature of this literature is that it furnished the material for and
reflects a dispute between a pantheistic and non-pantheistic interpretation

[19] A. Johns, JRAS (1955), pts. 3 and 4, pp. 73, 151.

[20] The schema summarizes the salient points of the three systems:

al-Jīlī (d. 1417)	Hamzah (d. ± 1600)	Faḍl Allāh (d. 1620)
al-'amā	Aḥadiyya (:al-Jīlī's ama)	Aḥadiyya
Aḥadiyya		Waḥda
		Wāḥidiyya
Huwiyya	ta 'ayyun awwal (containing two aspects:	'alam al-arwāh
Anniyya	aḥad	'alam al-mithāl
Wāḥidiyya	wāḥid)	'alam al-ajsām
		'alam al-insān kāmil
	ta 'ayyun thani	etc.
etc.	etc.	

[21] Gibb, loc. cit., p. 132.

of the Sufi emanation system. The pantheists declared that each stage of the emanation system was God Himself, the formal series being only aspects under which our mind sees Him. The opposing opinion represented by al-Ranīrī[22] declared that the emanations were not God, but an illusion of being created in somewhat the same way as a stick twirled rapidly creates the illusion of a continuous circle. With the death of Iskandar Muda in 1636, and the arrival of al-Ranīrī in Acheh in 1637, the books of Hamzah Pansuri were burnt, and numbers of his pupils were executed. It is only with al-Ranīrī that we can get some idea of the ideas of history to be found in these writers. So far this paper has treated their writings considered as material for the historian rather than as displaying their authors' notions of the nature and function of history. But on the whole, it must be admitted that to look for ideas of history in mystical writings is a little unrewarding. Al-Qushairi's remark in his treatise on Sufism of the nature of time: 'Something unreal in which we may predicate something real happening'[23] is quite alien to history as we understand it. 'Abd al-Ra'ūf quoted with approval to illustrate a point: 'The gnostic sees himself and all things from various aspects: as different from God, as a state of the Divine Essence, and as God Himself. And he sees God as a mirror in which he sees reflected in detail his own states as he sees himself a manifestation of God's Being—*and all this at one and the same time.*'[24] Serial time is plainly not of the first importance.

Apart from this there is the problem of what we are to define as mystical writing so that we know the limits of our data in the search for ideas of history. By it do we mean writings concerned strictly with the experimental knowledge of God, using the word in its proper sense; or do we mean a teleological view of the world accompanied by more or less vague effusions, if it is used in a more general sense? Then again, can chronicles, which among narratives of kings, kingdoms, and dynasties include stories of mystics—such as that of Siti Jenar—be properly called mystical writings in the sense of expressing ideas of history peculiar to mystics? Or can lives of Saints and the pedigrees of the various *Khalīfa* of the mystical orders be said to possess anything distinctive from the point of view of historical ideas? It must remain an open question.

Certainly the mystics had an attitude to the past, even if it only slips out

[22] Al-Ranīrī's career is interesting, and is perhaps representative of a certain class of religious teacher. Drewes in *Bijdragen*, iii (1955), p. 138 et seq., constructs an interesting background. He establishes that he came from Rander—a prosperous merchant town until it was destroyed by the Portuguese in 1530 and its trade diverted to Surat. Also, with regard to his mixed descent, that his ancestors were perhaps Shi-ite commercial immigrants who under local pressure became Sunni. On the basis of his name he considers him of Hadramaut descent. Al-Ranīrī studied in the Hadramaut, and on returning home and finding no outlet for his energies, travelled further east—to Acheh. It is not unlikely that he too belonged to a *tarīka*. For no matter how he attacked the Wujudiyya, he seems never to have attacked the *tarīka* as such.

[23] Al-Qushairi, *Risāla* (Cairo. 1947), p. 31. [24] JRAS, pts. I–II (1955), p. 67.

occasionally. In a text by 'Abd al-Ra'ūf of Singkel we read that the people of his time had fallen far from the heroism of the earlier Muslims; and since they were weak the practice of the dhikr: *Lā ilāhz illā'llāh* was just the thing for them. This attitude is not acquainted with the idea of progress, neither is it peculiar to mystics. But at any rate there is implicit in it an idea of history: a more or less atomic sequence of events, with things tending to get worse rather than better. It is worth while to muse of the bases for such an attitude: the writer has his heart and judgement firmly anchored on the kernel of history (in this case the mission of Muhammad) from which the ebb and flow of everything round about can be judged with security. Also implicit in the same premise is the tendency to make historical perspective revolve round the Good and the Bad in such a way that the past can never really be *known*, or for the sake of prescisians, attempted to be known, to use, Ranke's words 'as something immediate to God'.[25] It is the attitude behind the intellectual outlook which makes possible the idea of universal history; and in the last resort history becomes a branch of religious instruction.

These are rather broad generalizations to make on the basis of a passing sentence. However, al-Ranīrī was a historian as well as a mystic. And his historical writing may be taken as illustrating the attitude of an Indonesian Muslim mystic to history, even though I rather fear that no points will emerge not implicit in general Muslim historiography in Medieval India. Al-Ranīrī was from the Gujerat, but wrote many works in fluent Malay, and is a characteristic representative of this type of author. The fact of his Gujerat origin makes a convenient link with Muslim historical writing in Medieval India. He was a prolific writer, and among his principal works was the encyclopaedic *Bustān al-Salāṭīn* which he began in Acheh in 1637 during the reign of Sultan Iskandar, and perhaps never finished. The work has never been published in full, and unfortunately I have no extracts available, but the synopsis of the contents given by Dr. C. Hooykaas in *Perintis Sastera* gives some idea of the kind of work it was. It is divided into seven books. The first deals with the creation of Heaven and Earth in seven layers; the Light of Muḥammad, the Inscribed Tablet, the Pen and the Throne, and so on. Book two is about prophets and kings. The stories of the Prophets from Adam to Muḥammad are given; then the kings of Egypt up to the time of Alexander; then the kings of Arabia from pre-Islamic times until the time of Umar including the kings of Nejd and the Hijāz until the time of Muḥammad; the history of Muḥammad and the first four Caliphs. In the same book is a history of the Arabs under the Ummayads and the Abbassids; a history of the Muslim kings of Delhi; a history of the Muslim kings of Malacca and Pahang, and finally, from our point of view the most interesting, a history of the Muslim kings of

[25] Pieter Geyl, *Debates with Historians* (Groningen, 1955), p. 8.

Acheh and an account of some of the religious teachers there prior to and during the seventeenth century.

The third book is about just Kings and Capable Ministers; the fourth Righteous Kings and Saints of God; the fifth Tyrannous Kings and Incompetent Ministers who deceived their masters; the sixth Merciful and Compassionate Men and Mighty Warriors, and the seventh Intelligence and the Sciences.[26]

Two other works of his of historical value are *Nubdha fi da'wā'z-zill ma'a ṣāḥibihi*, an Arabic treatise compiled on the occasion of a dispute with the followers of Shams al-Dīn in the presence of Sultan Iskandar II, and the *Tibyān fi ma'rifat al-Adyān*—an account of the religions of the world up to the time of writing. A significant part of the book consists of a polemic against the alleged pantheism of his near contemporaries Hamzah Pansuri and Shams al-Dīn.[27]

Another Muslim historical work of the same general type, although whether its author would qualify as a mystic or not is open to question, is the *Tāj al-Salātīn* (the Crown of Princes) composed according to a Persian literary type by Bukhari Jauhari (or Bukhari of Johore) in 1603. Basically it is a work of religious instruction with examples culled from history of the qualities of Just and Righteous Kings, Infidel Kings, and the like. Just as in al-Rānīrī's work the virtues of the Good are inflated to incredibly gargantuan proportions. The works are to a high degree derivative. Dr. Voorhoeve has shown for example that more than a quarter of al-Rānīrī's *Tibyān fi ma'rifat al-Adyān* is a literal translation of *al-Tamhīd fi bayān al-Tauḥīd* by Abu Shakūr al-Sālimī.[28] And his comment on the Tibyan: 'The work gives a summary of pre-Muslim religions and the sects of Islam with the express purpose of warning the faithful against these errors in general, and in particular against the heterodox mysticism of the *Wujūdiyya*.'[29] This is fair comment on Indonesian Muslim historical writing of this period, mystical or otherwise. Al-Rānīrī's writing on his near contemporaries is useful to us as historical raw material, but to him and them it was for the most part purely polemic reporting.

As far as ideas of history goes this is rather a negative note. The best one can say is that the attitudes towards history which developed from various sources in Medieval Muslim India found a response in the Indonesian countries among writers of history there, and probably came from there. One admits that the data available for the area in question is hopelessly inadequate, but feels that a reviewer's comment on Rosenthal's *History of Muslim Historiography*, 'This is an interesting and important

[26] C. Hooykaas, *Perintis Sastera* (Groningen Djakarta, 1951), p. 148.
[27] See also *Bijdragen* (1955), iii, 152, where Dr. Voorhoeve gives a full bibliography of his works.
[28] *Twee Maleise Geschriften van Nûruddîn ar-Raniri* (Leiden, 1955), p. 9.
[29] Ibid., p. 7.

though hardly readable book . . . devoted to a subject which should be, but is not very exciting' is apt.

There are various other points of interest arising from this Sumatran mystical literature. The authors—Hamzah, Shams al-Dīn, al-Rānīrī and 'Abd al-Ra'ūf are the first authors writing in Malay known to us by name —which is an important stage in the development of a literature. It also represents a workmanlike if crude use of the language in the attempt to make it the vehicle for ideas of a most esoteric type taken from a different tradition of civilization. The struggle to do this played an important part in the development of the language which is in many respects parallel to the development of modern Indonesian.

In addition these mystical writings can contribute to an understanding of the form in which Islam reached Indonesia, and thus provide a basis which assists in the isolation of what is peculiarly Javanese in the later formulations of Javanese Islamic mysticism. For it must be admitted that most of the literature from Sumatra is concerned with the elaboration and analysis of schema, and as mystical writing in its own right (with the exception of Hamzah) is of little more than historical value. In Java the picture is very different. The stories and traditions are richer, and have a dimension totally lacking in those from Sumatra. They are of great interest both in themselves and as evidence of acculturation. When analysed and set against the prevailing political, social, and economic background they will be of great value to the historian.

One example can be taken from East Java, the history of which is nothing if not complicated when one considers the situation following the decline of Majapahit; the rivalry between Demak and Pengging and later the struggle between the agrarian inland Mataram and the Islamic coast towns—not to mention further complications following the spread of European influence. The story of Siti Jenar who was executed about the middle of the sixteenth century is famous in Java. It has become a nucleus for a large number of legends, and treated in many *Babad*; even today it is easy to obtain, printed locally. The following is a translation from one version:

As time passed Demak grew more and more prosperous, and the reputation of the Sultan and of the religious head of the state, Sunan Giri became known all over Java. There were many students taking religious instruction (*ngelmi*) from the *walis* but they all had differing doctrines to offer.

Among Siti Jenar's students was a son of Dipata Andayaningrat of Pengging, and Pangeran Panggung, a son of the Sultan. These studied with Siti Jenar, and as time went by, more and more students came to him in search of mystical knowledge. Many Fridays went by without their attending the mosque. Since this was so Sunan Giri summoned a meeting of the *walis* who crowded together in the mosque, and said softly: 'I have summoned you all to discuss Siti Jenar. He is devoting himself to mysticism to such an extent that he neglects the Friday prayer. If he is not stopped the mosques will soon be empty, for the Javanese naturally follow the teaching which makes the least demands on them.'

The *walis* replied respectfully: 'He should be summoned and asked to alter his conduct. If he refuses, he should be executed. There is a precedent for this in the book of Nawawi where it is mentioned that a Shaikh Mubarak was punished in the presence of the Prophet himself because he contravened the holy law by revealing hidden knowledge which was the prerogative of Muhammad—thus treating the law of the prophet with contempt. There is no knowing where the matter will stop.'

Sunan replied to this by ordering two *khatibs* to go to Siti Jenar and ask him to come to Giri. They set out without delay, and soon arrived. They entered his house and said respectfully: 'We are required to invite you to come with us to Giri.' But Siti Jenar replied: 'You must both realise that there *is* no Siti Jenar. Only God *is*.'

Thereupon the two messengers took their leave, and went straight back to Giri. They entered into the presence of the Sunan, and bowing said: 'Lord, we were sent to bring Siti Jenar, but he replies: "There *is* no Siti Jenar; only God *is*." '

Sunan Giri smiled, and replied softly: 'Then go back, and say that I require God to be brought into my presence.' The two messengers set out, and went straight to Siti Jenar. They addressed him respectfully, saying: 'God, you are requested to come to Sunan Giri.' But Siti Jenar replied: 'Now Siti Jenar is sitting here—you may report that.'

The two messengers thereupon set out again. They returned straight to Giri, and bowing reported this to the Sunan. Sunan Giri asked them softly to go back again and request Siti Jenar *and* God to come. They set out quickly, and after arriving delivered the king's order for Siti Jenar *and* God to go with them to Giri, and come before the Sunan.

Siti Jenar smiled, then set out with the two messengers followed by seven of his disciples. They went straight to Giri. After arriving they exchanged greetings with the *walis* and sat down. Sunan Giri asked him why he did not fulfil the Friday duty, thereby putting into effect the law of the Prophet, and making the mosque a centre of activity. But Siti Jenar replied: 'There *is* no Friday, there *is* no mosque. Only God truly is. Nothing has being other than He.'

Sunan Giri nodded to Sunan Kali who then spoke, at the same time drawing his sword, asking: 'What is this then?' Siti Jenar replied: 'God is manifest in it.' (*Allah ingkang katon iki.*) At once his neck was severed, his head fell, and his body rolled on the ground. Red blood flowed from him. Sunan Kali jeered: 'So God has red blood, and his body rolls over like a banana-palm trunk.'

But without any sound the blood suddenly became clear, and then white, giving a sweet perfume. At the same time it recited: 'There is but one God, and Muhammad is His prophet.' So the blood declared. Then body and blood both vanished. Sunan Kali commented: 'This is what happens when devils are slain, the body disappears.'

But then the voice of Siti Jenar was heard saying: 'What does death matter? If one places his trust in any other unity than that of the All-Highest he will be disappointed and not attain his goal—just like one suffering highway robbery.'

Sunan Giri then turned to the seven disciples, and asked them: 'Do you wish to follow your master?' They all so wished and were put to death. Their bodies too vanished.

The *Wali*-synod smiled (grimly) and gave thanks to God (Yang Sukma).

This is but one example from an unedited MS. reproduced in the T.B.G.[30] As Rinkes observes it has close affinities with the story of Mansur Hallaj; the number of legends woven round it are also somewhat the same in content. Just as—according to Muslim belief—only a phantasm of Christ was crucified, so the same substitution theories were elaborated around al-Hallaj and Siti Jenar.[31] With regard to the significance of the story from the standpoint of acculturation and the reaction of the Javanese to Islam, one can hardly do better than quote Schrieke—although with the caution that at the moment any form of rationalism of this kind can only be tentative: 'With the ecstatic sense of unity, which according to its psychic content and as the highest saving secret of life was a pre-Mohammadan possession of the Javanese, their minds associated merely the various terms, mental and emotional complexes which Arabian-Persian mysticism supplied. Hence too, the predeliction for the extreme pantheism of the "heretical" Siti Jenar, which outvies all positive religion and yet clothes itself in Moslem terms, and wishes to be interpreted as the true Islam.'[32]

Politically one can see in it a reflection, in general of the struggle between the Muslim coastal population under the leadership of the *panguku* of the holy *desa* of Giri against the Javanistic Islam of the agrarian and potentially rival kingdom of Mataram; and in particular of the rivalry between Demak and Pengging.[33] It is interesting to note the relative posi-

[30] Rinkes, De heiligen van Java II, T.B.G. 53, pp. 18 et seq.
[31] Rinkes, ibid. VI, T.B.G. 55, p. 37.
[32] Schrieke, op. cit., p. 237.　　　　　　　　[33] Rinkes, ibid. II, T.B.G. 53, p. 47.

tions of heterodoxy and orthodoxy reversed when Mataram gained power over the coastal towns. For under Sultan Agung (1613–45) there was a revival of Javanese theosophy, and his successor Mangkurat I (1646–77) even initiated a persecution of orthodox religious teachers.[34]

As a further background there is a new pattern of economic rivalries following on entrance of Europeans into the Indonesian countries, and a succession of struggles for power among the states of the archipelago and a series of commercial alliances both among themselves and with the European intruders.

This paper has perhaps indicated avenues of research rather than explored them. At least it may have shown something of the value of mystical writings from the standpoint of historical research and as examples of historiography. As far as the history of Islam is concerned it furnishes another illustration of the relevance of Massignon's remarks on the *tarīḳas*: 'The *tarīḳas* however cannot be completely neglected: and although their average moral level is very far below that of the great examples of the first Sufiya, the great part they have never ceased to play in the everyday life, humble but profound of the Muslim community promises important results to those who will undertake a thorough study of their rules and writings.'[35]

As far as the history of Indonesia is concerned they have given us some idea of the mental world of the Indonesian peoples, the ideas of history implicit in it, and the energy with which they threw themselves into the intellectual and spiritual life of the international system of which they were so integral a part, at least till towards the end of the seventeenth century.

That the religious, and particularly Islamic history of Indonesia is closely linked with politics and commerce is already well known, but it has not yet received sufficient emphasis of the right kind, nor has the intimate pattern between it and these varying conditioning factors—which both illuminate it and are illuminated—been carefully analysed. The extent of pan-Islamism among the various Indonesian states from Acheh to Ternate, and their relations with the Dutch company and with the non-Islamic states in the seventeenth century for example, is a fascinating theme. This is a first necessity. A second is that every stage of religious development must be closely documented from indigenous writings to the point of direct and ample quotation—translated into English—for only specialists can have an adequate knowledge of the wide linguistic field involved. Broad generalizations based on synopses are not only inadequate, they are misleading.

[34] Schrieke, op. cit, p. 77.   [35] Encyclopaedia of Islam, s.v. *Tarīḳa*.

5. THE NATURE OF THE BURMESE CHRONICLES

U TET HTOOT

Monks are forbidden by Buddha to indulge in idle talk on stories of kings, robbers, ministers, and generals, as indulgence in such idle talk is not conducive to spiritual development. But the commentary adds that if such stories are treated as themes showing the impermanence of all things—how even mighty kings cannot escape death—then it is permissible to indulge in such talk. Although the original injunction of the Buddha and the commentarial interpretation of it is meant for monks, not only Burmese monks but Burmese laymen as well take the interpretation of the commentary as their moral justification to write their chronicles. U Kala, a layman, and the compilers of the *Hman Nan* and Second Chronicles, monks, and laymen, all quote this interpretation of the commentary in the exordiums of their chronicles as justification for writing them. They have a secondary aim as well: to give moral instruction on the art of government to kings, ministers, generals, envoys, and other government officials, and quote, in their exordiums, extracts from Buddhist texts and works on Indian policy which set forth the qualities they should possess in the discharge of their duties.

In flavour the Burmese chronicles are not unlike Elizabethan chronicles such as those of Holinshed and Speed. As Camden's attitude to history can very well be applied to Burmese chronicles, it is not inappropriate to quote his words in his preface to his *History of the Reign of Queen Elizabeth*. 'Things manifest and evident I have not concealed; things doubtful I have interpreted favourably; things secret and abstruse I have not pried into. The hidden meaning of princes (saith that great master of history) and what they secretly design to search out, it is unlawful, it is doubtful and dangerous: pursue not therefore the search thereof. And, with Helicarnassaeus, I am angry with those curious inquisitive people who will need seek to know more than by the laws permitted.' The Burmese chroniclers might not have expressed themselves explicitly in these words but that they had such an attitude was reflected in their works down to as recently as 1918. They had their limitations. One can complain of them as Bacon, in his *History of Henry VII*, complained of 'the best writers of history, that they do not often enough summarily deliver and set down the most memorable laws' but, within their limitations, they were honest and did not distort history as imputed to them by Crawfurd.

The following remarks were written by Crawfurd in his *Journal*, published in 1829. 'I learnt last night, from good authority, that the Court Historiographer had recorded in the National Chronicle his account of the war with the English. It was to the following purport:— In the year 1186 and 1187, the Kalapyu or white strangers of the West, fastened a quarrel upon the Lord of the Golden Palace. They landed at Rangoon, took that place and Prome, and were permitted to advance as far as Yandabo, for the king, from motives of piety and regard to life, made no effort whatever to oppose them. The strangers had spent vast sums of money in their enterprise; and by the time they reached Yandabo, their resources were exhausted and they were in great distress. They petitioned the king, who, in his clemency and generosity, sent them large sums of money to pay their expenses back and ordered them out of the country.' It must be pointed out that Crawfurd was in Ava in 1827 but the compilation of the Hman Nan Chronicle was only begun in 1829 and took some three or four years. The account of the first Anglo-Burmese war, however, was written only in 1867 at the compilation of the Second Chronicle under the patronage of King Mindon. There the defeat of the Burmese army was faithfully recorded and the Yandabo Treaty with all its clauses was fully given. Henry Burney, in his valuable note in the twentieth volume of *Asiatic Researches*[1] also refuted the imputation of Crawfurd. As he wrote just after the completion of the *Hman Nan* Chronicle, I am giving his note in full.

The Burmese possess several histories of their own kings, as well as of the kings of Prome, Pagan, Zenmay, Toung-ngoo and Ta-thoung, relating fairly enough their disasters as well as successes, and bearing strong internal marks of authenticity, often supported by ancient stone inscriptions. About four years ago the present king of Ava appointed some of his most learned priests and officers to compile a new edition of the large Burmese History, called Maha Yazawen-dau-gyee. I possess a copy of this work in thirty-nine volumes. It commences with the creation of the world, according to the Buddhist system of cosmogony, and after giving some account of the kings of Magadha and Central India, and of the life of Gaudama, relates a history of the kings of Tagoung, Prome, Pegu, and Ava, coming down to the year 1821. The ground work of this compilation is taken from other histories written at various times, and principally from two works, copies of which I also possess.

One is a very popular history in twenty volumes, comprising a period from the creation of the world down to the Burmese year 1073 (A.D. 1721) written by a private individual named Moung Kula, who is said to have died about the time that the Peguers took Ava in 1751. The

[1] pp. 163–4 (1836).

other is a continuation of this history, compiled by an officer named
Pana Mengyee or Moutta Mengyee, and comprises a period from 1711
to 1819, to the death of the late king, in thirteen volumes. What Mr.
Crawfurd reported as to the account of the late war written by the royal
historiographer at Ava, is a very good story, but I have the best reason
for believing that he was incorrectly informed. There is no such officer
at Ava as a special historiographer, and the portion continuing the
history from 1821 to 1830 in eight or nine volumes, has only lately been
completed by a committee of officers and learned men, whose labours
have not yet been published. An abstract of the large history was prepared for me in 1830, by order of the king of Ava, and I then made a
translation of it.

U Kala's Chronicle

There were chroniclers before him. It is said that even as far back as
during the reign of a Pyu king, supposed to have flourished between 19 and
10 B.C., six wise men—Puppā Maṇi, Indriya, Kittiriya, Candriya, Sakka,
and Massa—had written a chronicle and an astronomical work; but U
Kala's chronicle was accepted as the standard work when the Hman Nan
Chronicle was compiled. We know very little about him. He wrote his
chronicle during the reign of Taninganwe (1714–33). There are three
versions of it—*Mahā Yazawin Gyi* (the great chronicle in twenty-one
volumes), *Yazawin Lat* (the middling or shorter chronicle in ten volumes),
and *Yazawin Choke* (the brief chronicle in one volume). As far as I know
the great chronicle, *Mahā Yazawin Gyi*, has not been published in full and
so I cannot say in which year he ended it. Burney was told at Ava that it
consisted of twenty volumes ending in the year 1721. A copy of the Yazawin
Lat, the shorter chronicle, is in The India Office Library (Chevilliot
3452). It ends in the year 1714 when Taninganwe ascended the throne. In
his colophon to his shorter version, U Kala said that he was a faithful
subject of Taninganwe and that he was a son of Dewa Tha Htay (Pali:
Deva Seṭṭhi).[2] In his colophon to the shorter version (Chevilliot 3452,
India Office Library), U Kala said that he collected the materials for his

---

[2] Seṭṭhi=banker or richman, titles given to rich men as king's bankers. In the year 1661, when
Pye ascended the throne, he gave Tha Htay titles to many men. Among them, a man called
Mya Kyauk was given the title of Dewa Tha Htay. He may very well have been U Kala's father.
Saya Pwa, in his introduction to his edition of U Kala's chronicle, says that he was, on his
mother's side, a descendant of a son of the Mohnyin Sawbwa called Sa Maw Khan, who served
under Bayinnaung in his campaigns in Siam and Chiengmai, and for distinguishing himself in
battles with an elephant was rewarded with titles and governorships of towns. Kaw Hla, Sa
Maw Khan's son, served under Nandabayin, Nyaungyan, and Anaukpetlun, winning titles and
the governorship of the town of Sale under them. He too distinguished himself in battle with an
elephant at Mone under the crown prince who later became Anaukpetlun. These are the few
facts we know about U Kala. We do not know the dates of his birth and death from published
Burmese sources. Burney's note is the only source so far where the year of his death was given.

chronicle from many *thamaings, mawguns* (accounts of founding of various cities, temples, etc.), traditional accounts of events, chronicles of kings and *ayedawbons* (memoirs on the reigns of certain kings). He did not mention all the names of the works he had used but in discussing certain facts, he mentioned three by name: an *ayedawbon* (probably a memoir on the reign of Bayinnaung), a chronicle written by a Royal Brahmin called *Punna Rāja Brahmana Yazawin*, and *Thakkarit Pon* (a work on chronological dates). We do not know the state of chronicles existing in his time and whether there was one on which he modelled his work. There were separate local chronicles about the dynasties that flourished in Tagaung, Prome, Pagan, and the Mon kingdoms of Lower Burma. There were others that brought together the chronicles of Tagaung, Prome, and Pagan into a continuous narrative. One of the earliest I have come across is *Zambu Kungya Po Yāzā Mū haung* (Chevilliot 3447, India Office Library). It was attributed to Po Yāzā or Wun Zin Min Yāzā who was appointed tutor to Min Khaung when he was crown prince by his father Minkyiswa Sawke (1368–1401). It is the only chronicle which mentions the name of the monk of the master of Narathihapate, the king of Pagan who fled before the Chinese, as Disāpāmokkha. Disāpāmokkha had left an inscription mentioning his negotiations with the Tartars after the fall of Pagan. His name and his negotiation are not mentioned either in U Kala's chronicle or the *Hman Nan* chronicle.

It is recorded that a monk called Hnget Pyittaung Shin Godhāvara wrote a chronicle in Pali treating the histories of Tagaung, Prome, and Pagan into a continuous narrative. Being a monk, he must have taken moral justification to write his chronicle from the gloss on the Buddha's injunction in the Pali commentary, as U Kala, though a layman, quoted the commercial gloss. Hnget Pyittaung Shin Godhāvara may have influenced U Kala and later Burmese chroniclers in respect of moral justification for the writing of chronicles.[3]

There was no chronicle before the appearance of U Kala's work that brought forward the history of Burma down to the year 1721 and hence it was regarded as the standard work, when the *Hman Nan* was compiled in 1829. As it was written in the best Burmese prose and had an epic quality, it became a model of Burmese historical writing down to the second decade of this century.[4]

[3] In a manuscript in the British Museum (Oriental 6453A) there is a misleading note in pencil saying Hnget Pyit Taung chronicle volume 7th, but it cannot be Hnget Pyittaung Shin Godhāvara's chronicle as it is written in Burmese instead of in Pali and it is almost word for word the same as U Kala's chronicle. It must be U Kala's chronicle owned by another monk having the same designation of Hnget Pyit Taung.

[4] Burney mentioned in his note a continuation of U Kala's chronicle from 1711 to 1829 by an officer named Pana Mengyee or Moutta Mengyee, but this work as well as its author is not mentioned in the standard bibliography of Burmese works, *Pitakat Thamaing*, nor in any other published Burmese sources.

The Hman Nan Chronicle

It was compiled at the request of Bagyidaw in 1829 to bring Burmese history up to date and to correct the errors in U Kala's chronicle. It covered the same ground as U Kala had done, following him mostly, but bringing the history of Burma down to the year 1821. It was apparently presented to Bagyidaw in 1832 (Monywe Sayadaw's *Rājovāda*). There are some points where the compilers of the *Hman Nan* differed from U Kala. Up to the latter's time Chiengmai was regarded as Suvaṇṇabhūmi (Golden Earth) instead of the Thaton region.[5] There were some who regarded Suvaṇṇabhūmi as somewhere in Siam. The compilers of the *Hman Nan* rejected these views and considered the Thaton region as more likely to have been Suvaṇṇabhūmi. They based their view on a passage in the commentary on the Anguttara Nikāya where it was said to be a place which could be reached by ship from Ceylon in seven days' sail under favourable monsoon wind, and it was also said to be a place where there were more creatures living in the water than on land. As Chiengmai was not in a coastal region they could not accept it as Suvaṇṇabhūmi. In the Kalyaṇī inscription the Thaton region was taken as Suvaṇṇabhūmi, with Sudhammaphra as its capital. As it was a coastal region, they thought it was more reasonable to accept it as Suvaṇṇabhūmi than Chiengmai.

They claimed too that their dates were more correct than those of U Kala as they based theirs on those found in the inscriptions. There had been interest in inscriptions since Bodawpaya ascended the throne. He wanted to check lands dedicated to pagodas and monasteries and if possible to get revenue from them, not for his personal use, but in order to spend it on religious works. The Twinthintaik Wun and the Thetpan Atwinwun were given charge of the inscriptions, some genuine and some copies, gathered in Amarapura. As the dates they had taken down were based on incorrect readings and incorrect copies, the dates in *Hman Nan* were no more correct than those in U Kala's chronicle.[6] Burmese scholars during Bodawpaya's reign were aware of the discrepancy between the traditional dates assigned to kings in the chronicles and those found in inscriptions. Already in 1810, Monywe Sayadaw, who took a leading part in the compilation of *Hman Nan* and who himself wrote a chronicle afterwards, admitted the discrepancy and urged people not to accept the dates he had worked out as final but said that under the circumstances those were the best that he could offer and that they should take them only after

[5] Bayinnaung, for example, forbade capture of prisoners of war when Chiengmai fell into his hands, saying it was the land of Suvaṇṇabhūmi from where Buddhism first came to Burma.

[6] This has been pointed out by Pagan Wundauk U Tin in his *Myanma Min Okchokpon*, and by U Hpe in his new Chronicle of Pagan, both of whom had worked in the Archaeological Department of Burma. The findings of the Archaeological Department and Professor Luce have not reached to the ordinary Burmese public as yet.

checking with those in the inscriptions or other available contemporary sources such as *ayegyins* or *mawguns* (laudatory verses extolling the cxploits of royal ancestors) for the dynasties that flourished after the fall of Pagan.[7]

The Second Chronicle

The compilation of *Dutiya Mahā Yazawin* or the Second Chronicle was begun in 1867 at the request of King Mindon. It brought forward the history of Burma from the year 1821 to the year 1869. The first part consisting of seven volumes ended in the year 1854, and the second part consisting of three volumes ended in the year 1869. Burney had mentioned a continuation of the *Hman Nan* from 1821 to 1830 by a committee of officers and learned men which had not been published as yet while he was at Ava, but this work was not mentioned by King Mindon in his request to compile the Second Chronicle; he asked the committee of compilers to start the continuation from the year 1821. There is no mention of this work in *Pitakat Thamaing*, the bibliography of Burmese works,[8] or in any other published Burmese sources. The committee of compilers was composed of monks and officers. The monks were the preceptors of the Queen of the Southern Chamber, Maung Daung Sayadaw and Pakhan Gyi Sayadaw. The officers were Kani Atwinwun, Maingkhaing Myosa Atwinwun, former Atwinwun to the Crown Prince, and two secretaries. It might interest English historians to know that Burney's attempt to reconcile Bagyidaw and Tharrawaddy, when the latter rebelled, is mentioned here. He must be the only Englishman mentioned in Burmese chronicles as one who had taken part in domestic politics. When it was finished Mindon gave the order that the *Hman Nan* should be known as the First Chronicle and the continuation as the Second Chronicle. It was only here that the account of the First Anglo-Burmese war was faithfully narrated and the Yandabo Treaty with all its clauses was recorded disproving what Crawfurd had said in his journal. The account of the Second Anglo-Burmese war too was given in this chronicle. The first part only of the Second Chronicle ending in the year 1854 was published as a separate volume in 1919.

The Konbaung Set and Thuthodhita (Pali = Susodhita)

After the annexation of Burma in 1886, Wetmasut Wundauk, Thandawsint Letnettaik Wun U Aung Min, Kani Sitke and U Tin (K.S.M.

---

[7] The compilers of the *Hman Nan* were learned men in the Pali Canon. Where U Kala had made wrong attributions to Pali works for his quotations or relied on non-canonical works such as the Lokapaññatti for his story of Upagupta and Asoka, they pointed out his mistakes and the non-canonical unorthodox nature of the work in question.

[8] See Bibliographical Notes (*a*) at the end of this paper.

and A.T.M. of Mandalay) wrote the continuations of the Second Chronicle down to the year 1885. I have not come across the accounts written by Wetmasut Wundauk and Thandawsint Letnettaik Wun U Aung Min. U Tin's account was the best known because he took out the account dealing with the Alaungpaya Dynasty from the *Hman Nan* and the Second Chronicle adding to it his continuation down to 1885 and published it as *Konbaung Set*, the chronicle dealing with the whole of the Alaungpaya Dynasty (or was his continuation just the work of Wetmasut Wundauk?)

The Thudhammawati Press published the whole of the *Hman Nan* and the Second Chronicle with a continuation down to 1885 naming it *Thuthodhita* Chronicle (Pali=susodhita, a word taken from the Pali verses in the exordium of *Hman Nan*, susodhita meaning corrected= purified=purified text). Kani Sitke and Maingkhaing Myosa Atwin Wun are mentioned in the introduction of this edition as each having written the continuation of the Second Chronicle but it does not mention whose continuation it has incorporated in this edition and so the last part in *Thuthodhita* can be either the work of Kani Sitke U Aung Min or Maingkhaing Myosa Atwinwun. The unusual feature in this continuation in the *Thuthodhita* Chronicle is the note of sympathy shown towards the murdered princes in the account of Thibaw's reign. Personal feeling such as this is very rarely shown in Burmese chronicles.

Monywe Chronicle

This chronicle has never been published. Monywe Sayadaw, a monk of Monywe Village, poet, scholar, and historian, was one of the leading compilers of the *Hman Nan*. As has been mentioned before, he had already worked out the dates for Burmese history in 1810 and his dates with slight changes were adopted in the *Hman Nan*. After finishing the compilation of the *Hman Nan*, he wrote another one on his return to his village. I have the manuscript of only the third part of this chronicle, dealing mostly with the entire reign of Alaungpaya. But being a monk and a poet, he gives more information in his chronicle about ecclesiastical matters, such as about many sects flourishing before the rise of Alaungpaya and also about poets flourishing before the fall of Ava in 1752. Also, being a great lover of his village, he mentions people from his village who figured in Burmese history. [9]

[9] For instance, he writes about one U Nay from his village who first served under the last king of Ava with titles Yanta Kyaw and Pyanchi Kyaw Din, under Alaungpaya first with the title Letwethondara and later after the conquest of Pegu, with that of Letwe Noratha, under Naungtaw Gyi with that of Sithu Kyaw Din, under Hsinbyushin with the titles Sithu Kyaw Din, Nemyo Mahā Kyaw Din, Nemyo Maha Thinkhaya Kyaw Din, under Singu with that of Mingyi Nemyo Mahā Kyaw Din, and under Bodawpaya with the title Maha Thiha Thūra. He was personal secretary to Alaungpaya and the writer of his orders and personal letters including those sent to the East India Company.

Alaung Mintaragyi Ayedawpon

Two memoirs on the reign of Alaungpaya are recorded in *Pitakat Thamaing*. One is attributed to Letwethondara, a native of Monywe mentioned by the Monywe Sayadaw. The other is attributed to Twinthin Taik Wun Mingyi Mahā Sīthū. The published memoir on the reign of Alaungpaya is attributed to him. It is interesting in that it seems like a draft work compared with the finished narrative on the reign of Alaungpaya in the *Hman Nan*.

Twinthin Taik Wun Mingyi Mahā Sīthū, poet, scholar, historian, and minister during the reign of Bodawpaya, also wrote a new chronicle of Burma, which is often referred to in the *Hman Nan*.

Arakanese Chronicles

I know of two chronicles of Arakan published in Burma. There may have been other chronicles published in Arakan itself. There are Arakanese Chronicles in manuscript both in the British Museum and India Office Library. *Danyawadī Ayedawbon* was written by Danyawadī Sayadaw in 1787, bringing the history of Arakan up to 1784, the date of the conquest of Arakan by Bodawpaya. He was one of the missionary monks sent by Bodawpaya to Arakan to take charge of the clergy in Sandoway district. In his colophon, he says that he bases his work on an old chronicle having forty-eight aṅgās.[10] His work is just a précis of the old chronicle.

Another work, *Danyawadī Yāzawinthit*, New Chronicle of Arakan, was written by Minkyaung Sayadaw U Pandi of Pegu in 1910. He ended his chronicle after the First Anglo-Burmese war of 1824–6.

Both these works are brief chronicles of Arakan based on older chronicles and so they cannot be taken as good examples of Arakanese historical writing. It is strange that both these works should make Philip De Brito one of the sons of Min Ba Gyi, grandfather of Min Yaza Gyi. Arakan, having as long a history as an independent kingdom as Burma proper, must have been rich in historical and literary materials. When the royal library from Arakan was brought to Bodawpaya, Mahā Dhamma Thingyan, the author of *Sāsanālaṅkāra*, complained that it did not even possess a complete set of the five volumes on the Vinaya[11] in Pali, the rest being all works of trifling secular literature.

Mon Chronicles

With regard to Mon chronicles, I am unable to write much about them. *Yazadirit Ayedawbon*, memoir in the reign of Yazadirit, is the most well

[10] One aṅgā has 12 palm leaves and so twenty-four pages of writing. The old chronicle must have had 576 palm leaves and double the amount in pages.

[11] i.e., Rules for the Buddhist Order.

known. There are two versions, one attributed to Binnya Dala, trusted Mon minister of Bayinnaung, and another to Gamaṇi Thingyan. The latter may be the fuller translation from Mon. *Yazadirit Ayedawbon* has great literary quality and it may have influenced Burmese historical style of writing a great deal.[12]

Religious History

The standard work is *Sāsanālaṅkāra* written by Maha Dhamma Thingyan in 1831. He was a great scholar of Pali and Sanskrit and as a monk he was known as Maung Daung Sayadaw. Bodawpaya made him Head of the Buddhist Order, but unfrocked him in 1813. Maung Daung, a village in Upper Burma near Ahlon, produced many famous monks and he was one of them.

The *Sāsanavaṁsa* is a history of the Buddhist religion in Burma written in Pali by another famous monk from Maung Daung village known as Maung Daung Sayadaw U Paññāsāmi. He based his work mainly on Mahā Dhamma Thingyan's *Sāsanālaṅkāra*. He was one of the monks who participated in the compilation of the Second Chronicle during the reign of King Mindon. His work *Sāsanavaṁsa*, written in 1861, is considered as another standard work in Burma. Mabel Bode based her Pali Literature of Burma on this work. It has now been translated into English by B. C. Law in the Sacred Books of the Buddhists series.

Sāsana-bahussuttappakāsani

Phayaphyu Sayadaw U Yāzinda wrote and published this work in 1928. It is interesting in that it gives information about the high-handed treatment meted out to his opponents by Atula Sayadaw while he was Head of the Buddhist Order under Alaungpaya. It also refers to the 'mad period of Bodawpaya' when Maung Daung Sayadaw and others were unfrocked by him. But this work is not comparable in quality to *Sāsanālaṅkāra* or *Sāsanavaṁsa*.

BIBLIOGRAPHICAL NOTES

(a) The following is a list of chronicles given in the *Pitakat Thamaing* a standard bibliography of Pali and Sanskrit texts and Burmese works of all aspects of Burmese literature written by Maingkhaing Myosa, who took part in the compilation of *Dutiya Yazawin* (Second Chronicle) and wrote a continua-

[12] Phayre's manuscript copy of the Burmese translation of Mon Chronicle (British Museum, Oriental 3462–3–4) is interesting in that Phayre adopted the name Nanda Bayin for the son of Bayinnaung. Nanda Bayin is very puzzling to the Burmese as it does not sound as a Burmese name. The Mon Chronicle might have used the last word 'Nanda' from his title as a prince and later combined it with the Burmese word 'Bayin' king. Nanda Bayin is known as Ngazūdāyaka in Burmese chronicles. Had Phayre any sound reason to adopt a Mon rather than a Burmese name?

tion of it down to the fall of Mandalay in 1885. As he was librarian at the Mandalay Palace, we may presume that these chronicles were regarded as standard works of reference during the reigns of Mindon and Thibaw. Some of them, the main works as well as a few unrecorded in this list, are in the India Office Library and the British Museum. Only a few from this list have been published in Burma.

1. *Majjhimadesa Yazawin.* Chronology of Sakyan kings of India based on Sumaṅgalavilāsinī Aṭṭhakathā, Linatthapakāsanī Tīkā (old version) and Sādhujanavilāsinī Ṭīkā (new version)—all Pali commentaries.
2. *Thīho Yazawin* (Thīho=Sīhala=Ceylon), Chronicle of Ceylon. Anon.
3. *Pagan Mahā Yazawin Paṭh*, Chronicle of Pagan (in Pali?), by Hnget Pyittaung Shin Godhāvara of Pagan (Monk).
4. *Pagan Yazawin*, Chronicle of Pagan, by a brahmin called Brahmaṇa or Rāja Brahmaṇa of Pagan.
5. *Pagan Yazawin*, Chronicle of Pagan. Anon.
6. *Toungoo Yazawin*, Chronicle of Toungoo. Anon.
7. *Yazawin Gyaw*, by Shin Thilawuntha (Monk), written in 882 B.E. (1520?) at Yindaw. Mostly about chronology of Kings of India and Ceylon and very little about Burmese kings. The only interesting thing is his reference to the existence of a Burmese chronicle about Prome, Pagan, Pinya, and Ava.
8. *Yazawin Gyoke*, by Shin Agga Dhammālaṅkāra (Monk).
9. *Thaton Yazawin*, Chronicle of Thaton. Anon.
10. *Mon Yazawin*, Chronicle of Mons. Anon.
11. *Zinme Yazawin*, Chronicle of Chiengmai
12. *Yakhaing Yazawin*, Chronicle of Arakan
    By Sīthū Gamaṇi Thingyan, who was Maharatanāpon Taiksoe (Chief of the custom house at Mandalay?)
13. *Yodaya Yazawin*, Chronicle of Siam. Anon.
14. *Tayok Yazawin*, Chronicle of China. Anon.
15. *Pūtakay Yazawin*, Chronicle of Portugal, by an unknown monk (?).
16. *Mahā Yazawingyi*
17. *Yazawin Lat*
18. *Yazawin Choke*
    U Kala's Chronicle, with shorter and brief or concise versions.
19. *Mahā Yazawinthit*, New Chronicle by Twinthin Taik Wun Mingyi Mahā Sīthū. He was given charge of inscriptions at Amarapūra by Bodawpaya.
20. *Hman Nan* Chronicle.
21. *Dutiya Mahā Yazawin*, Second Chronicle. Here Mainkhaing Myosa said that he (i.e. Mainkhaing Myosa Mingyi Mahā Thirizeyathu), Mahā Minhla Thinkhayā, former Atwinwun to the Crown Prince, and two secretaries Minhlazeyathu and Nemyo Sīthū-Yāza compiled this chronicle. He does not mention the two monks, Maung Daung Sayadaw and Thetpan Sayadaw and Kani Atwinwun, whose names were given as compilers in the introduction to the Second Chronicle. After they had compiled the Second Chronicle, Mainkhaing Myosa says that they continued compiling the history of Burma down to the year 1869 during Mindon's reign.

22. *Ngazu Dāyaka Min Ahmabon*, Memoir on the mistakes made by Ngazu Dāyahā Min (i.e. Nanda Bayin). Anon.
23. *Hanthawaddypa Min Ahmabon*, Memoir on the mistakes made by Hathawaddypa Min (i.e. Mahādhammayazadipati, the last king of Nyaung yan Dynasty of Ava). Anon.
24. *Yazawunthadīpaka*, by Maung O, otherwise known as Salin Minthagyi (Prince of Salin). He was brother-in-law of Bagyidaw. The English who went to Ava knew him as Minthagyi. Tharrawaddy executed him. He and Akyidaw Maung Ye wrote this work. (Akyidaw=Chief Steward of a prince or princess holding the superintendence of the estate in which his master or mistress lives. Was Maung Ye his Chief Steward?)
25. *Majjhimadesa-Sīhaladīpa-Myanma-Yazawingyoke*, Concise chronicle of India, Ceylon and Burma, by Nyaunggan Sayadaw (monk).
26. *Yazadhirit Ayebon*, Memoir on the reign of Yazadhirit by Bhinnyadala. A Mon who served under Bayinnaung as a minister. He plotted many times to assassinate Bayinnaung but the latter spared him as being a wise man. He was disgraced by Bayinnaung only when he meddled in military affairs in his campaigns in Siam during the latter part of his reign.
27. *Hanthawaddy Hsinbyumyashin Ayebon*, Memoir on the reign of Bayinnaung. Anon.
28. *Alaung Mintayagyi Ayebon*, Memoir on the reign of Alaungpaya by Letwe Noratha. See Monywe Sayadaw's account of him in my paper.
29. *Alaung Mintayagyi Ayebon*, Another memoir on the reign of Alaungpaya by Twinthintaik Wun Mingyi Maha Sīthu. I think this is the one which had been published from these two memoirs.
30. *Dhammazedi Aṭṭhuppatti satan*, Life of Mon king Dhammazedi. Anon.
31. *Mahā Pyinnyagyaw Lhyawk Hton*, Wise sayings of Arakanese minister, Maha Pyinnyagyaw. Anon.
32. *Yazawingyoke*, Concise chronicle. Anon.
33. *Wunthadīpani (Vaṁsadīpani)*, Religious History by the second Kyaw Aung San Hta Sayadaw.
34. *Wunthamāla (Vaṁsamāla)*, Religious History by Nyaunggan Sayadaw.
35. *Thathanawunthadīpani (Sāsanavaṁsadīpani)*, Religious History, by Monywe Sayadaw.
36. *Yazawin Thanbauk*, Mnemonic verses for kings and dates from Burmese history by Mingyi Atula Mahā Dhammika Yāza.
37. *Amarapura Myothamaing*, Account of Amarapura, by Atwinwun Nemyo Thīhathu.
38. *Maniyatanabon*, A new version of a chronicle of Wun Zin Min Yāzā, tutor and later minister to the first Minkhaung (1401–22), by Shin Saddhammalaṅkāra (monk). N.B. The old version (Chevilliot 3447, India Office Library) is not recorded in this list.

(b) *Chronicles and Ayegyins listed by the Monywe Sayadaw for consultation regarding dates in Burmese history.*

In reply to a request for dates of the reigns of Burmese kings and the changes of Burmese calendar (this had happened twice in Burmese history), the Monywe

Sayadaw worked out the dates of Burmese kings accompanied by mnemonic verses for them in 1810. (Samantacakkhu Dīpani, vol. i, Hanthawaddy Press, Rangoon.) He listed the following chronicles and Ayegyins for consultation.

Chronicles

1. *Yazawuntha Paṭh*, by Shin Vaziya (Vajira), monk. (Possibly No. 3 of Pitakat Thamaing attributed to Hnget Pyittaung Shin Godhāvara).
2. *Yazawuntha*, by Hnget Pyittaung Pathama Athet Godhāvara Sayadaw. There must be more than one Hnget Pyittaung Sayadaw (pathama athet= first upper) as he is known as the First Upper Hnget Pyittaung Godhāvara Sayadaw.
3. *Yazawuntha*, by Shin Thilawuntha (Sīlavaṁsa).
4. *Hanthawaddy Hsinbyumyashin Ayedawbon*, Memoir on the reign of Bayinnaung.
5. *Thamaingdaw Akye*, Royal account at length (?) It must mean thamaings in general (or was there a compendium of all thamaings, i.e. accounts of pagodas, cities, and kings in his day?).
6. *Puṇṇa Yazawin*, Chronicle by a Brahmin, No. 4 of Pitakat Thamaing.
7. *Thakaritpon Insauk-cha*, chronological columns. Referred to by U Kala.
8. Three versions of chronicles by U Kala.

List of Ayegyins

(The earlier dates given in these ayegyins may not be true but the dates given for contemporary events can be trusted. An ayegyin written in Tabinshwe Hti's reign will be useful for the dates of the events of that time. Some of the ayegyins written during the Alaungpaya dynasty recounted the whole history of Burma up to the time they were written. They therefore serve also as mnemonic verses for Burmese history. It was one of the requisites of a Burmese historian to learn one of the ayegyins, especially Paleiksa Ayegyin, by U Phyaw, by heart. The last one who could recite it by heart was the late Saya Pwa of Rangoon University.)

1. Ayegyin for Thakin Htwe, by Shin Thuye.
2. Ayegyin for Tabin Shwe Hti by Hlawka Thondaung Hmu (i.e. an officer commanding 3,000 hlawka boats).
3. Another Ayegyin for Tabin Shwe Hti by same.
4. Another Ayegyin for Tabin Shwe Hti by same.
4. Ditto, ditto.
5. Ayegyin for Mintaya Medaw (Queen Mother), by Nawaday.
6. Ayegyin for Nat Shin Medaw (Mother of Natshinnaung?), by Sikaing-sa.
7. Ayegyin for Yakhaingpa Mibaya, i.e. the Queen who was taken to Arakan. (Daughter of Nandabayin taken to Arakan in 1599 by Minyazagyi after the fall of Pegu?), by Sikaing-sa.
8. Ayegyin for Hanthawaddy Maha Upayazagyi (Crown Prince of Pegu), by Thinkhaya, governor of Talok Myo.
9. Ayegyin for Minye Kyaw Swa's son, known as the younger Crown Prince of Ava, by Thinkhaya, governor of Talokmyo.
10. Ayegyin for Bayin Hna-ma-daw (sister of the king), by Nawaday.
11. Ayegyin for Thakin Gyi, by Pe Thunge Sa (i.e. governor of Pe Thunge).
12. Ayegyin for Min Ye Dibha, by Shin Than Kho.
13. Ayegyin for Min Ye Na Ya, by Zeyya Yandameik.

14. Ayegyin for Yakhaing Minthami (Arakanese princess), by Adu Minnyo.
15. Ayegyin for Man Aung Yatana Min Thet Shay, by Mye-sun Wun Yaza Thuya Mya-O.
16. Ayegyin for Nga Singu Min, by Shin Buddhinkema (monk), former tutor to Maha Dhamma Yāzādipati while a young prince.
17. Ayegyin for Princess of Myedu, by Min Kyaw Htin (a young poet).
18. Ayegyin for Min Hteik U Nay, by Minye Min Hla Kyaw Htin Padethayaza.
19. Ayegyin for Min Yatana, alias Min Hteik U Nay, by same.
20. Luta style Nadawthwin Ayegyin (author unknown).
21. Ayegyin for Prince of Pintale, by Sein-ta-Kyaw Thu.
22. Ayegyin for Crown Princess, by same.
23. Ayegyin presented to Nga Singu Min (King Singu), by Paleik Sa Maung Hpyaw. (Best known Ayegyin.)
24. Ayegyin, by Letwe Thondara (for whom?).
25. Ayegyin for Bagyidaw while a Crown Prince, by Zeya Kyaw Thu Maung Toe. (The famous author of Yama Yagan, a burlesque of Ramayana.)
26. Ayegyin on royal genealogy, by Twinthin Wun Maha Sithū.
27. Ayegyin for the mother of Prince Hsinbyushin.
28. Ayegyin for the genealogy of the royal family, by Myin Khwasa Min Yaza.

6. A MON GENEALOGY OF KINGS: OBSERVATIONS ON *THE NIDĀNA ĀRAMBHAKATHĀ*

H. L. SHORTO

Lecturer in Mon, School of Oriental and African Studies

Introductory

It is, I hope, unnecessary to dwell on the inutility of seeking a strict idea of history among the Mons, or any other South East Asian people, before the prolonged and general contact with Western European systems of thought which arguably marks the true boundary between the 'medieval' and 'modern' periods in Further India, and which in their case began only with the British annexation of Tenasserim in 1826. By this time the Mon historiographical tradition was moribund as a result of the final destruction by Alaungpaya, not of the books—for such destruction as there was in fact provoked a considerable activity of rewriting and re-compiling—but of the dynasty and the political entity Rāmañña which alone provided it with a reason for existence.

The decision as to what classes of work should be regarded as 'historical' for the purposes of this symposium is thus inevitably arbitrary. The majority of the writings which are of prime importance to the historian fall into three groups: *rājāwaṅ*, or genealogies of kings; *dhātuwaṅ*, recording the histories of particular relic pagodas, with some other works; and *puṁ* or 'stories', biographies of the more prominent monarchs which usually incorporate a more summary account of the others of their dynasty. Of the few works accessible to other than native scholars, *Rājādhirāj*, known by its translations into Burmese and Thai, is the most celebrated of the *puṁ*; the 'Genealogy of kings' (*Rājāwaṅ tnow datow smiṅ*) published by Schmidt and later re-edited by Halliday is, in spite of its title, largely a record of successive royal benefactions to the Shwe Dagon pagoda; and *Gawampati* is a curious compilation of topographical and genealogical extracts written in compliment to an obscure mid-eighteenth-century kinglet. As sources, the *puṁ* are the most important class, but, as their name indicates, they are in intention no more than edifying works of literature, hardly germane to our present purpose; and while the principles underlying the composition of the relic histories are not without relevance for the study of the *rājāwaṅ*, there is a fundamental division between the two categories which justifies the limitation of our inquiry to the latter, to which the term 'history' may most usefully be restricted.

The Nidāna Ārambhakathā

There is a good deal of similarity between the various *rājāwaṅ*, and a general survey seems less adapted to disengage the principles animating . Mon historiography than the close examination of a representative example. For this purpose the *Nidāna Ārambhakathā* stands recommended not only by its representative character but also by its relative accessibility. It is printed at pages 9–34 and 45–61 of the second of the two volumes of historical texts issued from Pak Lat,[1] apparently to supply a lacuna at the beginning of the *Puṁ Dhammacetī*—since apart from page headings no indication is given that it is a separate work. Its brevity is not exceptional; Mon literature in general is characterized by a refreshing absence of prolixity, and historical texts (apart from *puṁ*) of any great length are rare, though in view of the cataclysms which overtook the Mon state between the sixteenth and eighteenth centuries one cannot confidently say that longer works were not composed during the period of Pegu's greatness. The author of the *Nidāna* alludes to the destruction of books, and the sacking of the capital will have resulted in the dispersal of large collections, but some copies must have remained in the districts; the destruction of the books is a favourite myth of the Mon historians.

The manuscript from which the *Nidāna* text was printed came from the National Library in Bangkok and is likely to have been of unusually early date. From a Pali colophon incorporated in the text it appears that the main part, originally entitled *Rāmañ'-uppatti-dīpaka*, was composed by a monk of Zingyaik after the extinction of Dhammacetī's line in 1538; later hands have resumed the story and taken it year by year up to the accession of the Pyi Min to the Ava throne in 1661. The annalistic character of this later continuation, which appears to be without parallel elsewhere, clearly derives from an extraneous tradition, which is most likely to be Burmese; if so, it offers a most valuable opportunity for discriminating Mon and Burmese elements in the general historiographical tradition of the country.

The work opens with an extremely summary account of the history of Thaton, omitting all mention of the first dynasty recorded in the *Uppanna Sudhammawatī-rājāwaṁsa-kathā*,[2] and entering in any detail only into the reign of Manuhaw (Manohara) and the conquest of the kingdom by Anuruddha or Anoratha. Unlike the *Uppanna*, it makes no reference to the coming of Buddhism to Burma. This section closes with an account of the brief resurgence of the Thaton kingdom after Anuruddha's conquest. The *Nidāna* then passes to the history of Haṁsāwatī or Pegu. It first

[1] (*Nidāna Rāmādhipatī-kathā* (or as on binding *Rājāwaṁsa Dhammacetī Mahāpiṭakadhara*), ed. Phra Candakanto (Pak Lat, Siam, 1912).)

[2] Printed at pp. 9–25 of the earlier Pak Lat volume (*Sudhammawatī-rājāwaṁsa; Siharājādhirāja waṁsa (Sudhammawatī; Gawampati; Rājādhirāj*), ed. Phra Candakanto (Pak Lat, 1910)).

recounts the legendary foundation of the city and its early history as a state contemporaneous with Thaton, including the well-known stories of Samala and Wimala, Prince Asaḥ, and Subhaddā and the heretical King Tissa. After a period of eclipse the line is resumed in the dynasty established in Martaban by Wā Row (Wagaru of the Burmese records), over whose activities the work again becomes discursive. From this point onwards the *Nidāna* generally follows the traditional account of Burmese history in so far as that relates to the rulers of Martaban and, after the establishment of the capital there in 1369, of Pegu. It differs from modern versions of the story chiefly in the matter of emphasis; Rājādhirāj, though his achievement is not disputed, is passed over briefly, while the stories of the stern justice of his grandson Bañā Barow are related at some length; and though Dhammacetī receives extended treatment from the clerkly author, his purification of the Religion gets far less attention than his construction of replicas of the sacred sites of Buddhism at Pegu. After Dhammacetī this original portion of the text carries the story rapidly to the death of Badhirarājā and the extinction of the dynasty in 1538.

The continuation, after a preamble in which the next reigning kings are identified, in a traditional formula, with incarnations of daemons who had waited on the Buddha when he visited Burma, takes up the story from the assumption of the Pegu throne by Tabin Shwe Hti in 1540, in a series of entries in which events are dated precisely by years, and after 1566 usually also by months and often days. It terminates in 1661, as already described, with a bare mention of the Pyi Min's accession to the throne of Ava, following on the circumstantial account of an apparently successful rebellion in Martaban.

Such, in effect, is the scope of Mon history. The *Nidāna* indeed is—as far as can be judged from the evidence—a purer exemplar of the Mon tradition of *rājāwaṅ*, less admixed with elements of *dhātuwaṅ* and other, extraneous, traditions, than most works; but in its principal themes, as in the period it embraces, it is typical enough. The only variable in these histories is the terminal date, some continuing their account into the eighteenth century, and some breaking off in the sixteenth, for the realm may rather be said to have petered out than to have terminated abruptly. The dynastic succession which it is their central purpose to record is at times tenuous; they span without embarrassment periods when the throne stood long unoccupied and the city[3] 'became a collection of large villages', and tell of kings ruling in Rāmañña at times when the orthodox account presents it merely as a province of Ava, so that the records of its final extinction vary. Geographically, the history of the Mons embraces the three capitals of Thaton, Martaban, and Pegu, though there is a tradition of other Mon kingdoms at Bassein, Dalla, and Lagunbyin in the fourteenth

[3] The Mon term *ḍuṅ* is used equally of the kingdom and its capital.

century, and we know from an inscription that Moulmein claimed to be a kingdom in the sixteenth; a brief history of Ye also exists.

The Contents of the Nidāna

The material contained in the original portion of the *Nidāna*, and in the Mon histories generally, may be analysed as follows:

(1) Dynastic information. For the earlier 'legendary' periods, this is often limited to lists of names, whereas for what would now be regarded as the 'historical' period it usually includes relationship to the previous king, age at accession, length of reign and date of death. These dates are in the main the only ones given in the Mon histories.

(2) Anecdotal material relating to the kings, often of an Alfred-and-the-cakes nature. This is especially designed to present each king as a distinct personality, and only rarely to relate the politically important events of his reign.

(3) Origin legends, designed among other things to validate a dynasty initially. After the extinction of a dynasty a fresh origin legend is often provided for its successor, which in the 'historical' period may take the form of a series of portents, as in the case of Wā Row; but in the eighteenth-century *Gawampati* a full-blown origin legend, involving the appearance of Indra and possession of a flying horse, is provided for the king in whose reign the work was written.

(4) Miscellaneous legends and traditions, such as the making of the magic drum of the kings of Thaton, and Prince Asaḥ's fight with the Indian. In many cases these seem extraneous to the main purpose of the *rājāwaṅ* and one may suspect that they have been included almost as an ornamental feature, because too well known to leave out. Under this head should probably be brought the traditions as to the coming of Buddhism to Burma, of the visits of Gavampati, the Buddha, and the Asokan missionaries Soṇa and Uttara; these, which do not appear in the *Nidāna*, belong properly to the tradition of the *dhātuwaṅ* and religious histories.

The Genealogy of Kings

In seeking to determine the function of the *rājāwaṅ* it is useful to look first at their most summary portions. These consist of little more than lists of the names of kings. The history of Thaton is almost entirely legendary, but all the accounts provide a full list of its rulers—even though these lists, while having certain names in common, vary to a degree which makes it impossible to reconstruct an archetypal tradition.

A connection between these bare enumerations and the more rounded accounts of the later parts of the *rājāwaṅ* is unexpectedly provided by the dynastic information incorporated in *Gawampati*. This consists of similarly summary lists in the form of Pali gāthās with nissaya,[4] followed by an expanded vernacular gloss; the form is precisely that of the *sakem*, religious works in which the Pali text is followed by a vernacular translation of the commentary. Now we know that the Mon kings bore at least three names: the Sanskrit regnal name, usually found only in inscriptions; the name, or names, by which they were generally known, which might or might not be identical with that which they bore before their accession; and the Pali name used in the genealogies. This last seems to have been in the nature of a nickname, and the glosses in *Gawampati* are explanations of why the nickname was conferred. Just such glosses are found embedded in the histories, and in many cases the characters of the kings are simply elaborations on them.

The two themes of origin (*uppana, ktuiw dadah*) and lineage (*rājāwań, tnow datow*) are the entwined threads on which the histories are strung. These latter are in effect legitimations of the monarchy; and in order to understand and use them it is necessary to consider what Mon ideas of realm and kingship were.

It is possible that a preoccupation with the genealogical theme is one of the autochthonous elements in South East Asian culture; among some of the pagan peoples of Indonesia such a preoccupation is sufficiently well known. But in any case the introduction into Burma of Buddhism, and of Indian ideas in general, at first offered two antithetical possibilities for the legitimation of the king, both of which are taken up in the eleventh-century inscriptions of Kyanzittha.[5] There was, first, the appeal to lineage, almost always coupled with some form of the Pallava tradition of a Nāga ancestress; and there was the appeal to reincarnation, which we find in a specifically Buddhist form combined with prophecies attributed to the Buddha and, in later texts, to his disciples. This latter justification is the more prominent in the inscriptions, and indeed never wholly disappears, being most freely cited in the final decadence when a series of chieftains, captains and successful rebels laid dubious claim to the throne of Pegu; but throughout the classical period it is merely subsidiary, lending some colour of Buddhist orthodoxy to the overshadowing genealogical theme.

It is characteristic of Buddhism in its later forms that, while its social ethic certainly assists political stability, it is, with its repudiation of caste and consequent neutrality towards status-systems generally, singularly lacking in doctrine designed to regulate the institution of monarchy. This in South East Asia was necessarily provided from Hindu sources, a development which led to a syncretism always nominally Buddhist but

[4] Fragments of such gāthās are occasionally incorporated in the *Nidāna* and other works.

[5] Though the kings of Pagan were Burmese, it is known that they were concerned to legitimize their claim to Rāmañña, and there is no doubt that Kyanzittha's Mon inscriptions reflect Mon ideas of kingship as well as Burmese ones.

incorporating without embarrassment many Hindu elements, especially in the political field, as well as residues of the autochthonous animism of the region. It is this essential, though unrealized, absence of contact between the religion of the monasteries and the rationale of kingship which accounts for the omission of religious elements from so many histories, and the ascendancy of the genealogical theme after an initial period of neglect.

The opposition thus existing between the *rājāwaṅ* and the *dhātuwaṅ* and religious histories does not preclude mutual influences, and the importance attached to the strict recital of the sequence of kings is paralleled, and undoubtedly reinforced, by that given to the succession of teachers from which a monk derived his authority. This *tnow datow* of the kings does not necessarily imply lineal descent, and certainly not the automatic succession of an eldest son or designated heir. Every occupant of the throne, every occupier of the capital for however brief a period, is listed in the genealogies: Jap Ban, whose brother was married to a princess of the blood and who in 1333 held the palace for a week after killing the heir apparent, till he was killed in his turn; the rebels Smiṅ Ḍot and Smiṅ Dhaw who successively held Pegu for a time in the interregnum after the death of Tabin Shwe Hti, all are numbered among the kings. The post-Anuruddha dynasty in Thaton was established by the Burmese general whom Anuruddha left behind as governor; Wā Row and his successors were Shans; Tabin Shwe Hti in 1544 cut his hair and 'became a Mon'. Once a king ascended the throne he was accepted by the nation irrespective of his ancestry, as the leader in whom were subsumed the fortunes of Rāmañña, the 'Mon country' successively embodied by Thaton, Martaban, and Pegu.

The king was the receptacle of a mystic power (*anubhau, trījah*), which in the earlier dynasties is usually attributed to possession of a specific magical object, often a *vahana*; indeed, the white elephant in later times probably served this same function. Sometimes a distinction is made between *trījah*, as derived from magical objects, and *anubhau*, resulting from spiritual attainments. Fluctuations in the fortunes of the people reflected this power, and a bad king was one who failed to preserve it as much as one whose administration was oppressive or faulty; so, while Manuhaw is in fact presented as a 'bad king' in the modern sense, his downfall is attributed to his allowing the sources of *anubhau* to be destroyed; because he unwrought 'the customs and usage of the men of old'. And Dhammacetī, the ex-monk and pattern of the pious Buddhist king, made ceremonial offerings at the fifty-one principal spirit shrines. Though the *rājāwaṅ* omit all reference to the practice, or take it for granted, other sources lead us to believe that *anubhau*, or the legitimate right of succession, descended in the female line and was assured to the king through marriage; such unions are recorded in the *Puṁ Dhammacetī* as late as the sixteenth century.

The revival of the Thaton monarchy after Anuruddha, the claim of

Moulmein to be a kingdom in the sixteenth century, and similar claims for Pegu recurrently through the seventeenth and eighteenth, can be explained in terms of modern political theory by a failure to establish adequate means of control of provinces by the centre; but no attempt seems to have been made to account for such resurgences by reference to contemporary ideas of king and state. Now the term *smiñ*, 'king', is not restricted to the ruler of Pegu, who from the sixteenth century onwards is increasingly referred to as *smiñ ekarāt*—in effect the high king, having several other *smiñ* under him, who might reside at court or be otherwise employed on royal service, or might in fact govern the provinces of which they were nominally 'kings'. The position of these minor *smiñ* was clearly equivocal, and they are sometimes specifically mentioned as laying claim to independent sovereignty. It seems that there was no means known to Pegu or Ava of extinguishing an extant kingdom; annexation meant placing a nominee on the throne, which then became feudally subject, so that the progressive unification of the country merely increased the possibility of rebellion as soon as central control slackened. This acceptance of kingdoms as persistent received paradoxical support from the teachings of Buddhism, which tended to show *anicca* as assailing the temporary embodiments of an institution rather than the institution itself. The resultant centrifugal trend was held in balance for a time by Mon nationalism, but as soon as Burmese expansion created a supra-national state it was able to assert itself unchecked.

The Concept of History in the Nidāna

The *rājāwañ*, and the *Nidāna* in particular, are primarily concerned to justify and legitimate the monarchy in the person of the reigning king, according to a highly stylized formula; in *Gawampati*, this traditional pattern has given way to a more elaborate literary form, but one which still has the apotheosis of the king at its core. The view of kingship which such texts subserve is a mystical, one would now say magical, one, and to this extent they themselves have to be regarded as part of a magical apparatus. But, though certain incidents are related several times with different participants, this appears to be less often due to the incorporation of a reigning king in a perennially re-enacted myth, as in Java, than to the filling out of blank periods of the chronicle by projecting historical events backwards into the mythological past; and from the diversity of the facts generally recorded we may infer their indicative, rather than optative, character. It is now time to examine this other material which has accreted round the genealogical core, to see whether it reveals the germ of any wider conception of history than that implicit in the record of the lineage.

There is very little that is not directly concerned with the kings and the general dynastic theme. Much of the anecdotal material, however, is plainly distinct from the genealogical glosses, which at times appear as almost irrelevant insertions, hardly congruent with the rest of the entry. In fact the reliability of these glosses is uneven; the order and form of the names may vary in different histories, so that when they are assigned to a known sequence of kings a given soubriquet may have to be variously interpreted. Thus the *Nidāna* identifies Bañā Barow, the traditional exemplar of the stern judge, with Sunakkharājā, and says somewhat inconsequentially: 'he was called Sunakkharājā because he sought to scratch merit from the ground like a dog', while in *Gawampati* this name is attached to a much earlier king 'who shall scratch himself up a kingdom like a dog'. It seems likely that the glosses, belonging as they do to the oldest elements of the text, furnished the impulse for the addition of further anecdotal material when their nature was imperfectly understood, and that the accretions were drawn from popular, largely verbal, tradition; for not only do these increase in volume as the times of the writer are approached, but—as in the case of Rājādhirāj—events adequately recorded in other written sources, and apparently relevant, may be passed over quite summarily. This is in contrast with the method of the religious histories, which often preserve with considerable accuracy passages known first from fifteenth-century inscriptions.

No attempt is made to present neighbouring states as partners in a historical process. The periodical incursions of Burmese, Shans and others are on a par with the activities of daemons and natural disasters, as elements of a hostile environment through which the nation is preserved by the kings' *anubhau*. There are passing references to Buddhism, as an institution fluctuating and indeed requiring periodical purgings, but generally flourishing; yet, though in Dhammacetī's time large areas of the country were still pagan, in particular most of the territory east of the Sittang, there is no citing of its introduction as a stage in a civilizing process. Even those works which draw more on the religious theme set the coming of the Sāsana almost at the beginning of historical time, making it a permanent concomitant of the abiding state.

The world picture which forms the ground of the *rājāwaṅ* is that of the continuing institution of the Mon nation, brought into being by a miraculous genesis which, like the biblical Creation, sets the beginning of relevant time, and renewed at the hours of greatest disaster by further supernatural interventions. The nation is wholly subsumed in the king: relations between states are a matter of embassies, when the fate of the whole people depends on the king's ability to give a wise or witty answer; wars are settled by the swords of the king's personal champions, or in the last resort of the king himself. (Sometimes he takes on a colour of the characteristic guileful folk-hero: Bañā Rām, a much admired monarch, 'was afraid of getting killed and so pretended to be humpbacked and walked with a stick; thus he lived to a ripe old age'. Yet he was called the Tiger.) But that the significance of the king is mystical rather than personal is shown by the relative unimportance, for the state's continuance, of his piety; a lewd king can redeem himself, like any other man, by late repentance, and a virtuous one damn himself by the wickedness of second childhood.

This concept of the world as a stasis is diametrically opposed to what now would be regarded as the essential precondition of any 'history' at all. The Mon chroniclers never considered that the kingship or the kingdom had come to an end; when this view imposed itself on them, they stopped writing. But the paradox only illustrates the necessity, when interpreting other cultures, of establishing their elements in terms of function in the total cultural system rather than approaching them with a ready-made definition of 'history' and seeking the most immediately plausible identification.

The Later Additions to the Nidāna

To point the foregoing conclusions, it is instructive to examine briefly the annals which have been added to the original *Rāmaññ'-uppatti-dīpaka,* and which I have suggested derive most probably from a historiographical tradition of Burmese origin. So far as this continuation represents an attempt to extend to the new rulers the justificatory and semi-magical intentions of the earlier work, it is in the behalf of Tabin Shwe Hti and his Burmese successors until Thalun gave up the attempt to rule the Mons and withdrew to Ava in 1635 that it was undertaken.

The annals are far less exclusively concerned with the kings. Their important activities are recorded (in itself noteworthy, since the *rājāwaṅ* are more selective in this respect), but as part of a general record of all events of import. There is no attempt to arrange this by topics into an ordered narrative; the progress of a campaign, for example, has to be extracted from among statements of other dissonant matters. The main consideration seems to be the establishing of an accurate chronology, in which respect the entries are meticulous; and astrological considerations are close to the surface. The existence of a more detailed contemporary record is to be suspected, for while the annals, apart from their wider scope, are much fuller than the *rājāwaṅ* proper, the entries are still terse enough to be in places cryptic to a modern reader. 'In [1587] the Franks came to Martaban.' 'In [1616], on Thursday, the seventh waxing of Phālguna, the great keel of Martaban was laid down.'

From such a record covering a century and a quarter, made close to the events in question, admittedly no broad historical picture emerges except to the forewarned modern reader; that is inherent in the jumble of the method; but enough is given of the fluctuating fortunes of states competing in a geographically circumscribed theatre, and of revolts in which the legitimate direction of allegiance is highly doubtful, to imply at least the possibility of an entirely new view. That no such new dynamic conception took root in Rāmañña was due to the centrifugal tendencies already mentioned; the record appropriately closes on a note of successful rebellion, such as paved the way for restoration, conservatism and ultimate eclipse.

Conclusion

It might seem after this analysis of a typical *rājāwaṅ* that the Mon historical writings are hardly of a significance to merit much attention from the modern historian. But the distinction that has been drawn between texts useful as sources and texts which are themselves entitled to the name of 'history' must be borne in mind. The set of ideas underlying the *rājāwaṅ* is perhaps more cosmological than truly historical; its influence certainly extends to a wider field than the restricted one considered here, a field whose surface has barely been scratched; and an understanding of it is essential to the proper utilization of the *puṁ* and all the other works which are nowadays grouped together as 'chronicles'.

7. SOME REMARKS ON MODERN INDONESIAN HISTORIOGRAPHY

BAMBANG OETOMO

Member of the Staff of the Sociological Institute, University of Leiden

As with those of many Asian peoples today, we can divide the Indonesian historical writings into a traditional and a modern section. The traditional section is made up of writings produced by Indonesians who were still living in a cultural milieu which was completely untouched by modern western ideas and values. On the other hand modern Indonesian historiography consists of historical writings of Indonesians who graduated from some kind of a modern western educational institution and who were thus influenced in some important respects by modern western ideas and values.

The traditional section of Indonesian historical writings will be treated by Professor Berg, Dr. Hooykaas, and Dr. Noorduyn. And we shall confine ourselves to the subject mentioned in the title of this paper.

Among Indonesian writers we find a few who have usually published their books or articles in the Dutch language, for example authors like Husein Djajadiningrat, Purbotjaroko, Priyono and Pryohutomo. Their writings will not be discussed in this paper, not only because those authors can be considered as belonging to the Dutch School, but also because their main interest is often merely directed to the literary aspects of traditional Indonesian culture.

Thus, our remarks will mainly concern the modern historical writings in the Indonesian language.

Modern historiography was practically unknown in Indonesian society before the nineteen-twenties. Its coming into existence was closely related to the rise of modern nationalist movement in Indonesia. Since this movement can be considered partly a result of modern education for Indonesians, we shall begin with a very brief review of the development of its institutions during the colonial period. Thereafter follows an outline of the nationalistic notion of Indonesian history.

Although the Dutch primary schools in Java were open to Indonesians since about 1820, until the last ten years of the nineteenth century their numbers at these schools remained very small. In 1847 there were for instance only thirty-seven Indonesian pupils at all Dutch primary schools on the island.[1] It was actually only after 1914 that thousands of Indonesians received a primary education along western lines.[2]

The first nationalist leaders, the promoters in 1908 of the first national association of Indonesians, the *Budi Utomo*, were graduates of the 'Java Medical School'[3] which was founded in 1851. Later on nationalist leaders were recruited from graduates of educational institutions on academic level such as the Bandung Higher Technical School (founded in 1920) and the Batavia Law School (founded in 1924). Between the years 1920 and 1940 about one hundred Indonesians went to Holland in order to get their degrees at the Dutch universities.

A remarkable fact in this development is that not one Indonesian completed courses in the science of history. We think this absolute lack of scientifically trained Indonesian historians has to a large extent determined the present condition of modern Indonesian historiography.

During the first years after its birth the nationalist movement formulated its aim as a 'respectable existence of the people' and 'a more harmonious development of country and peoples of the Netherlands Indies'.[4] In order to achieve this aim the early Indonesian nationalists followed 'quiet' methods such as founding national schools or stimulating native science, arts, and industry.

But when Sukarno's Partai Nasional Indonesia (PNI) came into existence in 1927 those quiet methods were abandoned. This party was based on the principle of self-determination and its leaders stated explicitly their determination to strive for a form of government responsible only to the Indonesian people itself. Thus they proclaimed a national struggle for independence to be achieved by their own powers and without the help from foreigners, against imperialism and capitalism, which were held responsible for the oppression of the Indonesian people. Moreover, it was believed by the PNI that such a struggle for freedom could only succeed by means of a nationalistic mass-action. Accordingly the quiet methods no longer sufficed and consequently mass-meetings were introduced in Indonesian life. The speeches and addresses at such meetings were calculated to stimulate national consciousness among the masses and to infuse them with enthusiasm for the fight for freedom.

It was in relation to this last point that the image of the past and ideas

[1] I. J. Brugmans, *De geschiedenis van het Onderwijs in Nederlands Indië* (*The History of Education in the Netherlands Indies*). (Groningen, 1938), p. 139.

[2] Cf. I. J. Brugmans, *De verbreiding van de Nederlandse taal in Indië* (*The Spread of the Dutch Language in the Indies*). (Koloniale Studieén, 1937), p. 58.

[3] B. H. M. Vlekke, *Geschiedenis van de Indische Archipel* (*History of Indian Archipelago*). (Roermond, 1947), p. 412.

[4] More information on Indonesian national movement can be found a.o. in: A. Vandenbosch, *The Dutch East Indies* (Berkeley, Los Angeles, 1944); G. M. Kahin, *Nationalism and Revolution in Indonesia* (New York, 1953); J. M. Pluvier, *Overzicht van de ontwikkeling der Nationale Beweging in Indonesië* (*Review of the Development of National Movement in Indonesia*) (The Hague, 1953).

on Indonesian history took shape and played a role in the nationalist movement.

Ir. Sukarno, who incidentally graduated from the Bandung Higher Technical School, was one of the first modern Indonesians to formulate ideas on their people's history. He explained those ideas in his defence (2 December 1930) when he was tried for 'subversive' action against the Dutch government.[5]

There are three ways to promote nationalism, Sukarno said, 'first we point out to the people that they have a glorious past, secondly we intensify the notion among our people that the present time is dark, and the third way is to show them the promising, pure and luminous future and how to get there'. Stated briefly his scheme consisted of a 'glorious past', a 'dark present', and a 'promising future'.[6]

The image of a glorious past is built up from stories about the 'greatness' of the empires and kingdoms of Sriwijaya, Malayu, Kediri, Singosari, Mojopait, and Mataram, and from the notion that during those glorious days the Indonesian colours were seen in Madagascar, Persia, and China. While reading or learning the history of those times every Indonesian, Sukarno believed, would feel a new spirit and new forces arising within himself; in this way the knowledge of a glorious past might revive the hope and national feelings of the people who would consequently obtain a new spirit and new powers.

Sukarno's conception of the dark present refers to conditions during the colonial period, from the days of the Dutch East Indies Company (founded in 1602) till his own times. Indeed, those conditions were painted by the PNI leader in the blackest colours.

The stern ferocious and greedy Company has sacrificed thousands of Indonesian lives while destroying whole kingdoms. Its policy was based on the principle of 'divide and rule', and even decent Dutch writers hold the opinion that the Company's ends and means were horrible. After the end of the Company's rule (1799) the 'Culture System' (introduced in 1830) in its turn took over the exploitation of the Indonesian people. This system, kept up by whippings and beatings, caused poverty, pauperism and famine, and brought the Indonesian masses into slavery. Lastly, modern imperialism (from 1870 onwards) made of the Indonesians a nation of wage-earners and a wage-earner among the nations. Imperialism checked the progress of Indonesian society, disorganized social life and left the individuals without civil rights to defend themsevles against its detrimental forces.[7]

[5] Ir. Sukarno's defence was translated in Dutch and published under the title: *Indonesië klaagt aan*[1] (*Indonesia Accuses*) (Amsterdam, 1931).   [6] *Indonesië klaagt aan*, p. 64.
[7] Chapter II of the same publication, pp. 18-36.

Reading those words in 1956 one might easily be led to ask what need there was of such a representation of the colonial period. The leader himself has provided the answer: 'The wretched lot of the people during the present colonial period will keep most strongly alive the nationalist sentiments amongst them.'[8] And the history of Indonesian nationalism thus far has clearly demonstrated how successful Sukarno has been in inciting the imagination of the masses and thus infusing them with enthusiasm for the fight against colonialism.

No doubt this enthusiasm as a result of Sukarno's words has formed one of the most powerful forces which had brought Indonesian nationalism to its victory after a battle of relatively short duration. Future historians will certainly ascribe much credit to Sukarno for his great contribution to the achievement of Indonesian independence.

It is comprehensible that, against this background of the nationalist struggle, no other Indonesian has yet tried to criticize or to correct intentionally and explicitly these concepts of Indonesian history. Only in a book by Pringgodigdo entitled *Sedjarah Pergerakan Rakjat Indonesia (History of the Indonesian People's Movement)* (Djakarta, 1949), we find an opinion on the causes of nationalism which is different from that expressed by Sukarno in his above-mentioned defence. While the latter saw the Indonesian movement caused exclusively by the deplorable condition of the people,[9] Pringgodigdo mentioned—in addition to the 'always present desire of the people for a better life'—other factors connected with its birth and growth. The author pointed to the Japanese victory over Russia in 1905, the Young-Turkish movement and the Chinese Revolution of 1911 as factors outside the country. The internal factors among others consist of the intellectual capacity of the Indonesians due to the growth of educational opportunities, the recognition by the Dutch government of the right of public meeting, the introduction of political institutions such as the Volksraad (People's Council) and the improved means of communication.[10]

But apart from Pringgodigdo the above-mentioned conception has exercised great influence upon every Indonesian historical writing even when it was written ten or more years after 1930, the year in which it was formulated for the first time.

For example, the glorious past was narrated by Muhammad Yamin in his book on Gadjah Mada (third printing, Djakarta, 1948), the prime minister of the kingdom of Mojopait between the years 1331 and 1364. It is a popular notion in Indonesia that Gadjah Mada was the first Indonesian politician who succeeded in unifying the archipelago. The importance of his position in present-day thinking is well illustrated by the fact that the University of Jogjakarta (founded in 1947) was named after him.

[8] Ibid., p. 65.   [9] Ibid., p. 41.   [10] *Pringgodigdo*, pp. 7–9.

When they speak of the 'Golden Age' of their history the Indonesians are referring to the days of Gadjah Mada.

A few quotations from Yamin's book will show the kind of images the Indonesians have of those days.

> Since the kingdom of Mojopait was a well-organized state, its social and political atmosphere provided a fruitful condition for the development of arts and literature. In general, cultural life was flourishing and the life of the people was profoundly affected by religion. Between the beginning of the fourteenth and the middle of the fifteenth century many books were composed, while the number of monuments in Eastern Java increased very much during the same period.
>
> In Gadjah Mada's time many inscriptions on stone or copper were published in order to commemorate important events or to be used as pieces of evidence. All recent as well as obsolete documents were kept and great care was taken that they would not just disappear.
>
> Justice was arranged in such a way that it satisfied the people's sense of justice. Sentences were passed in harmony of common and statute law. The Judges occupied a high position in society, they were inferior only to the king and his family.
>
> To promote the welfare of the country several central services were called into existence, for instance for taking care of the taxes, duties and condition of the roads. There were also special services for health, irrigation, traffic, agriculture and public security. Much attention was paid to the Departments of War and Commerce.[11]

Moreover Mr. Yamin imparted to his readers the existence of some kind of a representative government at that time. He wrote about a State's Council consisting of representatives from the islands outside Java and from other parts of the empire.[12]

Apart from that, in a textbook on Indonesian History by Sanusi Pané (*Sedjarah Indonesia*, fourth printing, Djakarta, 1950) which is being used in secondary schools, we find this evaluation of Mojopait:

> ... Its Golden Age during the days of Rajasanegara (the king) and Gadjah Mada can be compared with the time during which Europe was beginning to free herself from feudalism. At that time cities were formed, while trade and handicraft grew in importance.[13]

Here, too, the nationalistic perspective on Indonesian history is evident.

Another salient feature of modern Indonesian historical writing is the emphasis on the struggle against the Dutch government. In fact, all recent publications contain stories about leaders or personalities who played an important part in the several revolts against Dutch colonial government or

[11] M. Yamin, *Gadjah Mada*, pp. 28–31.   [12] Ibid., p. 29.   [13] S. Pané, Book I, p. 116.

in the early days of the national movement. To mention a few examples:

Diponegoro by Muhammad Yamin (1945) is a book on the hero of the Java War (1825–30). *Tuanku Imam Bondjol* by Dawis Datuk Madjolelo and Ahmad Marzuki (1951) is a story about the leader during the Padri (west coast of Sumatra) War from 1821–32. *Teku Umar dan* and *Tjut Nja Din* (written by Hazil in 1952) were leading personalities in the Acheh War (1873–1904). *Kartini* (by Mrs. Hurustiati Subandrio) was a prominent young woman living from 1879 till 1904 who is considered in Indonesia as the forerunner of the women's movement. A biography of Dr. Sutomo (who died in 1936), one of the promoters of *Budi Utomo*, was produced by Imam Supardi. And a life-history of Tjipto Mangunkusumo (who died in 1943), another prominent personality in the early days of national movement, was published by M. Balfas.

In these books the heroes are represented as brave, noble, energetic, steadfast, loyal, well-read, sacrificing, patriotic, poetical, and so on. There is no doubt that the production of this kind of literature is still functionally related to the nationalistic idea, and that they are intended to rouse their readers to the fight for freedom. Obviously, their moral lesson amounts to this: we have a glorious past, the present time is dark, let us fight for a promising future just like the sample set by our heroes.

We would like to stress the importance and necessity of such efforts to increase the numbers of Indonesians supporting the nationalist idea. Because, only with the greatest possible numbers of Indonesians on the side of nationalism can its fight against colonialism and for a better future be quickly brought to a successful end.

Since the functional character of modern Indonesian historiography has now been shown, one may not expect from its authors that they are solely directed by the search for the truth. In fact, we can observe that the desire to produce nationalistic literature is almost always much stronger than the desire to conform to scientific standards. Consequently, the value of those writings for the scientific study of Indonesian history is not evident. And this constitutes the other side of the medal with a functional historiography.

Up to this day modern Indonesian historiography has not yet produced new contributions to the science of history. No Indonesian has yet reported discoveries of new facts or unknown documents. Findings by Indonesians of new inter-relationships between already known facts or events still fail to appear. All the knowledge of the above-mentioned authors is based on Dutch literature or traditional literature which has been made accessible by Dutch scholars. Nevertheless, with the exception of Sukarno, not one writer made notes referring to the sources used, although two of the writers published a list of consulted works on the last page of their books.

A few words about the way Sukarno made use of the Dutch works written by Snouck Hurgronje, Colenbrander, Veth, Kielstra, Stokvis, Gonggrijp, and van Gelderen. Sukarno quoted only those parts of these works which supported his point of view. No sincere effort was made by him to arrive at an understanding of what had really happened during the colonial period. His sole object was to present a picture of a deplorable time. Thus he did not critically evaluate the facts and information derived from the consulted literature, nor did he strive for a well-balanced judgement on the period.

And although with later Indonesian writers their intention to present a preconceived picture was perhaps less prominent than with Sukarno, no essential change for the better has taken place, because scientific training has still been lacking. It is self-evident that accordingly, historical works which have been the fruits of real scholarship or of careful, critical, accurate and painstaking studies are non-existent. There is as yet no sign of a renaissance in Indonesian historiography. Of course, in considering this fact it should be borne in mind that the Indonesians achieved their independence only a few years ago.

Although the relative absence of scientific historiography will certainly not cause disaster to Indonesian society, we believe that such a state of affairs is rather unfortunate. In order to clarify this point we shall briefly outline the most important changes which have been taking place in the Indonesian society during the last century, with special reference to Java.

Before the appearance of Europeans in the archipelago social and cultural life was largely centred around the sacred position of the king. In such a context, religion, literature, sculpture, and political organization were not only intertwined and interrelated to each other, but they often also had the magical function of enforcing or legitimating the sacred power of the king. Society was mainly agrarian in character and its members considered the king as the origin of fertility of the soil, thus as a source of prosperity of his subjects. Moreover, to these subjects the king was also the guardian of the security of the whole community.[14]

Though at the end of the sixteenth century a spirit for trade and commerce was certainly present, it was not as prominent as among Europeans of the same days. Economically Indonesian culture remained on a peasant-village basis.

During the Dutch control of power Indonesian society on Java experienced profound changes. It began when the Dutch East Indies Company controlled the Indonesian waters necessary for the establishment of her trade monopoly.[15] This put an end to all Javanese shipping and overseas

---

[14] Cf. W. F. Wertheim, *Nederlandse cultuurinvloeden in Indonesië* (*Dutch Cultural Influences in Indonesia*) (Amsterdam, 1948), pp. 3-4.

[15] Cf. B. Schrieke, *Indonesian Sociological Studies*, pt. I (The Hague, 1955), pp. 72-73.

trade, thus, the economic development in this respect was checked for a long time.[16]

Afterwards, with the political control of the island well in Dutch hands, the Indonesian king was made subordinate to the Dutch Governor General, thus putting an end to the King's central function in his society, because, directives for administrative and other measures no longer originated from the Indonesian king, but from the Company's offices or from The Hague and Amsterdam. And often the measures introduced were based on reasons unknown or foreign to the king and his subjects. Consequently, sacred kingship, which for ages has formed the central basis of traditional Indonesian society and culture, was seriously undermined, and gradually the social order connected with it broke down.

Of course we have much oversimplified the picture of processes covering such a long period of time. We are fully aware that historical reality was far more complicated than outlined above. For example, although they have ruled out the political and social influence of the Indonesian king the Dutch maintained his bupati's (the king's governors for important cities) who continued living as much as possible according to their traditional way of life till the outbreak of the Pacific War. Thus, although cut off from their original context, many parts or elements of the traditional order remained in existence as survivals long after the actual breakdown of that order.

Besides the tendency towards social disintegration during Dutch rule we can also observe signs, however weak, pointing towards a process of social integration.

One of the most salient facts during this period was that the Dutch succeeded in bringing the most important parts of the Indonesian islands into one political and administrative unity. This development imparted to the Indonesians—peoples with a great diversity of cultures—the notion that they belong together. On such a basis an awareness of a common lot could grow and accordingly the formulation of a common will was made possible.

Another very important and interesting side of the history of Dutch rule is the process by which the Indonesians got acquainted with ideas, techniques, modes of thinking and values originating from the western world, through the introduction of modern educational institutions. In fact, all social and political weapons or instruments used by the Indonesian nationalists in fighting the Dutch were learned from or made possible by the modern education created in Indonesia by the Dutch themselves.

At the same time we know very well that it was not the explicit intention

[16] Or, in the words of Van Leur: 'The conquest of the spice islands by the Dutch East India Company put a stop to a complete branch of traditional trade and thus disorganized the whole of it.' *Indonesian Trade and Society* (The Hague, 1955, p. 122).

of colonial government to emancipate the Indonesians in the shortest possible time. The dominant motivation for maintaining their rule over Indonesia was in fact the desire for material profit to the home-country. Nevertheless, viewed historically, the existence of integrating factors in Dutch rule cannot be denied.

As demonstrated, Dutch measures caused a dissolution of the traditional order on one hand, and on the other they opened possibilities of modern development. However, the latter has been carried out unintentionally and unexplicitly, while many elements of the traditional order still received some support from the Dutch colonial government.

These circumstances conditioned a great deal the mental development of educated Indonesians. While today their behaviour is no longer motivated exclusively by traditional values, often statements such as 'We have our own "eastern" way of solving things' or 'We should save our own traditional eastern culture by guarding ourselves against western influences' can still be heard amongst them.

It is evident that such a state of mind has something to do with their attitude towards modern culture. Since the Dutch only quite recently introduced higher learning in Indonesia, the process of its transference to Indonesians could not have yielded many results by the end of colonial rule. And in comparison with other Asian peoples such as the Indians and Filipinos, the minds of educated Indonesians have generally not yet been seized by modern science or scientific attitude. We cannot yet observe amongst them an eager acceptance of the intrinsic essence of modern culture.

Seemingly the Indonesians have not yet made up their minds as to which direction they will move in social and cultural respects. It is clear how transitional is the character of present-day society and culture in Indonesia.

After the recognition of independence gradually more Indonesians expressed the view that they should live according to conditions also found with modern nations. If we are to take such statements seriously, it means that the Indonesians should promote social development in the direction of a society and culture in which first, the recognition of the ultimate value of human personality, second, modern science and achievements based on it, and lastly, elements from the Indonesian heritage, will be integrated successfully. In fact, it is our personal opinion that such is the only one direction in which the Indonesians should go, if they want to maintain themselves as an independent nation in this modern world.

In other words we think that history has called upon the Indonesians to modernize their society to a condition in which the best sides and highest achievements of modern culture can flourish unobstructedly. However, the starting point for this desired development can only be constituted by the present social and historical reality. And here we have touched the point where the science of history—apart from being a source for intellectual delight—can perform an important role in Indonesian efforts at social reconstruction.

In the first place history is of importance for the knowledge of present-day social reality. Because the present situation can only be adequately understood and comprehended if we have sufficient knowledge of past events and processes leading to it. Secondly, European and American history can provide a wealth of information on modern societies. The Indonesian may learn from it which are the best sides and highest achievements of modern culture, and, which events, processes, values, attitudes, and techniques have led to those sides and achievements. In general, the history of modern and western peoples may also produce lessons from their mistakes, giving opportunities to learners to take precautions in order to avoid the same mistakes.

It is understandable, however, that at this moment there can be little or no interest among Indonesians in studies in history. The market for such books is negligible and no one can find time for performing historical research. Actually, every branch of intellectual life is suffering from this lack of time for activity in it. This may be caused by the country's general condition, which still necessitates the consumption of all psychic energies in the daily struggle for the strengthening of the recently established social and political order, and for earning a living. It is self-evident then that there can be little opportunity for the sublimation of energies not fully exhausted into more cultural and intellectual achievements.

But apart from this there are of course other factors determining the present lack of interest in scientific historiography. First of all there was no living tradition of historiography. In this respect, modern educated Indonesians are completely cut off from traditional culture.

Moreover, since the Indonesian notions about their past were conditioned by their education at Dutch schools, their school-knowledge of Indonesian history consists largely of the Dutch perspective on it. Under these circumstances the Indonesians have learned at school that the heroes of revolts against the Dutch were usually cruel and unreliable terrorists. And the Indonesian defeats were always evaluated according to the Dutch colonial point of view. Every Indonesian educated at a Dutch school can still recount unpleasant memories of history lessons during his primary and secondary school years. Thus the subject of history was not only made unattractive to Indonesians but it also became unpopular amongst them.

Furthermore, higher learning was—as already stated—only recently introduced in Indonesia. Besides, it did not teach history in any of its curricula and as a consequence it could not encourage historical research among Indonesians, nor could it correct their historical notions, which were much influenced in one or another way, in a negative or positive sense, by the Dutch colonial perspective. Consequently the Indonesian understanding of the nature of the present transitional phase of their development remained scanty, while there is on the other hand no great interest in reliable knowledge concerning the present time, knowledge which might be useful for further social development.

Another explanatory factor can be found in the image the Indonesians cherished concerning Europeans or western peoples in general. Seen through Indonesian eyes Westerners in pre-war colonial society seemed only concerned with materialistic life. And, since relations between white and colonized people based on social equality were almost unknown in colonial Indonesia,[17] no real personal contacts took place between Dutch and Indonesian intellectuals. As a result of this, cultural exchange between them was impossible and accordingly the more valuable sides of modern Western and European culture remained unnoticed by most educated Indonesians. Thus, in their minds, western peoples live mainly for materialism and colonialism, both of which are sharply contrasted with Indonesian ideals of the 'spiritual East'. Along these lines the notion of the 'undesirable West' became prevalent among Indonesians, causing them to become uninterested in the backgrounds and history of western peoples.

For our last remark we shall turn again to the nationalists' scheme of history. According to this scheme Indonesian history should be divided into three stages, i.e. a glorious past, a colonial era full of troubles, difficulties and humiliations, and as a third stage a promising future. The implication of such a conception is clearly that all troubles, difficulties, and humiliations will be over as soon as the second stage passes into the third.

Now, in 1930 Sukarno's representation of the future was as follows:

No millions of guilders will flow any more to other countries. There will be a people's community with a social organization in harmony to its needs. The political structure will be as democratic as possible, arts and science flourishing, culture unobstructed. A Federated Republic of Indonesia will live in peace and friendship with other nations and the Indonesian colours will constitute an ornament at the firmament of the East. A powerful, outwardly and inwardly sound nation will be ours.[18]

We have already stated how powerfully and successfully this ideal functioned during the decades before the Indonesian Republic became reality. At the moment, however, the question arises whether such an expectation of the future formulated in 1930 can still serve as an inspiration for social action. Will it not be necessary to redirect or adjust the scheme to the

---

[17] This was indicated in the 'Verslag van de Commissie Visman' (Report of the Visman Commission), pt. II (New York, 1944), pp. 85 and 89.   [18] *Indonesië klaagt aan*, p. 67.

present needs until it can again become an inspiration for social action as powerful as it was before the international recognition of the Indonesian government? And will such a new inspiration be able to rouse more citizens to do their utmost in order to secure the moral, social, and political integrity of their Nation?

Only the future can disclose the answer to those questions.

8. MODERN HISTORICAL WRITING IN BURMESE, 1724-1942

A brief study of the Burmese chronicles
of the eighteenth and nineteenth centuries
and their influence upon historical writing.

TIN OHN

Lecturer in History, University of Rangoon

Early historical literature in Burmese exists in prose as well as in poetic form. The former consists of the *Thamaing*—annals of pagoda and kingdoms, the *Ayedawpon*—the memoirs and the *Yazawin*—(*Rajavamsa*) the chronicle of kings; the latter ranges from 'the Minset Linka' the list of kings in simple verse to the *Mawkun* the epic poems and 'the Egyin'—the historical ballads. The chronicles which form the bulk of the historical literature can be conveniently divided into two, the old chronicle and the standard chronicle, the distinction between the two being—the former tends to be limited in scope, either it confines to one dynasty or region while the other is more extensive.[1] The Tagaung and Thaton chronicles are the well-known old chronicles and the *Mahayazawin*—the Great chronicle by U Kala is one of the most important of the standard chronicles. This article is an attempt to study the eighteenth- and the nineteenth-century chronicles as the traditional form of historical writing in Burmese and to assess its influence upon later historians.[2]

The history of historical writing in Burmese is as old as that of the Burmese literature. The earliest of the Burmese writings namely the inscriptions of Pagan eleventh to thirteenth centuries, contain the traces of historical writing. The system of dates, the use of 'Sakaraj' which was so essential to the writing of chronicles, was fully developed in the inscriptions. The stories such as the prophecy of Buddha and the reincarnation of Indra as a king in Pagan (Kyansittha's inscription at Myakan pagoda), stories which became the stock-in-trade of the chroniclers to describe the founding of early kingdoms, also started with the inscriptions.

The chronicles were first written in the fifteenth century which was a great age in Burmese literature. Of the chronicles written between the

---

[1] The classification of chronicles into the old and standard was made by Professor U Pe Maung Tin in his *Glass Palace Chronicle*. Dr. Hla Pe suggested 'parochial' and 'national' as an alternative name for the old and the standard.

[2] The article is largely based upon the *Glass Palace Chronicle* by Professor U Pe Maung Tin and Professor G. H. Luce, and their articles in the *Journal of Burma Research Society*, and I gratefully acknowledge my debt to them.

fifteenth century and the end of the seventeenth century very few survive today. The oldest chronicle extant is the 'Celebrated Chronicle' by Shin Thila-wuntha, the great poet. It was based on the *Mahavamsa* and it deals mainly with the Buddhist kings of India and Ceylon. Information about Burma is limited to a list of kings of Pagan, Pinya, and Sagaing and it occupies one fifth of the book. It is therefore disappointing as a Burmese chronicle. The significance of the work, however, lies in the fact that for the first time the Burmese kings were linked up with those of India and Ceylon, thereby establishing a tradition which was to be developed further by later chroniclers.

The Tagaung Chronincle, the Tharehkittara Chronicle, the Hngeppyit-taung Chronicle, and the Pagan Chronicle are some of the Old Chronicles that survive today. Almost all these chronicles deal with particular places or periods. As to the authors many of them were monks. This explains the nature and scope of their works. Like the chronicles of India and Ceylon, the old chronicles give only the account of kings their lineage and activities, and there was the same emphasis on religion and morals. Most of the stories described are legendary in character. As regards the sources these authors owe as much to Pali works such as Commentaries, *Mahavamsa* and *Dipavamsa*, as to local traditions, especially those of the Mons. Some of the stories mentioned in relation to the early kingdoms in Burma are adaptations from Mon stories. One of these stories is that of the King Dwattabaung—the famous three-eyed king. In methods of writing, too, the Burmese chroniclers owed a great deal to the Mons who, through earlier contact with India and Ceylon had developed a high standard of literature. In the middle of the sixteenth century Binnya Dala, a Mon officer at the court of Bayinnaung, translated the *Rajadarit Ayedawpon* from Mon into Burmese. With its rich details and fine narrative, the *Ayedawpon* which is a kind of *Mein Kampf*—a biography of a king, his struggle to power and his struggle to retain it after he had achieved it, must have contributed greatly to the historical writing of the eighteenth and nineteenth centuries.

The eighteenth century is the age of great chronicles. U Kala wrote his monumental work, the *Mahayazawin*—the Great Chronicle—in 1724. Son of Thuhte Deva and Mani Awga (of Singaing), U Kala was a scion of a wealthy family on his paternal side and of a nobility on his maternal side. His heritage of wealth and nobility partly explains his success as a scholar. Like his great contemporary Gibbon, U Kala, because of his wealth was able to devote himself to a scholarly life. Generally the chroniclers were either monks or ministers and most of their works were naturally limited by their outlook, training, and interests. U Kala was neither a monk nor a minister and so his writings were free from the defects common to many of the other chroniclers, namely the narrow outlook and excessive moralizing of the monks and the extreme subservient tone of the ministers. His knowledge of the style of the official or 'Hluttaw' records was clearly reflected in his writings and a style noted for its simple and matter-of-fact prose and a dignified narrative. In compiling the *Mahayazawin*, U Kala consulted about seventy works ranging from Pali commentaries to local chronicles and inscriptions.[3]

The first two parts of the chronicle deal with the origin of the Universe, and of the Buddhist kings of Ancient India. The third part opens with the founding of Tharehkittara and Pagan. After dealing with the Pinya, Sagaing, Ava, and Toungoo dynasties, U Kala brings the narrative down to his time (i.e. the reign of Taninganwe Min, 1714–33). The *Mahayazawin* was the first to give a detailed account of the dynasties after the fall of Pagan.

In giving a continuous history of Burma, U Kala departed from the sectional or regional approach which was the marked feature of the Old Chronicles. Thus both in his method and his style of composition U Kala is unique among the chroniclers. The fact that *Mahayazawin* or U Kala *Yazawin*, as it is popularly called, has been used as one of the classics in studying Burmese literature at the University is in itself an eloquent tribute to its literary qualities. Thus, thanks to U Kala, a tradition that chronicle writing or historical writing should aim at truth as well as a high literary style was established. The *Mahayazawin* naturally became a model for later chronicles and in fact it is the principal basis of the *Hmannan* Chronicle in which large portions of it are incorporated verbatim.

The *Yazawinlat*—the Middle chronicle, the second work of U Kala is an abridged version of the first work. Some of the details, however, are different. The last chronicle of U Kala is known as the *Yazawingyok*, the abridged chronicle, which gives little more than a bare list of the kings contained in his bigger versions namely the *Mahayazawin*. No other works are known to have been written by him. Thus U Kala is the only one among the early writers who can be called a 'professional' chronicler.

The next important chronicle of the eighteenth century is known as the New Pagan Chronicle—which was written in 1785. Its author is unknown. But its style and content suggest that the author was probably a monk. This chronicle follows the traditional style of the old chronicle. It was regional and the story is confined to the Pagan dynasty. The religious fervour of the author is clearly shown from many moralizing passages of the chronicle. He quotes stories from the *Jatakas* to preach good sermons. The importance of this work lies in three things: (*a*) It is the first chronicle which connects the lineage of the Tagaung Kings with the Sakyan family. (*b*) The author shows a critical power in selecting materials from different sources. Sometimes he criticizes his sources. (*c*) 'He possesses literary gifts

[3] *Mahayazawingyi II*, published by Burma Research Society, 1932, Introduction, p. 6.

and he has produced a work of no mean order as a prose composition. He displays his literary taste in his selection, from various poetical sources, of sumptuous passages with which he adorns his narrative.'[4]

The New Chronicle, which was the last of the eighteenth-century chronicles, was written in 1798 by Twinthin Mahasithu, a great scholar, whom Bodawpaya appointed as one of the officers in charge of the inscriptions which he collected at Amarapura. Twinthin thus had a unique opportunity of checking the chronicles by means of inscriptions. Like U Kala, Twinthin brings the narrative in his chronicle down to his time (1752). He criticizes the older chronicles and puts forward new observations generally based on his readings of inscriptions. The New Chronicle is the first to make a serious attempt to check history by means of inscriptions.

The nineteenth century, which marked the highest stage of development in the writing of Chronicles was an age of official chroniclers. In 1829 a committee to compile an official chronicle was formed by order of King Bagyidaw. It consisted of learned monks, Brahmins, and ministers. The Monywe Sayadaw and Thawkapin Sayadaw acted as consulting editors. The former was a great scholar and a chronicler in his own right. All the members of the committee had been selected for their learning. As the preface says, the purpose was to compile a chronicle of kings that should be the standard, a balance, so to speak, for all duties of the king, for all affairs of state, for all matters of religion, and not a thing full of conflicting and false statements. To achieve this object the method was also laid down. 'The chronicle was to be purified by comparing it with other chronicles and a number of inscriptions, each with the other, and adopting the truth in the light of reason and the traditional books.'[5] The work of compilation took about four years. In the process the committee consulted not only the accounts of the dynasties of Pagan, Ava, Amarapura, and Toungoo, but also used Mon, Arakanese, and other records, and included them in their history. The compilers showed their learning and assiduity by drawing upon almost every form of literature ranging from Nikayas (the collection of Dharma) and commentaries to the inscriptions, in support of their view. They drastically revised many of the observations made by U Kala in the opening parts of his chronicle. New information such as the detailed account of the coming of Sakya kings in connection with the founding of Tagaung was added. The narrative of the chronicle was brought to the year 1821. The chronicle was known as the *Hmannan Yazawin*, the Glass Palace Chronicle after the name of the hall at the palace in which the authors met for compilation.

In 1867, Mindon Min ordered another committee to be formed in order to bring the chronicle up to date. Once again a committee of learned

---

[4] *The Glass Palace Chronicle*, Tin and Luce translation, p. xvi. [5] Ibid., p. ix.

monks and ministers met together and compiled a new chronicle from the
point where the Glass Palace Chronicle ended. The second chronicle
when completed brought events down to 1854. The king ordered that the
first official chronicle was to be known as the First *Mahayazawin* and the
new one compiled during his reign—the Second *Mahayazawin*. (This
official chronicle was continued in 1905 to cover the whole period of the
Konbaung dynasty. This was later published along with that portion of
the previous chronicle relating to the Konbaung dynasty. Hence the
chronicle came to be known as the *Konbaungset Yazawin*.)

With the compilation of the Second *Mahayazawin*, a standard chronicle
of Burma from the earliest times down to 1854 was completed. It was more
than a coincidence that the two chronicles were compiled in the aftermath
of the two wars with the British (the First 1824–5 and the Second 1852).
With their grand accounts of the glory and achievement of the past, the
two chronicles may be taken as a deliberate attempt on the part of the
king and his ministers to bolster up the morale of the court and the people
who had suffered a terrible shock as the result of the disastrous war.
Viewing these works in their proper historical context one can easily
understand their pompous and almost arrogant tone. In short, these
chronicles are the Burmese examples of writing history with a purpose.

As to their merits and demerits, the First and the Second *Mahayazawin*
share with other chronicles in their main defect, namely the narrowness of
scope. Only the accounts of the kings are given in the chronicles. It is the
fault of all chroniclers that they say little of the state of the people and the
country. In short, the awareness of society was conspicuously absent among
the chroniclers. Besides, the compilers had to gloss over incidents which
might have been unpleasant in the ears of the kings. Against these shortcomings much can be said in favour of the chronicles. They represent
Burmese history from the point of view of Ava. They portray the achievements of the Burmese and yet at the same time give a fair and generous
account of the achievements of the other races of Burma. As the compilers
had access to most of the sources of historical materials, the accounts given
in the chronicles are authentic and most comprehensive. The words attributed to the kings, ministers, and great generals are expressive and forceful
and above all they have the ring of truth. The best accounts of the royal
ceremonies such as coronations, enthronement of Uparaj, royal levees and
also the detailed accounts of wars are to be found in the chronicles.

The compilers were very scholarly and learned and hence one of the
great merits of the chronicles lies in their literary qualities. The diction
and the style of the narrative often match the dramatic moments it
describes. The chronicles contain many examples of good prose—and the
classic instance is the account of the Sino-Burmese wars of the reign of
Hsinbyushin. The clear and detailed account of the battles and sieges and

the thumbnail sketches of the personalities taking part in the fight, give a most realistic and graphic picture of the struggle.[6] The vivid and pungent style of narrative could be ranked among the best of historical literature.

Finally, the two *Mahayazawin*, written in the tradition of the chronicles, have their moral aspect. They teach good morals by examples. With the stories extolling good virtues, such as loyalty, self-sacrifice, and faith in the Three Gems, the *Mahayazawin* set out to give the essence of the Burmese way of life and culture. This fact explains why, in the 1920s with the beginning of national awakening, there was a popular demand for history (Burmese history) to be taught in schools.

The comparative study of the *Mahayazawin* with other chronicles such as the Siamese Chronicle, clearly shows us that the former, with a high degree of authenticity, both in its chronology and events, is a more reliable work. European scholars such as Sangermano, Phayre, and Mr. Harvey used the *Mahayazawin* as an authoritative source. In the words of Mr. Harvey, 'it is impossible to study these (Burmese chronicles), especially in conjunction with the other native records, without acquiring considerable respect for them. No other country on the mainland of Indo-China can show so impressive a continuity. The great record of substantially accurate dates goes back for no less than nine centuries and even the earlier legends have a substratum of truth.'[7] No better tribute could be paid to the chronicles.

The *Hmannan* or the Second *Mahayazawin*—1867 appears to be the last and the most important chronicle compiled under the Burmese kings. No other chronicles of note or historical works are recorded during the period 1867–85. The only exception is the *Raja Dharma Singaha*—'the kingly duties' (1878) written by Wetmasu Wun. It is a semi-historical work representing a modest attempt to explain the parliamentary government of England. The fact that such a treatise on government had been written by an administrator-scholar, one who had the earliest opportunity to visit the western countries, clearly shows that the Burmese intellectuals were fully aware of the world outside their own country and were quick enough to appreciate the new ideas. Yet this healthy development among the intellectuals was checked by the collapse of the Konbaung Dynasty. (Experiments in the form of enlightened schemes in economic and industrial fields also met a similar fate in 1885.)

The chronicle writing more than any other form of literature suffered in the decades following 1885. With no Burmese king to inspire and patronize, the Burmese literature suffered a serious setback. Chronicle writing also met the same fate. Besides the new regime brought about

---

[6] See 'Chinese Invasion', by Professor Luce, JBRS, xv, 115.
[7] *History of Burma*, G. E. Harvey, Introduction, p. xix.

drastic changes in the traditional values. Burmese for instance was supplanted by English as an official language. The subordination of the Burmese language to English also explains why the Burmese literature in general and the historical writing in particular had not developed fully as it should, although there has been a closer contact with the West.

After 1905 new 'historical' works most of which are chronicles, began to appear. They came as part of the new nationalism that spread in Asia. (In Burma the movement manifested itself in various forms such as Buddhistic revival and the formation of political organizations.) In fact, these writings are the literary manifestations of the new nationalism. To many Burmese scholars of the period, the writing of 'history' was an act of faith and a patriotic duty. Their main purpose was to defend the old regime against the slanderous attack of some English writers who in their zeal to justify the new government, misinterpreted and misread Burmese history. With few exceptions, most of the histories written between 1905–25 are the modified versions of the chronicles particularly the Glass Palace Chronicle. This is quite natural for the writers who had been brought up in the old-fashioned way of monastic schools and hence steeped in Burmese traditionalism, to model their work on that of the chronicles.

The first writer of note is U Pe, a former employee of the Burmese government and later a clerk at the Archaeological Department, and his only work is the *Rajavamsazalini*, the new Pagan History. The main importance of the work lies in the fact that the author, from his vast knowledge of the inscriptions, attempted to reconcile the conflicting views of the previous chronicles about some of the events in Pagan.

In 1905 U Tin compiled the *Konbaungset Mahayazawin* as a continuation to the second Mahayazawingyi. His work which covers the period 1854–85 was based on diaries and records of the royal court and memoirs and papers kept by the royal princes and ministers of the last regime. In 1922 U Tin revised his work and published it as part of the Glass Palace Chronicle under the title of *Konbaungset Mahayazawin*. Hence that part of the official chronicle beginning with the Konbaung dynasty was incorporated in U Tin's work and was known as the Konbaungset Chronicle. U Tin was a scholar of high repute and among his other works were the five volumes of the *Myanma Min Okchokpon Sadan*—the system of government under Burmese kings—a compilation based on the Hluttaw records, sittans, and royal orders.

In 1922 U Bi, a former translator at the High Court and a well-known Pali-scholar, published a series of chronicles known as the *Thuthawdita Mahayazawingyi*. The sixth and the last volume was published in 1933. These chronicles as the name signifies are the reprint with proper editing of the Glass Palace Chronicle and the *Konbaungset*.

The most notable writer of this period is U Lun, who began his career as a journalist, and has been in turn a poet, novelist, historian, and a nationalist. His prolific writings representing his varied interests and accomplishments form the bulk of the nationalist literature. U Lun, generally known as Thakin Kodaw Hmaing, who is still a prominent figure in the literary field, wrote his first history book in 1911 and it is known as the *Yazawinthankhaik* an abridged chronicle. His major work in history, the 'New Glass Palace Chronicle' was written in 1922. It is a modified version of the official chronicle with the first two parts relating to India and the learned discussions and Pali-stanzas left out. By excluding the early part relating to Indian history and by its use of simple prose, the chronicle reflects the growing nationalist aspirations to use Burmese as the sole medium of expression. It therefore reversed the traditional practice of using Pali words and Pali-stanzas as the indispensable part that lends dignity and sacredness to the literary works.

Apart from the chronicles of conventional type other historical subjects began to attract attention. Two works on the Treaty of Yandabo and its history, one by U Khin Nyunt (1923) and the other by U Shwe, both school teachers, marked a departure from the traditional form of 'history' writing. In 1926 U Thein (Hmawbi Saya Thein) wrote *Pazat Yazawin*— a history based on oral traditions. The work deals with the reign of King Bodawpaya and it describes the life of the king when he was a prince. It is a unique history in the sense that it gives an account of the king in his unusual surroundings. As a result, the picture of the king that appears from this book is one of a very human person stripped of the glamour of royalty.

However, towards the end of the 1920s, a gradual change in the method of historical writing occurred. The political awakening (the Wunthanu Movement), the spread of Western education, the writing of English historians on Burma, the publications of the Burma Research Society are some of the factors which inspired this change in the outlook and technique of the new 'historians'. Besides, by 1928 as there was a demand for school texts in history, the Burmese scholars of the period began to write history books for the use of the schools. U Po Kya, who was the Inspector of National Schools, was one of the pioneers, and he wrote the *Myanma Gonyee*—the achievement of the Burmese. Another set of short biographies soon appeared. These are the lives of Burmese Heroes namely, Minyek-yawswa, Bandoola, Tabinshwehti, Bayinnaung, and Alaungpaya, written by U Thein Maung, the editor of the *Sun Magazine*, and published in 1933. A short Burmese history for High Schools was written by U Ba Than and U Ohn Maung, and these texts are still in use at the schools. After the war, Major Ba Shin wrote the *Myanma Thamaing* in which for the first time there is an emphasis upon the ethnical and cultural developments. Moreover, the choice of the word *Thamaing* for the conventional word

Yazawin signifies the growing acceptance of the meaning of the word history in its wider sense. *Thamaing* unlike the word *Yazawin* has acquired a new connotation, namely, a history that covers political as well as economic, social, and cultural life of the people.

In the 1930's, with the founding of the Red Dragon Book Club, a number of semi-historical books were written and published. But the most important publication was the Political History of Burma by 'Fabian' U Ba Khine and published in 1937. The only historical work of its kind in Burmese, it gives a first hand and a reliable account of the contemporary politics and political history of Burma for the period 1885 to 1937. This represents the last and most notable of the historical writing for the period ending 1942.

From the above it is clear that the historical writing in Burmese has yet to be developed as a proper discipline on western lines. The late introduction of Western education into Burma, the reluctance on the part of the Burmese scholars who had the knowledge and flair for research to write in Burmese, and the lack of facilities and training in research are some of the factors which explain the paucity of historical writing in Burmese in the pre-war period. Since independence, however, the Government has adopted effective measures in order to remedy some of the shortcomings. Thus, for example, scores of students have been sent abroad for post-graduate training in historical research. Numerically, it constitutes a marked improvement over that of the pre-war practice, for before the war only two state scholars had been sent to England for post-graduate study in history. Besides, another encouraging sign is the growing number of Burmans taking up history teaching as a profession at the University. Whereas in the past almost all the honours graduates in history joined the civil service.

Two organizations stand out among the enlightened measures of the government. In 1947 the Translation Society was founded with a view to promote Burmese culture and Burmese literature. In 1955, Burma Historical Commission with U Kaung as Chairman was set up with an object to produce a standard history of Burma. Important and timely though these measures of the Government are, the main solution for the improvement of the historical writing lies in the training and production of more historians. In this the Rangoon University should play its part as a training centre of the future historians.

9. MODERN VIETNAMESE HISTORIOGRAPHY

P. J. HONEY

Lecturer in Vietnamese, School of Oriental and African Studies

The word 'modern' in the title of this paper is not a precise term, so that it is necessary at the outset to define what is meant by it. It is one of the two categories, traditional and modern, into which the historical writings on Viet Nam may be conveniently divided. A brief review of the whole of Vietnamese historiography will exemplify the full significance of these two terms, and will also serve, in some small measure, to fill the gap caused by the absence of a paper on the earlier historical writing on Viet Nam. This review will, in addition, provide information about the source material available to historians at the present time.

Documentation for the period of Vietnamese history prior to the seventeenth century is very sparse indeed. A number of factors are responsible for this, the more important being the unsettled condition of the country, a climate in which it is difficult to conserve books and papers, and the absence of any system for the preservation of archives or the organization of libraries. The long succession of wars and invasions led inevitably to the pillaging and destruction of collections of manuscripts. In the preface to his *Dại-Việt Thông-Sử* (*The Complete History of Dai-Viet*) the Vietnamese scholar Lê Qúy Dôn, who wrote at about the middle of the eighteenth century, had the following to say: 'The number of books was very small, and their preservation in the imperial libraries was neglected. There was no organisation to conserve the confidential documents of the imperial palace, and no mandarins were specifically charged with the care of the libraries. No regulations had been laid down to govern the task of verifying the contents of documents or of copying them, and no provision was made for their preservation.'

From the end of the second century B.C. to the middle of the tenth century A.D. Viet Nam was under Chinese domination, and it is to China that one must look for the most important historical sources for this period. A few such sources have already come to light, but the greater number still lie undiscovered in the libraries of China.

It is known that the Vietnamese scholars were producing a considerable output of writings during the dynasties of the Lý and the Trân. The decline of the Trân dynasty during the second half of the fourteenth century, however, brought about a series of invasions by Champa. A number of these Cham attacks reached the Vietnamese capital, and one can only speculate about the losses of books which resulted.

At the beginning of the fifteenth century the Chinese Ming dynasty successfully invaded Viet Nam. Their occupation of the country lasted only fourteen years but, during the course of it, the Chinese systematically removed all Vietnamese books and replaced them with Chinese classics. It is true that the Lê, who drove out the Chinese and founded the new dynasty, endeavoured to replace the lost books; but the Chinese had been very thorough. The revolt of Trân Cảo early in the sixteenth century led to the capture of the capital by the rebels and to further destruction.

The rebellion of the Tây Son and their subsequent defeat by Gia Long occupied the last quarter of the eighteenth century and caused widespread devastation throughout the whole country. The coming of the French in the nineteenth century led to further warfare and destruction, although this was later offset by the work of French scholars who studied and preserved historical documents, and particularly by the work of the École Française d'Extrême Orient. It is still too early to assess the losses which have been sustained during the war of independence, 1946–54, but these are certainly severe.

Nevertheless, some documents have survived all of these hazards and, as far as it is possible to ascertain, still exist today. Many of these are, at the present time, inaccessible and there is no indication that they will be available for study in the foreseeable future. The last war has left Viet Nam divided, and the future of libraries such as that of the École Française d'Extrême Orient is still unsettled. The situation in the country is explosive and fighting may break out again. It is likely to be several more years, at the very least, before it becomes possible to discover what can be salvaged.

The surviving traditional histories of Viet Nam are of two kinds, those written at the decree of the emperor by the mandarins of the court, and those written by private scholars unconnected with the court. The official imperial annals, or *Chánh-Sử*, record, reign by reign, the important happenings which took place in Viet Nam. These are not necessarily contemporary records of the events which they describe because each new dynasty compiled its own annals afresh, and the accounts of events which occurred prior to the composition of any particular set of annals was based upon earlier annals or other records. All of these *Chánh-Sử* have certain grave defects as truthful and useful historical documents. Since all were written by order of a particular dynasty, one of the principal objects of the authors was to please—or at least to avoid displeasing—the reigning dynasty. Consequently, they tended to belittle the achievements of earlier dynasties and to magnify those of the reigning dynasty. When these *Chánh-Sử* recorded contemporary happenings, they devoted too much space to the relatively unimportant court happenings and to the doings of the emperor, while glossing over or even omitting those happenings which might displease the emperor. These annals tell us very little of the actual conditions in the country, of the everyday life of the people, of trade, and of many other important factors. The earliest of the surviving *Chánh-Sử* is the *Đại-Việt Sử-Ky* (The History of Dai-Viet) which was compiled over a period dating from the middle of the thirteenth century A.D. up to the end of the seventeenth century A.D. The most recent is the *Khâm-Định Việt-Sử Thông-Giám Cương-Muc* (Texts and Commentaries Forming the Mirror of the Complete History of Viet Nam and Written by Imperial Decree) which was compiled by order of the Nguyên dynasty between 1856 and 1884.

Of the histories of Viet Nam written by private scholars only a very few survive today. The oldest is the *An-Nam Chi Lược* (Brief History of Annam) was written by Le Tac and dates from the thirteenth century A.D. Another, the *Việt Sử-Lược* (Short History of Viet Nam), was compiled during the sixteenth century A.D., but its author is unknown. The remainder of these private histories were written during the eighteenth and nineteenth centuries. Perhaps the principal value of such works is that they enable the official annals to be checked, and they fill in some of the lacunae which are found in the latter.

These two kinds of history typify what is meant in this paper by the term 'traditional history'. They both record events in chronological order but do not examine either causes or motives. No attempt is made in them to assess the relative importance of the happenings or their implications. When dealing with earlier periods they recount the events as set out in earlier chronicles, possibly altering the emphasis but never cross-checking and trying to evaluate the different sources.

The mandarins of the imperial court produced other works which may, if the term 'historiography' is interpreted liberally, be described as histories. These works are of four categories, namely the *Hoi-Diên* (collections of legislative and administrative documents), the *Ngoc-Phá* (genealogies of the imperial families), the *Thús-Lúc* (accounts of the doings of an emperor and his forebears), and the *Liêt-Truyên* (biographies of outstanding Vietnamese men and women). All of these, together with a number of geographical treatises of comparatively recent date, comprise the Vietnamese documentary sources for the history of Viet Nam.

A further complication arises in the case of these documents, the complication of language. All of them are written in Sino-Vietnamese characters which are no longer used by the Vietnamese people. These characters have been replaced by a form of writing known as Quốc-Ngữ, in which Roman letters are used, and are understood only by Vietnamese who have made a special study of them. Few of these documents have been transcribed into Quôc-Ngữ or translated into a European language, and this will have to be done before the texts can be used by the majority of modern historians. A start has been made in this task by one or two scholars. Mr. Maurice Durand, of the École Française d'Extrême Orient, undertook in 1949 the transcription into Quôc-Ngữ and the translation into French of the *Khâm-Định Viêt-Sử Thông-Giám Cương-Muc*. This work contains fifty-three chapters, of which only five had ever been translated and published. In the introduction to the first instalment of the translation, Mr. Durand writes: 'Notre but est d'offrir à tous, étrangers et Vietnamiens, l'accès à un texte important de l'histoire Vietnamienne et de contribuer par là à la renaissance toute prochaine des études vietnamiennes.' The first publication, containing the introductory chapter and chapter one, was completed in 1950, and the second one appeared in the Bulletin de l'École Française d'Extrême Orient in 1955.

With the arrival of the Europeans in the seventeenth century, there commenced a new source of information about the past of Viet Nam. These Europeans came to Viet Nam either as missionaries or as traders, and both groups sent reports of conditions and events back to Europe. A number of missionaries have written histories of Viet Nam, or descriptions of the country and its people. Alexandre de Rhodes, the celebrated Jesuit missionary, wrote the first of these, the *History of Tonking*, which was published in Rome in 1651, and many others have followed over the intervening three centuries. The majority of these histories described contemporary events or cited the annals for earlier ones. They cannot be said to have made any radical departure from the traditional style of history writing until comparatively recent times. The unpublished accounts and letters of the East India Company factory which was established in Tonking towards the end of the seventeenth century are a most valuable source of information about such subjects as economics and trade, currency, housing, trading practices, and so on. The early European sources have a very special value for the following two reasons. They are concerned particularly with aspects of Vietnamese life which are ignored by the official annals, and they apply European standards of values to things Vietnamese, thus enabling a more objective assessment to be made of conditions in Viet Nam.

The conception of modern historiography is one which was alien to the old Vietnamese civilization. It could never have developed of itself within this civilization, and consequently had to be brought in from outside. The coming of the French to Viet Nam in the middle of the nineteenth century marked the beginning of the collapse of this traditional civilization which had persisted with so little change for over two thousand years. Viet Nam, it is true, had been subject to a foreign power in the past, but that power was China, and the similarities between the cultures, religions, and ways of life of the two peoples were considerable. The French came from nine-teenth-century Europe, and the differences between the two peoples and countries could not have been greater. Under the influence of French education, the beliefs, codes of behaviour, and standards of values, which no Vietnamese before that period would ever have thought of questioning, were not only questioned but rejected and replaced. The effects of the French impact on Viet Nam have nowhere been fully appreciated, and they are still making themselves felt today in every facet of Vietnamese life. During the period of the French domination a new type of Vietnamese was developed, a person with the mind of a sceptic who would accept nothing which he could not verify from his own experience or by his own thinking. The modern Vietnamese is the very antithesis of his forbears who lived in pre-French times.

It would not be true to say that the imposition of French domination on Viet Nam marked the end of traditional Vietnamese historiography and the beginning of modern historiography. The spread of French ideas and education was a slow and uneven process, and even today there are Viet-namese scholars still alive who have steadfastly resisted French culture. The *Viêt-Nam Sử-Lược* (Brief History of Viet Nam), a very widely read history of Viet Nam, cannot be described as anything but traditional, yet it was first published in 1928 and republished as recently as 1948. This book was written by the celebrated Vietnamese scholar and nationalist Trân Trọng Kim, who died only two years ago. It is to French scholars to whom one must look for the earliest modern histories of Viet Nam.

When the French colonized Cochin China in 1858, little or nothing was known in Europe about Viet Nam. French scholars commenced to study the language and history of the country, but their early attempts at writing histories of Viet Nam were made with considerable trepidation. This was occasioned by the great gulf which separated the two civilizations and by the uncertainty felt by these scholars about their ability to understand and interpret Vietnamese civilization. In the preface to his book *Histoire Ancienne et Moderne de l'Annam, Tonking, et Cochinchine*, which was published in 1884, Launay wrote:

Nous croyons avoir, dans ces quelques pages, résumé avec assez d'exactitude tous les faits importants de l'histoire annamite. Quant aux jugements que nous avons quelquefois mêlés à notre recit, nous prions le lecteur de les acceuillir avec une indulgente réserve. L'historien doit montrer comment les événements se développent et s'enchaînent, il doit distribuer entre les personnages dont il raconte les actes, la part de responsabilité qui revient aux hommes dans la destinée des peuples. Mais cette tâche est bien difficile, quand il s'agit des époques fort éloignées de la nôtre, de peuple trés différents de nous par leurs croy-ances et leur institutions, par leurs idées, leurs usages, et leurs moeurs ...

This book, like the majority of early European histories of Viet Nam, was based almost entirely upon Vietnamese and Chinese official annals. The *Khâm-Định Việt-Sử Thông-Giám Cương-Mục* was not available to the earlier French historians of the colonial period, and the annals to which the writers refer are the *Đại-Việt Sử-Ký*. One cannot leave this early colonial period without mentioning a remarkable Vietnamese scholar who was one of the first of his race to absorb the new culture which the French had brought. This was Trương Vĩnh Ký, the author of the *Cours d'Histoire Annamite*, the most complete and detailed of all the histories written at that time.

Throughout the last quarter of the nineteenth century a number of French scholars devoted themselves to the investigation of the past of Viet Nam. The tendency of historians during this period, in contrast with that of their predecessors, was to make more detailed studies of specific periods or aspects of Vietnamese history. A more careful examination was made of source materials. Des Michels undertook the task of translating the text of the *Khâm-Định Việt-Sử Thông-Giám Cương-Mục*, a task which he unfortunately never lived to complete. Sainson translated and published the *An-Nam Chi-Lược*. Deveria published his *Histoire des Relations de la Chine avec l'Annam-Viet Nam du XVIe au XIXe Siècle* and his *La Frontière Sino-Annamite*. Others interested themselves in more recent history and particularly in the achievements of France in Indo-China. Vial, one of this latter school, published two books entitled *Les Premières Années de la Cochinchine* and *Nos Premières Années au Tonkin*. Historiographers had become less unsure of themselves than in earlier years by virtue of their longer acquaintance with Viet Nam. The writing of Vietnamese history was no longer regarded by them as a matter of writing about a country and a people which they did not fully understand, but as an undertaking which posed very much the same problems as the historiography of any other country. No Vietnamese scholars, with the sole exception of Trương Vĩnh Ký, published any noteworthy historical work during this period.

The establishment of the École Française d'Extrême Orient in 1900 provided a very powerful stimulus to the study of Vietnamese history. This school built up a very fine specialist library, and afforded facilities to historians and archaeologists to carry out research and field work in Viet Nam. It produced a bulletin in which these scholars were able to publish the results of their work and founded museums in Viet Nam where Vietnamese antiquities were displayed. It is hardly surprising, then, to find that the next quarter of a century was a most fruitful one from the point of view of the historian. Scholars of the calibre of Cadière, Maybon, and Maspéro were at that time engaged upon their historical research and publishing their findings. Many new aspects of the past of Viet Nam were studied. Lacroix and Schroeder wrote studies of numismatics in Viet Nam, while the French Military Authorities compiled a military history of Indo-China from 1664 onwards. Deloustal produced studies of the economic and financial resources of Viet Nam before the arrival of the French, and others on Vietnamese justice and law. The contributions of Cadière to Vietnamese historiography during this period were of very great value. He wrote on a number of different topics, publishing articles and books on the establishment of the Nguyen in Annam, the historical geography of Quanh Binh, the dating of the Vietnamese dynasties, and the historical documents relating to the period of Gia Long. Of all the historical works published at that time, the most outstanding is, perhaps, Maybon's *Histoire Moderne du Pays d'Annam* (1592–1820). This book is a most detailed study of the period, and is remarkable for the very large number of sources consulted by the author in the course of its preparation. Maybon made use of all the available historical material, studying the Vietnamese annals, missionary reports, accounts of European traders, and archaeological discoveries. Several societies were founded in Viet Nam for the study of all aspects of the history of Vietnamese civilization, and many of these published bulletins and reviews. Some of these publications such as the *Revue Indochinoise* and the *Bulletin des Amis du Vieux Hué*, to name but two, won international repute.

This was still a period of French historiography, however, and no Vietnamese scholar was yet producing any serious historical work. The reason for this phenomenon is that the Vietnamese people were still in the process of absorbing western ideas and western education. For reasons which are outside the scope of this paper, the Vietnamese people were not encouraged to travel overseas. During the First World War, France raised a Vietnamese force and shipped it to Europe. When the members of this force returned to Viet Nam at the end of the war, they carried back with them tales of the wonders of the western world. These reports stimulated in the Vietnamese people a desire to travel abroad and to learn for themselves about the world outside Viet Nam. A small number of Vietnamese, children of the wealthy families for the most part, went abroad to complete their education, but these were permitted to travel only to France.

It is possible to discern in Viet Nam during the late 1920s and throughout the 1930s the considerable effects which the new ideas, brought back by Vietnamese students and workers from Europe, were producing on the thought and behaviour of the Vietnamese people. Vietnamese nationalism had been strong throughout the whole period of the French domination, but during this era nationalism was being joined with socialism, Marxism, Trotskyism, and other political creeds imported from abroad. It manifested itself in the formation of underground political parties and sporadic revolts against French authority, but had not yet begun to make its effects felt in the sphere of historiography. Between the years 1928 and 1937 a

Vietnamese scholar, Lê Thành Cành, published a series of articles in the *Bulletin des Amis du Vieux Hué* entitled 'Notes Pour Servir a l'Histoire de l'Etablissment du Protectorat Français en Annam (1847–63)', and in 1937 and 1938 the Vietnamese statesman Pham Quynh wrote 'Essais Franco-Annamites' and 'Nouveaux Essais Franco-Annamites'. These may be looked upon as the first stirrings of a new and different interest in Vietnamese history being taken by the Vietnamese themselves.

In the years directly preceding the outbreak of the Second World War Vietnamese historiography was still a field which was almost entirely confined to French scholars. These continued to work under the auspices of the École Française d'Extrême Orient and independently, producing a steady flow of historical publications. A change of emphasis is discernible in these publications. Although many of the historians continued to interest themselves in the earlier periods of Vietnamese history, a much larger number than hitherto studied the French Colonial period. Problems of colonization were studied and commented on by men such as Robequain who wrote *L'Evolution Economique de l'Indochine Française*. Colonialism was a subject which was being widely discussed all over the world at that time, and it had many opponents both in the colonial countries themselves and in America. It was the colonial questions which induced two American scholars to interest themselves in Vietnamese history and to publish books on the subject. These scholars were T. E. Ennis who published *French Policy and Developments in Indo-China*, and Virginia Thompson, the authoress of *French Indo-China*. The French Government General in Indo-China produced a work in five volumes entitled *Contribution a l'Histoire des Mouvements Politiques de l'Indochine Française*, and a French scholar wrote *La Formation des Classes Sociales en Pays Annamite*, both of which foreshadowed the developments which were later to take place in Viet Nam.

The events of the Second World War, and the granting of 'independence' to Viet Nam by the defeated Japanese stirred the national pride of the Vietnamese people. Viet Nam, they felt, was regaining her lost independence and would once more be a free country—freer, in fact, than ever before, because she would no longer be dependent upon the Chinese emperor. The direct results of this surge of nationalism were the outbreak of a war of national liberation and the subsequent withdrawal of France from Indo-China after her defeat at Diện Biên Phủ. One of the indirect results was the writing of an unprecedented number of historical books and articles by Vietnamese authors. At first these took the form of hastily written biographies of Vietnamese patriots who had been put to death for taking part in revolts against French colonial rule, or histories and descriptions of such revolts. These were read avidly by the Vietnamese people which demanded more books and more information about the past history of Viet Nam. This demand has proved to be the incentive which has encouraged so many Vietnamese scholars to produce serious historical studies over the past ten years.

A Vietnamese renaissance would seem to have taken place during, or at the end of, the Second World War. At the outset it appeared to be one of the many manifestations of a belligerent nationalism, but time has proved that it was and is very much more profound than that. It is to be seen in all branches of Vietnamese culture, but most particularly in literature and historiography. In the course of the preparation of this paper, a date chart was prepared which extended from 1850 up to 1956. The title of every serious publication dealing with Vietnamese history was written on this chart opposite the date of its publication. The most striking feature of the completed chart is the distribution of the works of French and Vietnamese authors by date. In the period 1850–1939 the authors are nearly all French, very few Vietnamese names appearing at all. The chart for the years 1939–56 shows a great preponderance of Vietnamese names over French. The number of French scholars working in the field of Vietnamese history has decreased appreciably since the outbreak of the Second World War, but this decrease has been more than compensated by the surprising number of Vietnamese historians who have commenced to study and to write about Vietnamese history. The numbers of these Vietnamese historiographers are probably greater even than the date chart would suggest because it is not yet possible to ascertain what work has been done in the sphere of Vietnamese history by scholars living in the Viet Minh zone of Viet Nam. It has been possible to enter in the chart only such publications as are obtainable in French or in the non-communist zone of Viet Nam.

The recent historical writings of Vietnamese scholars have one feature in common; they are all written in a style which is very different from that of the traditional Vietnamese histories. They are part of modern Vietnamese historiography in every sense of this term. All of them contain evidence of painstaking research and publish lists of the sources consulted in the course of their preparation. A novel feature of many of these books is their interpretation of Vietnamese history in accordance with non-Vietnamese political philosophies. One of the most recent, and certainly the most detailed history of Viet Nam written since the end of the second World War is entitled *Le Viet Nam, Histoire et Civilisation*. This book is the work of the young Vietnamese scholar Lê Thanh Khôi, and in it the author presents a Marxist interpretation of Vietnamese history. Other books, Hoàng Xuân Hãn's *La-sơn Phu-Tu* to cite but one example, are the fruits of careful, critical, and accurate scholarship. Nor are these modern Vietnamese historiographers confining themselves to the study of the important political happenings, the major wars, or the doings of the court, but are carrying out historical research on many different facets of Viet

Nam's past. Within the past few years they have published books on such diverse topics as the history of Buddhism in Viet Nam, the social history of Viet Nam, the origins of the Vietnamese people, and the history of Vietnamese literature.

Non-Vietnamese historians have also been active since the end of the Second World War, although they are now outnumbered by their Vietnamese colleagues. Some of them have continued to write about the earlier periods—Janse and Malleret have published the results of their archaeological researches and Gaspardone, Lévy, and Stein have published their findings on the pre-French era, while others have confined themselves to the French colonial period. The subjects about which most has been written, however, are the Japanese occupation of Viet Nam and the Vietnamese struggle for independence from France. The most interesting and the best documented of the accounts of the Japanese occupation was written by the Governor General of Indo China at that time, Admiral Decoux. This book, the title of which is *A la Barre de l'Indochine*, was written as an apologia for the conduct of affairs in Indo China by Decoux and presents a most lucid account of the dealings between the French and Japanese at a political level. General Sabattier has written a military history of the same period.

Of the histories of the Vietnamese struggle for independence from French rule, two stand out from the remainder by virtue of the amount of research which has gone into their preparation and for their dispassionate and unbiased presentation of the material. One of these, *The Struggle for Indo-China*, is the work of an American scholar, Ellen Hammer. The fact that such a book should have been written by an American is an indication of the keen interest which has been taken in Vietnamese studies by Americans in recent years. The second history, *Histoire du Viet Nam du 1940 à 1952*, was written by a French historian, Devillers. An excellent feature of this book is its copious references to the source material used, the references being provided in the form of footnotes. A number of other books have been, or are being written about this period, and these include the personal records of men who played leading parts in the events which took place. Prominent in this latter category is *Histoire d'une Paix Manquée*, by Jean Sainteny, who is at present the accredited French representative to the Viet Minh Government of North Viet Nam.

Modern Vietnamese historiography is still in its very early beginnings. The old Vietnamese civilization embodied the writing of history, or rather the recording of contemporary events for the information of posterity. The origins of this practice in Viet Nam are not known, but it appears probable that it was copied from the Chinese custom. The overthrow of reigning dynasties and their replacement by other dynasties necessitated the rewriting of the chronicles; for it was necessary to record that the preceding dynasty was not the rightful one and that its emperors were usurpers or rebels. Change, innovation, and independent thinking were all discouraged by this old civilization which had reached a stage of complete stagnation by the middle of the nineteenth century. Since all three of these are necessary prerequisites for modern historiography, it would have been impossible for this to develop inside Viet Nam.

With the coming of the French to Viet Nam, there was introduced an influence which was to prove fatal to the old culture of the country. The development of a new culture to take the place of the old was a slow and gradual process. French scholars had to point the way in all branches of scholarship, and the introduction of nineteenth-century European ideas was strongly resisted by Vietnamese traditionalists. Nevertheless, by the 1930s the overwhelming majority of Viet Nam's intellectual leaders had undergone a French education and were eager to compete with and to rival French achievements in all fields. Under the influence of such men, Vietnamese national pride and the desire for independence from France rose to unprecedented heights. The train of international events presented the Vietnamese people with the opportunity to break away from French colonial rule, and that same spirit which encouraged them to do so, also encouraged Vietnamese scholars to bring about a renaissance in Vietnamese arts and science. The past ten years have seen only the first fruits of this renaissance in historiography, as in all other branches of study.

The French historians who devoted themselves to the study of Viet Nam's past during the nineteenth and twentieth centuries produced a large number of historical works of the highest quality. These historians laid the foundations of modern Vietnamese historiography since they introduced a fresh conception of history writing to the Vietnamese peoples and provided models for the Vietnamese historians to copy. These French historians carried out a most necessary preliminary survey of Vietnamese history and preserved intact much historical source-material which would, but for their efforts, have been lost for ever.

A beginning has been made, but most of the work still remains to be done. Historical materials must be sought and, when discovered, be made generally available. Archaeological work must be extended in Viet Nam. Much work has still to be devoted to the study, assessment, and translation of the material already available. The present political situation in Viet Nam threatens to make these undertakings difficult, if not impossible, in the immediate future. Nevertheless, with so many Vietnamese scholars engaged in the study of Vietnamese history and achieving such a high standard of work, the future of modern Vietnamese historiography cannot be described as anything but one of great promise.

PART II
WESTERN WRITINGS

10. SOME WRITINGS ON SOUTH EAST ASIAN PRE-HISTORY[1]

A. H. CHRISTIE

Lecturer in the Art and Archaeology of South East Asia, School of Oriental and African Studies

For those whose concern is with the growth and development of man, with his physical and mental evolution, South East Asia provides a comprehensive field of research. From the Pliocene-Pleistocene boundary to the establishment of the Republik Indonesia there is more or less continuous evidence for human evolution and for the growth of social institutions: for local developments and regional variations; for alien intrusions—some to be rejected, others to be absorbed or assimilated; for the diffusion of ideas and of material culture. Though the historian, confronted with *Pithecanthropus erectus*, *Meganthropus sp.*, *Homo modjokertensis* and the like, may exclaim with Aquinas, 'Quid curae nobis de generibus et speciebus?', these are, in fact, units in the whole train of events connected with the growth of nations in South East Asia, and form an integral part of the region's history. Dubois, Oppenoorth, von Koenigswald, and Weidenreich, no less than Brandes, Krom, Coedès, and van Leur, have contributed to its historical study. But although it seems likely that the historian will ultimately be compelled to take into account the remoter periods of human history, if he is to present an adequate account of the growth of nations, it has seemed best to limit the present paper to a period upon the fringe of conventional history, to a period which the compilers of the *Concise Oxford Dictionary*, with sublime disregard for regions other than Western Europe, include within '*ancient h.*' (usually to A.D. 476).

The historian may be tempted to argue that in South East Asia this period scarcely falls within his conspectus, since, for the centuries prior to A.D. 500, documentation is inconsiderable. Yet reflection suggests that its events are demonstrably significant for the subsequent history of the area and can be neglected only at the grave risk of falsifying the study of later epochs. For if the concept South East Asia is indeed valid, a hypothesis which has yet to be demonstrated formally, though there exists a body of evidence which points to its general acceptability—in contrast to the older concept of Further India—it can be shown without any difficulty that the basic pattern or patterns of development were already in existence by the sixth century of the Christian era. Primary sources, contemporary

---

[1] *History*: continuous methodical record of public events; study of growth of nations; whole train of events connected with nation, person, things (*Concise Oxford Dictionary*).

and synchoric with the events to which they relate, are more or less non-existent. The few inscriptions, which belong entirely to the last years of the period in question, are of considerable interest in themselves, but they scarcely suffice to provide any coherent picture of early South East Asian history. Secondary sources, that is, records more or less contemporary with the events to which they refer, but written outside the theatre of such events, are rather more adequate, though confined almost wholly to one restricted type, Chinese writings. Their interpretation therefore presents certain intrinsic difficulties. Quite apart from the barrier of language (the number of historians of South East Asia with any competence in Chinese is, and has been, very limited indeed), there is the especial problem implicit in the treatment of 'barbarians' in Chinese documents. Nevertheless, this material is of the greatest value as is shown by the publications of such scholars as Paul Pelliot and M. R. A. Stein. Certain difficulties, too, are presented by the tertiary sources, that is to say, by historic records compiled after the events to which they purport to refer.[2] Those which deal with events in this period in a historical manner are very few, while the greater part are difficult to interpret on account of their legendary and mythopoeic style. As Professor Berg has shown, methods may be devised to deal with this problem, but much has yet to be done, before they can be utilized satisfactorily, though the work of Przyluski should be noted in this connection.

Numerous studies by divers hands exist—the works of M. Coedès, Professor Krom, and Professor Hall may be cited as illustrations—studies which attempt a synthesis of this period of the history of South East Asia, a period of about a thousand years centred about the beginning of the Christian era. But it is significant that none of these is able to present any coherent account without calling upon the resources of extra-historical disciplines, linguistic, anthropological, archaeological. In utilizing material drawn from a study other than his own, the historian inevitably faces difficulties: the data is different from his own, the statements are made in answer to different questions. Nor, for the most part, is he in a position to judge whether the technical aspects of the investigation of which he wishes to use the results are satisfactory. The historian may subject the evidence which he wishes to use from other fields to his own discipline. If he does so, then it seems that he is bound to treat such 'testaments' drawn from another speciality as 'brute facts' in his own. This appears to give rise to certain theoretical implications which may deserve further study. The alternative appears to be for the historian to include, for example, material remains within his corpus of documentation. But if he does this, he has either to treat such objects as being no different from conventional docu-

---

[2] Strictly, tertiary sources should be subdivided in accordance with their origin in relation to the events to which they refer, but for present purposes such a sub-division seems unnecessary.

mentary sources, or to equip himself to undertake their study in terms of the discipline of archaeology. Perhaps this last is the ideal, but individuals with an adequate formation in these two branches of the study of the past, history and archaeology, are inevitably rare. The more usual practice is for the historian to accept archaeological statements as part of his documentary sources. It may therefore be useful to examine a number of such statements which refer to the early history of South East Asia, to consider the methods used by their authors in arriving at the various conclusions which they present, and to try to establish the ideas and theories of cultural history, the intellectual climate in which they worked. In order, again, to limit the scope of this paper, this analysis will be confined almost entirely to archaeological evidence.

The earliest account of the prehistoric material from South East Asia appears to be that of G. E. Rumphius who devoted two chapters of his *Amboinsche Rariteitkamer* (Amsterdam, 1705) to stone and bronze axes. Although he was aware of the close similarity between the specimens he recorded and man-made objects, Rumphius seems to have held that they were in fact thunderbolts. Unlike the inhabitants of the region who shared, as they still do, this belief, Rumphius was not content to let the matter rest there, but, true to the spirit of his age, propounded a scientific explanation of the tools, which in his view were the products of terrestrial effluvia fused into stone or metal forms by the action of lightning. From then onwards various accounts were published of neolithic and later objects, and towards the end of the nineteenth century considerable attention began to be paid to one special group of finds, the famous bronze drums. A. B. Meyer, W. Foy, G. W. W. C. van Hoevell, and others published articles dealing with these, but the most significant publication was by Franz Heger whose *Alte Metalltrommeln aus Sudost-Asiens* appeared at Leipzig in 1902. Heger compiled a corpus of all the drums known at that time, described them in detail, with many illustrations, and showed that there were four types. Of his classification, Heger Type I is that which concerns the present paper. Further specimens have been published since, notably by Parmentier and Goloubew, but these, while increasing the number of examples, have not upset Heger's fundamental classification. Various hypotheses were put forward as to the origin of the drums: J. D. E. Schmeltz (1896) favoured India, while F. Hirth postulated a Chinese origin (1890, 1904). J. J. M. De Groot (1901) considered that they should be assigned to the southern barbarians known to the Chinese as *Man*. This view seems to have been shared by Heger, though his reasons were rather more archaeological since he based himself upon the known distribution of the three earliest specimens then discovered, a distribution which pointed to a centre upon the southern borders of China, notably in Tonkin and northern Annam (1903). Parmentier (1918) took another step forward, when he drew attention to similarities between the decor of the drums and that of certain bronze weapons found in Tonkin. These formed part of a private collection, that of M. A. d'Argence, which had been acquired by L'École Française d'Extrême-Orient. The similarities were undoubtedly true, but since the objects to which the drums were compared were also without provenance, the importance of the discovery, though considerable, was to some extent lessened. However, in 1924 Pajot undertook certain excavations at Dong-so'n, as a result of which Goloubew (1930) published the first account of the culture to which the drums and the other related objects belonged. In consequence, the material now had a setting and, at least potentially, a chronology, and considered studies of its importance and its relation to other material and cultures, both in South East Asia and in neighbouring regions, were possible on a scientific basis.

Before an analysis of these studies is undertaken, certain other points must be touched upon. For the location of his material in time, and indeed in most other aspects of his research, the archaeologist relies upon three factors: stratigraphy, association, typology. Two of these depend, in their turn, upon the method of excavation. Thus, stratigraphical relations can only be established by scrupulous care during the excavation, and depend upon continuing and personal observations of soil changes and other indications during the removal of the earth and in the vertical sections which are exposed at various stages of the work. Similarly, association can only be established during the course of the excavation, by precise observation and recording of the objects found in their stratigraphical context, due attention being paid to the possibility of intrusions, assignable to a variety of causes, which will invalidate conclusions drawn from superficial observations.[3] Further, in order that other scholars may judge the data upon which the excavator bases his own conclusions as to stratigraphy and association, it is incumbent upon him to publish his report with adequate plans and sections, as well as a comprehensive account of the salient features of the site, to facilitate the work of later investigators. These are minimal requirements if an excavation is to be any more than a more or less unscientific method of replenishing museum cases with a diversity of objects uncritically labelled. For Pajot's excavation at Dong-so'n these desiderata are significantly lacking. A brief narrative account (1927) and a few general observations by Goloubew (1937) provide absolutely no data for the establishment of either stratigraphical or associational conclusions. In view of the categorical nature of this criticism it is perhaps desirable to present the paragraph from the 1927 report which purports to analyse the chronology and nature of the site. There are no plans, no sections, nor

---

[3] Association may also be established as a result of context and situation. Thus, the finding of rock paintings, for instance, in the vicinity of specific aggregates of archaeological material in a number of places may also permit of certain conclusions based upon association.

even photographs of the graves or of the site in the process of excavation.

The manufacturer of the bronzes and the discovery of several *sapéques* appear to allow the attribution of this ensemble to the Han period. There existed there, in an excellent strategic and commercial position, an agglomeration which seemed to exist for some distance to the East, to the locality of the present bed of the Song Ma, which used to flow further away from the hill. Among the objects discovered some seem to have been buried with bodies which were discovered in extended burials. Certain bronze vessels still bear shreds of coarse material, preserved through being impregnated with copper oxide, others retain traces of red ochre. Other objects could represent household equipment (*le mobilier d'habitation*) built on platforms excavated in the side of the hill. M. Pajot recognised borders of potter's clay which may have edged hearths. Many objects, bronze vessels, heaps of pottery were lying in the earth along the line of the stream, as if the huts had been overthrown violently by some natural disaster, for instance by a typhoon. (*Beaucoup de pièces, vases de bronze, piles de poteries, gisaient dans la terre, couchées de l'aval vers l'amont, comme si les cases avaient été renversées violemment par un accident naturel, un typhon par exemple*) (1928: 467).

The presumption is inevitable: the processes by which this material found its way into the collections of EFEO can be described as excavations only in the most general sense. Such a conclusion must inevitably undermine much of Goloubew's argument, based upon the association of Chinese objects with the Dong-so'n material, and a further fact, not hitherto taken into account in discussions of this site, must also be noted. A *sapéquerie* in the vicinity of Dong-so'n was briefly noted (1925: 642), though no information of any importance is given. Thus any conclusions based upon the Chinese coinage alleged to have been found in a Dong-so'n context must be viewed with the gravest suspicion, not only because of the totally inadequate nature of the report, and indeed, by reasonable presumption, of the excavation itself, but also because of this indication of local coining.

Despite these manifest disadvantages, various scholars have published studies of the Dong-so'n culture. It is true that further excavations at the site were undertaken by Janse, whose preliminary report (1936) gives promise of a more scientific approach to the problems in the field. Unfortunately, his excavations appear to have revealed no clearly datable objects which might, by association, throw light upon the chronological problem of Dong-so'n, while his definitive report is still awaited, some twenty years after the excavations. The historian must, therefore, fall back upon those studies, or such parts of them, which rely upon typological analysis for the elucidation of the Dong-so'n culture, its dating, its relations, and its significance in the early history of South East Asia. Three names, in particular, are associated with such investigations: Goloubew, Heine-Geldern, and Karlgren. None of these scholars has been directly associated with the excavation of Dong-so'n material, though Goloubew had a long archaeological experience of Indo-China. Karlgren's principle activities have been connected with the development of Chinese civilization and culture where he has established a dual reputation as linguist and art historian. Heine-Geldern has for many years been engaged upon a synthesis of eastern cultural history, particularly in its formative period, an activity which may perhaps be summarized as a continuation of Menghin's work upon the Stone Age in a restricted field.

In a major study (1930), followed by a feuilleton (1937) which seems to have been a manifestation of internecine warfare in French academic circles, Goloubew set out his views upon *L'âge du Bronze au Tonkin et dans le Nord-Annam*. Part of his papers depend upon arguments from stratigraphy and association which cannot be sustained by the facts, or rather by the absolute absence of these. Karlgren (1942) has noted:

> The lack of reliable data concerning the crucial parts of Pajot's finds places us in an awkward position when trying to estimate the purport of these finds. Were the Wang Mang coins (and the Wu-shu coins) as well as the above-mentioned Chinese 'Han' specimens (the sword, two Hu flasks, the mirror) found in one grave or in several? And how do these graves stand, from the point of view of excavation conditions, in relation to the other graves which did not (?) contain such objects (Goloubew's phrase 'the vast necropolis of Dong-so'n' suggests a considerable number of graves)? It is obvious that, if there were many graves, they need not all have belonged to one brief period, such as 'the middle or latter part of the 1st c. A.D.', but may very well extend over several generations, perhaps several centuries—indeed this seems the most likely (1942: 5).

From his expert knowledge of the Chinese material Karlgren has demonstrated certain errors in Goloubew's proposals and has established a range of dates from the fourth century B.C. to the first century A.D. From these he concludes:

> This does not necessarily mean that some of the graves in Dong-so'n are to be dated quite as early as the 4th–3rd c. B.C. Imported Chinese treasures were surely not buried immediately but were used by the living for some time, before they were deposited as gifts in the graves. On the other hand, it is hardly likely that even those imported specimens from the 4th–3rd c. B.C. were kept and used for four centuries before they were buried in the Dong-so'n settlement. There is every probability that the Dong-so'n graves extend over a considerable period,

some of them being much earlier than the 1st c. A.D., others being posterior to Wang Mang and hence dating from that century (1942:7-7.)

But if the context of the Chinese finds is uncertain, as Karlgren himself has pointed out, the criticisms which he has made of Goloubew may be applied equally to the paragraph just cited. There is in fact some evidence for Chinese burials of various dates in and about Dong-so'n, so that it is not even necessary that the Chinese objects should pertain to indigenous burials. There is another point of which Karlgren seems not to be aware. The collection of *chinoiserie* is a cultural phenomenon as strongly established in S.E. Asia as in Europe or in America, and of much longer standing. In these circumstances, it is probably unwise to be dogmatic about the pre-inhumation history of Chinese objects in South East Asia.

Nevertheless, in his amplification of Parmentier's thesis to which reference has already been made, and in his study of the Dong-so'n material as a whole, Goloubew made a notable contribution to the subject. In addition to presenting a reasonably well-documented corpus of the material culture, he attempted its interpretation, in South East Asian terms for the most part, and sought to explain certain aspects of it in the light of existing ethnographic data. In this he was, in part, following the lead of Finot who wrote of the Hanoi drum:

> Should one not recognise in this precisely those Indonesians whom linguistics and ethnography show us as established at first on the coasts of Indochina, and then, abandoning these shores to new arrivals, going to carry into the islands of the archipelago their language, of which the mainland has preserved but the debris, and their customs which it has quickly forgotten? (1919: 216).

(Finot, it should be noted, had been anticipated to some extent by Hubert (1903: 44) who referred certain skeletal material, as well as decorative motifs to ' les specimens les plus purs de ce qu'on appelle, en la distinguant sans doute à tort de la malaise, la race indonésienne'.) Although this procedure is undoubtedly open to criticism, it is difficult to see what other method can be used, in areas and periods for which primary or secondary documentation is inadequate or non-existent, if archaeology is to attempt the interpretation as well as the cataloguing of its finds. It is not clear that Goloubew was aware of the objections to the method which he used, nor is it clear whether, in so doing, he was considering his material in accordance with any particular theoretical approach. (An example of such an approach, and of what, to an unbeliever, appear its almost incredible shortcomings, can be found in the writings of Professor George Thomson. It has to be admitted that a similar situation is not unknown in archaeological works which propound an inevitable evolutionary sequence: crude stone, polished stone, copper, bronze, iron—evidence to the contrary not-withstanding.) But Goloubew's synthesis, these provisos apart, is of considerable value: a criticism which may be thought of some force is that he seems to have preferred to interpret his material in the light of the present, rather than be reference to its contemporaries or by searching for its origins.

Both Professor Heine-Geldern and Professor Karlgren, on the other hand devote large parts of their studies to the elucidation of the relation between Dong-so'n and other cultures in its vicinity, though the former (1937) is also concerned with its position in the Pacific Islands and South East Asia today. Both primarily base their conclusions upon what appears, at first sight, to be typology. It may be said, not unfairly, that for Karlgren Dong-so'n is fundamentally Chinese:

> We have demonstrated, by a long series of *points d'appui*, that the affinities between the early Dong-so'n art of the primary drums of type I and the Chinese culture are affinities not with the art of the Han but with the art of the pre-Han Huai style. The oldest interrelations are those revealed on the one hand by the Huai sword found in Dong-so'n, which cannot very well be older than the 4th–3rd c. B.C., on the other hand by the hunting-scene vessels, likewise of the 4th–3rd c. B.C. We may thus with a large measure of probability date the early Dong-so'n culture in the 4th–3rd c. B.C. It flourished for some centuries, and a late stage of the same culture is revealed by the grave finds in the village of Dong-so'n. The early Dong-so'n culture was a neighbour of and closely related to—certainly to a large extent influenced by—the Huai style of Central China. It is fully explainable from these premises, and we need no speculations about world-wide emigrations and hypothetical intermediate 'Central-Asian' cultures in order to interpret the facts of its birth (1942: 24–25).

The excerpt serves also to introduce the standpoint of Heine-Geldern who presents his own case thus:

> The decorative designs found on bronzes of the Dong-so'n Culture in Indo-China as well as in Indonesia, double spiral circles linked by tangents, meanderlike patterns, etc., are of western origin and closely related to, and indeed in many cases identical with, those of the Hallstatt Culture of Europe, the Thraco-Cimmerian Culture of the lower Danubian regions and South Russia, and the Early Iron Age of Caucasia. All these cultures were interrelated, and flourished side by side until the Cimmerians were driven from South Russia by the Scythians around 700 B.C. The numerous types of weapons, tools, ornaments, and decorative designs of Hallstattian, Thraco-Cimmerian, and Caucasian

affiliations which are found in the late Chou and Dongson Cultures of China and Indo-China must therefore have been brought to East Asia by western invaders who had left their homelands before the Scythian conquest of South Russia, i.e. at the latest during the 8th century B.C. It is highly probable that the barbarian tribes who in 771 B.C. destroyed the Western Chou Kingdom belonged to this same ethnic wave. In China, the decorative designs of western origin were immediately amalgamated with indigenous ones, thereby originating the Late Chou style of art. On the contrary, the decorative designs of the Dongson Culture perpetuate the western forms almost unchanged. From this we may infer that one stream of western invaders had branched off at the western confines of China and went directly to Yunnan and Indo-China where their influence created the Dongson culture probably during the 8th and 7th centuries B.C. (1945: 147).

By what methods, by what criteria do these two distinguished authorities arrive at such divergent views of a single culture presenting a single corpus of material for study?

Two points may be made at the outset. Karlgren himself, as has already been remarked, has demonstrated the unreliability of the associational evidence upon which he relies in part. Neither the Huai sword, nor 'the grave finds in the village of Dong-so'n can, therefore, be regarded as particularly convincing arguments. In the case of Heine-Geldern it will be obvious to those familiar with the material that 'numerous types of weapons, tools . . . of Hallstattian, Thraco-Cimmerian, and Caucasian affinities' are not, in fact, found in the Dong-so'n culture which is notable for highly specialized types for the most part which seem to be peculiarly its own. It may even be thought that the constellation Hallstatt, Thraco-Cimmerian, Caucasian requires to be justified rather than assumed. Nor is any mention made of a major technological distinction, the fact that the western cultures are iron-using while Dong-so'n is a bronze culture, and one which relied upon a bronze formula with an approximate 20 per cent. lead content which is apparently unique in its general application. But it is in the items omitted from the citation from Heine-Geldern, 'ornaments and decorative designs' that both these scholars find the essence of their arguments. The principles which are implicit in this method must be examined: neither scholar appears to have considered it worthy of discussion.

Neither Professor Karlgren nor Professor Heine-Geldern has attempted to compare the Dong-so'n culture as a whole with those to which they wish to relate it. Nor has either been able to find direct parallels between the greater part of this material and that of their preferred sources, whether Huai or western. The Dong-so'n drums, the characteristic pediform axes remain *sui generis*. Thus the prime basis for typology, the comparison of like with like, as a whole or item by item, does not exist here. Mention has already been made of the technological difference between Dong-so'n and the western cultures; a slighter, but significant difference exists between Dong-so'n bronze and that of China which is based upon a quite other alloy formula. Both these scholars depend upon the comparisons of isolated elements from the total decoration of whole objects. Thus Karlgren in his attempt to assign Dong-so'n to the Huai style depends upon certain linear motifs, as for instance those of the Mu'o'ng drum. Such motifs occupy perhaps a third of the decorated surface of the drum. These he divides into six categories: 'central star', 'granulation line as filling of a band', 'saw-teeth pattern', 'slanting-stroke band or rope pattern', 'circles with tangents', 'concentric circular zones'.[4] Now Karlgren can adduce no single object of the Huai style, let alone a drum of any type, which shows the combination of these six motifs and decorative techniques which are found on the Mu'o'ng specimen. Instead he invokes a whole series of diverse objects which together exhibit the motifs in question. But the ultimate weakness of his method is noted in passing:

> Under the preceding 11 points we have produced evidence to show that almost all the decor elements—*apart from the principal scenes* [my italics]— on the early drums of the Dong-so'n culture are such as are familiar and important motifs in the Huai style of the pre-Han era (1942: 14).

It is true that he subsequently claims that in the case of the principal themes 'we can find evidence of strong affinity on some fundamental points', but this, in its turn involves similar divorcing of individual items from their context, a procedure open to the same criticism, and he is quite unable to produce an instance which parallels the totality of a single Dong-so'n theme in this category.

A characteristic specimen of Heine-Geldern's comparative method runs as follows:

> The Batavia Museum possesses two magnificent bronze axes from the little island of Roti. Their extremely rich ornamentation includes, in addition to human figures which resemble to an astonishing degree anthropomorphic designs of Melanesia (more especially of the Solomon Islands), circles with tangents of Dong-son character and motifs of stars with curved points which recall certain motifs of the bronze age of Hungary and Transylvania, and of the late Bronze Age (Montelius period IV and V) of North Germany and Scandinavia. Should we see a real relationship here? That does not seem to me to be completely mpossible (1937: 190).

[4] In all he considers eleven points but none of the objects includes them all. For the purpose of the present discussion, the Mu'o'ng drum serves to illustrate the principle at issue.

Once again, those familiar with the material will recognize how the relationship between the parts of the design, and the proportion between linear and anthropomorphic elements, is disregarded in this type of analysis. It should be noted that Heine-Geldern has to some extent followed Janse and Goloubew in his Hallstattian comparisons, though he has perhaps taken matters further than either of these scholars, who, on the whole, confined their instances to objects rather than elements of the decor upon material which is unknown to the West.

What remains to be considered is the theory, the frame of reference in which these scholars have undertaken their studies. Neither appears to have set out on any occasion the principles upon which his work is based. In the case of Professor Karlgren, the method seems to be a natural extension of that which he has used in his study of Chinese bronzes. Its failure, for in the view of the present writer its inadequacy is manifest, must be attributed to a signal lack of recognition that to compare a series of objects which form a homogeneous group, either by internal comparative analysis, or with another group of the same general order and in the same cultural province, is not the same as to select isolates from such a group for comparison with other isolates from a wholly different series. This failure, coupled with an understandable sinocentricity, is the crux of the matter.

A contributory factor may be the traditional approach to the study of Chinese bronzes. Virtually none of these, nor indeed of the great mass of Chinese archaeological material, has any satisfactory archaeological context of provenance. Their study therefore has been a matter of *Kunsthistorischemethode* rather than of archaeology. An inevitable concomitant of this has been that objects have been treated as antiquities, and have tended to acquire virtues which are unrelated to their context, to be treated as unique and individual. To the archaeologist *pur sang*, on the other hand, the merits of an object derive from its context, and from its association with other objects, none of them having necessarily any particular artistic or aesthetic value.[5]

Professor Heine-Geldern, it has already been suggested, is concerned to extend, for a more limited region, Menghin's synthesis, his *Weltgeschichte der Steinzeit*. It appears from his various essays relating to South East Asian material that he is always concerned to present his material in terms of world relations and derivations. His position is perhaps revealed by a passing suggestion (1945: 149) that, with due precautions, the ideas of Perry should be reconsidered. Professor Heine-Geldern is a diffusionist, not, be it understood, of the extreme, Children of the Sun, School, but certainly predisposed to consider his material in terms of *Urheimaten* and

---

[5] This point is discussed by Childe (1956) and has recently formed part of the Inaugural Lecture, 'The Study of Chinese Antiquities' by Professor S. Hansford, which will be published shortly.

Volkerwanderungen. The relative importance to be assigned to diffusion and to spontaneous discovery is still a matter for debate, but a scholar who has worked for most of his life in the home of the *Kulturkreislehre* may be assumed to have read the observations of Bernheim, to whom Graebner expressly refers, on the uncritical approach to material. He writes of those who

> not seldom lump together reports without discrimination, whether or not the information applies to the same time and place and culture level (1908: 610).

In the final analysis, it may be thought that neither Professor Karlgren nor Professor Heine-Geldern has in fact established any very definite methodological or theoretical approach to a complex and difficult question. Neither conforms to the strict canons of comparative archaeology. It would seem to follow, therefore, that the historian who decides to accept or adopt their 'statements' as his own, does so at his peril. On the other hand, if he treats *their* 'statements' as *his* 'brute facts', he is faced with another problem, that of the criteria of judgement which he is to bring to the assessment of the documents with which he is confronted. Childe has written:

> The archaeological record is constituted of the fossilized results of human behaviour, and it is the archaeologist's business to reconstitute that behaviour as far as he can and so to recapture the thoughts that behaviour expressed. In so far as he can do that, he becomes a historian (1956: 1).

Perhaps, in some corollary of this statement, the solution may be found. It may well be that, while for the archaeologists time and space are facts of geography and geology, they remain for the historian abstractions, co-ordinates of his frame of reference. If this is so, then methods must be found to include material objects within the statistical data which are the biographical facts of a community.

> For, god wot, thing is never lasse the sooth
> Though every wight ne may hit nat y-see.

BIBLIOGRAPHY

BEFEO, xxiv (Hanoi, 1925), p. 642.

BEFEO, xxvii (Hanoi, 1928), pp. 466–8.

E. Bernheim, *Lehrbuch der historischen Methode und der Geschichtsphilosophie* (Leipzig, 1908).

V. G. Childe, *Piecing together the Past* (London, 1956).

L. Finot, *L'Asie française* (Paris, 1919).

W. Foy, *Über alte Bronzetrommeln aus Südostasien Mitteilungen der Anthropologischen Gesellschaft in Wien XXXIII* (Vienna, 1903), pp. 390–409.

V. Goloubew, 'L'âge du bronze au Tonkin et dans le Nord-Annam', BEFEO, xxix (Hanoi, 1930).

— *L'archéologie du Tonkin et les fouilles de Dong-so'n* (Hanoi, 1937).

J. J. M. de Groot, *Die antiken Bronze-Pauken im ostindischen Archipel und auf dem Festlande von Südostasien Mitteilungen des Seminars fur orientalische Sprachen* (Berlin, 1901), pp. 76–113.

F. Heger, *Alte Metalltrommeln aus Südost-Asien* (Leipzig, 1902).

F. Heger, *CR analytique des séances: Ier Congrès International des Etudes d'Extrême-Orient* (Hanoi, 1903).

R. von Heine-Geldern, 'L'art prébouddhique de la Chine et de l'Asia du Aud-Est et son influence en Océanie', RAA, xi (Paris, 1937).

R. von Heine-Geldern, *Prehistoric Research in the Netherlands Indies.*

— *Science and Scientists in the Netherlands Indies* (New York, 1945), pp. 129–67.

F. Hirth, *Über hinterindische Bronze-Trommeln. T'oung Pao I* (1890), 137–42.

F. Hirth, *Chinesische Ansichten über Bronze-Trommeln Mitteilungen des Seminars für orientalische Sprachen* (Berlin, 1904), pp. 200–57.

G. W. W. C. van Hoevell, *Mitteilungen über die Kesseltrommel zu Bontobangun, Insel Saleyer.*

— *Internationales Archiv für Ethnographie*, xvi, 155–7.

H. Hubert, *CR analytique des séances: Ier Congrès International des Etudes d'Extrême-Orient* (Hanoi, 1903).

O. Janse, 'Rapport préliminaire d'une mission archéologique en Indochine' (iii).

— 'La station et la nécropole "indonésiennes" de Dong-son (Thanh-Hoa), Annam du Nord', RAA, x (Paris, 1936).

B. Karlgren, 'The date of the early Dong-so'n culture', BMFEA, xiv (Stockholm, 1942).

A. B. Meyer and W. Foy, *Bronze-Pauken aus Südost-Asien Königliches Ethnographisches Museum zu Dresden, XI* (Dresden, 1897).

H. Parmentier, 'Ancien tambours de bronze', BEFEO, xviii (Hanoi, 1918).

G. E. Rumphius, *Amboinsche Rariteitkamer* (Amsterdam, 1705).

I. D. E. Schmeltz, *Bronze-Pauken im Indischen Archipel Internationales Archiv für Enthnographie, IX* (1896).

11. HISTORICAL WRITING ON INDONESIA (EARLY PERIOD)

J. G. DE CASPARIS

Lecturer in the History of Ancient India, School of Oriental and African Studies

Introductory

In this paper main attention is drawn to principles, and especially to the approach of scholars writing on the older history of Indonesia.

Research may be roughly divided into three periods of very unequal length. The first period begins towards the end of the eighteenth century, when Europeans showed the first signs of interest in older Indonesian culture, and ends in 1926 with the first true account of older Indonesian history. The second period runs from 1926 to 1942, the Japanese occupation. The third and last period, from 1942 to 1956, comprises the Japanese occupation, the struggle for freedom of the Indonesian people (1945 to 1949 inclusive) and the beginning of the national reconstruction (1950 to 1956). This year marks a good ending point since it is hoped that a new period of research will start with the first parliament and government elected by the people. Finally, something will be added about the present state of historical studies and the prospects for the immediate future.

First Period

Although the Dutch East India Company had occupied parts of Indonesia since the beginning of the seventeenth century, no clear signs of interest in Indonesian culture and history can be noted prior to the latter part of the eighteenth century.[1] This new attitude was not only due to the extension of the power of the Company, which more and more had become a territorial power by then, but rather to the more enlightened age. In the period of Locke, Voltaire, and Rousseau, of industrial revolution, American independence, and French revolution, Europeans became aware of the existence of other cultures than their own. In the same period when Sir William Jones disclosed great works of Persian and Sanskrit literature to Europe (1771–94), the first society to study the culture of the Indonesian peoples was founded in Java (1778).[2] Especially from the British interim period (1810–16) on, this society became the centre for studies in Indonesian culture and history. This interim period also marks the beginning

---

[1] There have been a few occasional exceptions, which do not, however, change the picture as a whole.

[2] On the work of Jones, cf. especially J. E. van Lohuizen-de Leeuw, 'Sir William Jones, 1746–1794', *Orientalia Neerlandica* (1946), pp. 288–97.

of historical research on Indonesia, inaugurated by people such as Raffles, Crawfurd, Baker, and Mackenzie.

Raffles' *History of Java* is an admirable piece of work for the time. It was based on materials collected by a staff of collaborators. These materials not only consisted of various traditions and legends, but included for the first time Old Javanese inscriptions. Transcriptions and translations were the work of the Sultan of Sungĕnĕb (Madura), and were unreliable or even fantastic. It is very striking that, in the beginning of the nineteenth century very little was known in Java about Indonesian history prior to the sixteenth century A.D.

For about half a century after its publication, Raffles' history remained an authoritative source for the history of Java, although many new materials were added (especially by Sieburgh, Van Hoëvell, Brumund, Friedrich, and Hoepermans).[3] Research was very limited, even after the erection of the Royal Institute at The Hague in 1851.[4]

Only in the last three decennia of the nineteenth century do we see an entirely new development. Here, too, external circumstances exercised great influence. The two main factors which led to a more intensive study of Indonesia's past were: (a) the opening of the Suez Canal (1869), which made closer contact between Europe and the Netherlands Indies possible, and (b) the influence of liberalism in the Netherlands. The latter factor is particularly important since, in principle, it was commonly held that colonies should be governed in behalf of the subject peoples themselves. Although the practice was very different from the attractive theory (the most cruel colonial wars in Atjeh were stated to be waged in the interest of the Atjehnese—to liberate them from the yoke of feudal lords), it cannot be denied that the new policy greatly stimulated cultural research.[5] It is self-evident that an essential condition of making such a policy successful was to have reliable knowledge about Indonesian culture and history. As a matter of fact, a new generation of scholars, almost exclusively Dutch, opened new fields of research on a sound basis. The greatest among them was probably Hendrik Kern, who mastered the fields of Sanskrit philology, Buddhology, Indo-European linguistics, and became one of the

[3] Cf. H. J. Heeren, 'Vergeten voorlopers der Indonesische oudheidkunde', *Orientatie*, 46, 1954, 673–83. For the work of Sieburgh there is an excellent monograph by J. V. de Bruyn, *H. N. Sieburgh en zijn beteekenis voor de Javaansche Oudheidkunde* (1937). For Hoepermans: W. F. Stutterheim, 'Een fuselier uit de vorige eeuw (Hoepermans) als oudheidkundige', *Djåwå* (1925), v, 73–79. Stutterheim does recognize the merits of Hoepermans, but describes his work in a rather ironical style.

[4] The complete name was 'Koninklijk Instituut voor de Taal-, Land- en Volkenkunde van Nederlandsch-Indië' (Royal Institute for the Linguistics, Geography and Ethnology of the Netherlands Indies). Since a couple of years the name has been changed to 'Koninklijk Instituut voor de Taal-, Land- en Volkenkunde'.

[5] To a certain extent this is even true with the Atjeh war itself. Thus, the well-known study by Snouck Hurgronje, *De Atjehers* (1893–5), translated into English in 1906 *The Achenese* was connected with the Dutch Government's policy in North Sumatra.

pioneers of comparative Indonesian linguistics, Old Javanese literature, and epigraphy.[6] The activity of Brandes concerned mainly the three latter fields, more recent Javanese literature and archaeology.[7] Besides Brandes and Kern, also Cohen Stuart and Holle published important studies on epigraphy, which is an important source for the entire older history of Indonesia and almost the only one for considerable periods.[8] Groeneveldt not only published an important catalogue of the Jakarta Museum, but also compiled and translated the indispensable Chinese references to the older history of this area.[9] An Old Javanese code of law, compared with Indian *dharmaçāstras*, was published by Jonker.[10] Van der Tuuk published a voluminous Old Javanese dictionary, based upon the study of numerous manuscripts and Balinese exegesis.[11] Old Javanese literary texts were published by Juynboll[12] and Gunning.[13]

The institution in 1901 of an Archaeological Commission for the preservation and study of ancient monuments constitutes the first clear effort of the Netherlands East Indies Government to stimulate research on the older period. This commission, which was replaced by an Archaeological Service twelve years later (1913), was extremely active, so that a mass of knowledge about Indonesia's past was collected.[14]

[6] Kern has published numerous historical inscriptions with translations and notes (between 1877 and 1911). Further, I mention Kern's edition and translation of the *Nāgarakṛtāgama*, one of the main historical texts in Old Javanese. A complete bibliography is given at the end of the *Verspreide Geschriften* (1913–20).

[7] Some of the most important publications by Brandes are: (*a*) the first publication on the Kalasan inscription (A.D. 778) in *Tijdschr. Bat. Gen.* (1886), xxxi, 240–60; (*b*) an important study on Old Javanese society in the ninth century A.D. with an analysis of the Indian and Indonesian elements in this culture, 'Een jayapattra of acte van eene rechterlijke uitspraak van Çaka 849', ibid. (1889), xxxii, 98–149. One of Brandes' conclusions in this article concerns the well-known ten fields of Javanese culture which are considered 'original', i.e. not borrowed from the Hindus. It is curious that both this article and a study by Kern on the 'Urheimat' of the Indonesians are still regularly quoted or used in modern Indonesian publications; (*c*) a large collection of transcripts of Old Javanese and Sumatranese inscriptions by Brandes was published after Brandes' death by Krom under the title 'Oud-Javaansche Oorkonden' in *Verhand. Bat. Gen.* (1913), lx; (*d*) Brandes' Pararaton edition with translation and copious notes is one of his major works on Javanese historiography. It was first published in 1896, but a second edition was published by the care of Krom in 1920 (with numerous additional notes by Krom, Jonker, Kraemer, and Poerbatjaraka). Finally, Brandes wrote great monographs and other studies about Old Javanese temples. He was one of the very few scholars who tried to study the history of Java in all of its phases.

[8] Holle, *Tabel van Oud- en Nieuw-Indische alphabetten* (1882) is still the only existing survey of the development of script in Indonesia. A. B. Cohen Stuart, *Kawi oorkonden in facsimile* (1875) is a still valuable collection of transcripts of Old Javanese inscriptions.

[9] W. P. Groeneveldt, *Catalogus der Archeologische Verzameling van het Bataviaasch Genootschap van Kunsten en Wetenschappen* (1887); 'Notes on the Malay Archipelago and Malacca, compiled from Chinese sources', *Verhand. Bat. Gen* (1876), xxxix.

[10] J. C. G. Jonker, *Een Oud-Javaansch wetbcek, vergeleken met de Indische rechtsbronnen* (1885).

[11] H. N. van der Tuuk, *Kawi-Balineesch-Nederlandsch Woordenboek*, four volumes (1897–1912).

[12] H. H. Juynboll, *Drie boeken van het Oudjavaansche Mahābhārata* (1893); *Ādiparwa* (1906); *Wirātaparwa* (1912).   [13] J. G. H. Gunning, *Bhāratayuddha* (1903).

[14] The results were published in the yearly reports of the 'Commissie in Nederlandsch-Indië voor Oudheidkundig Onderzoek' (1901–12).

I shall not go into details about the numerous new discoveries,[15] but prefer to add a few words about the approach to Indonesian history by the generation of scholars just mentioned. An outstanding feature is their sincere admiration for older Javanese culture. Often the greatness of the older culture is contrasted with what they considered the rather deplorable state of more recent Indonesian culture, a difference sometimes attributed to the influence of Islam. Usually—and most clearly by Kern—the greatness of the ancient culture was attributed mainly to Hindu colonizers; as a consequence, older Javanese art was more appreciated than its later phases, for deviation from the Indian 'prototypes' was considered a kind of degeneration. Archaeological and historical research was almost limited to Java. This was due not only to practical circumstances such as easy communications and cheap labour, but also to the more imposing qualities of Old Javanese monuments.

The scholars working in this period were almost exclusively Dutch. Specialized training for philological, archaeological, and historical work for the older period did not exist. Kern, for instance, had studied Sanskrit philology and comparative Indo-European linguistics. It is therefore understandable that he approached Indonesian culture mainly from the Indian point of view. On the whole, contact with Indonesian circles was not intensive; it was rather considered that the Indonesians of the end of the nineteenth and the beginning of the twentieth century knew and understood very little of their own history and, unlike Western Europe, had not the means to acquire such knowledge. One should not forget that it was considered almost self-evident that only Western science could solve the great problems of the past. After all, had not the West succeeded in solving some of the great riddles of hieroglyphs, cuneiform writing, and Brāhmī writing in India? Indonesian co-operation was considered rather useless, except to supply information as to the existence of temple ruins, manuscripts, etc. The paternalist attitude was no less clear in historical research than in most of the other fields.

Finally, a typical feature of this research on older Indonesian culture was that the above scholars paid little or no interest to more recent Indonesian history (i.e. from about A.D. 1500 on). The latter was more or less implicitly considered a part of European history, to be studied by historians trained in Western, especially Dutch, history, by officers of the Civil Service of the Netherlands East Indies, archivists, etc.[16]

Most of the above features, though in a more moderate form, remain

---

[15] These discoveries are fully dealt with by Krom in his *Hindoe-Javaansche Geschiedenis* (1931), second edition.

[16] One consequence was that there arose a considerable gap between the treatment of older and more recent Indonesian history. The handbooks on more recent Indonesian history (from about the sixteenth century on) were mostly outspokenly Europe-centred. Cf. *infra*, p. 150.

characteristic for the Dutch approach to Indonesian history in the subsequent periods also.

Second Period

The first two decades of the twentieth century still belong to the previous period as far as research on older Indonesian history is concerned. Most of the scholars mentioned on p. 123 continued their research essentially in the same lines as in the end of the nineteenth century.[17] In addition to these scholars I should mention G. P. Rouffaer, one of the very few amateurs working in this field.[18] Rouffaer strikes us by his fervent enthusiasm, his wide knowledge of Javanese culture in all its aspects, and not least by his bold hypotheses.[19]

The erection in 1908 of the first Indonesian nationalist movement, the Budi Utomo, did not much to change the attitude of Western historians. It had, however, some influence, since it called attention to the fact that far too little had been done to promote Indonesian culture. It thus acted as an, unfortunately rather weak, stimulus to historical research.

The First World War may have had a more direct influence. For four years the communications between Holland and Indonesia had been suspended, and it was realized that Indonesia depended too much on Europe and that it was necessary to provide better educational facilities. As a matter of fact, soon after the war a Technical College and Faculties of Law and Medicine were opened in Java. An increasing number of Indonesians studied at Dutch universities. In Holland, a new Academic Statute made an introduction to both the older and the more recent history of Indonesia obligatory for future civil officers, while specific training for Aryan (Indo-Iranian) and for Indonesian languages and cultures was established.[20]

The dominating figure of this period, as far as older Indonesian history and archaeology are concerned, was Krom.[21] Krom worked in Indonesia from 1910 to 1915 and again in 1921, first as the president of the Archaeological Commission and, from 1913 on, as the first chief of the Archaeological Service. An astounding mass of work was finished during that

[17] As a matter of fact, the more important works written during the first two decades of the twentieth century have already been included in the above survey.

[18] Cf. N. J. Krom, 'Herdenking van Dr. G. P. Rouffaer', *Bijdr. Kon. Inst.* (1928), lxxxiv, 163–288.

[19] As a typical example I may quote Rouffaer's article 'Was Malaka emporium vóór 1400 A.D. genaamd Malajoer, en waar lag Woerawari, Ma-hasin, Langka, Batoesawar?', *Bijdr. Kon. Inst.* (1921), lxxvii, 1–174 and 359–604.

[20] The former opened possibilities of specializing, e.g. on older Indonesian history. The latter was an adequate introduction to future research in Indonesian languages and literatures.

[21] Cf. A. J. Bernet Kempers, 'In Memoriam Prof. Dr. N. J. Krom', *Oudheidk. Versl. 1941–1947* (1949), pp. 1–14 (with complete bibliography).

time;[22] in addition, Krom collected ample materials for his books on Hindu-Javanese History[23] and Hindu-Javanese Art,[24] which were to become the basis of all future studies. Nothing needs to be said here about the merits of these books; instead it is necessary to stress a few points about Krom's approach to older Indonesian culture.

The term 'Hindu-Javanese', which we find in the titles of the two handbooks, reflects Krom's basic ideas about pre-Islamic Indonesia. Whereas most of the earlier scholars considered older Indonesian culture a form of Hindu culture transplanted on Indonesian soil,[25] Krom always used the term 'Hindu-Javanese' to indicate that this culture was a harmonious combination of Indian and Indonesian elements.[26] According to Krom, the artists who constructed the great Javanese monuments were neither Hindus nor Javanese, but 'Hindu-Javanese', i.e. Javanese who followed the cultural traditions of the Hindus.[27] This culture may have been started by the offspring of Hindu settlers married to Javanese women.[28] Krom further agreed that no real Indian 'prototype' could be found, a circumstance which he mainly attributed to the scarcity of well-preserved Indian monuments of the period immediately preceding 'colonization', i.e. the first centuries A.D.[29] Since we have no Hindu-Javanese monuments older than the eighth century A.D., the gap of at least three or four centuries would explain why already the oldest preserved monuments in Java are typically 'Hindu-Javanese'.[30] Whereas for the older period (the monuments of Central Java) the former half of the compound is stressed, a gradual shift of the accent is noted during the development of 'Hindu-Javanese' culture.[31]

Krom's Hindu-Javanese History is still the only account of older Indonesian history which is both trustworthy and detailed. In addition to his main work on archaeology, Krom had made an intensive study of inscriptions and of the main historical works in Old Javanese. Although very critical-minded, Krom always tried to be fair towards theories brought forward by previous scholars. Owing to this latter feature, he never forgot to mention previous theories and to discuss them if he thought them

[22] Thus, the list of books and articles published by Krom from 1913 to 1921 inclusive counts about eighty numbers.

[23] *Hindoe-Javaansche Geschiedenis*, first impression 1926, second impression 1931.

[24] *Inleiding tot de Hindoe-Javaansche Kunst*, first edition in two volumes (1919); second edition in three volumes (1923).

[25] An important exception should be made for Brandes, whose ideas strike us as 'modern'. Cf. note 7 above.

[26] Krom gave his last and, in my opinion, best survey of his ideas on 'Hindu-Javanese' culture in his *Het Oude Java en zijn Kunst*, second edition (1943), ch. I, pp. 1–39.

[27] *Hindoe-Javaansche Geschiedenis*, second edition (1931), p. 129.

[28] *Het Oude Java en zijn Kunst*, pp. 19 f.

[29] Ibid., p. 17. Cf. also *Hindoe-Javaansche Geschiedenis*, second edition, pp. 128 f.

[30] Cf. *Hindoe-Javaansche Geschiedenis*, second edition, p. 128.

[31] Cf. *Het Oude Java en zijn Kunst*, p. 119.

serious.[32] As a consequence, his Hindu-Javanese History is full of discussions, often lengthy, on the reading of a word in some inscription, on the interpretation of a passage in an Old Javanese text or on the conclusions to be drawn from such materials. It is an advantage in so far as it makes the study of previous publications on such subjects almost superfluous, but also a drawback since it makes a great portion of his book almost unreadable.[33] Another drawback is that Krom was not really a historian. One gets the impression that history was for him a kind of necessary evil which he had to go through in order to get a fuller understanding of the monuments.[34] He is little concerned about economic affairs, and social groups and their development receive little attention from him, although the inscriptions furnish ample materials,[35] so that we get the impression that history consists essentially of the solution of a great number of puzzles.[36] Another drawback is that Krom was not sufficiently trained in Indonesian languages and cultures.[37] Although Krom was essentially free from colonial prejudices, one may find traces of a colonial outlook[38].

[32] Theories which Krom did not think serious were usually referred to in notes. This happened e.g. with some extravagant theories of Moens.

[33] Such lengthy discussions may concern the mere date of an inscription (e.g. *Hindoe-Javaansche Geschiedenis*, second edition, pp. 190-2), the identification of a single name (e.g., ibid., pp. 240-2), a critical discussion of various theories on a definite detail (e.g., ibid., pp. 206-9 and 272-9), etc.

[34] Krom's profound interest in the monuments appears throughout his *Hindoe-Javaansche Geschiedenis*. Thus, he gives often lengthy discussions about problems of 'Hindu-Javanese' art (e.g., op. cit., pp. 126-9), whereas corresponding problems in other fields (such as those in literary works, economic and social history) do not get the attention which they deserve. Moreover, if one compares Krom's history with his handbook on 'Hindu-Javanese' art (cf. *supra*, note 24), one is struck by the fact that the latter, though dealing with a detail of history, is far more elaborate than the former; its text is even longer. Krom's approach to Indonesian history was essentially that of an archaeologist; this is probably why he took no real interest in more recent Indonesian history. Owing to this approach Krom presumed a clear break in Indonesian history at the end of the Majapahit period, 'when control over Java was no longer in Hindu-Javanese hands, but had been taken over by Islamic rulers' (op. cit., p. 467). The above remarks are not at all meant to belittle Krom's historical work, but rather to stress his approach.

[35] It is true, however, that materials about social and economic history are not as easily accessible as dynastic and archaeological data. The parts of the inscriptions dealing with social and economic affairs are not easily understood, mainly as a consequence of difficulties in the meaning and interpretation of the numerous technical terms. On the other hand, Krom used such materials whenever the interpretation did not meet with serious difficulties (e.g., op. cit., p. 198).   [36] Some characteristic examples were mentioned in note 33 above.

[37] Krom sometimes made curious mistakes in interpreting written Old Javanese sources. As an example of such a mistake due to insufficient knowledge of Old Javanese I may quote Krom's conclusions based on the beginning of the Perot and Argapura inscriptions (*Hindoe-Javaansche Geschiedenis*, pp. 156 f.). Cf. *Prasasti Indonesia* (1956), ii, 218 ff.

[38] In another connection (*Orientatie* (1954), xlvi, 642), I quoted the beginning of Krom's part in Stapel's *Geschiedenis van Nederlandsch-Indië* (1938-40). The initial sentence, freely translated, runs as follows: 'History of the countries which would once become the Netherlands Indies starts with the arrival of the Hindus.' Such a sentence gives the impression as if Krom described the history of the 'Hindu Indies' preceding that of the Netherlands Indies. Several Indonesians told me that the impression made upon them by Krom's history was that of a view on Indonesia from outside. In addition they got the impression that Krom tries to give the credit to foreigners (i.e. Indians) whenever the materials give him a choice to do so.

Throughout his academic career (1915–40) he continued his studies, essentially in the same line as before.[39] In 1938 Krom gave again a rather detailed account of 'Hindu-Javanese' history, but in a form which is, in several respects, disappointing.[40]

The influence of Krom's History has been enormous; as a matter of fact, no other detailed account of older Indonesian history (excepting that mentioned in note 40) has been written since 1931.[41] The flow of articles and also larger works concerning several aspects and numerous details has, however, been impressive for these twenty-five years, so that it is, at present, very difficult to get a clear view of the progress which has been made. Only the essential points can be mentioned here.[42]

The first important point to be noted is that Krom's work provided a solid basis to further research, since it gave precise knowledge about what exactly was known about the problems of older history in 1931, and to know how far one is, is an essential condition to progress. On every page of Krom's 'Hindu-Javanese History', the reader may note what is still to be done. In numerous cases, Krom gives us all the materials available for a certain detail and the conclusions which may be drawn; instead of choosing himself, Krom leaves the reader free in his choice, although he usually shows a preference for one particular conclusion. And indeed, in such cases, the reader is not bound to the preference shown by Krom, but may examine the materials himself and arrive at some other conclusion. This way of describing history is not only irritating for many readers who want to know facts, but it also gives the wrong impression, especially to 'outsiders', that almost nothing definite is known with certainty.[43] On the other hand, it is impossible to deny that Krom's way of describing history has greatly stimulated later research.

The second important point is that since Krom's History the study of

[39] It is striking that neither Stutterheim's nor Moens' work had real influence upon Krom's ideas. [40] Cf. *infra*, pp. 144–45.

[41] It should be stressed that such a work is very urgently needed. A few years ago (cf. *Orientatie* (1954), xlvi, 655) I thought that a new handbook should be based upon Krom's *Geschiedenis*, but I am now convinced—by the Conference on Historical Writing on the peoples of Asia more than by anything else—that this is not desirable. In one respect, however, I think that Krom's method should be followed, viz., in the attempt to give a relatively full account of the studies, theories, etc., published during the last forty years or so. The main text should, however, be mainly descriptive, whereas references, detailed discussion of sources, controversial matters, etc., should be removed from the main text, wherever possible, and referred to a separate volume. The description itself ought to be given a strong methodological basis in keeping with the results of contemporary historial thought. Finally, I think that such a history should deal with Indonesia within the frame of world history in general and the history of South East Asia in particular.

[42] The reader is also referred to *Orientatie* (1954), xlvi, 626–64.

[43] Anyone who has worked in Indonesia in this field will be familiar with this kind of remarks, which are only partly true. On the whole, we do know more about more recent history (from the sixteenth century on) than about the older period, especially as far as the more concrete facts are concerned. On the other hand, the views on more modern history are, as a rule far more distorted by either extremely nationalist or outspoken Europe-centred views.

older Indonesian history became 'internationalized' to a certain degree. Whereas before 1926 research was mainly limited to Dutch scholars,[44] the following period shows us an increasing number of Indian, British, and French scholars working in this field. Indonesian scholars took an increasing interest in these studies, but the number of research workers on older history was very small.

The work of Indian scholars on Indonesian history requires a separate treatment, not only on account of its importance, but still more because the Indian approach to Indonesian history differs from that of most other scholars.

Although isolated tokens of interest in Indonesian history are visible before the end of the nineteenth century,[45] it was not till after the First World War that Indian scholars began to study systematically the influence of Indian culture outside India. The Greater India Society, founded in 1926, started a regular Journal in 1934.[46] The aim of the Greater India Society appears clearly from the foreword by Rabindranath Tagore to the first number of this journal:[47]

> To know my country in truth one has to travel to that age when she realised her soul, and thus transcended her physical boundaries; when she revealed her being in a radiant magnanimity which illumined the Eastern horizon making her recognized as their own by those in alien shores who were awakened into a great surprise of life; and not now when she has withdrawn herself within a narrow barrier of obscurity, into a miserly pride of exclusiveness, into a poverty of mind that humbly revolves round itself in an unmeaning repetition of a past that has lost its light and has no message to the pilgrims of the future.

This quotation shows clearly that the Greater India Society should be considered a part of the national revival in India. The Indian scholars are therefore less interested in Indonesian culture as a whole than in its Indian components. One finds, however, many different shades in the views of Indian scholars. Some of them use regularly terms such as 'ancient Indian colonies', in which 'colonies' seems to imply also political domination. Thus, R. C. Majumdar writes, in a recent account (1950): 'The art of Java and Kambuja was no doubt derived from India and fostered by the Indian rulers of these colonies.'[48] Such formulations, which suggest colonial empires ruled by Indians, go far beyond the discrete limits posed by Krom

---

[44] There are a few important exceptions such as Cœdès and Ferrand, but they do not change the picture as a whole.

[45] Thus, an Indian scholar, R. G. Bhandarkar, published the Kalasan inscription as early as 1887 (*Journal of the Bombay Branch of the Royal Asiatic Society*, xvii).

[46] Cf. L. Finot, BEFEO (1927), xxvii, 504–7.

[47] *Journal of the Greater India Society* (1934), i, Preface.

[48] R. C. Majumdar in R. C. Majumdar, H. C. Raychaudhuri, and Kalikinkar Datta, *An advanced History of India* (1950), p. 221.

and may create serious misunderstandings.[49] I have often heard terms such as 'cultural imperialism' from Indonesians when referring to Indian studies about Indonesian history and culture.[50] The frequent use of terms such as Indian colonies and Indian rulers instead of old Indonesian empires and princes[51] creates serious misunderstandings which interfere with successful co-operation between India and Indonesia in the cultural field.[52] Fortunately, most Indian scholars take a more moderate view and avoid terms such as those mentioned above; they prefer terms such as 'Indian cultural expansion' or merely 'influence'.

Although the Indian approach has found little response among Dutch and Indonesian scholars, Indian scholarship has furnished ample materials for Indonesian history. A few examples will be sufficient. B. Ch. Chhabra published numerous studies on Sanskrit inscriptions in Indonesia. His doctoral thesis, entitled *Expansion of Indo-Aryan Culture during Pallava Rule*,[53] deals with a great number of Sanskrit inscriptions in South East Asia and gives important corrections to the readings and interpretations in previous publications. It has, however, been noted that the title does not quite agree with the contents of this book, for no clear evidence of Pallava influence appears from the inscriptions dealt with by Chhabra.[54] More recently, the same author published an important article about *yūpa* inscriptions in India,[55] an article which is indirectly important for our knowledge of Indian influence in Indonesia. As is well known, the oldest epigraphic remains in Indonesia are seven inscribed *yūpas* from East Kalimantan.[56] On account of their script and some other features,[57] these

[49] As a matter of fact, not even one example of a king in Indonesia claiming Indian origin is known up to now. An example considered certain by Krom (*Hindoe-Javaansche Geschiedenis*, p. 125) proved to be based upon wrong reading and interpretation of a passage in the Tjanggal inscription (cf. W. F. Stutterheim, 'Notes on cultural relations between South India and Java', *Tijdschr. Bat. Gen.* (1939), lxxix, 73–84; J. Ph. Vogel, 'Aanteekeningen op de inscriptie van Tjanggal in Midden-Java', *Bijdr. Kon. Inst.* c, (1941), 443–7; R. Ng. Poerbatjaraka, *Riwajat Indonesia* (1952), i, 56–58).

[50] I have often been struck by remarks made by distinguished Indian guests when visiting musea and monuments in Indonesia. Remarks such as: 'We have all that in India too' are not rare and may be irritating to Indonesians. An Indian diplomat thought it obvious that Barabuḍur was built by Indians ('of course with Indonesian workmen').

[51] Cf. the quotation in note 48 above, which is one example out of many.

[52] As a matter of fact, there has been very little co-operation between the two countries in historical and archaeological fields, except in the exchange of a few cultural missions.

[53] Also printed in the *Journal and Proceedings of the Asiatic Society of Bengal*, Letters (1935), i, 1–64.

[54] Cf. W. F. Stutterheim in *Djåwå* (1934), xiv, 235–8.

[55] B. Ch. Chhabra, 'Yūpa inscriptions', *India Antiqua, a Volume of Oriental Studies presented to Jean Philippe Vogel, C.I.E.*, pp. 77–82.

[56] J. Ph. Vogel, 'The Yūpa inscriptions of King Mūlavarman', *Bijdr. Kon. Inst.* (1918), lxxiv, 167–232; B. Ch. Chhabra, 'Three more yūpa inscriptions of King Mūlavarman from Kutei (East Borneo)', *Journ. Gr. India Soc.* (1945), xii, 14–17 and *Tijdschr. Bat. Gen.* (1949), lxxxiii, 370–4.

[57] Cf. Krom, *Hindoe-Javaansche Geschiedenis*, p. 72: 'Behalve taal en schrift is ook de inhoud der inscripties Voor-Indisch; deze doorlezend zou men ze evengoed in het Pallava-land zelfs als in Borneo ontstaan kunnen achten' (i.e.: 'In addition to the script and the language, also the con-

inscriptions have rightly been attributed to influence from Southern India, especially the Pallava empire,[58] but it now appears from Chhabra's article that all inscriptions of this kind in India (twelve in all) originate from Rajputana, Mathura, and Allahabad.[59] Another Indian scholar who has done important work for Indonesian history is K. A. Nilakanta Sastri. I will mention especially his important articles about Kaṭāha,[60] Çrīvijaya[61] Agastya,[62] about a Tamil inscription from North West Sumatra[63] and another from Takuapa[64] and, finally, an excellent little book about South Indian influences in South East Asia.[65] R. C. Majumdar wrote important articles about the Çailendras and Çrīvijaya;[66] in another book[67] he gave us a picture of old Indonesia, especially for Indian readers. A large book by H. Bh. Sarkar on Javanese and Balinese literature[68] is hardly satisfactory;[69] it contains, however, numerous materials which prove useful. The same scholar discussed also a number of Old Javanese inscriptions with translations into English;[70] the author seems not sufficiently versed in Old Javanese grammar and literature to give satisfactory translations of these difficult texts.[71] An important discovery was made by Manomahan Ghosh when he read the book by Sarkar mentioned in note 69; he concluded from a translation of some strophes of the Old Javanese *Rāmāyaṇa* that the latter poem is based upon the Sanskrit *Bhaṭṭikāvya*.[72]

The above survey[73] may give an impression of the subjects dealt with

tents of the inscriptions are Indian; when reading them, one could even presume that they had been written in the Pallava country as well as in Borneo'). This statement seems, however, to be in conflict with Krom's discussion on Waprakeçwara, which precedes and that on Kuṇḍungga which follows on page 73.

[58] Cf. the articles mentioned in note 56.

[59] Cf. the list and the map in Chhabra's article quoted in note 55 above on pp. 78 f.

[60] K. A. Nilakanta Sastri, 'Kaṭāha', *Journ. Gr. India Soc.* (1938), v, 128–46.

[61] K. A. Nilakanta Sastri, 'Srī Vijaya', BEFEO (1940), xl, 2, 239–310.

[62] K. A. Nilakanta Sastri, 'Agastya', *Tijdschr. Bat. Gen.* (1936), lxxvi, 471–545.

[63] K. A. Nilakanta Sastri, 'Takuapa and its Tamil inscription', *Journ. Mal. Br. Royal Asiat. Soc.* (1949), xxii, pt. 1, 25–31.

[64] K. A. Nilakanta Sastri, 'A Tamil merchant-guild in Sumatra', *Tijdschr. Bat. Gen.* (1932), lxxii, 314–27.

[65] K. A. Nilakanta Sastri, *South Indian Influences in the Far East* (1949).

[66] R. C. Majumdar, 'Les rois Çailendra de Suvarṇadvīpa', BEFEO (1933), xxxiii, 121–41; 'The Śailendra Empire (up to the end of the tenth century A.D.)', *Journ. Gr. Indian Soc.* (1934), i, 11–27.

[67] R. C. Majumdar, *Ancient Indian Colonies in the Far East* (1938), ii, Suvarṇadvīpa.

[68] H. Bh. Sarkar, *Indian Influences on the Literature of Java and Bali* (1934).

[69] Cf. Th. Pigeaud, *Djawa* (1935), xv, 97–98; J. Gonda, *Indische Gids* (1935), pp. 637–43.

[70] E.g., 'Literary and epigraphic notes', *Journ. Gr. India Soc.* (1936), iii, 108–12.

[71] In addition, Sarkar bases his translations exclusively on a published transcription without consulting the original stone, copper plate, or photographs.

[72] Cf. R. Ng. Poerbatjaraka, *Kepustakaan Djawa* (1952), pp. 2 f.; C. Hooykaas, 'The Old-Javanese Rāmāyaṇa Kakawin with special reference to the problem of interpolation in Kakawins', *Verhand. Kon. Inst.* (1955), xvi.

[73] The survey is, of course, far from being complete. The number of books and articles on the older period of Indonesia by Indian authors, as far as I have listed them, amounts to well over a hundred; I hope, however, that I have succeeded in choosing the most representative examples.

by Indian authors. Although the larger works about Indonesian culture often remain unsatisfactory because the authors almost limit their research to Indian influences, I think that the main contribution of Indian scholars is the numerous new data which they discovered; more precise knowledge about the Indian elements in the older Indonesian culture makes it possible to determine the extent of the Indian influence; this again is a necessary condition to understand the development of Indonesian culture.

The interest of non-Dutch European scholars in older Indonesian history increased in the period from 1931 to 1942. There was excellent co-operation between the cultural institutes in Indonesia (especially the Archaeological Service and the Royal Batavian Society) and similar institutes in Malaya (Malay Branch of the Royal Asiatic Society) and Indochina (École Française d'Extrême Orient). Each took notice of the other's discoveries,[74] commented upon them and used them. However, British and French scholars were, as a rule, too busy with their own fields of research, so that they had few opportunities to specialize on Indonesia.[75] Generally speaking, the British scholars dealt mainly with problems common to Indonesia and Malaya, whereas the French scholars discussed similar problems with reference to Indochina. Among the former, I will mention especially Sir R. O. Winstedt, whose very numerous publications on the history and the culture of Malaya are obviously important for the Indonesian history, too,[76] and Sir Roland Braddell, whose valuable studies on ancient geography (including the location of ancient cities and empires mentioned in Chinese and other sources) have a direct importance for the

---

In this connection I should mention also a new quarterly (replacing the old Journal of the Greater India Society), viz., The Indo-Asian Culture, published by the Indian Council for Cultural Relations under the presidency of Maulana Abul Kalam Azad since 1953. The object of the Indian Council is 'to establish, revive and strengthen cultural relations between India and other countries'. Unlike the older journal it is meant for the general educated public. The majority of the articles which have appeared up to now deal with Indian Culture itself, but there is also a considerable number of articles on Indian elements in Asian cultures outside India.

[74] Especially discussions of new books, new materials and new articles. There have even been abbreviated translations (cf. *infra*, note 147).

[75] A major handicap was also the language, for Dutch scholars used almost exclusively Dutch in their publications. It is, of course, impossible to have the vast Dutch literature on Indonesian history translated into English or French. A new handbook, such as that alluded to in note 41 above, should be written in one of the major world languages, while it should give extensive translations of the more important quotations. Only then could the extensive materials be made accessible to the world outside Holland—including Indonesia, where the number of those reading Dutch is rapidly decreasing.

[76] R. O. Winstedt, 'A History of Malaya', *Journ. Mal. Branch Royal As. Soc.*, xiii, pt. I, 1–270; 'The Chronicles of Pasai', ibid. (1938), xvi, pt. II, 24–35; 'The Malay Annals', ibid. (1938), xvi, pt. III, 1–126; 'The Malay Annals again', ibid. (1949), xxii, pt. I, 178–80; 'A History of Malay Literature', ibid. (1939), xvii, pt. III; 'Kingship and Enthronement in Malaya', *Journ. Royal As. Soc.* (1945), pp. 134–45 (reprint in *Journ. Mal. Br. Royal As. Soc.* (1947), xx, 128–39); 'The date, authorship, etc., of the Malay Romance of Alexander the Great', *Journ. Mal. Br. Royal As. Soc.* (1938), xvi, pt. II, 1–23; 'A Pañji Tale from Kĕlantan', ibid. (1949), xxii, pt. I, 53–61, and numerous other publications.

study of older Indonesian history.[77] H. G. Quaritch Wales not only published important works on Siamese state ceremonies[78] and ancient administration[79]—which are indirectly important for a better understanding of the older Indonesian states—but also did very valuable research in Kĕdah,[80] which is directly important for Indonesian history. Kĕdah is situated on a cross-road of civilizations; the numerous discoveries in that region show us not only direct Indian influence, but also influences from the hinduized Indonesian empires in Sumatra and, presumably, in Java, too; finally, there is influence from Thailand and, presumably, from other regions, too.[81] Continued research and study of the discoveries in that area may clear up many problems which seem confusing at present. Although Burma is rather far away from Indonesia, I do not doubt that the important research by G. H. Luce, Pe Maung Tin, and others will prove valuable for Indonesian history, too.[82]

French scholars have contributed very much to our knowledge of ancient South East Asia, including Indonesia, especially since the foundation of the École Française d'Extrême-Orient in 1901.[83] I need not remind the reader that the publication by George Cœdès of the Ligor epigraph in 1918, with the study based on it, has completely changed our views on the older history of Indonesia (prior to about the twelfth century).[84] In 1930 Cœdès re-edited the Old Malay texts of Çrīvijaya with translations, notes, and a glossary.[85] This edition has remained fundamental. G. Ferrand published another edition of these most important epigraphs in 1932.[86] Further, I may mention important publications by Cœdès on the Çailendra dynasty,[87] on the last period of Çrīvijaya,[88] on the iconographic

[77] R. Braddell, 'Notes on Ancient Times in Malaya', *Journ. Mal. Br. Royal As. Soc.* (1947), xx, pt. I, 161–86, and (1947), pt. II, 1–19; ibid. (1949), xxii, pt. I, 1–25.

[78] H. G. Quaritch Wales, *Siamese State Ceremonies*, 1934; 'Archaeological Researches', *Journ. Mal. Br. Royal As. Soc.* (1940), xviii, pt. I, 1–85; *The Making of Greater India* (1951); *Ancient South East Asian Warfare* (1952), and numerous other publications.

[79] *Ancient Siamese Government and Administration* (1934).

[80] Cf. the second publication of those mentioned in note 78.

[81] There must certainly have been influence from Çrīvijaya, but owing to the scarcity of archaeological remains in South Sumatra its extent could hardly be ascertained.

[82] According to information kindly supplied by Dr. Luce during my stay at Rangoon in July 1954, there seem to be numerous points of agreement both in state and in village organization.

[83] A brief survey on the work of the École Française d'Extrême Orient in various fields is given in the commemoration volume issued at the fiftieth anniversary of that School. *Vid.* 'Cinquante Ans d'Orientalisme Francais', *Soc. Et. Indoch., Nouv. Sér.* (1951), xxvi, 409–577; as far as Indonesia is concerned, cf. especially the survey by Cœdès, ibid., pp. 460–2.

[84] G. Cœdès, 'Le Royaume de Çrīvijaya', BEFEO (1918), xxviii, Fasc. 6, 1–36.

[85] G. Cœdès, 'Les inscriptions malaises de Çrīvijaya', BEFEO (1930), xxx, 29–80.

[86] G. Ferrand, 'Quatre textes epigraphiques malayo-sanskrits de Sumatra et de Banka', *Journ. Asiat.* (1932), ccxxi, 271–426.

[87] G. Cœdès, 'On the Origin of the Çailendras of Indonesia', *Journ. Gr. India Soc.* (1934), i, 66–70; 'Le Çailendra "Tueur des Heros ennemis" ', *Bingkisan Budi* (1950), pp. 58–70.

[88] G. Cœdès, 'A propos de la chûte du Royaume de Çrīviyaya', *Bijdr. Kon. Inst.* (1927), lxxxiii, 468–72.

collections of the Bankok Museum (a part of which comes from regions dominated or influenced by Çrīvijaya).[89] In addition, his numerous studies about ancient Cambodia are obviously important for Indonesia, too.[90] The same is true with the publications by Pelliot on Chinese sources.[91] We still do not know much about relations between Indonesia and Indochina in ancient times, but the work of Coral Rémusat[92] and Stern[93] tends to show Old Javanese influence on ninth-century Khmer art;[94] an example of Campā influence on fourteenth-century Javanese art seems to be more doubtful,[95] but might be connected with connubial relations between Java and Campā.[96] Another French scholar, Sylvain Lévi, published important articles on parts of Sanskrit and Pāli texts such as the *Rāmāyaṇa*,[97] *Niddesa*, and *Bṛhatkathā*[98] in connection with the

[89] G. Cœdès, 'Les collections archéologiques du Musée National de Bangkok', *Ars Asiatica* (1927), xii.

[90] Among his numerous publications on ancient Cambodia I will mention the 'Études Cambodgiennes', a series of studies published in the BEFEO from 1911 on. The hitherto last study in this series is 'Études Cambodgiennes XXXIX: L'épigraphie des monuments de Jayavarman VII', BEFEO (1947–50, but published in 1951), xliv, Fasc. 1, 97–119. A no less imposing series is the 'Inscriptions du Cambodge', six volumes of inscriptions in Sanskrit and Khmer from Cambodia, with complete transcriptions, translations, introductions, notes, indexes etc., published by the E.F.E.O. as the third part of the *Collection de Textes et Documents sur l'Indochine*. The six volumes of the 'Inscriptions du Cambodge' were published in 1937, 1942, 1951, 1952, 1953, and 1954.

[91] P. Pelliot, 'Deux Itinéraires', BEFEO (1904), iv, 132–413.

[92] G. de Coral-Rémusat, *Journ. Asiat.* (1933), p. 190.

[93] Philippe Stern, BEFEO (1938), xxxviii, 127 f.

[94] This influence has been connected with data in the inscription of Sdok Kak Thom, according to which Jayavarman II came back from Java before he started to reign at Angkor.

[95] Cf. Krom, *Hindoe-Javaansche Geschiedenis*[2], p. 423: 'Één jaar later, in 1371, kwam Tjaṇḍi Pari, N. W. van Porong, tot stand, een gebouw met sterk Camsche motieven en welicht aan een vreemdelingenkolonie uit dat land toe te schrijven, waar voortdurende troebelem uitwijken naar den vreemde in de hand kunnen hebben gewerkt' (i.e.: One year later, in 1371 A.D. Tjaṇḍi Pari, to the South West of Porong (which itself is situated 15 miles due south of Surabaja) was erected —a building with strong Cham features, which should perhaps be attributed to a colony of foreigners from that country, where continuous internal quarrels may have promoted flight to other countries). A similar statement is given by Krom in *Het Oude Java en zijn Kunst*, second impression, 1943), p. 153. However, Henri Parmentier, one of the best authorities on Cham art, is less certain about this influence; cf. *L'Art architectural hindou dans l'Inde et en Extrême-Orient*, p. 87: 'le Tj Pari qui peut montrer une influence chame'. Cœdès, who usually mentions all materials on cultural relations between Indonesia and Indochina in his *Etats Hindouisés*, does not at all mention Tjaṇḍi Pari, presumably because he considered the reference too uncertain. It is true that Tjaṇḍi Pari shows some unusual features in its ornamentation, but it seems that new research is necessary before Cham influence may be postulated.

[96] About connubial relations between Campā and Java at the end of the thirteenth and the first half of the fourteenth century, cf. Krom, *Hindoe-Javaansche Geschiedenis*[2], pp. 332 f.; Coedès, *Etats Hindouisés*, p. 362; Berg, 'De geschiedenis van Pril Majapahit. I. Het mysterie van de vier dochters van Kṛtanagara', *Indonesië* (1951), iv, 481–520, especially pp. 500–3 and 516.

[97] S. Lévi, 'Pour l'histoire du Rāmāyaṇa', *Journ. Asiat.* (1918).

[98] S. Lévi, 'Ptolemée, le Niddesa et la Bṛhatkathā, *Etudes Asiatiques E.F.E.O.* (1925), ii, 1–55. Cf. also 'Notes sur la géographie ancienne de l'Inde', *Journ. Asiat* (1925), pp. 46–57, and 'Kouen-Louen et Dvīpāntara', *Bijdr. Kon. Inst.* (1931), lxxxviii, 621–7.

beginnings of contact between India and South East Asia; the same scholar identified a relief series of Barabuḍur[99] and collected Sanskrit texts from Bali.[100] Penetrating studies on the Barabuḍur were published by Paul Mus.[101]

The above survey may have shown that British and French scholars contributed very much to the study of older Indonesian history; on the other hand, it appears that Indonesia was never the main field of their studies. Therefore, the main subjects discussed by the above authors are common to several areas in South East Asia; the studies on Çrīvijaya, on Chinese sources, on Indian influence and on cultural relations between the various areas are typical examples. The main importance of British and French research is not the study of the materials for the history of Indonesia proper—although such research was not at all absent—but rather what might be termed an extension of the field of Indonesian problems: the latter became parts of more general problems common to the whole area of South East Asia, although this term was not used at that time. As a matter of fact, such research as that mentioned above has paved the way for research on South East Asia after the last war.

The greater part of the research on the older history of Indonesia in the period between 1926 and 1941 was done by Dutch and some Indonesian scholars. Progress in the first five years of this period appears clearly from a comparison between the first impression of Krom's Hindu-Javanese History (1926) and its second impression (1931). If a few publications of 1925, which could not, or not fully, be used in Krom's first edition, are included, the most important studies in these years were: the studies on the Nālandā inscription,[102], the inscriptions of Kĕlurak, Kalasan, and Ratubaka,[100], the Gaṇḍavyūha reliefs on the Barabuḍur,[104], all by Bosch; Stutterheim's studies on the ruins on the Ratubaka plateau,[105] on a very important inscription from Kĕḍu,[106], on 'a Javanese period in Sumatran

[99] S. Levi, *Mahākarmavibhaṅga et Karmavibhaṅgopadeça* (1932). Cf. also N. J. Krom, 'Het Karmawibhangga op Barabuḍur', *Meded. Kon. Akad. Wetensch., Afd. Lett.*, lxxvi, B, 215–83.

[100] S. Levi, 'Sanskrit Texts from Bali', *Gaekwad's Orient. Ser.* (1933), lxvii.

[101] P. Mus, *Barabuḍur. Esquisse d'une histoire du Bouddhisme fondée sur la critique archéologique des textes*. Avec préface de G. Cœdès (1935).

[102] F. D. K. Bosch, 'Een Oorkonde van het Groote Klooster te Nālandā', *Tijdschr. Bat. Gen.* 925, lxv, 509–88.

[103] F. D. K. Bosch, 'De inscriptie van Keloerak', ibid. (1928), lxviii, 1–64 (with two appendixes on the inscriptions of Kalasan and Ratubaka respectively).

[104] F. D. K. Bosch, 'De beteekenis der reliëfs van de derde en vierde gaanderij van Baraboedoer', *Oudheidk. Versl.* (1929), pp. 179–243; 'De Bhadracarī', *Bijdr. Kon. Inst.* (1938), xcvii, 241–93.

[105] W. F. Stutterheim, 'De bouwvallen op de heuvel van Ratoe Baka bij Prambanan', *Djåwå* (1926), vi, 129–36.

[106] W. F. Stutterheim, 'Een belangrijke oorkonde uit de Kĕḍoe', *Tijdschr. Bat. Gen.* (1927), lxvii, 173–216.

history',[107] on Balinese antiquities[108] and on the Barabuḍur;[109] Vogel's excellent re-edition of the Pūrṇavarman inscriptions;[110] Cœdès's re-edition of all the Çrīvijaya epigraphs in Old Malay known at that time;[111] Berg's studies on the 'Middle-Javanese historical tradition',[112] on the study of Old Javanese language and literature,[113] on the *kidungs Rangga Lawe*,[114] *Harṣa-Wijaya*,[115] *Kidung Suṇḍa*;[116] Poerbatjaraka's studies on Agastya,[117] on the Old Javanese *Rāmāyaṇa*,[118] *Arjunawiwāha*,[119] and *Smaradahana*;[120] finally, numerous discussions of new discoveries in the reports of the Archaeological Service, mainly by Bosch.[121] This list, which is far from being complete,[122] serves to give an impression of the intensity of research in these few years.[123] Since all the above-mentioned scholars continue their publications during the period from 1931 to 1941, their approach to older Indonesian history can better be dealt with in the following part of this survey.

The new trends in historical research on older Indonesian history, which are already distinguishable in the period from 1926 to 1931, but

---

[107] *A Javanese Period in Sumatran History* (1929). This publication is really a kind of pamphlet directed against Krom's views in the first impression of the *Hindoe-Javaansche Geschiedenis* and especially against Krom's inaugural speech in the Leiden University entitled 'De Sumatraansche periode der Javaansche geschiedenis' (i.e. The Sumatran period of Javanese history) (1919).

[108] W. F. Stutterheim, *Oudheden van Bali. Het oude rijk van Pedjeng*, pt. I, text (1929); pt. II, plates (1930).

[109] W. F. Stutterheim, *Tjaṇḍi Baraboedoer. Naam, Vorm en Beteekenis* (1929).

[110] J. Ph. Vogel, 'The Earliest Sanskrit Inscriptions of Java', *Public. Oudheidk. Dienst* (1925) i, 15–35, plates 27 to 35.

[111] G. Cœdès, 'Les inscriptions malaises de Çrīvijaya', BEFEO (1930), xxx, 29–80 (with Old Malay word index).

[112] C. C. Berg, *De Middeljavaansche historische traditie* (1927).

[113] C. C. Berg, *Inleiding tot de studie van het Oudjavaansch* (1928).

[114] C. C. Berg, 'Rangga Lawe', *Bibl. Javanica* (1930), i.

[115] C. C. Berg, 'Een nieuwe redactie van de roman van Raden Wijaya. Kidung Harṣa-Wijaya', *Bijdr. Kon. Inst.* (1931), lxxxviii, 1–238.

[116] C. C. Berg, 'Kidung Suṇḍa', *Bijdr. Kon. Inst.* (1927), lxxxiii, 1–161. Cf. also 'Iets over de historische Kidung Sorandaka', *Feestb. Bat. Gen.* (1929), i, 22–34.

[117] R. Ng. Poerbatjaraka, *Agastya in den Indischen Archipel* (1926).

[118] R. Ng. Poerbatjaraka, 'De datering van het Oud-Javaansche *Rāmāyaṇa*', *Gedenkschr. Kon. Inst.* (1926), pp. 265–72. More in detail: 'Het Oud-Javaansche *Rāmāyaṇa*', *Tijdschr. Bat. Gen.* (1932), lxxii, 151–214. On this problem, cf. also C. Hooykaas, 'The Old-Javanese *Rāmāyaṇa* Kakawin with special reference to the problem of interpolation in Kakawins', *Verhand. Kon. Inst.* (1955), xvi.

[119] R. Ng. Poerbatjaraka, 'Arjuna-Wiwāha', *Bijdr. Kon. Inst.* (1926), lxxxii.

[120] R. Ng. Poerbatjaraka, 'Smaradahana', *Bibl. Javanica* (1931), iii.

[121] *Vid.* the archaeological reports (Oudheidkunig Verslag) from 1916 to 1930 inclusive and all the other publications of the Archaeological Service in Indonesia during that period. All these publications were directed by Bosch, who, in addition, published himself numerous reports on special questions, transcriptions of epigraphic materials, etc., in that series.

[122] In this portion, too, only the most important studies could be mentioned—mainly those which are important for the approach to Indonesian history.

[123] One gets an excellent impression of the intensity of research during this period from the two large volumes of the *Feestbundel* of the 'Koninklijk Bataviaasch Genootschap', issued at its 150th anniversary in 1928.

appear more clearly in the ten years which follow, may be briefly summarized. As a rule, these scholars stress the original Indonesian features of the older culture. This is partly due to the more intensive study of Indonesian culture in its manifold aspects,[124] partly a reaction against Indian research which laid too great stress on Indian elements in Indonesian culture.[125] Another feature is the more regular exchange of opinions between the scholars working on Indonesian, Malay, and Indochinese history and culture. Finally, I will stress the thoroughness of research in this period; this feature is very striking if one reads any study of before about 1920 immediately after a study on a similar subject written after 1926. One is struck by the *naiveté* of conclusions, often generalized, which were based upon scanty evidence, in the older period of research.[126] On the other hand, research between 1931 and 1941 is often rather sophisticated; it is, moreover, often very polemical. Especially the latter feature strikes us

[124] In this connection I may mention the studies by Rassers in the anthropological field, such as *De Pandji Roman* (1922), which, although not dealing with history, had a great influence on research in this period. Another important anthropological work of this period is K. A. H. Hidding, *Nji Pohadji Sangjang Sri* (1929). These studies stressed the original Indonesian basis of older Indonesian culture, whereas the older generation had laid too great a stress upon the Indian elements. The edition and translation of the *Tantu Panggĕlaran* by Th. G. Th. Pigeaud, published in 1924, showed that also Old Javanese literature had produced works which were not based upon Indian prototypes. In this period, too, were published important studies on Indonesian music, especially J. Kunst and Kunst-van Wely, *De toonkunst van Bali* (1925), and J. Kunst and R. Goris, *Hindoe-Javaansche muziekinstrumenten* (1927). These studies showed the fundamental originality of Indonesian music in spite of Indian influence. All these studies, though somewhat outside the purely historical field, had great influence on historical studies and gradually changed the approach.

[125] Such features strike us even in the work of a great scholar as Kern. When something in Old Javanese inscriptions or literature did not agree with Indian literature or philosophy, Kern often started to use a slightly ironical style; cf., for instance, his commentary on the first strophes of the *Nāgarakṛtāgama* (H. Kern, *Het Oud-Javaansche Lofdicht Nāgarakṛtāgama van Prapañca* (1365 A.D.). Met aantekeningen van Dr. N. J. Krom (1919), pp. 21–24. Or his discussions of the language, etc., of Ādityavarman's inscriptions, e.g. in *Verspreide Geschriften* (1917), vii, 163–75.

[125] As a rule, the publications of the Greater India Society (and of Indian scholars working in the same line) were rather coolly received by scholars of this group. Cf., for instance, Stutterheim's discussion of Chhabra's doctoral thesis (mentioned on p. 6 above) in *Djâwâ* (1934), xiv, 235–8; Pigeaud's discussion of Sarkar's book on old Javanese and Balinese literature (cf. *supra*, note 68) in *Djâwâ* (1935), xv, 96–98; cf. also G. W. J. Drewes, *Internationale belangstelling voor het Oudjavaansch* (a public lecture given on 16 April 1935). Cf. also W. F. Stutterheim, 'The meaning of the Hindu-Javanese caṇḍi', *Journ. Amer. Orient. Soc.* (1931), li, 1–15, and 'Iets over de prae-hinduistische bijzettingsgebruiken op Java', *Meded. Kon. Acad. Wet* (1939), Lett., N.R., ii, 105–40, and *Indian influences in Old Balinese art* (1935). Stutterheim may have gone too far, possibly as a reaction against Indian views. The best recent discussion of some of the main problems involved is F. D. K. Bosch, 'Uit de grensgebieden tussen Indische invloedsspheer en Oud-Inheems volksgeloof of Java', *Bijdr. Kon. Inst.* (1954), cx, 1–19. In this study, Bosch first gives two 'extreme' views, first that of O. C. Gangoly, 'Relation between Indian and Indonesian Culture', *Journ. Gr. India Soc.* (1940), vii, 51–69, as typical of the Greater India circles, and then that of Stutterheim. After that, Bosch exposes his own views, which constitute a kind of Middle Road. Bosch considers Old Javanese culture basically Indian, but changed by various kinds of javanization.

[126] One gets a clear idea of the difference in research of before and after about 1920 when reading Krom's *Hindoe-Javaansche Geschiedenis* (second impression), for instance, pp. 206–9.

unfavourably; a difference of opinion on often minor questions resulted in quarrels which sometimes took ridiculous proportions.[127] This feature is presumably due to the structure of colonial society. Just as the private entrepreneurs tried by any means to accumulate sufficient means to be able to withdraw to Europe as soon as was possible, also the civil officers, who had to serve for a period fixed in advance, tried to retire with the highest possible pension. An ambitious attitude pervaded the whole European group in Indonesia.[128] It is understandable that even research workers were influenced by this attitude to some degree.

W. F. Stutterheim is perhaps the most typical example of this group of scholars.[129] Although he was trained for linguistic research in Indonesia[130] he soon became an archaeologist in the widest sense of the term. He worked in Indonesia from 1924 until his death in 1942 and published an astounding number of articles and larger works during this period (his bibliography comprises more than two hundred titles) in addition to his other activities.[131] Unlike Krom, he always lived in close contact with Indonesian circles. Also his approach differed essentially from that of Krom, since he studied older Indonesian culture for its own value. Stutterheim was not particularly interested in whether important elements of older Indonesian culture had come from India or elsewhere; he always stressed that research should be concentrated on how these foreign elements were assimilated in Indonesian culture. He used to insist that the Old

[127] Here, too, Stutterheim gives the most typical examples. When something was published which did not agree with his views, his reactions were unnecessarily sharp, often in an ironical way. Often, sharp criticism was directed against the work of Krom; cf. especially his reactions against Krom's article 'Een ontdekking van een toren der stilte op Java' (i.e. Discovery of a Tower of Silence in Java), *Wereldkroniek* (1925), p. 1034, in his article 'Tjandi Dadi een "Tower of Silence"?', *Bijdr. Kon. Inst.* (1925), lxxxi, 543–41. Cf. another example of Stutterheim's polemical style in his article 'Koning Tĕguh op een oorkonde', *Tijdschr. Bat. Gen.* (1940), lxxx, 345–66 (directed against Berg's opinion that king Dharmawangça Tĕguh mentioned in the Wirāṭaparwan might have been identical with Airlangga). A final example is the article by G. W. J. Drewes, 'Over werkelijke en vermeende geschiedschrijving in de Nieuw-Javaansche literatur', *Djåwå* (1939), xix, 244–57 (directed against Berg's opinions in 'Javaansche Geschiedschrijving', in F. W. Stapel, *De Geschiedenis van Nederlandsch-Indië* (1939), ii).

[128] Partly this is also a consequence of the relatively small number of scholars working in the field of older Indonesian history, where everybody knew everybody else; so criticisms were usually far more personal than in medicine or physics, where the number of scholars, working in the entire world, was many times larger. Moreover, the colonial career was short, about half of the length of a career in Europe, so that the few desirable posts should be attained in as short a time as possible. Everybody tended to go his own way.

[129] Cf. R. Goris in his preface to the posthumous publication of W. F. Stutterheim, 'De Kraton van Majapahit', *Verhand. Kon. Inst.* (1948), vii, pp. iii–ix, and A. J. Bernet Kempers, 'In Memoriam Dr. W. F. Stutterheim', *Oudheidk. Versl. 1941–47* (1949), pp. 15–28 (with detailed bibiliography).

[130] Viz. the special university education meant in the first place for future civil officers charged with linguistic research in the Indonesian Archipelago ('Taal-ambtenaar' in Dutch).

[131] Thus, Stutterheim was, for instance, Director of a secondary school from 1926 to 1936 and Chief of the Archaeological Service from 1936 to 1942. Stutterheim was an excellent organizer and administrator, which certainly took a good deal of his time.

Javanese *caṇḍi* is something essentially different from an Indian temple[132] and sometimes compared Indian influence in Indonesia with Greek and Roman influence in Western Europe. As far as possible he avoided terms such as 'Hindu-Javanese' because they might give the impression that older Indonesian culture was a mixture or a synthesis of Hindu and Javanese cultures: the Old Javanese culture should rightly be considered an Indonesian culture in which Indian influence, however great it may be, is only something accessory.[133]

Stutterheim published a considerable number of inscriptions, always with translations and copious notes. Some of these editions are real masterpieces, in which the author introduces us into the complicated older Javanese society.[134] His 'archaeological notes' amount to fifty;[135] in each

[132] In his article on the meaning of the Hindu-Javanese caṇḍi, quoted in note 125 above, he showed that the *caṇḍis* are not just places where some deity was worshipped, but rather funeral temples in which the objects of worship were kings identified with Hindu gods after their apotheosis. He further assumed that this was a typical Indonesian custom, some kind of continuation in a new form of ancient Indonesian animism; cf. for greater details, W. F. Stutterheim, 'Iets over de Prae-Hinduistische bijzettingsgebruiken op Java', *Meded. Kon. Acad. Wet., Lett.*, N.R. (1939), ii, 105–40. For a more recent discussion of these views cf. *supra*, note 125.

[133] Therefore, the fundamental problem for Stutterheim was not where exactly the Indian elements came from (the central problem for scholars in the Greater India Society and affiliated circles), but rather how these foreign elements became integrated in the pattern of older Indonesian culture.

[134] Some of his most important editions of Old Javanese epigraphs are: (1) W. F. Stutterheim, 'Een oordkonde op koper uit het Singasarische', *Tijdschr. Bat. Gen.* (1925), lxv, 208–81 (edition of an inscription of King Siṇḍok dated A.D. 929 with a very detailed discussion of the meaning of old Javanese terms for various arts and crafts, definitions of crimes, etc.); (2) W. F. Stutterheim, 'Een belangrijke oorkonde uit de Kĕḍoe', *Tijdschr. Bat. Gen.* (1927), lxvii, 173–216; (3) W. F. Stuttheim, 'Inscriptie op een zuiltje van Papringan', *Tijdschr. Bat. Gen.* (1933), lxxiii, 96–101; (4) W. F. Stutterheim, 'Beschreven lingga van Krapjak', *Tijdschr. Bat. Gen.* (1934), lxxiv, 85–93; (5) W. F. Stutterheim, 'Een vrij overzetveer te Wanagiri (M.N.) in A.D. 903', *Tijdschr. Bat. Gen.* (1934), lxxiv, 269–95 (transcription, translation and discussion of an inscription of king Balitung in the beginning of the tenth century A.D.; the king gave important privileges, such as freedom of taxation, to a number of people in exchange of the duty of transporting all travellers from one side of the river to another without demanding any fee; the inscription gives important materials for our knowledge of Old Javanese society; (6) W. F. Stutterheim, 'A newly discovered pre-Nāgarī inscription on Bali', *Acta Orient.* (1934), xii, 126–32 (this is a very interesting bilingual inscription, partly in Pre-Nāgarī, partly in Old Javanese script; after Stutterheim, the stone was discussed by L.-C. Damais, 'La colonette de Sanur. Études Balinaises, I', BEFEO (1947–50), xliv, Fasc. 1, 121–8; and finally by R. Goris, *Prasasti Bali*, I (1954), No. 103, pp. 64 f.; and II (1954), No. 103, p. 131; Damais dated the stone A.D. 903); (7) 'Epigraphica, I–V', *Tidjschr. Bat. Gen.* (1935), lxxv, 420–67 (the most interesting document is No. III, a sentence accordingly to which somebody is considered to have been wrongly accused of being a Khmer; the text proves that such a designation was taken as an offence; this fact would not have been some kind of xenophobia, but was mainly due to the social position of foreigners, who not rarely exercised the ungrateful profession of claiming taxes for the king); (8) 'A Malay shā'ir in Old Sumatran characters of A.D. 1380', *Acta Orient* (1936), xiv, 268–79 (on this inscription from Minye Tudjoh in Atjeh cf. also C. Hooykaas, *Perintis Sastera* (1951), pp. 73 f., with photographs, and G. E. Marrison, 'A Malay Poem in Old Sumatran Characters', *Journ. Mal. Br. Royal As. Soc.*, xxiv, pt. I, 162–5. Marrison gave important corrections to Stutterheim's transcription and proved that the strophes are not a shā'ir, but are composed in an Indian metre, viz., Upajāti); (9) 'Een inscriptie van Lombok', *Djåwå*, xvii, 309 f. (discussion on the only stone inscription known of the island of Lombok; the

of these the author deals with some little problem: the meaning of a statue, the date of a temple, the interpretation of a word in a text or in an inscription, an argument which might strengthen or invalidate some previous theory, etc; some of these notes merely call attention to some little problem and suggest a possible solution.[136] Among his larger works I will mention especially his excellent account of Balinese antiquities[137] and his last publication on the *kraton* of Majapahit.[138] In the latter, Stutterheim gives a new interpretation of the *Nāgarakṛtāgama* portion dealing with the heart of the greatest ancient Indonesian empire. Kern's translation had failed owing to insufficient knowledge of later *kratons*; Stutterheim, on the contrary, could use his precise knowledge of the Surakarta court, the results of excavations in the ancient Majapahit area and, finally, the corrected translation of Ma-Huan's description.[139] In this way, Stutterheim has succeeded in reviving one of the most important political and cultural centres of ancient South East Asia.

document is of the Majapahit period and shows Javanese influence); (10) 'Een van Balitung uit A.D. 905)', *Inscr. Ned.-Indië* (1940), i, 3–28 (edition of a copper plate inscription of Balitung with introduction, translation and discussion; especially important is the discussion on different kind of Old Javanese tools); (11) W. F. Stutterheim, 'Oorkonde van Ḍang Ācārya Munīndra', ibid. (1940), i, 33–49 (discussion of a rare kind of document in Old Javanese epigraphy, dealing with the payment of a debt; the text is important also for our knowledge of the monetary system used in Java in ancient times); (12) W. F. Stutterheim, 'Koning Tĕguh op een oorkonde', *Tijdschr. Bat. Gen.* (1940), lxxx, 345–66 (document which proves that king Dharmawangça Teguh was indeed a historical person to be distinguished from Airlangga; cf. note 127 above, and L. C. Damais, 'Études d'Épigraphie Indonésienne', III, BEFEO(1952), xlvi, Fasc. 1, 70 f., No. 169, and L. C. Damais, 'Études d'Épigraphie Indonésienne', IV, BEFEO (1955), xlvii, Fasc. 1, 123 f.).

[135] W. F. Stutterheim, 'Oudheidkundige Aanteekeningen', I–VIII, *Birdj. Kon. Inst.* (1929), lxxxv, 479–510; IX–XVI, ibid. (1930), lxxxvi, 302–12; XVII–XXVIII, ibid. (1932), lxxxix, 97–116 and 261–89; XXIX–XXXVIII, ibid. (1933), xc, 267–99; XXXIX–XLV, ibid. (1935), xcii, 181–210; XLVI–L, ibid. (1937), xcv, 397–424.

[136] The subtitles of these archaeological notes often end in a point of interrogation. Thus the title of archaeological note No. XLIII runs: 'Is 1049 the year of the death of Airlangga?' in translation. In this note Stutterheim discussed a queer representation, viz., Rāhu biting the sun while *ṛṣi*'s are visible in the sky. The three main elements, Rāhu, the Sun, and the *ṛṣi*'s, are frequently used as symbolic cipher words (respectively 9, 1 or 12, and 7). Choosing the cipher value 1 for the Sun, Stutterheim combines the three elements to 971. Since the year must be interpreted in the Çaka era with elapsed years, this would agree with A.D. 1049. Since, further, the site of discovery could be connected with Airlangga, Stutterheim concluded that it could denote only the death of that king, whose last known inscription is of the end of A.D. 1042. It is obvious that this interpretation is very uncertain: first, there is no certainty that the representation does have a cipher value; second, if it does, it is by no means certain that 9, 7, and 1 are meant (thus, the sun is taken to mean 1, although it has more often the value 12 on account of the twelve horses which draw the solar chariot); third, the order in which these elements should be combined to form a cipher seems unusual; fourth, even if the representation does mean 971 Çaka and is to be connected with Airlangga, there is no proof that it denotes the year of the king's death; it could, for instance, refer to the date in which some important ceremony connected with the death of Airlangga took place. We therefore conclude that the point of interrogation after Stutterheim's subtitle could not well be omitted. On the other hand, Stutterheim's interpretation is very attractive and would certainly agree with other data. Future discoveries might confirm it or otherwise. In spite of all this uncertainty, this note has undoubtedly a useful function, especially in stimulating future research. This is true with most of the 'Oudheidkundige Aanteekeningen'; they are given as suggestions, always worthy of consideration, not as real solutions.

The approach of R. Ng. Poerbatjaraka is rather different from that of Stutterheim. Poerbatjaraka in particular specialized on old and modern Javanese literature and epigraphy. I have already mentioned his text editions of the *Smaradahana* and the *Arjunawiwāha*, as well as his study on the Old Javanese *Rāmāyaṇa*. The last-mentioned study[140] was followed by a far more detailed study about the same poem in 1932.[141]. There, Poerbatjaraka proved beyond reasonable doubt that the Old Javanese version of the Rāmāyaṇa, which is one of the finest poetical works of Old Javanese literature, was composed in the Central-Javanese period (end of the ninth or beginning of the tenth century A.D.). The arguments are based upon a detailed analysis of the language, metrics, titles of officials, and the description of a temple complex in the poem. A still unpublished inscription[142] and a new study by Hooykaas[143] confirm Poerbatjaraka's conclusion. The same scholar edited a number of Old Javanese inscriptions with their translations,[144] an interesting Old Javanese text of the last period of Majapahit[145] and, together with Hooykaas, a translation of the *Bhāratayuddha*.[146] Some recent publications by Poerbatjaraka will be discussed in my survey of the third period.

J. L. Moens was one of the few 'outsiders' (he was a civil engineer by profession) who succeeded in acquiring the full esteem of professional historians and archaeologists. He not only published a valuable treatise on ancient geography (especially the location of empires and cities mentioned in Chinese and other foreign sources),[147] but also valuable studies on the

[137] W. F. Stutterheim, *Oudheden van Bali. Het oude rijk van Pedjeng*, two volumes; I, text (1929), II, plates (1930).

[138] W. F. Stutterheim, 'De kraton van Majapahit', *Verhand. Kon. Inst.* (1948), vii (published after Stutterheim's death).

[139] J. J. L. Duyvendak, 'Ma-huan re-examined', *Verhand. Kon. Acad. Wet.*, Afd. Lett., N.R. (1933), xxxii, 1–74.

[140] R. Ng. Poerbatjaraka, 'De datering van het Oud-Javaansche Rāmāyaṇa', *Gedenkschr. Kon. Inst.* (1926), 265–72.

[141] R. Ng. Poerbatjaraka, 'Het Oud-Javaansche Rāmāyaṇa', *Tijdschr. Bat. Gen.* (1932), lxxii, 151–214.

[142] Now published in *Pras. Indon* (1956), ii, No. XI, 280–330; cf. especially pp. 287 f.

[143] C. Hooykaas, 'The Old-Javanese Rāmāyaṇa with special reference to the problem of interpolation in Kakawins', *Verhand. Kon. Inst.* (1955), xvi.

[144] A number of inscriptions is edited by Poerbatjaraka in 'Agastya in den Indischen Archipel', doct. thesis, 1926. Other publications on epigraphy are: R. Ng. Poerbatjaraka, 'De Batoe-Toelis by Buitenzorg', *Tijdschr. Bat. Gen.* (1921), lix, 392–4; R. Ng. Poertbatjaraka, 'De inscriptie van het Mahākṣobhyabeeld te Simpang (Soerabaja)', *Bijdr. Kon. Inst.* (1922), lviii, 426–62; R. Ng. Poerbatjaraka, 'Vier oorkonden in koper', *Tijdschr. Bat. Gen.* (1936), lxxvi, 373–3; R. Ng. Poerbatjaraka, 'Oorkonde van Krtarājasa uit A.D. 1296', *Inscr. Ned.-Indië* (1940), i, 33–49 (with an introduction by Stutterheim). Finally, Poerbatjaraka discussed a number of inscriptions (all before about A.D. 750) in the first volume of *Riwajat Indonesia* (cf. *infra*, p. 16).

[145] R. Ng. Poerbatjaraka, 'Dewa Roetji', *Djâwâ* (1940), xx, 5–83.

[146] R. Ng. Poerbatjaraka and C. Hooykaas, 'Bhārata-Juddha', *Djâwâ* (1934), xiv, 1–87.

[147] J. L. Moens, 'Çrīvijaya, Yāva en Kaṭāha', *Tijdschr. Bat. Gen.* (1937), lxxvii, 317–487 (with two plates and four maps). Abbreviated English translation in *Journ. Malay Br. Royal As. Soc.* (1939), 1–108.

meaning of art, especially its religious background.[148] Moens lacked a sound archaeological and philological training and therefore often committed mistakes, which did not encourage full confidence in his conclusions, but many of his often original and fresh views require more consideration than they have had so far. [149]

The publications of R. Goris mainly concern Old Javanese and (Old) Balinese[150] religion and epigraphy. He published a number of Old Javanese inscriptions,[151] gave important accounts of Balinese ceremonies[152] and an excellent doctoral thesis about Old Javanese and Balinese theology.[153] An article about historical and sociological data from Old Balinese inscriptions[154] is still the only trustworthy account about this subject. I need not stress that the history of Bali, although only a tiny part of Indonesia, is rather important, especially on account of the close relations with East Java; in many a case, Old Balinese inscriptions yield important materials for a correct understanding of the history of the great Indonesian centres in East Java. In addition, Bali has a very strong tradition, uninterrupted by the coming of Islam; as a consequence, the interpretation of ancient documents of Bali is less uncertain than that of the corresponding Old Javanese documents. On the other hand, the old inscriptions of Bali may prove to be a great help in interpreting the old documents of Java. Goris concentrated upon this kind of research, and its main results will be briefly mentioned in the last part of this survey.

[148] J. L. Moens, 'Tjandi Mendut', *Tijdschr. Bat. Gen.* (1919–21), lix, 529–80; 'Het Buddhisme op Java en Sumatra in zijn laatste bloeiperiode', *Tijdschr. Bat. Gen.* (1924), lxiv, 521–80.

[149] Moens' articles always require careful consideration, although many of his conclusions are based upon scanty evidence. Sometimes such an uncertain conclusion becomes again the basis of another theory; cf. for instance, his conclusions about Kaṭāha in the article quoted in note 147 (especially pp. 415 ff.). A good discussion of Moens' views on the location of ancient empires is K. A. Nilakanta Sastri, 'Notes on the Historical Geography of the Malay Peninsula and the Archipelago', *Journ. Gr. India Soc.* (1940), vii, 15–42. For some of his conclusions on Old Javanese iconography, cf. W. F. Stutterheim, 'Het Berlijnsche Ardhanārī-beeld en de bijzettingsbeelden van Kĕrtanagara', *Tijdschr. Bat. Gen.* (1933), lxxiii, 292–306 (which is some kind of very critical epilogue to an article by Moens on the same subject). As a rule, however, Stutterheim appreciated the work of Moens, whereas Krom did not take it very seriously. In the circles of the Malay Branch of the Royal Asiatic Society, Moens' conclusions on ancient geography received very serious attention. Cf., for instance, Braddell's notes (quoted in note 77 above).

[150] R. Goris, 'Enkele mededelingen nopens de oorkonden gesteld in het Oud-Balisch', *Djâwâ* (1936), xvi, 88–101; 'Enkele historische en sociologische gegevens uit Balische oorkonden', *Tijdschr. Bat. Gen.* (1941), lxxxi, 279–94. Of his main work on Balinese epigraphy, two volumes have already appeared (cf. *infra*, note 203).

[151] R. Goris, 'De inscriptie van Koeboeran Tjandi', *Tijdschr. Bat. Gen.* (1930), lxx, 157–70; 'De Oud-Javaansche inscripties uit het Sri-Wedari-Museum te Soerakarta', *Oudheidk. Versl.* 1928, 1ste en 2de Kwartaal, Bijlage B, pp. 63–70; cf. also ibid., p. 32. Cf. also his article 'De eenheid der Matarāmsche dynastie', *Feestb. Bat. Gen.* (*1958*), i, 202–6.

[152] R. Goris, 'De Poera Besakih, Bali's rijkstempel', *Djâwâ* (1937), xvii, 261–70; 'Bali's tempelwezen', ibid. (1938), xviii, 30–46; 'Een merkwaardige plechtigheid in een bijzonder heiligdom', *Djâwâ* (1939), xix, 46–53.

[153] R. Goris, *Bijdrage tot de kennis der Oud-Javaansche en Balineesche theologie* (1926).

[154] Cf. *supra*, note 150, the second quotation.

P. V. van Stein Callenfels was one of the strangest figures in this field. Successively civil officer, coffee planter, prehistorian, and expert on art and inscriptions, he exercised more influence by his astounding personality than by his publications. He lived almost always among Indonesians and had acquired enormous knowledge of the Javanese society. Even more than Stutterheim, he stressed the Indonesian basis of Old Javanese culture. His publications were not frequent and sometimes rather careless, but some of his ideas were sound and stimulating.[155]

F. D. K. Bosch conducted the Archaeological Service for twenty years (from 1916 to 1936). His principal studies concern the development of older Indonesian art.[156] He also published a number of historical inscriptions[157] and some penetrating studies on the relation between Indian and Indonesian elements in older Indonesian culture. Since, however, some of his major works were published after the last war, they can better be discussed in the last part of this survey.

Also the publications of C. C. Berg extend over the second and third period of research. Berg's approach to older Indonesian history is mainly that of older Javanese and Balinese literature. Whereas most of the scholars before based their accounts on inscriptions, Chinese materials and, of the literary works, the *Nāgarakṛtāgama* and the *Pararaton*, Berg added a number of other historical works to our sources of older Indonesian history. Although these sources date from a considerable time after the events, they frequently contain accounts based on older and more reliable traditions,

[155] Cf. W. F. Stutterheim in the Preface to *Oudheidk. Versl.* 1937 (published in 1938), and N. J. Krom, 'Levensbericht van P. V. van Stein Callenfels', *Jaarboek Kon. Akad., Wet., 1937-38* (published in 1938), pp. 219-25 (with bibliography). According to Stutterheim, the two greatest merits of Van Stein Callenfels were: (*a*) that he had shown the great importance of the Javanese element in so-called Hindu-Javanese culture and therefore paved the way to a better understanding of that culture, and (2) that he was the first scholar who placed the prehistory of Indonesia upon a firm basis.

[156] F. D. K. Bosch, 'Een hypothese omtrent den oorsprong der Hindoe-Javaansche kunst', *Handelingen Eerste Congres Taal- Land- en Volkenkunde van Java* (1921), pp. 93-169. In this publication, Bosch proved that the so-called Hindu-Javanese temples were constructed by Javanese, who applied their knowledge of Indian handbooks. Some other publications by Bosch have been mentioned in notes 102, 103, and 104 above.

[157] Among the more recent epigraphic studies by Bosch I may mention: (1) 'De Inscriptie van Ligor', *Tijdschr. Bat. Gen.* (1941), lxxxi, 26-38; (2) 'De inscriptie van Kebon Kopi', *Bijdr. Kon. Inst.* (1941), c, 49-53. The former is a discussion of the Ligor inscription, one of the decisive documents for the interpretation of Çailendra rule in Java and Çrīvijaya. Bosch there refutes the interpretation proposed by Majumdar (BEFEO (1933), xxxiii, 127), but agrees with Chhabra's interpretation, according to which the text begins with the four-lined part and continues at the other side ('Expansion of Indo-Aryan Culture during Pallava Rule', *Journ. As. Soc. Bengal* (1938), i, 162). A later study by Bosch in which the same problem is discussed again will be mentioned in note 209 below. In the second article Bosch discussed one of the few inscriptions from West Java. Both the date of the document (expressed with symbolic cipher words) and its contents give rise to difficulties in interpretation. Bosch concluded that the text was engraved in the ninth century A.D., and that West Java was liberated from suzerainty of Çrīvijaya. The language of the document is Old Malay.

partly independent of the *Pararaton*. In a number of very detailed articles on episodes of the history of the Singhasari and Majapahit empires, Berg uses these sources and shows that in this way a solution, more satisfactory than that exclusively based upon *Pararaton*, *Nāgarakṛtāgama*, and inscriptions, may be arrived at. Many an episode in the Pararaton is an abbreviated version of a fuller account preserved in 'Middle-Javanese'[158] historical tradition, and cannot be satisfactorily interpreted without comparing this fuller account.[159] In another detailed study, Berg showed that purely literary works also may furnish important historical materials, since they were usually written by court poets for important occasions. Berg proved that the *Arjunawiwāha* was probably written at the occasion of the marriage of king Airlangga with a Sumatran princess; the court poet, in describing Arjuna's asceticism, struggle against demons, victory, and marriage, was giving at the same time a laudatory poem on king Airlangga, whose life may be divided into similar periods.[160] Finally, I will briefly mention Berg's treatise on Javanese historiography,[161] which gives completely new views about the aim and the background of Javanese historical writing. Berg gradually developed a new method of research on older Javanese history. Since the full consequences of this method have been taken in the most recent period of research, they will be discussed in the last part of this survey.

N. J. Krom continued his publications in this entire period. Although he was very well informed on the immense progress in research, one gets the impression that his fundamental views on older Indonesian history did not change in proportion to the new discoveries. Also his publications after 1931 are not numerous. They include an excellent article about the

---

[158] C. C. Berg, *De Middeljavaansche Historische Traditie*, doctoral thesis (Leiden, 1927). The book gives, *inter alia*, chapters on the history of the kingdom of Gelgel in Bali, especially its importance for the study of Old Javanese culture and an analysis of a number of works on the history of Majapahit written in Bali between about 1550 and 1600. Berg proved that the *Pararaton* is not the 'mother of historical *kidungs*', as Brandes had presumed; on the contrary, both the *Pararaton* and the *kidung* literature are derived from a 'broth' of historical tradition, though neither at the same time, nor at the same place. Sometimes the *Pararaton* gives a very abbreviated account on some episode, so that we are unable to ascertain its meaning without further materials. In that case, a comparison with *kidung* versions of the same episode may prove very valuable in determining the exact meaning of the *Pararaton* account. Sometimes, however, a *Pararaton* and a *kidung* version of some episode are based upon a different tradition. In such cases, we may prefer a *kidung* version to the *Pararaton* if it appears more likely, or if it better agrees with other data (such as inscriptions).

[159] In *Hindoe-Javaansche Geschiedenis*[2], pp. 351 ff., for instance, Krom followed Berg's account in op. cit., pp. 48–52 in order to get a more satisfactory survey on the events between the fall of Singhasari and the foundation of Majapahit.

[160] C. C. Berg, 'De *Arjunawiwāha*. Er-Langga's levensloop en bruiloftslied?', *Bijdr. Kon. Inst.* (1939), xcvii, 19–94. Cf. J. E. van Lohuizen-de Leeuw, 'The Beginnings of Old-Javanese Historical Literature', ibid. (1956), cxii, 383–94.

[161] C. C. Berg, 'Javaansche Geschiedschrijving', in F. W. Stapel, *Geschiedenis van Nederlandsch-Indië* (1939), ii, 7–148.

Karmavibhaṅga reliefs on the Barabuḍur,[162] an interesting discussion of the results of new excavations in the Palembang region,[163] and a new survey of the older Indonesian history.[164] The last-mentioned publication is a part of what was to be a monumental history of the Dutch East Indies, to be written by a large number of scholars under the redaction of F. W. Stapel. Five volumes have appeared between 1938 and 1940.[165] One of the dangers of this kind of publication is that each scholar treats his subject in his own way, and this danger has not been avoided in this case. In addition, there is a striking lack of proportion between the different parts. Thus, the older Indonesian history (approximately from the fifth to the fifteenth century) takes less than 190 pp. in Volume I, whereas a complete volume is needed to describe the eighteenth century. The latter volume, by the way, hardly teaches us anything about the history of Indonesia during that period. It is almost exclusively devoted to the Dutch East India Company. I have already called attention to the curious title of Krom's part for the older Indonesian history, viz., 'The Hindu Age';[166] in such a publication, this title is hardly misplaced, since Indonesia, in the later ages, is viewed from the Dutch East India Company's ships in the harbours of Bantěn and 'Batavia' or from its dusty offices in the city.[167] Krom's survey is not very satisfactory; the new views on Indonesian history have not sufficiently been taken into account; great portions are essentially condensations of Krom's larger work of 1931 and cannot sometimes be fully understood without consulting the *Hindu-Javanese History*. The recent Indonesian translation (entitled 'Zaman Hindu') can only be defended on the ground that very little serious literature on older Indonesian history is available in an Indonesian language.

J. C. van Leur is the last scholar to be mentioned in this brief account, especially since his approach is entirely different from that of all the scholars hitherto mentioned. Van Leur was essentially an economist,[168]

[162] N. J. Krom, 'Het Karmawibhangga op Borobudur', *Meded. Kon. Acad. Wet.*, Afd. Letteren (1933), lxxvi, B, 215–83 (based upon Sylvain Levi's study mentioned in note 99 above).

[163] N. J. Krom, 'De heiligdommen van Palembang', ibid., N.R. (1938), i, 397–423. This article is a critical discussion of the results of research in the Palembang region by F. M. Schnitger; cf. note 173 below. A very brief discussion of Schnitger's discoveries was given by Krom in 'Antiquities of Palembang', *Annual Bibliography of Indian Archaeology for the year 1932* (1933), 29–33.

[164] N. J. Krom, 'Het Hindoe-Tijdperk', in F. W. Stapel, *Geschiedenis van Nederlandsch-Indië* (1938), i, 112–298.

[165] The sixth volume on the twentieth century, to be written by Brugmans, never appeared.

[166] Cf. *Orientatie* (1954), xlvi, 641–3.

[167] J. C. van Leur, *Tijdschr. Bat. Gen.* (1930), lxxix, 589–95.

[168] Van Leur was, however, trained as a civil officer in the Netherlands East Indies administration. His main field of study was socio-economics, where he was strongly influenced by Max Weber. Van Leur studied Indonesian history from a viewpoint completely different from that of the other scholars. He mainly limited his research to the seventeenth and eighteenth centuries, but the pattern of Asian trade which he sketched in his main work, *Eenige beschouwingen betreffende den ouden Aziatischen handel* (1934) (i.e., Some reflections on the old Asian trade), is not limited to the seventeenth and eighteenth century, but may be applied (of course, with some changes) to

who examined the data of the Dutch East India Company in order to get a better idea of the Asiatic commerce of the pre-capitalist age. Van Leur proved that the importance of this commerce had been grossly underestimated in the past and, as a consequence, the prevailing ideas about the seventeenth and eighteenth centuries need thorough revision. Although Van Leur specialized in the seventeenth and eighteenth centuries, with which all his main works deal, it cannot be denied that his publications open wide views for the study of the older history, too. Van Leur sometimes discussed essential parts of the older history, such as the background of Indian influence,[169] but had no opportunity to continue his research owing to his premature death.[170] An important aspect of the work of Van Leur is that it constitutes an effort to treat the history of Indonesia as a whole. Owing to several factors—not only the difference in sources, but still more the completely different approach—there has been an almost complete separation in the research on the periods before and after the impact of the West.[171] Van Leur's approach would make it possible—at least in principle—to bridge the gap between these two parts of Indonesian history.

In the above survey the work of only a few scholars could be discussed with some detail. I need not add that many other scholars worked on problems of Indonesian history during this period, such as A. J. Bernet Kempers, who published an excellent study on the relations between Nālandā and Indo-Javanese art,[172] F. M. Schnitger, who started excavations in several parts of Sumatra,[173] K. C. Crucq, who published a number

the earlier period, too. Both his main work and some other studies were recently published in English in an abbreviated version, which is more readable than the original Dutch text (J. C. van Leur, *Indonesian Trade and Society* (1955)).

[169] J. C. van Leur, *Eenige beschouwingen betreffende den ouden Aziatischen handel*, pp. 114–56. Considering the position of Indian traders in Indonesia in more modern times, Van Leur refutes the opinion (cf. Krom, *Hindoe-Javaansche Geschiedenis*², pp. 89 ff.) that Indian culture would have been brought to Indonesia mainly by Indian traders, but gives the main credit to Indonesian ruling circles who appealed to Indian priests and other experts. For the importance of Van Leur's ideas, cf. especially F. D. K. Bosch, 'Het vraagstuk van de Hindoe-kolonisatie van den Archipel' (1946) (i.e. the problem of Hindu colonization of the (Indonesian) Archipelago).

[170] Van Leur fell as a naval officer in the Battle of Java in the beginning of 1942.

[171] As a typical example I may quote the discussions on the erection of a study group for Indonesian History in addition to the older study group for Linguistics, Geography and Ethnology of Indonesia (cf. *Jaarboek Bat. Gen.* (1939), vi, 54 and 62). In 1938 it was decided that the new study group should be limited to more recent history, whereas prehistory, archaeology, and older history would remain within the study group of Linguistics, Geography, and Ethnology.

[172] A. J. Bernet Kempers, *The bronzes of Nālandā and Hindu-Javanese Art* (1933).

[173] F. M. Schnitger, *The Archaeology of Hindoo Sumatra* (1937). Some smaller publications by the same author are: (a) *Oudheidkundige Vondsten in Palembang*, 4 vols. (1935); *Oudheidkundige Vondsten in Padang Lawas* (1936); *Hindoe-Oudheden aan de Batang Hari*, 2 vols. (vol. ii: Appendix) (1936); 'Vondsten te Moeara Takoes', *Tijdschr. Bat. Gen.* (1936), lxxvi, 331 f.; 'De tempel van Simangambat (Zuid Tapanoeli)', ibid. (1936), pp. 334–6; 'De herkomst van het Kĕrtanagara-beeld te Berlijn', ibid. (1936), pp. 328–30; 'Het grootste Hindoe-beeld van Sumatra', *Tijdschr. Aardr. Gen.*, IIde Serie (1937), liv, 570–5 (on a huge Bhairava statue from Sungai Langsat); 'Five reliefs at Poelo in Tapanuli', *Journ. Gr. India Soc.* (1937), iv, 43 f.; 'Three Indo-Javanese Gangā images', ibid. (1937), iv, 122–4; *Forgotten Kingdoms in Sumatra* (1939) (cf. Winstedt, *Journ. Royal Asiat. Soc.* (1939), pp. 646 f.).

of epigraphic notes,[174] H. Maclaine Pont, who excavated parts of the ancient *kraton* of Majapahit,[175] M. A. Muusses with some articles on archaeological and epigraphic subjects,[176] and a few others.[177]

To end my survey on the period from 1926 to 1942 it might be good to consider the main results achieved in these sixteen years. The age of startling discoveries and of pioneering belongs to the past, although important discoveries were still regularly made. On the other hand, a new generation of scholars, better trained for their tasks than those in the first period, re-examined and re-interpreted the epigraphic, literary, and archaeological sources and arrived at conclusions which seem to change not only the details, but gradually even the great lines of the picture drawn at the beginning of this period. No real attempt to rewrite the history of Indonesia on the basis of the new results was, however, undertaken; this was partly due to serious disagreements between the research scholars; even on some fundamental questions no *communis opinio* had as yet been established. Some great lines along which research developed in these sixteen years can, however, be distinguished: increasing stress laid upon the Indonesian fundaments of the older culture, the beginning of co-operation in research of different areas in South East Asia and the beginning of economical and sociological studies on ancient Indonesia.

Third Period

Not much needs to be said here about research during the Japanese

[174] K. C. Crucq, 'Epigraphische Aanteekeningen', I, *Oudheidk. Versl. 1930*, Bijl. F, pp. 216–34; II, ibid., Bijl. G, pp. 235–9.

[175] H. Maclaine Pont, 'Madjapahit; poging te reconstructie van het stadsplan' (i.e.: Majapahit; attempt at reconstruction of the plan of the city), *Oudheidk. Versl. 1924*, pp. 36–75; ibid. 1924, pp. 157–99; ibid. 1926, pp. 100–29.

[176] M. A. Muusses, 'Singhawikramawardhana', *Feestbundel Bat. Gen.* (1929), ii, 207–14 (attempt at illuminating fifteenth-century history of Majapahit; cf. W. F. Stutterheim, *Jaarb. Bat. Gen.* (1938), v, 117–19).

[177] It is impossible and unnecessary to give a somewhat exhaustive list of publications on older Indonesian history during this period. I only add a few references: F. W. van Naerssen, 'Twee koperen oorkonden van Balitung in het Koloniaal Instituut te Amsterdam', *Bijdr. Kon. Inst.* (1937), xcv, 441–61 (good publication of two interesting documents of the beginning of the tenth century A.D.); F. H. van Naerssen, 'Hindoejavaansche overblijfselen op Sumbawa', *Tijdschr. Aardr. Gen.*, 2nd ser. (1938), lv, 90–100 (based upon unpublished notes by Rouffaer; in addition to the materials given in this article, some other remains of the Majapahit period were discovered a few years ago by a team conducted by G. J. Held; these confirm the data about Dompo in the *Nāgarakṛtāgama* and *Pararaton*); H. K. J. Cowan, 'Bijdrage tot de kennis van de geschiedenis van het rijk Samoedra-Pasé', *Tijdschr. Bat. Gen.* (1938), lxxviii, 204–14; Th. P. Galestin, *Houtbouw op Ostjavaansche tempelreliefs* (1936); J. Blom, *Antiquities of Singasari*, doct. thesis (1939); G. W. J. Drewes, 'Over werkelijke en vermeende geschiedschrijving in de Nieuwjavaansche litteratuur' (i.e. On real and pretended Historiography in modern Javanese Literature; mainly a critical discussion of the publication mentioned in note 161 above), *Djåwå* (1939), xix, 244–57; J. Ph. Vogel, 'Aanteekeningen op de inscriptie van Tjanggal in Midden-Java', *Bijdr. Kon. Inst.* (1942), c, 443–7 (some important notes on the interpretation of the oldest dated document of Java); cf. also Stutterheim, 'Note on cultural relations between South India and Java', *Tijdschr. Bat. Gen.* (1938), lxxix, 73–84, and *infra*, p. 16.

occupation of Indonesia (from March 1942 to August 1945). As a matter
of fact, research almost completely stopped during these years in Indonesia.[178] It is true that some research continued in the Netherlands and in
other European countries. Thus, the Dutch 'Bijdragen' were continued;
even a doctoral thesis on historical inscriptions in German and Danish
collections appeared during the war.[179] We do not, however, notice important new developments in views on Indonesian history.

Much more should be said about the most recent period, from 1945 to
1956. As is well known, the Republic of Indonesia proclaimed her independence in 1945, but her sovereignty was not recognized by all countries
until the last days of 1949 after some very serious armed conflicts with the
Netherlands. After the complete transfer of sovereignty all cultural institutes were taken over by or came under the control of the Government of
the Republic of Indonesia. Especially from 1950 on, national education
programmes with national history as an important component have constituted an object of both public and private concern.

It may be understood that the young republic had not much time to
devote to historical research between 1945 and 1950. The works on Indonesian history written in these years were either textbooks for primary or
secondary education or works which had a function in the national struggle. The works of the former group cannot be discussed here in detail.
They were emergency books written by authors who had neither sufficient
training nor materials at their disposal. Among the textbooks for secondary
instruction the most widely used was Sanusi Pane, *Sedjarah Indonesia*, in four
volumes. The author, who has great merit as a poet and a prose writer
strongly influenced by Indian culture, has not succeeded in giving a reliable
account of older Indonesian history (in the first volume); this part contains
a considerable number of misunderstandings and hardly takes account of
the progress in our knowledge since 1931.

Among the works of the second group I will mention two books by
Muhammad Yamin, *Diponegoro* and *Gadjah Mada*. The former deals with
the greatest national hero of the nineteenth century; his biography aimed
at giving a brilliant example for the struggle for independence. The latter
deals with the great minister of the fourteenth century, who used all means
to unite all the Indonesian islands under the crown of Majapahit. The
materials for this book were mostly taken from Krom's history, but differently interpreted. The unity of Indonesia is strongly stressed and this again

[178] Contrary to what happened in the Netherlands, all periodicals on older Indonesian history
and culture (such as the 'Tijdschrift', 'Verhandelingen', 'Jaarboek', 'Bibliotheca Javanica' of the
Royal Batavian Society; 'Djåwå' of the 'Java Instituut'; 'Mededeelingen van de Kirtya Liefrinck-
van der Tuuk', etc.) were stopped during the Japanese occupation. As far as I know, no books on
older history were published in Indonesia during this period; therefore, as far as publications are
concerned, the Japanese occupation seems to be a complete blank. Cf., however, *infra*, note 185.
[179] F. H. van Naerssen, *Oudjavaansche Oorkonden in Duitsche en Deensche Verzamelingen* (1943).

may be easily understood since the book was composed in a time when Indonesia was divided into a Republican and a Federalist part; in the latter, a number of autonomous states was erected under Dutch supervision.[180] Both these books are well written and have been best-sellers, so that several editions have been necessary. They give an extremely nationalistic view of history, but free from distortions. That they represent a more or less official view may be concluded from the introductions by President Sukarno. In this connection, I may mention several books by the same author, although they do not belong to this period. In the first place, there are three theatre pieces based on older history; the first one is named *Ken Arok dan Ken Dedes* (first performed in 1928, printed in 1934, and reprinted in 1952); the other two, which have not been printed, but repeatedly played, are based on the struggle of king Airlangga, related in the Calcutta inscription[181] and the events concerning Çrīvijaya and the Çailendras according to the Nālandā inscription.[182] The events are dramatized, and, although the historical sources are followed for the great lines, many modern thoughts are put into the mouth of the main figures. A few years ago, Yamin published a book entitled *6000 tahun sang Marah-Putih*, in which he tried to prove that red and white, the colours of the Indonesian flag, have been national colours for six thousand years.[183] The same author is preparing monographs on Airlangga and Ādityavarman.[184]

Some research was continued in the Prambanan region in Central Java (Plaosan, Ratubaka) in spite of the difficult circumstances.[185]

Finally, I will mention the erection of the first national university during this period, the 'Gadjah Mada' at Djogjakarta.[186] National history was taught there by such able scholars as Dr. Poerbatjaraka and Dr. Prijono.

During the same period, some research was done in the Dutch-controlled federal area, where work was taken up again in the Archaeological Service and elsewhere. The old Tijdschrift reappeared from 1948 on, but irregularly.[187] In Holland, the 'Bijdragen' were continued and a new periodical, *Indonesië*, appeared (1948 ff.); in the latter, numerous articles on Indonesian history were published. Of the larger books published in

[180] Cf. George McTurnan Kahin, *Nationalism and Revolution in Indonesia* (1952), *passim*.

[181] Muh. Yamin, *Kesetiaan Narottama kepada prabu Airlangga* (i.e.: The Loyalty of Narottama towards king Airlangga).

[182] Muh. Yamin, *Djikalau Dewi Tara berkata* (i.e.: If Queen Tārā could relate).

[183] Muh. Yamin, *6000 tahun Sang Merah Putih* (1954).

[184] In addition, a doctoral thesis on the state organization of the Majapahit empire is now being printed.

[185] A survey of archaeological work from 1942 to 1948 was given by Suhamir in *Oudheidk. Versl.* 1948 (published in 1950), Bijl. A, pp. 20–41. For the two following years, cf. *Oudheidk. Versl. 1949* (published in 1950), pp. 1–25, and *Laporan Tahunan Dinas Purbakala Republik Indonesia 1950* (published in 1952), pp. 4–21.

[186] The only other university in Indonesia at that time was at Djakarta in the Dutch occupied zone.

[187] The last numbers appeared in 1952 after considerable financial and other difficulties.

this period I mention B. Vlekke, *Nusantara*[188] and H. J. de Graaf, *Geschiedenis van Indonesië*.[189] These books hold in common the assumption that the older history of about ten centuries only constitutes a kind of introduction, so that the titles give a wrong impression. The impression they give is as though Indonesian history only began to be interesting when regular contact between Europe and Indonesia was established. Both books stress once more the gap between the older and the more recent history of Indonesia: for the traditional historian who looks at the world from some place in Western Europe, Indonesian history before the impact with the West is still a field outside his scope of interest. This moreover appears from the history programmes of Dutch universities. In an 'Apparatus for the study of history' composed by the well-known Dutch historian, J. M. Romein, in 1949,[190] one looks in vain for titles of works on the history of Asian countries before about A.D. 1500. Although Romein, who seems free from colonial prejudices, taught at an Indonesian university from 1952 to 1953, it does not seem that his ideas have fundamentally changed about this subject.[191]

[188] B. Vlekke, *Nusantara, A History of the East Indian Archipelago* (1943). This book was published in the United States during the war, but a second edition appeared in Dutch after the war with the title *Geschiedenis van den Indischen Archipel* (1946). The portion on older history is superficial and hardly more than a short extract from Krom's *Hindoe-Javaansche Geschiedenis* in a popular form, whereas the vast literature which appeared after Krom's work has hardly been consulted.

[189] H. J. de Graaf, *Geschiedenis van Indonesië* (1948). On the whole, the part of this book dealing with older history is far better than that of the work mentioned in note 188, since also other literature but Krom's book has been consulted, though not sufficiently. Here, too, the part dealing with Indonesian history of before the sixteenth century constitutes only a tiny part of the book.

[190] J. M. Romein, *Apparaat voor de studie der geschiedenis* (1949). The book is a critical bibliography on general history with a tremendous number of titles accompanied by brief notes on each title. It was especially adapted to the use by students in the History Department of the Municipal University at Amsterdam. It is curious that general history does not seem to include the history of Asian countries. On Indonesian history only one book was mentioned, viz., the five volumes of Stapel's work mentioned on p. 11—curiously enough, between works on Dutch history (which is a good judgement on that work, with the exception of the first volume and the part of the second volume written by Berg).

[191] According to a newspaper report Professor Romein declared after his return from Indonesia that progress in the field of Indonesian history had been unsatisfactory because there were hardly any real historians working in Indonesia, but only archaeologists, philologists, etc. I think that this statement is due to insufficient knowledge of the source-materials of older Indonesian history. In this respect, there is a great difference between the European and most of the Asian source-materials. The historian of the countries of Western Europe would have access to most of the materials without making profound philological and archaeological studies (although it would be extremely useful if he did), but his colleague in South or South East Asia could not do much useful work without such studies—at least as far as the older history is concerned. The latter is usually faced with few, but extremely difficult, materials. Even if the data have been well published by philologists and archaeologists, there are almost always controversies on their interpretation as sources. The historian should be sufficiently trained in philology, archaeology, and several other branches as well (such as palaeography, customary law and ethnology) to have an independent opinion on the interpretation of his sources, whereas the traditional training for historians of Europe will not prove a great help. On the other hand, it cannot be denied that much more would have been achieved if the philologists and archaeologists working on older Indonesian history had had some training in general history, too. As a matter of fact, specialized

An important consequence of Indonesia's struggle for independence was that Indonesian affairs became a matter of world-wide interest; it is no longer something which exclusively or even especially concerned the Netherlands. The world's interest naturally focused around the more recent, especially the contemporary, history. For the older history, how- ever, Dutch scholarship had, and still has, a considerable advance owing to a longer tradition of studies and more direct contacts with Indonesia. Scholars in other European countries may have been no less interested, but had more limited means for detailed study at their disposal.[192]

Another important consequence of the more recent political develop- ments is the concept of South East Asia. Probably the South East Asia Command during the Pacific war has had some influence on the origina- tion of the term, which was at least unusual before the war. Anyhow, it is now fully realized that the countries of South East Asia have numerous common features and common interests.[193] Attempts have been made to treat also the history of older South East Asia as a whole, although it seems that the present state of knowledge makes it inevitable that such a history is composed of separate histories of each of the South East Asian coun- tries.[194] A very important work on the older history of this area was pub- lished by Cœdès in 1948, viz., *Les états hindouisés d'Indochine et d'Indonésie*.[195] There, the history of South East Asia is divided into a number of periods

training in the history of Indonesia has never existed in Dutch Universities. The programmes of Indonesian Universities are better adapted to the education of historians on History of Indonesia, although we still find some separation between the older and the more recent history. Thus, the University of Djakarta offers two possibilities: first, there is the branch 'Sedjarah Kuno dan Ilmu Purbakala Indonesia' (i.e.: Old History and Archaeology of Indonesia), which comprises *inter alia* the study of archaeology, prehistory, cultural anthropology, general linguistics, Old and Modern Javanese, but no modern history or history of European countries; second, there is the branch 'Sedjarah' (History) with general historical education in the first part of the studies (roughly corresponding with Bachelor of Arts) and the possibility of specializing on Indonesian History in its second part. In the latter case, however, the accent is laid on more recent Indo- nesian history.

[192] A major handicap for students outside the Netherlands is the language question: the great majority of the studies on Indonesian history is in Dutch. In addition, libraries outside Indonesia and the Netherlands do not seem to have sufficient periodicals and books to make detailed research on Indonesian history possible.

[193] A number of the peoples of South East Asia are originally related, sometimes very closely (Indonesia, Malaya, and the Philippines; Thai and Laos), so that there must be a similar cul- tural background. More important perhaps is the fact that all the peoples of South East Asia underwent more or less strong Indian influence, which was an essential factor in shaping their cultures, especially the refined court cultures. Numerous common features are obscured by present political differences: some of the countries follow a neutral foreign policy, others are members of the S.E.A.T.O., one is in the British Commonwealth, and another within the com- munist sphere of influence.

[194] This is not only true with South East Asia, but applies as well to other areas such as Western Europe, where mutual relations between the different countries have certainly been far more intensive than between the countries of South East Asia.

[195] This is, in fact, the second edition of the *Histoire ancienne des Etats hindouisés d'Extrême Orient*, published in 1944 at Hanoi. The second edition appeared four years later in the series 'Histoire du Monde' edited under the direction of M. E. Cavaignac.

based on common features as far as proved possible,[196] but within these periods each part of the area is treated separately. The reader is thus given the opportunity to note that the events in the separate areas are often in some way interrelated and that events in one area may have consequences for other areas. Cœdès did not stress such relations (although he occasionally suggests them), certainly because he rightly considered that much research still has to be done before more precise knowledge is acquired. I think that this is an important task for the future.[197]

In the last part of this paper, it is necessary to give a few details about research during the last six years. Special reference is made to research in Indonesia itself. I need not add that it is extremely difficult to get a clear idea of the progress in such recent times, especially at a place where books from abroad arrive with considerable delay. The survey which follows is therefore provisional.

When the Republic of Indonesia saw its independence recognized by the Netherlands and the entire world, a period of real reconstruction could begin. Education was an essential part of this effort and the teaching of national history was an important part of any educational programme. However, there were (and still are) tremendous difficulties to be overcome. The question was how to teach national history with only very few qualified teachers and no reliable textbooks. Similar difficulties existed for the universities. An emergency training centre for history teachers was established at Jakarta in the beginning of 1950, soon followed by similar centres in other towns.[198] In 1951 a Commission for National History,

[196] The history of ancient South East Asia is divided into twelve periods varying in length between two centuries and about thirty years, preceded by two introductory chapters and rounded off by a Conclusion. The title of the second edition of the work shows that particular attention is given to Indonesia and Indochina. Each chapter bears a title in which the period is briefly characterized. The titles of ch. XIII and ch. XIV (respectively the decline and the fall of the Hindu Empires) are chosen with reference to the mainland of South East Asia. For an Indonesian it is really strange that the history of the great Majapahit empire is dealt with in these chapters.

[197] The materials given by Cœdès seem to make a few general conclusions possible. Thus, one can draw the conclusion that there was no scope for more than one great naval power in South East Asia (consecutively Fu-nan, Çrīvijaya, Majapahit, and Malacca). It may be understood that China was always particularly interested in the country which held that naval power. One sees it clearly in the beginning of the fifteenth century, when China seems no longer interested in Majapahit, but establishes good relations with Malacca. Is it not curious that the first Javanese embassy arriving in China after a long interruption at the end of 992 A.D., takes place just at the time when (East) Java becomes a naval power capable of attacking Çrīvijaya? (cf. Groeneveldt, *Notes*, pp. 17 f.). There seems to have been some balance of power in South East Asia in ancient times. On the other hand, not much is known yet about relations between the South East Asian countries in ancient times; for a very interesting hypothesis cf. F. D. K. Bosch, 'De laatste der Pāṇḍawa's', *Bijdr. Kon. Inst.* (1948), xiv, 541–71. Cf. also Cœdès, *Etats hindouisés*, pp. 154, 168, 171 ff., 210, and *supra*, notes 92–96.

[198] These training centres were intended especially for those already teaching history at secondary schools, but without having good diplomas. They were established at Djakarta, Bandung, Semarang, Bukittinggi, and Medan. Lectures are given in the evening in order to enable the candidates to continue their teaching task in the morning. The basic training course

composed of Indonesian and also a few Dutch scholars, was established but never yielded any concrete results.[199] Some of the older institutes still exist, but show few signs of activity. This especially applies to the former 'Royal Batavian Society for Arts and Sciences' which became the 'Lembaga Kebudajaan Indonesia' (Institute for Indonesian Culture) in 1950. Its Museum and Library are in an excellent condition, but receive insufficient funds to remain up to date by new acquisitions. A few issues of the 'Tijd-schrift' have still appeared, but very irregularly; it now seems to have ceased altogether. On the other hand, some new periodicals have taken its place. Thus, the Institute for Language and Culture of the University of Indonesia at Jakarta publishes *Bahasa dan Budaja* (Language and Cul-ture). Most articles concern problems of the Indonesian national language, and sociology, but questions about history are not completely absent. The Department of Culture of the Ministry of Education publishes a periodical named *Budaja* (Culture). The Archaeological Service continues its pub-lications of Annual Reports and of a new periodical called *Amerta*, three issues of which have appeared up to now. As with the other publications mentioned above, it is less concerned with research than with the effort of stimulating the interest of larger circles in archaeological work.

It looks as though there is, at present, a serious crisis in historical research. It is true that practical difficulties are largely responsible for this state of affairs. The few specialized scholars all have other tasks, which take all or almost all of their energy; they are usually engaged at two or even more universities, sometimes more than a thousand miles apart. Lecturing tasks of more than twenty hours a week are not exceptional. A university lecturer has hardly the time to read the publications on his own subject, even if he succeeds in obtaining them. It is obvious that not much serious research may be expected in these circumstances. It can also be under-stood that the Government attaches more importance to national educa-tion than to research.

But practical difficulties do not account for everything; there may be a more serious crisis at the background. I think it is what might be termed an ambivalent attitude towards the past. This is especially true for the history of the last three to four centuries. The prevailing attitude of the cultivated Indonesian is one of extreme nationalism. He sees the last three to four centuries mainly in terms of foreign interference in his country's

lasts for two years and comprises the history of (*a*) Indonesia, (*b*) South Asia and Middle East, (*c*) Europe and the United States, (*d*) East Asia. In addition to this basic training course, there is a possibility of a further two years' course with specialization in one of the four above-mentioned fields.

[199] The task of this Commission may be continued by the Madjelis Ilmu Pengetahuan Indo-nesia (Indonesian Scientific Council) which, at present, consists of two Branches, viz., Science and Humaniora. The Council has a small governing body which assists the Government in promoting Science and Letters, and a larger advisory body.

domestic affairs, occupation by foreign troops, foreign rule and suppression. He might be aware that not only foreign countries are to blame, for such events have only been possible because the Indonesian society was divided. As a rule, he is really interested only in the resistance movements, especially in figures such as Sultan Agung, Trunodjojo, Suropati, Diponegoro, Imam Bondjol, Teuku Umar, and the main figures in the national struggle for freedom since the beginning of this century. Obviously this attitude is not favourable for real historical research.

There are different kinds of psychological resistance towards the older periods. First there are strict Moslim circles who consider the pre-Islamic period as a dark age which need not be studied seriously; these circles are fortunately rare. Other circles think of the older period in terms of feudalism; one may admire the beautiful temples of the past, but one should not forget how much the people suffered in order to construct them. The still clear remnants of feudalism in the modern society lend substance to the above opinion, especially among the younger generation. Finally, the most serious kind of resistance concerns less history itself than our knowledge about older history. It is often brought forward that almost nothing definite is known, that older history consists rather of theories than of facts. As a matter of fact, a university teacher may explain to his students that Chö-po, frequently mentioned in Chinese sources, represents Java according to Cœdès, Sumatra according to Ferrand, a part of the Malay peninsula according to Moens, and Western Borneo according to Braddell. Students will smile and ask the teacher which of the above opinions is correct. If they do not get a clear reply, they will ask again why the history of their own country is so very different from European history, a question which may put the teacher in a difficult position. I myself used to answer that still a lot of research has to be done before we get certainty. Recently, I discussed the theories of Professor Berg on Singhasari and Majapahit. One of the comments of the students was: 'of course the theory of a Dutchman'. They felt it as an attempt to minimize the greatness of a figure such as Ken Angrok and of an empire such as Majapahit—an attempt which they seemed to connect with the political attitude of the Netherlands in recent times.

Whatever one may think about such comments, they reflect a great deal of public opinion. This attitude may be unscientific, but it should never be forgotten that their history means something more to the Indonesians than just a number of academic questions. On the other hand, the above comments reflect some of the dissatisfaction with the results of Western research up to now.

In spite of these different kinds of resistance, there is great interest in national history. Indonesian books on historical subjects, whatever their quality, are best-sellers. Lectures on history attract numerous listeners.

References to national history are frequent in public speeches (even in the election campaigns last year) and in newspaper articles.

Real research has not been intensive in Indonesia for these last six years, but it has not, fortunately, been completely absent. Poerbatjaraka, whose publications have been discussed above, published two larger books in this period. In *Kepustakaan Djawa* (written in co-operation with Tardjan Hadidjaja), he gave a brief discussion of no less than eighty-four literary works in Old and Modern Javanese.[200] In *Riwajat Indonesia*, Djilid 1, he discussed the earliest history up to the end of the eighth century. It is an excellent little book, in which a clear and readable account of this period is given. Unfortunately, the subsequent volumes have not appeared up to now.

Muh. Yamin published not only his *6000 tahun Sang Merah-Putih* during this period, but also a number of newspaper articles on historical subjects. One of these deserves particular attention since it is a new attempt to divide Indonesian history into five great periods (*Pantjawarsa*),[201] viz., 'the beginning of history' (up to the beginning of the Christian era), 'the basis of history' (from 0 to 600), 'the national period' (from 600 to 1500), 'the international period' (from 1500 to 1900) and 'the age of the Proclamation' (from 1900 on). This division has, I think, great advantages over the divisions hitherto accepted. Thus, the term 'colonial period' has rightly been avoided; one could object against 'international period', which may easily be misunderstood, but it is difficult to find a more suitable term; the term 'age of the Proclamation' is a happy choice since it stresses the most important aspect of the last fifty-six years for Indonesia. It is the exact opposite of the Dutch-centred view which has given the title 'the reign of Queen Wilhelmina' to approximately the same period of Indonesian history.

L. C. Damais published a number of articles on epigraphic studies in the *Bulletin de l' Ecole Française d' Extrême-Orient*. These studies based on precise calculations of Old Javanese dates will give a sounder chronological basis to a future description of the older Indonesian history.[202]

[200] R. Ng. Poerbatjaraka and Tardjan Hadidjaja, *Kepustakaan Djawa*, i.e. 'Javanese Literature', published by the Djambatan (Djakarta/Amsterdam, 1952). An edition in the Javanese language (*Kapustakan Djawi*) appeared at the same time. Javanese literature is discussed in seven chapters: I. The oldest group (before about A.D. 1000), consisting of sixteen works all in prose except for the Old Javanese Rāmāyaṇa, II. Kakawin's of the Kaḍiri period (ten works), III. Kakawin's of the Majapahit period (ten works), IV. Prose works in Middle Javanese language (end of the Majapahit period; five works), V. Poetry in Middle Javanese (five works), VI. Islamic literature of the sixteenth, seventeenth, and first half of the eighteenth century, and VII. Literature of the beginning of the Surakarta period (in the last chapters fourteen and twenty-four works respectively).

[201] This division of Indonesian history was also discussed by the author in a public lecture given at Malang in June 1955. It will be dealt with in detail in a new publication by the same author, viz., a book on the state government and administration of the Majapahit empire, which is still in print.

[202] The main publications by L. C. Damais are: (1) 'Epigraphische Aantekeningen' (I. Lokapāla—Kayuwangi, II. Kāmeçwara I—Bāmeçwara, III. Çṛngga—Kṛtajaya, IV. Çrī Jayawarṣa Çāstraprabhu, V. Jayabhūpati van Suṇḍa, VI. Sang Ratu—Çrī Mahārāja, VII. Sang Ratu i

Finally, I will mention the work on Old Balinese inscriptions by R. Goris. Recently the first two volumes of his new edition of *Prasasti Bali* have appeared with complete translations into Dutch, detailed introduction, word index, etc. This edition deals with all the epigraphic materials from Bali earlier than A.D. 1040.[203] It is hardly necessary to add that the importance of this edition is not limited to those interested in Bali; not only are the events in Bali often connected with those in Java, but there is also much in older Balinese culture which is common to a considerable part of Indonesia, so that this new edition will certainly prove useful to the study of the older Indonesian history as a whole. I further mention two other works by the same author, first a brief outline of older Balinese history in Indonesian[204] and second, a collection of plates on Balinese culture with copious explanations.[205]

In the Netherlands research continued, though mainly by the older generation of scholars. I have already mentioned some important publications by Bosch of before 1942. In this period of research, Bosch published an important article on older Indonesian culture, partly a discussion of new theories of Quaritch Wales.[206] One of the conclusions, which is fully guaranteed by the facts in my opinion, is that the Indian influence in Indonesia was not so much the result of an Indian effort to expand their culture as rather of Indonesian initiative in assimilating those elements of Indian culture to which they felt attracted. This effort was primarily a consequence of the great number of Indonesians who visited sacred spots and studied with famous Indian teachers. A perhaps not very precise, but presumably strong, argument in favour of this interpretation is the text which was used for half of all the reliefs of Java's greatest monument, the

Halu, VIII. Centraal gezag of koningkrijkjes?), *Tijdschr. Bat. Gen.* (1949), lxxxiii, 1–26; (2) 'Études d'Épigraphie Indonésienne', I. Méthode de réduction des dates javanaises en dates européennes, II. La date des inscriptions en ère de Sañjaya, BEFEO (1951), xlv, Fasc. 1, 1–64, III. Liste des principales inscriptions datées de l'Indonésie, ibid. (1952), xlvi, Fasc. 1, 1–105, IV. Discussion de la date des inscriptions, ibid. (1955), xlvii, Fasc. 1, 7–290; (3) 'Études Balinaises', I. La colonette de Sanur, II. L'inscription sancrite de Pejeng, in *Mélanges publiés en l'honneur du Cinquantenaire de l'École Francaise d'Extrême-Orient,* BEFEO (1947–50, 1951), xliv, Fasc. 1, 121–40. For a detailed discussion of Damais' method in reducing Old Javanese dates, cf. F. D. K. Bosch, *Bijdr. Kon. Inst.* (1956), cxii, 331–3.

[203] Roelof Goris, *Prasasti Bali, Inscriptions vóór Anak Wungçu* (1954), I. with Introduction and Transcriptions, II. with translations into Dutch, summaries in Indonesian and in English, Word Index, Chronological list of the inscriptions, Alphabetic Index of the sites of discovery of the inscriptions and ten plates.

[204] R. Goris, *Sedjarah Bali Kuno* (1948).

[205] R. Goris (Text) and P. L. Dronkers (Photography); *Bali, Atlas Kebudajaan, Cults and Customs*, with the help of A. N. J. Th. à Th. van der Hoop, R. Bonnet, no date. This book gives a fine collection of more than two hundred photographs on various aspects of old and modern Balinese Culture with introductions and brief explanatory notes in Indonesian, English, and Dutch.

[206] F. D. K. Bosch, ' "Local Genius" en Oud-Javaanse Kunst', *Meded. Kon. Akad. Wet., Afd. Lett., N.R.* (1952), xv, 1–25. Cf. H. G. Quaritch Wales, 'Culture Change in Greater India', *Journ. Royal As. Soc.* (1948), pp. 2–32; 'The Dong-son Genius and the Evolution of Cham Art', ibid. (1949), pp. 34–45; *The Making of Greater India* (1951).

Gaṇḍavyūha on Barabuḍur. This text describes the wanderings of the merchant sons of Sudhana, who travels throughout India and visits no less than sixty-four teachers before he finds the highest truth. Might Sudhana be a symbol of the Javanese pilgrims and students who went to the holy spots in India and to the great teachers at Nālandā and elsewhere? asks Bosch, and I think we may answer in the affirmative, in view of the numerous other materials given by Bosch, which fit in well with this view. Especially the eclectic features of Indian elements in Indonesian culture are satisfactorily explained in this way.[207] It is further noted that Van Leur arrived at similar conclusions based on the patterns of commerce in older Indonesia.[208] Among other publications by Bosch I mention a new hypothesis on the Çailendra problem,[209] based upon a new interpretation of the Ligor inscription by Cœdès;[210] further a very interesting address on the relations between Indochina and Indonesia, pronounced at the occasion of the fiftieth anniversary of the École Française d'Extrême-Orient.[211] A comparison with an article by Stutterheim published a quarter of a century earlier shows how much our ideas have changed in a relatively short period.[212] Finally, I will mention an important article by Bosch on the relations between Indian influence and original Indonesian beliefs in Java,[213] in which an attempt at determining Indian and Indonesian elements in older Javanese culture is made. Contrary to the theories of Stutterheim and others, Bosch considers the Old Javanese culture essentially Indian, whereas the Indonesian elements, however important they may be, are limited to several kinds of substitution and extension of Indian elements.

It appears from the above that the most recent discussion on the relation between Indian and Indonesian elements in older Indonesian culture again stresses the Indian basis of that culture and therefore seems to come nearer to Krom's views than similar discussions in the second part of our second period did. The problem is very important, not only for Indonesian

[207] Cf. Bosch, art. cit., pp. 20 f. Cf. also p. 6 above (Chhabra's studies on the *yupa* inscriptions). From a new discovery (the construction of an Abhayagirivihāra in Central Java in A.D. 792) it appears that not only the Indian continent, but also the island of Ceylon should be reckoned with. Krom (e.g. in *Het oude Java en zijn Kunst*, second impression (1943), pp. 14 ff.) laid far too much stress upon South East India.

[208] Cf. note 169 above.

[209] F. D. K. Bosch, 'Çrīvijaya, de Çailendra- en de Sañjaayvaṃca', *Bijdr. Kon. Inst.* (1952) cviii, 113–23.

[210] G. Cœdès, 'Le Çailendra "tueur des heros ennemis" ', *Bingkisan Budi* (1950), pp. 58–70.

[211] F. D. K. Bosch, 'Les rapports entre l'Indochine et l'Indonésie', in L. Malleret, *Le Cinquantenaire de l'Ecole Française d'Extrême-Orient. Compte Rendu des Fêtes et Ceremonies* (1953), pp. 85–9.

[212] W. F. Stutterheim, 'Histoire des rapports entre l'Indochine et Java dans les temps anciens', *Extrême Asie* (1928), xxiv, 603–9.

[213] F. D. K. Bosch, 'Uit de grensgebieden tussen Indische invloedssfeer en Oud-Inheems volksgeloof op Java' (i.e.: From the frontier area between the sphere of Indian influence and Indonesian popular faith in Java), *Bijdr. Kon. Inst.* (1954), cx, 1–19.

history, but even for a correct appreciation of the extent of Indian influence in South East Asia as a whole.

Many important materials, also related with this problem, may be found in Gonda's *Sanskrit in Indonesia*.[214] The author, whose sound scholarship in Sanskrit and Indonesian linguistics and philology needs no comment, gives us an almost exhaustive treatise on the study of Sanskrit and Sanskrit literature in Indonesia.

I will briefly mention an article by E. B. Vogler on the development of architecture during the so-called Central Javanese period. The author proposes a new analysis of the styles of Central Javanese buildings of that period, in which he distinguishes five sub-periods. If his conclusions may be relied upon—his main materials are stylistic developments of ornamental patterns such as the *kāla-makara*—they may give us clues also to political developments still imperfectly known from epigraphy.[215]

An article by H. J. de Graaf[216] deals with the much-discussed problem of when Majapahit fell. On the basis of Cortesão's edition of Tomé Pires' *Suma Oriental*, he compared the main sources on the last period of the famous empire again. It is regrettable that the author has not used some important materials published after Krom's account, especially Stutterheim's edition of an inscription of Kṛtawijaya.[217] It would have appeared that the succession of Girīndrawardhana (which, by the way, is not the name of a new dynasty) was a regular one, so that the myth of a Kaḍirian conquest of Majapahit in 1478 should disappear from our historical accounts.[218] This example shows clearly how difficult it is to deal with

---

[214] J. Gonda, *Sanskrit in Indonesia*, Sarasvatī Vihāra Series (1952), vol. 28.

[215] E. B. Vogler, 'Ontwikkeling van de gwijde bouwkunst in het Hindoeistische Midden-Java' (i.e.: Development of religious architecture in Hinduistic Central Java), *Bijdr. Kon. Inst.* (1953), cix, 249–72.

[216] H. J. de Graaf, 'Tomé Pires' *Suma Oriental* en het tijdperk van godsdienstovergang op Java' (i.e.: The *Suma Oriental* by Tomé Pires and the period of religious change in Java), *Bijdr. Kon. Inst.* (1952), cviii, 132–71 (comparison of Tomé Pires' account with a number of other traditions on the end of the Majapahit empire; the author concludes that the last Hindu Javanese royal residence, that of Kaḍiri, fell about A.D. 1526). Another interesting article by the same author is 'Titels en Namen van Javaanse Vorsten en Groten uit de 16e en 17e Eeuw' (i.e.: Titles and Names of Javanese Kings and Dignitaries in the sixteenth and seventeenth centuries), *Bijdr. Kon. Inst.* (1953), cix, 62–82. Although dealing with a later period, the article is important for older history, too.

[217] W. F. Stutterheim, *Jaarv. Bat. Gen.* (1938), v, 117–19. The term 'edition' is not quite correct. Stutterheim gives only some extracts of this very lengthy document. A complete publication is in preparation.

[218] The opinion that Majapahit was conquered by Kaḍiri in or about A.D. 1478 is based upon Krom, *Geschiedenis*, second impression, pp. 448 ff. It is a conjectural conclusion based upon the then available materials. Krom's basic mistake is that he interpreted the title 'Lord of Dahana-pura' in the inscription of A.D. 1486 as 'King of Kaḍiri', whereas it is nothing but an honorary title (there was always a prince or a princess in the Majapahit court who held such a title; if it is stated that some British king was succeeded by the Prince of Wales, this would not mean that England was conquered by Wales). As a matter of fact, the inscription of Kṛtawijaya, dated A.D. 1446, gives the name of the Bhaṭāra i Kling, Çrī Girīndrawardhana as one of the last mentioned (that means: youngest) princes at the Majapahit court. The battles to which inscriptions and Pararaton allude appear to be nothing else but quarrels between several princes.

such problems without sufficient acquaintance with the epigraphic sources.[219] In another article, the same author gave an interesting collection of titles of Javanese princes of the seventeenth and eighteenth centuries.[220]

The articles published by Berg during this period[221] give a completely new vision on older Indonesian history. These studies are more or less a continuation of the older studies by the same author mentioned above. The author applies his basic ideas about Javanese culture in general, and about linguistics and comparative mythology to arrive at a new evaluation of the sources of the older Javanese history, especially the Singhasari and Majapahit periods. Contrary to Krom, who considered the inscriptions, the *Nāgarakṛtāgama* and most of the factual materials of the *Pararaton* as absolutely reliable sources (provided, of course, that we are able to read, translate, and interpret them correctly), Berg views these materials as products of essentially the same culture that also produced the *Babad Tanah Djawi* and the *Pustaka Radja*; Krom grossly simplified when he considered the first group reliable, the second unreliable. Both groups, according to Berg, are based on the same or similar structural principles. Neither may be considered historiography in the modern sense of the term, whereas both groups may, in principle, be used to acquire knowledge about the history, provided that we have correct insight into the structural principles on which the works are based.

One direct consequence of the application of these views is that the first group of texts descends in value, whereas the second one mounts. Inscriptions lose their lofty position of factual evidence; so does the *Nāgarakṛtā-gama*. On the other hand, the *Babad Tanah Djawi* and Balinese historical works of the sixteenth century or later may be used to interpret the *Nāgarakṛtāgama* and epigraphic materials.

However attractive these principles may be, their application seems extremely difficult. The most awkward point is how to obtain correct insight into the structural principles of Javanese historiography which become the basis of the new analysis of our historical sources. At present, there is still much which remains subjective. It seems especially dangerous

---

[219] In order to avoid any misunderstanding, it is necessary to add that the scholars to be blamed are those who did not publish such materials in the proper way. Thanks to Krom's *Geschiedenis* we have an almost complete account of all research on older Indonesian history of before 1931, so that research after that year stood upon a reliable basis, until the number of new materials, new interpretations, etc., accumulated in such a way, that no scholar has any guarantee that he has not overlooked something important or even decisive for his own interpretations.

[220] H. J. de Graaf, 'Titels en Namen van Javaanse Vorsten en Groten uit de 16e en 17e Eeuw' (i.e.: Titles and Names of Javanese Kings and Dignitaries in the sixteenth and seventeenth Centuries), *Bijdr. Kon. Inst.* (1953), cix, 62–82. The importance of this study is not limited to the sixteenth and seventeenth centuries. The same is true with H. J. de Graaf, 'De regering van Panembahan Sénapati Ingalaga', *Verhand. Kon. Inst.* (1953), xiii.

[221] Some of the most important of Berg's studies are enumerated by Bosch in *Bijdr. Kon. Inst.* (1956), cxii, note 1 to p. 1.

to me to let the results of such an analysis prevail against epigraphic or textual evidence the reading and interpretation of which seem to be beyond doubt (such as the numerous inscriptions of king Siṇḍok, the Calcutta inscription of Airlangga, the inscription on the back of the Cāmuṇḍā of Singosari, etc.). Some of the main results which seem to follow from this new interpretation of source-materials are unfortunately only negative. Thus, Airlangga's ancestors (including Pu Siṇḍok) become fiction instead of history and the same happened to the division of Airlangga's empire into Janggala and Pañjalu;[222] the first two kings of the Singhasari empire become imaginary and even the imposing greatness of Majapahit becomes a myth. I cannot go into details about the way in which Berg arrives at such conclusions. The real basis is sometimes extremely weak[223] or even imaginary.[224] In spite of these objec-

[222] C. C. Berg, 'Herkomst, vorm en functie der Middeljavaanse rijksdelingstheorie' (i.e.: Origin, Form and Function of the Middle Javanese Theory on the Division of the Empire), *Verhand. Kon. Acad. Wet.* (1953), Afd. Lett., N.R., lix, No. 1.

[223] Cf. F. D. K. Bosch, 'C. C. Berg and Ancient Javanese History', *Bijdr. Kon. Inst.* (1956), cxii, 1–24, and, again, C. C. Berg, 'Gedachtenwisseling over Javaanse Geschiedschrijving' (i.e.: Discussion on Javanese Historiography), *Indonesië* (1956), ix, 177–216. I agree that strength of arguments is sometimes a subjective question. Thus, Berg's arguments for the non-existence of Ken Angrok and Anuṣapati as historical kings of Singhasari (cf. C. C. Berg, 'De evolutie der Javaanse geschiedschrijving', *Meded. Kon. Acad. Wet.* (1951), Afd. Lett., N.R., xiv, No. 2, 121–46) seem weak to me on the same grounds as those given by Bosch (art. cit., 4–9).

[224] As an example of an imaginary basis I may mention the so-called Saḍeng War (C. C. Berg, 'De Saḍeng-oorlog en de Mythe van Groot-Majapahit', *Indonesië* (1951), v, 385–422). As a matter of fact, its basis is a conjectural, and certainly wrong, reading of the fragmentary inscription at the back of the Cāmuṇḍā statue from Ardimuljo (near Singosari, East Java). This very interesting statue was discovered in 1927 (cf. *Oudheidk. Verslag* 1928, p. 27), and a first attempt at reading the text of the inscription was made by Goris (ibid., p. 32). Goris then read the ciphers of the (Çaka) year in the first line of the inscription as .254. In the next year, Stutterheim discussed the date and the meaning of a number of East Javanese groups of images (W. F. Stutterheim, 'De dateering van eenige Oost-Javaansche beeldengroepen', *Tijdschr. Bat. Gen.* (1936), lxxvi, 249–320), where he proposed an interesting explanation of the Cāmuṇḍā image and its inscription (art. cit., pp. 315–20). On the basis of the date concluded to by Goris he connected the demonic features of the statue with the suppression of the Saḍeng revolt, mentioned both in the *Nāgarakṛtāgama* and the *Pararaton* for the year Çaka 1253. He further concluded from the Cāmuṇḍā statue and its inscription that the Saḍeng revolt (which he located in the very Eastern part of the island of Java, as Brandes and Krom had suggested before) must have been a very dangerous episode. Some years later again, Berg devoted a very detailed study to the meaning of the *Nāgarakṛtāgama* and *Pararaton* passages dealing with the Saḍeng revolt and the circumstances under which Gadjah Mada arrived at the lofty position of a *patih amangkubumi* (*Bijdr. Kon. Inst.* (1939), xcviii, 1–74), but did not deal with the Cāmuṇḍā inscription in that connection. Finally, in the first-mentioned article in *Indonesië*, v, Berg analysed the Saḍeng episode again; following Stutterheim's interpretation of the text of the Cāmuṇḍā inscription, he proposed an entirely new explanation of the event, according to which Saḍeng would have been a hidden allusion to an expedition against Bali. Whatever the strength of other arguments (which I cannot discuss in this note), Stutterheim's conjecture about the Cāmuṇḍā inscription cannot be accepted by any means: the reading of the date by Goris is certainly wrong, for no trace of a 5 is visible on the stone; then there is no reason to complete the final syllable, *sa* to *saḍeng* as Stutterheim had done. As a matter of fact, the last fragment of the inscription was found back by 1940; it proves that *sa* is the beginning of *sakaladvīpāntara*. Finally, a few years ago, the date of the inscription was calculated by Damais on the basis of those elements which are still clearly visible ('Études

tions, I think that not only Berg's principles (if moderately and carefully applied), but also a number of his results[225] will greatly assist progress

d'Épigraphie Indonésienne', III. Liste des principales inscriptions datées de l'Indonesie', BEFEO, xlvi, Fasc. 1, 72 f., No. 175; and 'Études d'Épigraphie Indonésienne', IV. Discussion de la date des inscriptions', ibid. (1955), xlvii, Fasc. 1, 151 ff.); the result of this calculation was 17 April A.D. 1292, i.e. during the reign of Kṛtanagara, some months before Jayakatwang's attack on Singhasari. The calculation by Damais may not be beyond doubt—although it seems sound—but it may be added that both the type of script and the title of the king agree with Kṛtanagara. On these grounds, I think that there is no more any reason to connect the demonic image with the Saḍeng episode. This strongly affects the results of Berg's article in *Indonesië* (1951), v, 385 ff.; at least, an important additional argument to consider the Saḍeng episode not as a local revolt, but as a struggle against the Nusantara is lost. It should also be added that the date of the Cāmuṇḍā inscription would lead to a different view on Kṛtanagara's policy. The very threatening tone against the *sakaladvīpāntara* in this inscription (cf. art. cit., pp. 401 ff.) could not well be attributed to a king whose aim was friendship with the Nusantara; it would rather point to another kind of Kṛtanagara, a policy of *parcere subjectis sed debellare superbos*. But then Berg's interdict theory would also have to be revised: for Gadjah Mada's policy, instead of being opposed to Kṛtanagara's programme, would be its logical continuation after an interruption of forty years during which Majapahit faced internal revolts. Personally, I am inclined to accept the latter view and its consequences. If indeed the Pamalayu has taken place in A.D. 1292 (cf. Berg, 'Kĕrtanagara, de miskende empirebuilder', *Orientatie* (1950), xxxiv, 16 ff., and *Indonesië* (1951), v, 197), it may have been a direct consequence of the menace contained in the Cāmuṇḍā inscription. This, again, would make the timing of Jayakatwang's revolt understandable. Also Berg's treatment of epigraphic sources is sometimes unconvincing. In 'Herkomst, Vorn en Functie der Middeljavaanse Rijksdelingstheorie', *Verhand. Kon. Akad. Wetensch.* (1953), Efd. Lett., N.R., lix, No. 1, 118, he mentioned an inscription dated A.D. 1135 and referred the reader to Krom, *Hindoe-Javaansche Geschiedenis*, second edition, p. 294. On both sides of the royal seal at the head of this inscription there is a short text in ornamental letters of the Kaḍiri period. Krom mentioned Brandes' reading *sang jalma wiyati* and noted that the first word should be read *pañjalu* in his opinion. This may have given the impression that the reading of *pañjalu* is uncertain, which, in fact, it is not. It is true that Brandes had given a different reading, but that was in 1887 in the very beginning of epigraphic studies. As a matter of fact, Krom's reading is beyond doubt. The second and last word of this brief motto is *jayati*. So the motto reads: 'Pañjalu is victorious' and proves that Pañjalu was indeed the official name of the Kaḍiri empire in A.D. 1135. As far as *sang juru pañjalu* (in an edict dated A.D. 1116) is concerned (cf. Berg, loc. cit.), Berg's explanation cannot be maintained; in such expressions, *juru* is always followed by a topographic name and denotes some kind of administrative chief. This point might seem a minor objection, but it is not: as a matter of fact, it is a very serious objection against Berg's opinion that Pañjalu would have denoted the Singhasari highlands until after Jayanagara's death in 1328. Another imaginary basis is, I think, the 'Proto-Pararaton' (Berg, 'De evolutie der Javaanse geschiedschrijving', *Meded. Kon. Akad. Wet.* (1951), N.R., xiv, No. 2, 121–46). For this point, the reader is referred to Bosch, 'C. C. Berg and Ancient Javanese History', *Bijdr. Kon. Inst.* (1956), cxii, 1–24, and, more in particular, ibid., pp. 4–9.

[225] The objections against Berg's interpretations mentioned in note 224 do not affect the greatness of the work as a whole. Even if some of the more 'extremist' conclusions (such as those about 'Saḍeng', 'Proto-Pararaton', the 'interdict') could not be accepted in the very form in which they were given, I think that some middle road will be found. Where exactly this middle path would run has to be fixed in each particular case. It seems impossible to me that we should return to Krom's method. Principally, Krom judged the value of historical sources in black and white colours, the former to be followed, the latter to be shunned. To the former belong, *inter alia*, inscriptions (except, of course, the non-authentic ones), the *Nāgarakṛtāgama*, most of the Chinese sources; their reliability poses no problem, provided that we are able to give a satisfactory interpretation of these texts. To the latter group belong the non-authentic inscriptions and the relatively recent historical accounts in Javanese and Balinese literature. It is true that also Krom allowed for some mixed or intermediate colours. The Pararaton, for instance, contains much

on the difficult road towards a new conception of the older history of Indonesia.[226]

The reader may have concluded from the last part of this paper that the study of this part of the history of Indonesia is, at present, in some kind of serious crisis. The inheritance which the Republic of Indonesia received from the former colony in the field of history represents much sound scholarship and gives a reliable basis to future research, but it is in some ways disappointing. The gap existing between the results of more recent Dutch research and the Indonesian need to develop education in its future is very wide. Responsible circles in Indonesia fully realize that Western research is still needed, but they are unwilling to accept Western assistance unless the West should fully comply with Indonesian ideals. May this Conference, the first ever undertaken on such a broad basis, succeed in finding a way out of the present crisis and thus pave the way towards future co-operation, which will be in the interest of all the parties concerned.

sound materials, but also much unreliable stuff, since it is a compilation. The *kidungs* occupy an intermediate position. Berg, on the contrary, has always stressed that there are no such things as absolutely white or black sources. All historical sources should be viewed as products of the same people and constitute an integral part of its culture. We have no right to isolate some of these products to treat them as history in the Western meaning of the term. This principle is undoubtedly correct; it means a great advance compared with Krom's view, which now strikes us as somewhat simplistic. The main difficulty, however, is the correct application of this lofty principle. One has, unfortunately, to confess that Old Javanese culture is still insufficiently known to us. It is certainly as complex as any culture is bound to be and, therefore, an attractive but dangerous thing to work with. In practice, the application of Berg's principle seems to mean that a particular element of Old Javanese culture is interpreted with the help of another element which appears to be well known. This happened, in my opinion, with Berg's judgement on Prapañca; cf. Bosch in the article quoted in the end of note 224, pp. 12 ff. I, personally, agree with the view expressed by Bosch. Of course, Prapañca was a child of his time, but even then he must have been a very outstanding figure, who tried to ascertain the truth as well as he could with the data at his disposal. Considering his erudition I do not think that such childish calculations as those attributed to him by Berg (for instance, in the 'Evolutie der Javaanse Geschiedschrijving' p. 15) would have entered his mind. Moreover, Prapañca certainly had many sources at his disposal which are lost at present. Especially as far as royal charters and other inscriptions are concerned, we may have only a very small part of the materials which once were accessible to Prapañca. It is true that we have no charters of Ken Angrok and Anusapati, but Prapañca may have had. On the whole, I think that the presence or absence of charters issued by the kings is a question of mere chance. The distribution of the available inscriptions over the Old Javanese period seems to confirm this point. We have only very few inscriptions of the long and glorious reign of Hayam Wuruk—far less than, for instance, of Balitung and Siṇḍok. In addition, it should not be forgotten that only royal charters pertaining to religious foundations were engraved in stone and metal; for all the other charters easier materials (such as the leaves of the *lontar* palm) were used. Sources of this kind must have been accessible to Prapañca, whereas they are lost to us. It cannot be denied that, wherever we have the opportunity to control Prapañca's historical data with the help of epigraphic materials, they agree. So I think that, as a matter of principle, it is still correct to assume the correctness of Prapañca's data unless there are really strong reasons to conclude to the contrary. This as far as concrete data are concerned. Towards Prapañca's interpretations a freer attitude may be adopted. I also doubt whether Berg's views with reference to historical inscriptions could be accepted. It should not be forgotten that the inscriptions which we call 'historical' have never been intended as sources of history; they were legal documents dealing with temple grounds and similar questions. Historical materials are always accessory, however important they may seem to us: to be considered legal, a document must be dated; it must give the names of the king and other authorities who issued it; further, the king's motives must be added; they are not rarely connected with historical events (in many cases, the king gives privileges to those who proved faithful to him in difficult circumstances). Such historical facts would not probably have been distorted since distortions might have seriously interfered with the legal value of the document.

[226] I regret that I had no opportunity of using a few recent publications at the time when I was preparing my paper for the London Conference. This is especially to be regretted for the book by D. G. E. Hall, *A History of South East Asia* (1955). Contrary to the work by Cœdès (cf. *supra*, notes 195-7), Hall's History is not limited to old history only. It therefore bridges the serious gap between old and more recent history, which was regretted in note 16 above. Unlike the books by Vlekke and De Graaf (cf. notes 188 f. above), old history fully gets the place it deserves in Hall's History. As far as the treatment of older Indonesian history is concerned, it may be stated that also the numerous modern studies, such as those by Berg, are fully taken into account.

12. THE WORK OF PROFESSOR KROM

C. C. BERG

Professor of Indonesian Linguistics, University of Leiden

1. In the course of the nineteenth century the history of the indigenous populations of Indonesia began to arouse increased general interest. As far as Java was concerned, the publication of a Javanese dictionary by Gericke and Roorda in 1847 ff. made the existing manuscript source materials more or less accessible. One of the first texts to be published and to be translated into Dutch was the story of Baron Sěkenḍer (Alexander), by Cohen Stuart in 1850; he considered the publication useful for various groups of students, but felt that the story itself was no more than a product of fantasy and confused ideas. The synopsis of the indigenous history of Java in prose, published by Meinsma in 1874 under the title *Babad Tanah Djawi*, also was regarded primarily as a text book for language students, so that as late as 1938 a suggestion to have the text published in Roman characters and translated into Dutch, on behalf of scholars who were not acquainted with Javanese, met with some resistance; in spite of this, Olthof's translation was published in 1941.

2. A large-scale study of the documents bearing upon the history of Java as the Javanese themselves conceived it was carried out by Brandes from 1884 to 1905. Brandes was appointed Government Philologist in 1884 and was instructed to specialize in Old Javanese and Javanese antiquities. To his admirable energy and broadness of vision we owe many books and articles on various subjects in the fields of archaeology and history, as well as the organization of the Archaeological Service of the Netherlands Indies, now the Dinas Purbakala Indonesia. Brandes lived in Batavia, where he had at his disposal the library of the Batavia Society of Arts and Science as well as its rich collections of manuscripts, statues, and objects of art and ethnological value.

In 1888, Brandes published an article on the early history of Java (TBG 32, 368 ff.) in which he (1) gave a survey of the genealogies to be found in different books of the Babad-cycle, (2) mentioned the Javanese theory about the loss of early literature in the years around the fall of the Majapahit empire, and (3) emphasized the importance of the difference between the historical tradition preserved in Bali and the Central Javanese one. As to the latter point, it should be borne in mind that Brandes was acquainted with the excerpts of Javanese books existing in Bali which were published by Friederich in his Bali Report of 1849 (VBG 22). As a comparative study of these excerpts and some inscriptions had given him the impression that the Balinese tradition was the more reliable one, and as he wanted to know as many historical facts as possible in connection with his archaeological studies, Brandes decided to devote his attention in the following few years to the Angrok story, some manuscripts of which he had been able to acquire. He published the text in 1896 (VBG 49/1); it is one of the best text editions that we have in this field.

In 1894, after Brandes had prepared the manuscript, but before it was printed, he made a trip to Lombok which resulted in his finding a copy of the *Nāgarakrtāgama*, written in 1365 by the Buddhist high priest Prapanca, in Cakranagara, Lombok, to judge from the name, the very place where this Buddhist text was 'at home'. Not until eight years later did Brandes have the text printed (in 1902, VBG 54/1), and then without even an introduction to draw attention to this remarkable book and its importance for the study of the archaeology of the Majapahit period. After his death some minor fragments of a translation were found amongst his papers; Bosch published them in TBG 58, 528 ff., more as an act of piety, however, than because of their importance at that moment. One of Brandes' best friends, Rouffaer, says in his obituary notice (Singasari Monograph, 1909) that in 1898, when they met in Holland, Brandes was very touchy on the subject of a *Nāgarakrtāgama* edition, and that in the next few years too he refused to discuss the possibility of his publishing a translation.

I am inclined to think that Brandes' discovery of 1894 had made him unhappy, in a way. He was extremely conscientious of the duties of his office and he had a very busy life. A provisional reading of the rather difficult poem must have made him realize that the *Nāgarakrtāgama* was more important than the *Pararaton*, from an archaeologist's point of view, and that in any case a careful analysis of the text would force him to rewrite his *Pararaton* manuscript. If his decision to publish the *Pararaton* first, without even mentioning the *Nāgarakrtāgama*, was taken in a state of hesitation between the good and the better solution, the mistake he made in the appendix of his *Pararaton* book is easily understood. In this appendix we find a theory on the genesis of the *Babad Tanah Jawi* which would have been a masterpiece in 1885 or 1886, but was quite incompatible with Brandes' own views of 1893 ff. Brandes says, as a matter of fact, that the *Babad Tanah Jawi* developed out of a manual containing useful informations for poets and had acquired the appearance of a history book only as a result of its growth which caused some adapter to rearrange the materials according to a principle of organization, which happened to be that of chronological order. I fail to see how this theory was reconcilable with the evidence of earlier historiographical activity provided by the *Pararaton* itself, but I can imagine Brandes adding an obsolete manuscript of an earlier article to the main text of his *Pararaton* book in a state of confusion.

I mention this question because of the effect Brandes' publication of 1896 had upon the course of research in the following years. In the context of this publication Brandes' remark in the appendix could but discourage Babad research by those who were not primarily interested in the enthno-psychological aspect of the Javanese documents, but in search of sources of information. In this way the importance of the *Babad Tanah Jawi* as a clue to understanding the Javanese practice of historiography was completely lost sight of.

3. The *Nāgarakrtāgama* was published for the second time, and translated into Dutch at that, by Kern, in a series of articles in BKI which appeared between 1905 and 1914. Kern was a pioneer in the field of Indonesian studies and as such one of the most deserving scholars of the Netherlands. The *Nāgarakrtāgama* translation has been only one of Kern's manifold activities, and this explains why it was at the same time very welcome and yet rather superficial. Even as it was, it furthered the study of Indonesian archaeology a good deal; it enabled Krom, for one, to do the subsequent work of comparing the *Pararaton* and the *Nāgarakrtāgama* in detail.

4. Krom's first contributions dealt with *Nāgarakrtāgama* puzzles: one of his earliest, devoted to Prapanca's statement on the structure of the royal family of Majapahit, was published as early as 1910. Of Krom's books, I should like here to call attention to his publication of Brandes' transcripts of Javanese inscriptions in 1913, his commentary upon Kern's *Nāgarakrtāgama* translation (in the 1919 edition of the *Nāgarakrtāgama*), his Introduction to Hindu-Javanese art in 1919, his new edition of the *Pararaton* in 1920, his book on Hindu-Javanese history of 1926 (second edition 1931), and his synopsis of Hindu-Javanese history in GNI 1.

It should be borne in mind that Krom was neither an historian, nor an orientalist by profession, though he was interested in history from the start. In 1908 he concluded his university studies in Latin and Greek with a thesis (written in Latin) on the Germanic tribes who lived in the Netherlands in early days. After serving in the Leiden Museum of Antiquities from 1907 to 1910, he was appointed to the staff of the Archaeological Service of the Netherlands Indies, whose chief he became in 1913. His main interest in the Indonesian field was the study of temples, especially of the Barabuḍur. However, the necessity to deal with problems of chronology made him devote a part of his time to history; problems of history made him work in Javanese texts; and in order to read Javanese texts he had to learn Javanese. As far as Javanistics was concerned, in twenty years of acquaintance and ten years of co-operation I had plenty of opportunity to observe that Krom was not really interested in studies of Javanese literature and social life. This is in accordance with the highly pragmatic character of his book on Javanese history; I could conceive of no history book better adapted to what seemed to be the needs of the archaeologists than Krom's Hindu-Javanese History: it is accurate and exhaustive, gives a complete survey of the relevant facts we know as well as bibliographical notes on them, is concise, but clear, and devotes attention to all such by-questions as archaeologists are interested in. The method applied by Krom was the same as that of his predecessors, viz., to put aside intrinsically improbable assertions, in case of conflicting assertions to select the most probable one, and to reject the others, for the time being.

After a first chapter on the sources which we derive our information from, the second chapter deals with questions of Java's prehistory. It is a pleasure to read it, as Krom gives a brilliant exposé of the main questions concerning the origin of the Javanese nation and a survey of the various opinions and arguments. I ought, perhaps, to have mentioned the survey first, as it seems to me that the structure of the second chapter has to a great extent been influenced by the incidental combination of subjects which happen to have been discussed; the Madagascar problem, for instance, has little to do with the history of Java, but it is given a full page in Krom's book, as it had drawn much earlier scholarly attention.

In chapters III, IV, V, and VI of his book Krom gives a digest of what is known or said about events in and around Java in the first millennium of our era, and more particularly between 732, the year of the first dated inscription of Java, and 927, the year of the last inscription preceding the inscriptions of 'king' Siṇḍok. The number of the inscriptions which this knowledge and those assertions are based on—it is not certain whether any Javanese book is older than A.D. 1000—may be called considerable, if we compare Java in this respect with the other Indonesian islands, but it is extremely small in proportion to the length of the period and the geographical size of Java. From the viewpoint of cultural evolution these centuries were very important: the Barabuḍur and the other great temples of Central Java were built, Hinduism and Buddhism seem to have clashed in Java, and the Chinese were interested in what happened in the 'Southern Islands'. Lack of narrative material prevents us, however, from seeing the connections between the details revealed by the highlights. The Javanese themselves must have had some idea of the history of their country in the eighth and ninth centuries, as inscriptions dated for a short period in a Sanjaya era betray their ability to fix chronologically king Sanjaya who had lived two centuries before; moreover, this Sanjaya is mentioned in remnants of a chronicle in Old-Sundanese. The explanation suggests itself that a later usurper may have destroyed such documents as were a danger to his claims, but this is no more than a sheer possibility. In a way the available data of the first millennium are prehistorical, as they represent isolated bits of information. On the other hand, the Barabuḍur is not a typically prehistorical find. One would need an intermediary term between 'prehistorical' and 'historical' to characterize the data discussed in these chapters of Krom's book.

Different again are the materials discussed in chapters VII, VIII, and IX. Krom would not hesitate to call them historical, I am sure, as the genealogy of the Erlangga Hymn was authentic in his opinion; the opposite possibility is not discussed in HJG, though Krom mentions on p. 144 Bosch's tentative suggestion as to the unreliability of a similar genealogy in an inscription of 907. Moreover, Krom believed Prapanca's story (Nag. 68, anno 1365) about the partition of Erlangga's realm after his death to be essentially true so that he suggests an uninterrupted series of kings from the eighth or in any case from the ninth century to 1922 (the year of what he calls the 'fall of Kĕdiri') including Sinḍok in the second quarter of the tenth century, Erlangga in the first half of the eleventh century, and Jayabhaya, the royal patron of the poem *Bhāratayuddha*, around 1150. I do not share his view, as both the contents of the first part of the Erlangga Hymn and Prapanca's story about the partition of Erlangga's realm are fictitious in my opinion. This goes to say that I am inclined to classify the whole period covered by these chapters under the same head as chapters III–VI.

The period covered by chapters X, XI, and XII is the only one, I think, that justifies the noun in the title of Krom's book. Krom lets it start in 1222, the year in which Angrok came to power in Tumapĕl, the later capital of Singasari, as he believes in the historicity of the 'first two kings' of the new dynasty, Angrok/Rājasa and Anusapati, whom I believe to be fictitious. Apart from this controversial question, we have at our disposal, say for the years 1250 to 1400, a story which integrates the various bits of information into one picture. It depends on our evaluation of the *Pararaton* and the *Nāgarakrtāgama* whether this picture is primarily acceptable or primarily tendentious. At any rate, this period has survived in the memory of the Javanese, first through the *Pararaton* and the *Nāgarakrtāgama*, later on, in a modified form, in the *Babad Tanah Jawi*, the seventeenth-century state myth of Mataram which is still largely known in Java. The most important figures of this period were Wiṣnuwardhana (died 1268), Krtanagara (died 1292), Wijaya/Krtarājasajayawardhana (died 1309), who survived in the *Babad Tanah Jawi* as Bra-Wijaya, his daughter Tribhuwanottunggadewi Jayawiṣnuwardhani (died *c.* 1370) and her son Ayamwuruk/Rājasanagara (born 1334). The most important events were the invasion of K'ubilai Khan's expeditionary force in 1293, the result of which was the foundation of the dynasty of Majapahit, and the expansion of Majapahit's power in Java and over the other islands which made the fourteenth century the golden age of Java's past in contemporaneous as well as in later stories.

The last chapter in Krom's book is devoted to the fifteenth century. Our notions of this period are rather vague, but much more accurate than those of the centuries preceding 1250. Krom discusses the information provided by the inscriptions and the *Pararaton* with as much devotion to his task as we observe in the rest of his book; the anti-climactic character of this chapter is due to a gradual decay of the Majapahit empire, and perhaps also, or at least partially, a result of the destruction of documents about the fifteenth century in the years of the rise of Mataram.

5. In this paper I shall confine myself to major objections against Krom's book on what he and his predecessors have not quite adequately called 'Hindu-Javanese' history.

In the first place, Krom should not have narrowed down his survey to the period before 1500. His argument is (HJG 5 and 467) that Hindu-Javanese history ended when Muslim kings came to power. That after the fall of Majapahit a Muslim king came to power is no more than a theory, however, issuing from the author of the second *Babad Tanah Jawi* who used the assertion for magical purposes, then accepted by the Javanese who had lost sight of the circumstances under which the *Babad Tanah Jawi* developed, and provisionally believed in by Brandes, in 1888, when no other sources of information were as yet available. In my opinion it is inconsistent to reject the *Babad Tanah Jawi* as a source of information and still to believe in the story about Java's conversion to Islam that it tells. It must be emphasized that Java's history is not a combination of two discontinuous parts; the civilization of Majapahit continued to exist in Mataram, and until the present century at that, though it goes without saying that in the course of the years some elements of culture have been added and others dropped. The present question has two aspects, I think. On the one hand Krom was free to write a book about whatever part of the history of Java he liked to discuss, and we must be grateful to him that he has written the book he wrote. On the other hand, Krom's decision has been influenced by the error of thinking of Java's history as being discontinuous, and the effect of this error has been, indeed, that the early history of Java is now a special subject of study in the Dutch universities, quite distinct from the study of the later centuries. It is, of course, the underlying error which I combat, not Krom's preference.

Krom's second error is intimately connected with the first one, but much more important as to its effect. If Krom had included the history of Mataram into what he called 'Hindu-Javanese' history, he would have regarded the *Babad Tanah Jawi* as a part of the early Javanese literature, and this might have induced him to infer a general appreciation of the 'history books' of Majapahit from our knowledge of the *Babad Tanah Jawi*. A man who understands the *Babad Tanah Jawi* is liable to doubt the pedigree of the Erlangga Hymn in the Calcutta inscription (1041) as intrinsically unreliable and to reject the story about the partition of Erlangga's realm into the kingdoms of Janggala and Kĕḍiri as intrinsically improbable (as we have no reason to believe that Prapanca had access to sources of information, owing to lack of continuity as far as central authority was concerned). It seems unlikely that such a man would try to write a book like Krom's Hindu-Javanese history, but if he would, he would emphasize the discontinuity of central authority and the continuity of Java's pattern of culture, whereas Krom's book starts from the conception of continuity of central power and discontinuity of the pattern of culture. I am fully aware of the fact that this is not Krom's fault, after all. The basic difficulty is that (1) before Brandes, 'complete' histories of Java have resulted from the uncritical and even more or less puerile desire to do for Java the same work as had been done before in the countries of the Western world, where, however, the situation was fundamentally different, because of the lasting effect of Greece's discovery of science; (2) Brandes' need of facts for his archaeological studies made him prefer the Balinese tradition to the Central Javanese one, though the former was not essentially different from the latter, and made him block in this way the road to the *understanding* of Javanese historiography.

In every society there are transmitted some types of utterances which evoke a type of executive behaviour. There are other types which produce no response other than to impel the further social transmission of the utterance. This latter type we may term 'myths' from the moment the society as a whole has accepted them. Each history in the sense of a story about the past is liable to develop into a myth. As one dealing with a myth a historian who avails himself of local sources of information wants some knowledge of the principles of mythology and an awareness of the relative positions of science and the traditional myth complexes in the society whose historiography he exploits. Krom's book contains a chapter dealing with his sources, of course, and the question of the value of these sources is discussed from time to time; it lacks, however, an introductory chapter about Java's pattern of culture as a result of which omission the book itself is not syntypical, that is, not written on the basis of a clear conception of what a given pattern of culture allows of or does not tolerate. It is interesting to state that Rassers' book on the Panji romance, which contains important chapters on Javanese historiography and which was written between 1919 and 1926, the years of Krom's introduction to Javanese art and his Hindu-Javanese history (which is the elaboration of chapter II of the introduction) respectively, has made practically no impression upon Krom; one need not agree with the details of Rassers' book to acknowledge the value of his approach.

It is questionable whether the book I have in mind could have been written immediately, i.e. before a competent scholar like Krom had framed the wrong picture. This consideration should have kept the author of a review in check, because his task should have been to do justice to the writer of the book reviewed. I for one make a daily use of Krom's book, and this is the best proof of appreciation I could imagine. This paper, however, is not a review—because Krom's book is past reviewing—but a contribution to a joint effort to find out the best principles of delving into the past of man in South East Asia. In this situation I feel free to make remarks which otherwise would have seemed both unfriendly and improper. Moreover, no one is obliged to prefer my viewpoint to Krom's.

A third question, perhaps a little outside the scope of our discussion, regards the function of Krom's book within a curriculum. The students at the University of Leiden who, in former times, prepared for an office in the Civil Service of the Netherlands Indies had to pass an examination in which one of the subjects was 'old and new history of the Netherlands Indies'. The practical reason for the study of history seems to be to make people appreciate the present day as the resultant of a number of forces which have been operating in the past. The history of the Dutch administration ought to be relevant to whomsoever had to play a part in it. A clear conception of the ideology of the nation in whose behalf a civil servant works—whether in the previous colonial situation or in the present situation of international agencies rendering special services—is of no smaller importance to him. I fail to see, however, why future civil servants should know a lot of facts which are no longer relevant to the present situation nor of any use to their study of other subjects. Krom's Hindu-Javanese history is a story about kings and their achievements in which we find scattered remarks about elements of culture. I for one would prefer a history of culture and elements of civilization in which the reader would find scattered remarks about kings. I am afraid that in this respect, too, the archaeologist in Krom has dictated his conceptions to the historian.

ABBREVIATIONS

BKI—*Bijdragen tot de Taal-, Land- en Volkenkunde* (The Hague).

GNI—*Geschiedenis van Nederlandsch Indië* (History of the Netherlands Indies), ed. F. W. Stapel (Amsterdam, 1938 ff.).

HJG—N. J. Krom, *Hindoe-Javaansche Geschiedenis*, second edition (The Hague, 1931).

TBG—*Tijdschrift voor Indische Taal-, Land- en Volkenkunde*, published by the Batavia Society of Arts and Sciences.

VBG—*Verhandelingen van het Bataviaasch Genootschap van Kunsten en Wetenschappen* (Batavia).

13. SOME ASPECTS OF PORTUGUESE HISTORICAL WRITING OF THE SIXTEENTH AND SEVENTEENTH CENTURIES ON SOUTH EAST ASIA

THE LATE I. A. MACGREGOR

Formerly Lecturer in History, University of Malaya (Singapore)

The years from 1515 to 1650 included a golden age of Portuguese historical writing. In the same period Portuguese historians showed much interest in Asia. Occurrences there became a main subject of chronicles of kings of Portugal: the authors almost ignored affairs at home for tales of ventures in foreign parts.

A critic might urge that the Portuguese writers related only a small part of Asian history: namely, the feats of their countrymen in the East. Few would deny that these form the dominant theme of the histories, though not always of historical compilations such as descriptions and reports. Yet sixteenth- and seventeenth-century chronicles of Portugal and its *conquista da İndia* yield valuable evidence for the history of Asia: in South East Asia they have made especially notable contributions to our knowledge of the past in Burma, Malaya, Sumatra, Java, and the Moluccas. Later Portuguese works have done far less. This paper therefore tries to define some characteristics of the earlier and more important Portuguese historical writings on South East Asia.

In the first hundred and fifty years after the opening of the Cape route Portuguese wrote three types of historical works on 'India beyond the Ganges'. Men serving in Asia wrote reports; laymen in Portugal and the East composed histories, chiefly about secular affairs; priests put together chronicles and biographies which primarily recorded Christian missionary endeavour.

1. *Reports*

Allusions to history in the reports are sometimes scattered and fragmentary. Two things make it fair to consider them with the continuous and methodical stories of the chronicles: the first is the intent of the writers: the second is the influence of what they wrote. A man who sent home a report almost certainly hoped that it would win a larger audience than the ordinary letter from India. (With a wider circulation went greater influence.) Reports were not historical writing on the grand scale, but they gave a number of people information—occasionally their only information; they sometimes strengthened prejudice; they disseminated legend;

and, now and then, they helped to build up Portuguese attitudes to various problems in Asia.

Reports fall into three classes: first, descriptions of countries or places, supplemented, in varying degree, by incomplete narratives of events which occurred in them before or during the authors' stay in Asia; second, numerical summaries: they generally give military or financial information but make reference to past events; third, printed reports from missionaries. In the first class are the *Suma Oriental* of Tomé Pires, the *Book* of Duarte Barbosa, the *Information* of Gabriel Rebello, the *Treatise* of Gaspar da Cruz, the *Report on the Golden Chersonese* and *Description of Malacca, Meridional India and Cathay* of Manoel Godinho de Eredia and the books on the fortresses and cities of Portuguese India by António Bocarro and Pero Barreto de Résende. The numerical summaries include the anonymous *Lembranças de cousas da Índia*, Simão Botelho's *Tombo do Estado da Índia*, António de Abreu's *Orcamento do Estado da Índia do que remde*,[1] Luis de Figueredo Falcão's *Book*, and Pero Barreto de Résende's *Livro da receita e despesa pertencente ás fortalezas do Estado da Índia*.[2] The last class is covered by the printed letters from missionaries in the East.

Except for Barbosa, all the writers of descriptions spent some time in South East Asia. The first was Tomé Pires, whose *Suma Oriental* has been called the most important and complete account of the East produced in the first half of the sixteenth century,[3] and the claim is justified for South East Asia (which Pires treated much more fully than India). Apart from a visit to Java in 1513, Pires lived in Malacca from 1512 to 1515, began his work during his stay and finished it soon after. His intention was to 'speak not only of the division of the parts, provinces, kingdoms and regions and their boundaries, but also of the dealings and trade that they have with one another . . . It is this that ennobles kingdoms and makes their people great.'[4] He faithfully remembered his aim and gave most space to economic matters on which, as Government Accountant in Malacca, he was well placed to give accurate information: for South East Asia he could base some assertions on statistics of trading voyages and on his own experience and observation in Malacca and Java. That he did get material from the accounts of trading voyages seems clear from his description of Pegu; the figures for trade and the accompanying report of the first Portuguese trading voyage to Martaban in 1512–13 appear to have influenced what he wrote. He certainly knew the accounts, for he audited them, adding marginal comments and calculations, the former sometimes acid, the latter not always correct.

---

[1] Lisbon, Arquivo Nacional da Torre do Tombo, Livraria, No. 320.
[2] Lisbon, National Library, Fundo Geral, No. 1783.
[3] A. Cortesão, *The Suma Oriental of Tomé Pires* (1944), p. xiii.
[4] Ibid., p. 4.

Pires often mingled history with descriptions of islands of the Malay Archipelago: the tendency was less marked in his accounts of other lands in South East Asia, except Malacca. The historical evidence of the *Suma* is especially valuable for Java, as Dr. H. C. de Graaf has shown recently: it is fairly ample for Sumatra. It is fullest for Malacca, on which it yields information about the coming of Islam, local marriage customs, methods of justice and government, communities of foreign residents and payments of tribute, as well as data on economic affairs. It also includes an outline history of the sultanate of Malacca based on local memories and traditions and, just possibly, on evidence at second hand from written sources.[5] This document is the earliest extant history of Malacca. All in all, the *Suma* has, as Sir Richard Winstedt has said, 'the most valuable of all Portuguese accounts of Malacca under the Malay Sultans'.[6]

Pires was not above error. Like some fellow officials of the same period, he was enthusiastic about the riches of South East Asia, where he hoped Portuguese trade would win high profits. But fervour outran caution when he described the resources of the Malay Archipelago. He almost certainly exaggerated the size of harvests of pepper in Java and Sumatra and of cloves in the Moluccas, while his information about other products, such as the 'enormous quantities' of tamarinds in Java, is not always above suspicion.[7] He knew that Pegu and Siam were wealthy, but did not imagine that they were 'more plenteous' than Java:[8] as for China, he admitted its large area, but thought its consequence unduly magnified: 'things of China', he wrote, 'are made out to be great, riches, pomp and state in both land and people and other tales which it would be easier to believe as true of our Portugal than of China'.[9] Both the tone and the division of space in the *Suma* tended to stress the importance of the Archipelago and to play down that of China and the northern parts of South East Asia. Pires may have been right when he wrote that 'this part of the world'—by which he seems to have meant South East Asia and China— 'is richer and more prized than the world of the Indies',[10] but he got the constituents of the newly revealed segment in the wrong proportion. He was not the first to do so, nor was he the last. But he did nothing to check a false impression.

The *Suma* is naturally not exhaustive, but it is not even as full as it might have been. For example, the account of Pegu declares that 'there is great profit in bringing rice and lac and all the rest of it from Pegu to Malacca',[11] but it does not reveal that in 1512 and 1513 merchants bought rice at Martaban for about one tenth of its price in the north Sumatran

---

[5] Ibid., pp. 229, 232.
[6] Sir R. O. Winstedt, *Malaya and its History* (1953), p. 156.
[7] A. Cortesão, *The Suma Oriental of Tomé Pires* (1944), p. 513; also p. 180.
[8] Ibid., p. 97.
[9] Ibid., p. 116.
[10] Ibid., p. 286.
[11] Ibid., p. 98.

port of Pasai. Yet Pires must have known this fact.[12] It is equally true that he had more to say about the history of Malacca under the Sultans than under the Portuguese: he even confessed that he deliberately passed over the details of a war in Portuguese times because 'many things of the kind happen in Malacca that are not written about'.[13] And at the end of the *Suma*, where he mentioned a date after the conquest, it is clearly wrong. External evidence shows that it is some months out and even if, as Sr. Cortesão suggests, Pires merely wrote 1514 for 1515, he still failed to make the day of the week agree with the day of the month.[14] Charity would suppose a copyist's mistake. Pires was a valuable historian, but by no means infallible.

Readers of the *Suma* have to remember that Pires was pleading a case. He wrote the *Suma* for king Manuel, whom he wished to impress with the worth of Malacca. He wanted to persuade the monarch to cherish his distant possession, to provide it—perhaps partly in Pires himself—with 'excellent officials, expert traders and lovers of peace' and to see that it was 'supplied, looked after, praised and favoured and not neglected'.[15] Even if it were only moderately governed and favoured, it 'could never in the world decline'. Pires' propagandist intention probably explains at least some of his exaggerations and also the way he glossed over difficulties at Malacca, including the dearness of its food and the troubles after the Portuguese conquest.

One difficulty Pires did not palliate was the general danger from Muslims. Instead, he strove to turn it into an argument for strengthening the Portuguese position at Malacca. The city was profitable but endangered by 'Moors': to check the danger Malacca must be strong: the Moors could then be destroyed, Christianity extended and trade secured—such was his reasoning.[16] It was marked by hostility to Muslims and a desire to serve God and Mammon at the same time. In this attitude, even more than in his exaggeration of the resources of the Archipelago, Pires spoke for many Portuguese besides himself. Later in the sixteenth century other Portuguese writers on South East Asia expressed similar sentiments.

The *Book* of Duarte Barbosa is mainly description. It contains but little history of South East Asia and most of what it has relates to the time after the arrival of the Portuguese at Malacca. Barbosa never visited South East Asia before and probably never after[17] he wrote his work, apparently in

---

[12] The accounts of the first Portuguese trading voyage to Martaban reveal it.

[13] A. Cortesão, *The Suma Oriental of Tomé Pires* . . . (1944), p. 281.

[14] Ibid., p. 287.

[15] Ibid., p. 286; see also pp. 228, 283.   [16] Ibid., p. 286.

[17] E. Reis, *O noticiarista das Índias: Duarte Barbosa* (1948), pp. 91–104; Fernão Lopes de Castanheda, *História do descobrimento e conquesta da India pelos Portugueses* (1924–33), iii, 313, 321. Dames' theory, in M. Longworth Dames (ed.), *The Book of Duarte Barbosa* (1918–21), i, pp. xlv–li, no longer seems tenable. See also F. M. de Sousa Viterbo, *Trabalhos nauticos dos Portuguezes nos seculos XVI e XVII* (1898), pt. I, p. 43.

1518–19.[18] The nearest he got was the Malabar Coast where he lived for many years[19] and served for some time as an official. For all the slightness of his historical references to South East Asia, he at least fostered, if he did not create, a legend about Malacca: to wit, that gold came there 'in such abundance that the leading merchants dealing in it do not value their estates nor keep their accounts except in bahars of gold, which bahars are four quintals each'.[20] Supplies of gold were not nearly so abundant as Barbosa thought and the practice of reckoning by weight in gold dated from pre-Portuguese times, when the city had no currency except small change. Even then merchants probably counted their wealth in catis rather than bahars.[21]

Gabriel Rebello spent thirteen years in the Moluccas and then composed his *Information* in 1569.[22] It includes a description of the islands and some history of them in the period before the Portuguese arrived. The story of later events is scanty and somewhat inaccurate up to the time when Rebello reached Ternate: thereafter it improves greatly. The *Information* is biassed in favour of sultan Hairun of Ternate, who appears in a different light in some letters from Jesuit missionaries. Rebello's view has persisted, partly because Couto accepted much of it. There is no evidence that Barbosa or Rebello used material from archives, but Rebello may have seen documents at Ternate.

Gaspar da Cruz was a Dominican missionary: nine-tenths of his *Treatise*, published in 1570, is about China. Apart from passing references, it mentions South East Asia only in the first chapter, where it deals with Cruz's visit to Cambodia in 1555–6. The chief value of the section is its indication of the survival of Ang Chan and of Brahman influence in Cambodia in 1556.

Manoel Godinho de Eredia (1563–before 1629)[23] was not primarily a historian. The son of a Portuguese captain and a 'princess' from the Celebes, he was born and partly educated at Malacca before going to Goa where he became Government Cosmographer. His chief interests were geography and exploration, though he himself might have added mathematics and a hostile critic self-glorification.[24] His *Report on the Golden*

---

[18] E. Reis, ibid., p. 100.

[19] C. 1500/02 – ?; 1511–16; 1517–29±?

[20] M. L. Dames, *The Book of Duarte Barbosa* (1918–21), ii, 175.

[21] In 1540 a Portuguese Captain of Malacca clamoured about the scandal when his predecessor was alleged to have carried away but one bahar of gold (Pero de Faria to the King, Malacca, 23 November 1540, in Lisbon, Arquivo Nacional da Torre do Tombo, Corpo Cronológico, 1–68–88). See also A. Cortesão, *The Suma Oriental of Tomé Pires* . . . (1944), pp. 249 and 259, where the quantities of 50 and 120 quintals of gold were considered great fortunes.

[22] *Informação das cousas de Maluco*, published by the Royal Academy of Lisbon in 1856. Rebello's first draft, composed in 1561, was called *Histório das islas de Maluco*.

[23] Goa, Arquivo Geral e Histórico, Monções do Reino, vol. 13A, No. 86, p. 12.

[24] E.g., F. M. de Sousa Viterbo.

Chersonese was written between 1597 and 1600: the dedication of his *Description* is dated in 1613: both works have a considerable number of historical references to times before and after the coming of the Portuguese, more especially in Malaya, Sumatra, and Java. Eredia did not claim to have used government archives: he based his work on traditions and oral and written evidence that he sometimes tended to accept without much discrimination. Thus, when dealing with the beginnings of Christianity in the Celebes, he sensibly drew on a copy of an 'authentic account' which had been kept in the archives of the see of Malacca: in the same work he inserted a copy of a certificate of a Portuguese about a visit to a mythical island.[25] Elsewhere, Eredia reproduced a couple of tall stories on dubious authority—in one case the evidence was both verbal and secondhand.[26] The historical information in Eredia's descriptions only sometimes merits careful attention: he was not always the most judicious of authors.[27]

Such a character could be more fairly claimed for António Bocarro and Pero Barreto de Résende. The former became keeper of the archives at Goa and chronicler of Portuguese India in 1631: the latter served as secretary to the Count of Linhares during his term as Viceroy, 1629–35. A command from the king caused Bocarro to write his *Description*, which Résende studied and to some extent copied, providing a corrected and more complete version. The authors generally kept to description, but their few excursions into the history of South East Asia are valuable: both men were in a good position to know the truth about the more recent events they mentioned. In addition, Résende visited Malacca.

Historical writing in the numerical summaries is naturally briefer and more incidental than in the descriptions. The anonymous *Lembrança de cousas da India* (1525) was apparently written in Asia: it has information about Portuguese losses in Sumatra and Malaya between 1522 and 1524. The *Tombo do Estado da India* (1554) has a short account of taxes in Malacca under the last sultan and in the first forty odd years of Portuguese rule. The author, Simão Botelho, was one of the Vedores da Fazenda (royal Financial Superintendents) in Asia: he visited Malacca to reform the fiscal system and served there as Captain (1544–5). His statements have weighty authority. The summaries of Abreu (1574), Falcão (1607), and Résende (1634) contain few historical references.[28]

The printed letters from Jesuit missionaries were much more detailed. From the early days of the Society, its members in different places corresponded regularly with the General in Rome. Because of difficulties of

[25] J. V. Mills (ed.), 'Eredia's Description of Malacca, Meridional India and Cathay', *Journal of Malayan Branch of Royal Asiatic Soc.* (1930), viii, pt. 1, 55, 64.
[26] Ibid., pp. 251, 253.
[27] Among other things he repeated the legend about the bahars of gold; see ibid., p. 17.
[28] Garcia da Orta, *Coloquios dos simples e drogas e cousas medicinas da India* (1563) and António Nunes, *O livro dos pesos e medidas*, written in 1554, are descriptive rather than historical.

communication, news from Asia came in only once a year, more particularly in the report from the Provincial. This document was a comprehensive review of the mission's progress in the past year: from about 1550 it was made in a fixed form. It went from India to Portugal and thence to Rome, sometimes with Spanish and Latin copies. From Rome the Jesuit headquarters sent shortened versions to the houses of the Society in Spain, Italy, Germany, and Flanders. To save the trouble of making handwritten copies the printing of letters began in Rome in 1552.[29] Previously a few other letters from missionaries were printed in Paris and Portugal: more followed in later years. Altogether missives printed between 1545 and 1640 formed a corpus of history of the Society's activities in Asia, with references to secular events.

The earliest publications appeared in 1545 and 1546. One of them, entitled *Copia di una littera di Nove Delle Indie Orientale*, described the missionary successes of the Portuguese in Asia with much exaggeration. It included a short recapitulation of the letter of António de Paiva which told of conversions he had made in the Celebes.[30] Subsequently, printed letters of St. Francis Xavier referred to events in South East Asia. The most well-known compilation from the missionaries' letters is perhaps that of Fernão Guerreiro, whose *Relations* (1601–11) included an account of the early and middle parts of Felipe de Brito's adventures at Syriam.

The printed letters were not always accurate or complete histories of the events they recounted. Original letters based on rumour sometimes misled Guerreiro, whose story of the Syriam episode is marred by exaggerations, omissions, and undue glorification of Felipe de Brito. At the same time, the Jesuits in Rome were drastic editors. They cut out harsh observations and judgements and 'vain amplifications and hyperboles . . . which must not be tolerated' and they sometimes omitted references to non-Christian religious customs because they did not consider such things edifying. Occasionally, they left out items which they thought strained belief.[31] Yet, for all their faults, the printed letters were no mean contribution to the history of the Portuguese in South East Asia in the sixteenth and seventeenth centuries.

2. *Secular Histories*

The secular historians number at least twenty-one and comprise eight official chroniclers and thirteen men who began and sometimes finished their works without the king's sanction or knowledge. Three, possibly four

[29] G. Schurhammer, S.J.: *Die Zeitgenossischen Quellen zur Geschichte Portugiesisch-Asiens und seiner Nachbarlander zur Zeit des Hl. Franz* (1538–52) (1931), 'Sources of the Catalogue: Jesuit Correspondence'.

[30] G. Schurhammer, S.J., 'Historical Research into the life of St. Francis Xavier in the sixteenth century', *Revista da Historia* (Portugal) (1923), xii, 194–5.

[31] G. Schurhammer, S.J., *Die Zeitgenossischen Quellen* . . ., ibid.

unofficial writers visited South East Asia: another three and two chroniclers commissioned by the king spent many years in India. The more accurate historians were not always those with oriental experience. Though António Galvão, Fernão Mendes Pinto, and Eredia all knew waters east of Achin Head, they all made important mistakes. Galvão's *Treatise* seems to have sent the first Portuguese voyagers to the Moluccas far off their course,[32] Pinto is notoriously unreliable, and Eredia's *History of the services and martyrdom of Luis Monteiro Coutinho* has several slips and probably one major confusion.

Pinto wrote vivid prose: so did another unofficial writer—Gaspar Correa, who lived in India for about fifty years. Modern writers have occasionally tended to equate vividness with truth. The late Aubrey Bell could write of Correa that the '*Lendas* are infinitely preferable to the sleek periods of Barros and often as reliable, being legendary in little beyond their title, as understood by the ignorant . . . They have a harsh flavour of religious fervour and lust for gold and an intense atmosphere of the East—*sangre e incenso, cravo e escravaria*, St. James fighting for the Christians, St. Thomas transformed into a peacock, all in a region of horror and enchantment.'[33] As for Pinto, Maurice Collis admitted the difficulty of disentangling the varying degrees of historical value in his statements, but concluded that 'his description of sixteenth century Asia is authentic to the last detail'.[34] It is true that the pictures of Correa and Pinto are bold and firm, but it would be hard to prove that they showed conditions in South East Asia better than the *Decades* of João de Barros. But Barros, an official historian, never got nearer India than the coast of Guinea.

Men like Barros had an advantage over their unsponsored rivals. In the sixteenth century nearly all Portuguese in the East were, at least technically, servants of the Crown. The government in Lisbon strove to direct their actions and reward their services: it never ceased to receive their requests and complaints. Every year scores of letters passed between the king and his subjects in Asia. It follows that the royal archives formed the biggest and most authoritative assembly of evidence about the deeds, circumstances, and aims of the Portuguese in the East. Historians favoured by the king could see this collection as a matter of course.

In many ways Barros (1496–1570) was an official historian *par excellence*. He wrote under royal patronage, but voluntarily and out of conviction; he probably saw more documents on his subject than any man before or since; he commanded a stately prose style; and he set out not merely to record but to celebrate and justify. He grew up at court when national enterprise and self-confidence were flowering at home and overseas.

[32] H. Leitão, *Os Portugueses em Solor e Timor de 1515 á 1702* (1948), p. 50.
[33] A. F. G. Bell, *Portuguese Literature* (1922), p. 201.
[34] M. Collis, *The Grand Peregrination* (1949), pp. 301–2.

Portuguese were then comparing their achievements with those of heroes of classical antiquity. The time and place of Barros' upbringing encouraged him to believe that the history of the Portuguese in Asia was a great and epic theme—an *epopeia*. By 1520 he had planned to write about it.

Before he could begin he became an official at India House in Lisbon, where he served first as Treasurer (1523–8) and then as Factor (1533–67). This employment delayed his progress as an author: he did not publish his first *Décadas da Ásia* until 1552. The second followed in 1553, the third in 1563. He left the fourth Decade unfinished. Lavanha edited it rather drastically and published it in 1615. The first three Decades take the story down to 1526: the last prolongs it to 1539.

Barros had a deep interest in theology and the moral sciences and his writings were nearly always didactic.[35] When he came to write history he took a high view of its ethical nature. In his *Panegyrics* on king John III (1533) and Infanta D. Maria (1555) he used historical allusions as the 'cement for the moral lesson'.[36] And in the Prologue to *Decade III* he declared:

> History is a field where is sown every divine, moral, rational and instrumental doctrine. Whoever pastures on its fruit will be furnished in understanding and memory for living the just and perfect life . . . Writings which do not have the utility of instruction, besides wasting time which is the most precious thing in life, fill the mind with dust from the torrents of words and deeds they convey.[37]

Barros never doubted the fundamentally moral and religious nature of Portuguese conquests in the East. In the first chapter of the first *Decade* he asserted that the kings of Portugal had continually warred against Muslims in Europe and afterwards in Africa. Portuguese in Asia now fought another battle in the same campaign: they too smote the infidel and spread the faith. Activity overseas was a religious enterprise, its history a means of preaching Christian zeal.[38]

> I am certain (he wrote) that the kingdom whose employment lies in spreading the Gospel and the conversion of infidels and pagans ought to be thought happier than that which is occupied in seducing Catholics from correct doctrines; and the kingdom which, sword in hand, attacks the chief power of these infidels and heathens ought to be thought happier than that which calls and brings them in to shed its own blood. And, finally, that kingdom should be thought happiest which, in the

[35] For an admirable short study of the chroniclers João de Barros, Diogo do Couto, Antonio Bocarro and their works see C. R. Boxer, 'Three Historians of Portuguese Asia', *Boletim do Instituto Português de Hongkong* (July 1948), No. 1, pp. 13–44.

[36] João de Barros, *Panegíricos* (ed. by M. Rodrigues Lapa) (1937), p. xxvi.

[37] Barros, *Ásia* (1777), v, Prologue; see also ibid., vii, 536.

[38] Barros, *Ásia* (1777), v, 408–9.

last judgement, can shew triumphs in these works, so that it may merit the title of a faithful servant who has learned to put the talent of his chances out to usury. And because the kingdom of Portugal has always laboured to merit this name before God, it has been a faithful servant in great matters. Here indeed it may be said with truth that in the area which Fortune gave it in Europe, it was the first to throw back the Moors beyond the sea: it was the first to pass over to Africa: and what it has taken (there) it has defended till now, with the exception of what it has abandoned as unsuitable. And it was the first to pass into Asia where it achieved the deeds told in this work. Finally, as to their quality, just as Jesus Christ compared the spread of the Gospel to that of a grain of mustard seed in comparison with other seeds: in the same way can we, by virtue of its extension and illustrious deeds, adding to the church and its own glory, compare this kingdom in greatness with the other kingdoms of Europe, both in size and population, to a grain of mustard seed that has produced such a large tree that its size, power and doctrine overshadows the greater part of the territories (in Asia) which are mentioned in the previous chapter.[39]

The *Decades* stressed the official theory of the ethos of Portuguese expansion: religion joined to love of country. As a Christian, Barros could record events in Asia and hold up Portugal as a model of religious zeal: as a Portuguese, he could glory in victories won for religion, insist on describing them in Portuguese and mock men who studied the annals of Greece and Rome but knew nothing of the achievements of their own country.[40]

Blindness to faults is not usually a trait of moralists. Barros was no exception: he saw cracks in the façade of empire. The underlying purpose might be noble, but evils existed. No official could fail to note abuses, no historian ignore them. Moralist, official, and historian, Barros was well aware of the bad side of things. Though he stressed his belief in the basic goodness of the Portuguese enterprise, he reminded his countrymen of their duties in the East.[41] He also slipped into the *Decades* encouraging examples of individual virtue.[42] Here and there he mentioned specific abuses and gave advice on how to remedy them.[43]

Barros thought that truthfulness was the first and chiefest part of history. He assailed flattery, exaggeration, and concealment of misfortunes or justly earned praise. Yet he put limits on frankness, saying that 'in some matters it ought not to be so great, especially in matters which concern the infamy of anyone, that there may be said of it the very just saying that it

[39] Barros, *Ásia* (1777), ii, 348–9.
[40] Barros, *Ásia* (1777), v, Prologue.
[41] Barros, *Panegíricos* (ed. by M. Rodrigues Lapa) (1937), p. xxviii.
[42] E.g., Barros, *Ásia* (1777), vi, 523–34.
[43] E.g., Barros, *Ásia* (1777), v, 98; vi, 99–100, 543.

is cruel, though perhaps true'. He condemned Suetonius and Paulo Jovio for revealing men's vices.[44]

Barros himself has not escaped attack. The four chief accusations against him are: first, that he omitted men's misdeeds; second, that he was partial in the distribution of praise; third, that he dealt in detail with some small matters and passed over others of importance; and fourth, that his statements occasionally clash with those of original documents. On every charge except the last he has some excuse. It is true that he left out some actions which reflected no credit on the Portuguese. He was reasonably open about it: his declaration against recording human vices lies in the Prologue to *Decade III* and in *Decade II* he had already recalled that his intention was to write of the wars of Portuguese against infidels and not of their disputes among themselves.[45] On the other hand, he was not always so detached. His history of events in South East Asia mentions a considerable number of quarrels, blunders, and even crimes of Portuguese. The second point—the allegation of partiality—is hard to sustain or disprove. In Barros' time a stream of contradictory reports went to Lisbon from Asia: with the best will in the world, it must sometimes have been very difficult to strike a true balance between them. Today, with many documents destroyed, the difficulty is often greater. As for detail, Barros did break in on the story of Diogo Lopes de Sequeira at Malacca at a vital moment for an excursus on the game of chess, but such parentheses are rare. A modern historian is more likely to complain that Barros said little about economic and administrative matters and a great deal on the minutiae of small battles and sieges. The omission is grave but scarcely just as a ground for criticism. The history of military and naval expeditions and campaigns was what Barros set out to write. The fourth charge is the most serious. R. S. Whiteway supported it in his *Rise of Portuguese Power in India*.[46] This is not without its curious side for Whiteway's account of the Portuguese at Malacca is less correct than Barros'. The Portuguese writer did make mistakes: less excusably, he exaggerated occasionally.[47]

Perhaps a yet stronger criticism stems from the position of Barros as an official historian. Professor Butterfield has written: 'I do not personally believe that there is a government in Europe which wants the public to know all the truth.'[48] He has gone on to point out the peril of the official historian developing 'a security consciousness even more pronounced than that of the professional Foreign Office official'.[49] Whatever the reason, on

[44] Barros, *Ásia* (1777), v, Prologue.
[45] Barros, *Ásia* (1777), iii, 321.
[46] R. S. Whiteway, *Rise of Portuguese Power in India 1497–1550* (1899), p. xi.
[47] E.g., *Ásia* (1777), vi, 476, where Barros seems to have exaggerated the price of rice at Malacca during the troubles of the 1520s.
[48] H. Butterfield, *History and Human Relations* (1951), p. 186.
[49] Ibid., p. 205.

at least two occasions Barros left out important information on Portuguese activities in South East Asia. First, he failed to carry the story of Cristovão de Mendonça's voyage of 1522 beyond the port of Pasai. Sr. Cortesão thinks that the reason was the Crown's wish to keep new discoveries secret —the *política de sigillo*.[50] Second, and worse, Barros said nothing to show that in 1525 the home government considered and probably ordered a withdrawal from the Moluccas, if the Spaniards appeared in the islands in force.[51] Instead, the Portuguese were to hold a base in Java. This might almost be described as a 'pivotal fact', because it indicates that the Crown was ready to give up the finer spices. It is not surprising that Barros did not mention the matter. Rivalry with Spain was not dead when he wrote, and the Portuguese government cannot then have wished to see a confession of its weakness appear in print.

Barros' attitude to Asians has often led to criticism. He maintained that Asian vessels could sail the seas only with Portuguese permission: ships without it were fair prize. Barros thought that the papal grants of Asia to Portugal gave the Portuguese a legal right to control the Eastern Seas. Unlike his near-contemporary, Francisco de Vitoria, Barros never seems to have doubted that the pope could 'distribute among the faithful of the Catholic Church the lands in the power of those not subject to its yoke'.[52]

It is also probable that hostility to Muslims biassed Barros' judgement of men like Sang Stia.

If it is easy to criticize, it is hard not to praise. Admit Barros' faults and much good work remains. Compare him with other Portuguese chroniclers: his writings on South East Asia generally have fewer mistakes and omissions and his knowledge is more broadly based. He may have seen few private papers, but he undoubtedly studied many official documents. Moreover, he knew notable actors in the history he wrote. Fernão Peres de Andrade, who served in Malacca 1511–13 and revisited the city in 1516–17 and 1518, was a colleague and friend. Barros found space to reproduce his *ipsissima verba* in an account of an incident on the coast of Indochina. Duarte Coelho, who saw much of South East Asia between 1511 and 1528, was an acquaintance of whom Barros had a high opinion.[53] Barros also seems to have known Jorge de Albuquerque, a relative of Coelho's by marriage, twice Captain of Malacca and one of a group of persons who served in the Archipelago at various times from 1514 to 1530. Other acquaintances included Domingos de Seixas, who spent over twenty years in Siam, and Duarte de Resende, once factor in the Moluccas. Business at India House almost certainly made Barros known to a good number of

[50] A. Baião, H. Cidade, and M. Murias (eds.), *História da expansão portuguesa no mundo* (1939), ii, 157–9.
[51] Lisbon, Arquivo Nacional da Torre do Tombo, Gavetas Antigas, 20–7–38.
[52] Barros, *Ásia* (1777), i, 218; see also p. 219.
[53] Luis de Sousa, *Anais de dom João III* (1938), ii, 234.

people who had been to one or other of the parts of South East Asia visited by Portuguese. By drawing on their knowledge Barros gave his history greater authority. Evidence from the lips of men who had served in South East Asia did not merely add detail. It also probably helped to save the *Decades* from some of the dangers of books written by careful observers distant in time and place from the events they describe. Such works, it has been alleged, portray a resemblance of reality, but at the same time distort it.

Barros was keen to paint a true picture of the East. He sought information on its geography: he investigated its history for times prior to the arrival of the Portuguese. His interest in geography led him to plan and partly write a Latin description of the countries of the world, based on a comparison of ancient and modern evidence. In the *Decades* he always set the scene before he told the story. General geographical description introduced the main narrative of the activities of the Portuguese in each part of South East Asia: reports on smaller areas preface accounts of travels through, visits to or battles in them. Barros described many places in South East Asia, including the Singapore Strait, the Malay capital on the island of Bintan, the river Muar, Acheh and the hill fort at Mariaco in Tidore. Now and then, he exaggerated, but at least he gave his readers some idea of the localities where events occurred. Today his words have the added value of showing the sort of circumstances which Barros, a well-informed official, imagined to surround the Portuguese in Asia.

From an early stage in his work Barros realized that conditions east of Ceylon—*Ceilão para dentro*—were different from those in India. He saw that the states on the west coast of India were sometimes small and nearly always ruled or much influenced by Muslims. East of Ceylon there were great kingdoms, though many small ones too: moreover, many South East Asian countries were not Muslim. Among the chief 'heathen' states of the Orient Barros counted Bengal, Pegu, and Siam. 'Their power and their riches', he wrote, 'were so great that the pen fears to begin describing them'. 'As for China,' he went on, 'we can only say that it is greater than all these others in size, power, riches and policy.'[54] Barros was especially impressed by what he heard of the Celestial Empire. Among the heathen Chinese, he said, were all the things which the Greeks and Romans praised. In an aside to his description of Canton, he added, with what seems almost a modern note, that jobs were found for all and there were no beggars.[55]

In his account of South East Asia Barros corrected the mistake of Pires. He did not overemphasize the importance of the Archipelago. At the same time, he did not sacrifice the idea that the East Indies were wealthy: he

[54] Barros, *Asia* (1777), ii, 350, 351.
[55] Barros, *Asia* (1777), v, 194, 204.

merely uttered temperate praise. He was reserved about the profits that the Crown drew from the islands. This may have been due to personal caution or official secretiveness: as factor of India House, Barros should have known the figures.

Like Pires, Barros had much interest in the history of countries in South East Asia before the coming of the Portuguese. He tried to find a chronicle of Malacca, but failed. He therefore repeated the evidence of traditions. He gave a version of the Parameswara story, which he may have got with other matters from Pires' *Suma*.[56] The *Decades* are fairly rich in historical references to the sultanate of Malacca and to Acheh and Pasai and Ternate: they have fewer such allusions to other places in South East Asia.

When he wrote of the lands the Muslims dominated on the shores of the Arabian Sea Barros could apply his idea of Portuguese expansion as war against Muslims. With the same thought in mind Barros justified the conquest of Malacca. He considered that God had moved Albuquerque and his men to seize the city for the glory of His holy faith, so that

> from thence it might be spread and diffused through those great regions of the East that were so barren of the merits of His redemption, and also for the extinction of that fire of Mohammed which was beginning to burn in all those parts.[57]

Barros appears to have held to one general theory about the course of Portuguese history in the East. Briefly, it was a belief in an uneven but ascending line of victories until Albuquerque's death: thereafter decline set in.

> And [in 1516] (he wrote at the beginning of *Decade III*) there also came home a great number of fidalgos and knights nursed in the school of Francisco de Almeida and Afonso de Albuquerque, in whose times men considered honour to lie in the means by which it was gotten and not in business by which fortune might be acquired, as from that time they began to do very freely, with which the affairs of India entered a new period, turning more on greed for the latter than the former, so that they are now in the situation in which we now see them.[58]

Barros did not say that he excepted South East Asia from the general decay. That was scarcely fair. Despite severe difficulties at Malacca, Portuguese activities in South East Asia reached a peak in the decade after Albuquerque's death. Nor did they do so as a result of a change of policy. Albuquerque foresaw and encouraged an increase of Portuguese enterprise in the Far East. Barros faithfully recorded the voyages and

[56] A. Cortesão, *The Suma Oriental of Tomé Pires* . . . (1944), pp. 135–6.
[57] Barros, *Ásia*: Selection with notes by A. Baião (1946), iii, 258.
[58] Barros, *Ásia* (1777), v, 10.

expeditions, but seems to have remained unimpressed. He may have thought some of them unwise. The *Decades* betray some impatience with the plans of the last years of king Manuel: Barros apparently felt that they outstripped the means of the government to carry them out. In one place the historian listed several large projects which the king ordered a successor of Albuquerque to effect: somewhat testily, Barros noted that the mere thought of these designs was enough to weary the mind, let alone their execution. Though an official writer, Barros was not an uncritical apologist of every royal decision. On the other hand, he certainly blamed the decline mostly on the misbehaviour of the king's servants in the East. This view was to become almost traditional with historians of the Portuguese in Asia.

The general assumptions of Barros were not utterly false. War against Muslims was more to the front in king Manuel's reign than later on. It did represent an ideal, whatever other things crept in as well. Barros' fault was to try to see matters too rigidly. He tended to try to force the scheme of history of the Portuguese in Asia into a framework which could not hold it. Even in the Arabian Sea, Portuguese enterprise was not all related to a crusade against Muslims. There was no sudden and catastrophic decline after Albuquerque's death: there was great if ill-regulated expansion. Virtuous and dutiful Portuguese did not disappear from the East after 1515, nor were all men honest and true before that date. In detail Barros recognized these things: it was only his general theories that were set so firm. And Barros probably kept to his theories because they fitted in with his ideas as a moralist and patriot. They gave a moral basis for past glories, an explanation of present misfortune, a hero to venerate and a lesson for future conduct.

It follows that Barros' work on South East Asia has two sides. The one is formed by assumptions which tended to hide or at least blur the significance of a period of ambitious expansion. The other is a history of that expansion written by a man who had exceptional chances of collecting evidence for it. Barros generally used his materials with care and enthusiasm. The result is a long story, rich in detail and fairly accurate. It may have been too long for sixteenth-century taste: Faria e Sousa claimed that people did not read the *Decades* because of their bulk. Be that as it may, they were a task well done. Barros even took pains over small matters like Portuguese names—a subject which could easily have led to confusion. He sometimes showed a very balanced judgement and occasionally surprising tolerance. In a sense, he did his work too well. Too many later authors were content to abstract, copy or translate what he wrote.

The official successor to Barros was Diogo do Couto (1542–1616). Couto was not of fidalgo blood, but, like Barros, he grew up at court. Unlike Barros, he spent most of his life in India (1559–69, 1571–1616). He was keeper of the archives at Goa and chronicler of the Portuguese in Asia from 1594/1604 till his death. He covered the story of the Portuguese in the East between 1526 and 1599 in nine *Decades* that are usually reckoned as the fourth to the twelfth in the sponsored history. His work suffered many setbacks: the known surviving texts of the eighth, ninth, eleventh, and twelfth *Decades* are incomplete or summaries of lost or stolen originals. Couto was an eager collector of information. He based his work on material from the archives at Goa, on evidence given orally by Asians, and Portuguese, and on private documents such as Rebello's *Information*.

The parts of Couto's *Decades* which deal with South East Asia are of great but unequal value. Among the best things is the account of civil strife in Burma at the beginning of the reign of Bayinnaung. At least as good is the narrative of Portuguese relations with Johore in the 1580s. Two things explain the high quality of the second story. It appeared in *Decade X* which was the first and longest Couto wrote: he finished it in 1593 and sent it home in 1600, only a few years after the occurrence of the events it describes. Further, Couto was a friend of dom Paulo de Lima, who may have provided first-hand testimony about the successful attack on Johore Lama in 1587. Certainly, *Decade X* has more detailed history of events in Malaya than Couto's other volumes.

Couto's work has considerable faults, but he was not to blame for them all. He complained that he could find no documents to tell him what happened in the Moluccas in the 1560s. To supply deficiency he said he had discovered only one reliable witness—Gabriel Rebello, on whose *Information* Couto expressed his dependence.[59] This was fair and honourable, but perhaps Couto need not have swallowed Rebello's story as completely as he did: and he could have said more about Christian missions in the Spice Islands. In a later *Decade* there is a break in Couto's narrative between 1575 and 1580—a vital period for the history of events in Malayan waters. Here again Couto could plead good excuse: the theft of the manuscript of *Decade IX* caused the gap. He was not always so innocent. Stolen papers cannot wholly explain why he now and then made little reference to important matters like the plans for the conquest of Acheh. Nor do they justify the odd slip which has occasionally confused or misled later historians.[60]

Couto has won praise for truthfulness. 'His supreme preoccupation',

[59] Couto, *Asia* (1778–88), Decade VIII, p. 418; also pp. 98, 207.

[60] E.g., Sir R. O. Winstedt, 'A History of Johore', *Journal of Malayan Branch of Royal Asiatic Soc.* (1932), x, pt. III, 21, mentions Couto's reference to the sultan of Johore of 1568 being urged to avenge the death of his brother on the Achinese. This occurs in Couto, *Asia* (1778–88), xviii, 144, but on p. 168 Couto spoke of the sultan of 1568 as the grandson of the sultan who lost Malacca to the Portuguese in 1511. On pp. 130–1 Couto asserted that the sultan Salaudim of Johore who was killed by the Achinese was a son of the sultan who lost Malacca to the Portuguese. It would seem that the statement on p. 144 is a slip.

Prof. M. Rodrigues Lapa has written, 'was to speak the truth: he would do so, cost what it might. The love of truth is in Couto a kind of vice.'[61] Couto was certainly outspoken, even cantankerous. He frankly revealed blunders and wrongdoings and it is doubtful if he often consciously hid such truths as he knew and thought important to the story. In the complete manuscripts it is possible that lack of evidence led to many of his mistakes and omissions. His work indicates that, less than a century after the Portuguese began their activities in Asia, the documents for their history were sometimes more scarce in Goa than in Europe.

Despite his regard for truth Couto could leave it aside or at least embellish it to flatter or satisfy a friend or patron. In *Decade IV* he admitted that he lacked details about dom Estevão da Gama's attack on the capital of Johore. Indeed, his information was so poor that he thought that Gama made only one expedition to the Johore river, not two. Yet Couto seems to have been anxious to please his patron, the Count of Vidigueira, Viceroy of India 1596–1600 and a collateral descendant of dom Estevão. He therefore inserted a grandiloquent description of the capital. He showed the same readiness for a purple patch in *Decade X*, where he practically copied Barros' encomium on Malacca in 1511 and applied it without acknowledgement to Johore Lama in 1587. Presumably, he wished to flatter the memory of his friend dom Paulo de Lima, the conqueror of the place.

Couto introduced no new major explanation of the position of the Portuguese in the East. Broadly speaking, he accepted Barros' ideas about the original purpose of the Portuguese and the policy of their kings.[62] He dated the beginning of the decline of Portuguese power later than Barros,[63] but held roughly the same views about its cause. In impressive detail he reiterated the complaints about the changed attitude of Portuguese and the misdeeds of officials, criticizing the servants of the Crown both in Asia and Portugal. Like Barros, Couto more than once censured the actions of the king.

In Couto's hands the history kept the character that Barros had given it. Style and tone had altered, but the content was largely the same: Couto too dwelt most on wars and sieges and referred only by the way to administrative and economic affairs. When he wrote of campaigns on the west coast of India he often described events in places he knew: occasionally he told of battles in which he had taken part. His work on South East Asia did not have this advantage. Couto never entered the region of *Ceilão para dentro* and some of his writing about it does not equal his best

[61] Couto, *O Soldado Prático* (ed. by M. Rodrigues Lapa) (1937), p. xxx.
[62] See Couto, *Ásia*, Decade VI, Bk. 4, cap. 7.
[63] See C. R. Boxer, 'The Portuguese in the East, 1500–1800', *Portugal and Brazil: an introduction*, ed. by H. V. Livermore and W. J. Entwistle (1953), p. 211.

work. On the credit side, it must be granted that he accomplished a great deal. He covered a long period and a vast ground; he gave information on many topics, both of purely Asian history and of the history of the Portuguese in Asia.

Couto's *Life of dom Paulo de Lima* and *History of dom Estevão da Gama's peace with Johore and his government of India*; *and of dom Cristovão in Abyssinia and dom Pedro da Silva in Malacca*[64] were mainly extracts from the *Decades*, though the *History* has fuller references to some matters in Malaya in 1535–6. The *Diálogo do Soldado Prático*[65] is concerned with abuses in the Portuguese government of their possessions in Asia: it only rarely and in passing makes specific reference to South East Asia.

António Bocarro was a far less prolific writer than Couto. He added only one *Decade*[66] to the series: it is usually known as the thirteenth. Bocarro's *Decade* is supposed to cover only the time of the viceroyalty of dom Jerónimo de Azevedo, 1612–17, but here and there it ranges further back. It includes the story of Felipe de Brito at Syriam and says much about the Portuguese in Malayan waters. Bocarro has been praised as a severe but impartial judge of men and affairs: his work provides a painstaking account of a short period. He also composed an *História de Maluco no tempo de Gonçalo Pereira Marramaque e Sancho de Vasconcellos*, which he dedicated to king Philip in 1636.[67] It concentrated on the period between 1565 and 1575.

Official chroniclers of the lives of sixteenth-century kings of Portugal devoted much space to affairs in the East. Damião de Goes (1501–74) became keeper of the archives in Lisbon in 1548: ten years later he began to write a life of king Manuel at the request of Cardinal dom Henrique, a son of the 'Fortunate' king. Goes carried out his task in nine years: his *Chrónica do felicíssimo Rei D. Emanuel da gloriosa memória* appeared in four parts in 1566 and 1567.

Goes grew up at the court of king Manuel, but spent many years of his adult life abroad before he returned to Portugal for good in 1545. By that time he was a humanist of European repute: 'Traveller and diplomatist, scholar, singer and musician, he was a man of many friends', including Erasmus, Luis Vives, and Cardinal Sadoletto.[68] Goes has been called 'one of the most accomplished men of his time',[69] but his chronicle of king Manuel is not a profound work. He advanced no idea of the use or scope of history beyond a statement that the chief business of the chronicler was

[64] The History is preserved at Lisbon, Arquivo Nacional da Torre do Tombo, S. Lourenço, vol. vi.

[65] Written in reign of dom Sebastian and revised 1610–12; first published 1790.

[66] First published 1876.

[67] Preserved at Lisbon, National Library, Fundo Geral, No. 474.

[68] A. F. G. Bell, *Portuguese Literature* (1922), p. 213.

[69] Ibid.

to distribute praise and blame. He accepted the official theory of Portuguese expansion as activity 'not so much for the extension of our empire as for the expansion of our beliefs'.[70] He spoke of the natural hostility between Christians and Muslims.[71]

The *Chrónica do felicíssimo Rei D. Emanuel* makes no major contribution to the history of South East Asia. As Tiele long ago pointed out, Goes took his account of affairs in Asia mainly from the history of Castanheda:[72] in some places he did not even copy very carefully.[73] He could certainly have made greater use of the archives he controlled. Goes never visited Asia.

The remaining official chroniclers are less important. Dom Jerónimo Osório (1506–80), Bishop of Silves and a fine Latinist, wrote his *De rebus Emmanuelis regis* (1571) at the instance of Cardinal dom Henrique. He based the work on Goes' chronicle, notes given him by Goes, and evidence from other writings and people.[74] He relied most on Goes' chronicle, whose story of events in the East he repeated with little variation, except for the occasional added comment. Two keepers of the archives at Lisbon undertook to write chronicles of king John III. António de Castilho is said to have written one of them by 1589: surviving extracts suggest that the Indian portions merely copied earlier authors.[75] Francisco de Andrade (*c.* 1540–1614) published his *Chrónica do muyto alto e muyto poderoso Rey destes Reinos de Portugal, Dom João o III deste Nome* in 1613. He had a lot to say about the East. Unfortunately, the main source of his statements was the *Lendas* of Gaspar Correa. Some years after Andrade's death, king Philip IV commissioned Frei Luís de Sousa (1555–1632) to write another chronicle of John III: Sousa began but did not complete his *Anais de D. João III*. A good deal of the Indian sections of the work summarizes Barros' *Decades*.[76]

There are five groups of unofficial historians. One group comprises Fernão Lopes de Castanheda and Gaspar Correa, who wrote long chronicles and had experience of the East: another consists solely of Albuquerque's son who used his father's papers and wrote his father's

[70] Damião de Goes: *Opúsculos Historicos* (ed. by Dias de Carvalho) (1945), p. 86.

[71] E.g., Goes, *Chrónica do felicíssimo Rei D. Emanuel* (1909–12), v, 90.

[72] P. A. Tiele, 'De Europeërs in den Maleischen Archipel', *Bijdragen tot de Taal-, Land- en Volkenkunde van Nederlandsch-Indie*, Volgreeks 4, deel 1 (1877), p. 328.

[73] Goes apparently thought that the Quelins (Klings) of Malacca came from Kilwa and he seems to have mistaken what Castanheda said about the site of the camp of sultan Mahmud's son after the conquest of Malacca. See Fernão Lopes de Castanheda, *História do descobrimento e conquista da Índia pelos Portugueses* (1924–33), i, 458; ii, 153; and Goes, *Chrónica do felicíssimo Rei D. Emanuel* (1909–12), v, 87; vi, 77.

[74] Dom J. Osório, *Da vida e feitos de el-Rei D. Manuel*, translated into Portuguese by F. M. do Nascimento and edited by J. Ferreira (1944), i, 12.

[75] A fragment of Castilho's MS. is preserved in Evora Public Library and District Archives, Codex CIII/2–22.

[76] A. F. G. Bell, *Portuguese Literature* (1922), p. 243.

biography. Fernão Mendes Pinto and António Galvão are in a third section which contains writers who spent some time in Asia but wrote works other than chronicles. Then comes a little set of men who composed biographies and chronicles referring to events in South East Asia in the 1570s and 1580s: it includes Jorge de Lemos, Manoel Godinho de Eredia, João dos Santos, António de Ataíde and the anonymous author of the *Vida de Mathias de Albuquerque*. Finally, there are historians who stayed at or near home and had no direct contact with India. Manuel de Faria e Sousa and Jacinto Freire de Andrade fall into this last category.

Fernão Lopes de Castanheda (1500–59) was the first unofficial historian to publish work which touched on the history of South East Asia. Eight books of his *História do descobrimento e conquista da Índia pelos Portugueses* appeared in print between 1551 and 1561. Castanheda wrote to preserve the memory of deeds the Portuguese had wrought in Asia: he believed that they had surpassed the feats of the heroes of Homer and Livy.[77] He quoted and apparently accepted the idea that the Portuguese in Asia were 'in charge of the honour of Christianity'.[78]

Castanheda went to India in 1528. He soon began to look for information about the history of the Portuguese in the East. He questioned captains and fidalgos who had served in old campaigns: he examined letters and memorials. He said that he had visited the places where the things he described had happened. Couto asserted that Castanheda got as far as the Moluccas: it is possible, but there is no proof.[79] Castanheda returned to Portugal in 1538. He spent several years getting further details from other writings and from people who had returned from Asia. He worked over his materials for years, checking one piece of evidence against another. The idea that conformity of evidence indicated the 'reality of a matter' guided him when he wrote.[80]

Unlike Barros, Castanheda does not seem to have thought that the Portuguese enterprise in Asia declined markedly after the death of Albuquerque. Dissimilar experience may have bred this difference of attitude. As Treasurer and then Factor of India House, Barros must have known that activities in the East had run the kings of Portugal deep into debt. He must also have learned of many scandals in Portuguese government in Asia. Castanheda never served as an official, rarely gave much space in his *History* to financial matters and wrote chiefly of wars, battles, and disputes. He went to the East when Portuguese confidence was still fairly high. He sailed from Lisbon with Nuno da Cunha and 'the most

[77] F. L. de Castanheda, *História do descobrimento e conquista da India pelos Portugueses* (1924–33), ii, 1.
[78] Ibid., ii, 46.
[79] Ibid., i, 3; Couto, *Ásia*, Decade IV, Book 5, cap. 1.
[80] F. L. de Castanheda, *História do descobrimento e conquista da Índia pelos Portugueses* (1924–33), ii, 2.

splendid body of men who till that time had gone to India'.[81] He stayed in Asia at a time when the Portuguese waged many wars and won some long-desired successes. Outward circumstances can have done little to make him believe in a steady failure of strength of Portugal overseas. That is not to imply that he could see no faults. Nor did he, like Barros, occasionally shrink from revealing quarrels and intrigues: the strife over the governorship in 1527 takes up almost a whole book of the *History*. Castanheda narrated both good and bad deeds, presumably in the happy confidence that the first outweighed the second.

The importance of Castanheda's work lies principally in its detailed history of the Portuguese in Asia between 1498 and 1542. The long chronicle reflects his overriding interest in the actions of his countrymen and, above all, in their military achievements. With that interest went a suspicion of Muslims,[82] perhaps strengthened by residence in Asia. The *History* has further value as a check on Barros' point of view and accuracy. Castanheda wrote without Barros' moral purpose, but also without Barros' fear of ultimate failure. It follows that he did not shroud Portuguese expansion with any pessimism. At the same time, it is useful to compare the *History* with Barros' *Decades*, for Castanheda often drew his story from what was virtually private evidence, while Barros relied much on materials from royal archives. The comparison is sometimes to the disadvantage of the *History*. The source of Castanheda's evidence may explain errors such as his idea that sultan Mahmud of Malacca died soon after the Portuguese captured the city.

Castanheda showed less interest in geography than Barros, and here and there, the *History* described places in South East Asia at some length: Pegu, Malacca, and the Moluccas received such treatment. Castanheda was not always accurate: his account of Malacca repeated the tale of the merchants and their bahars of gold. Descriptions of other countries and places in South East Asia are generally briefer. Reference to the history of South East Asia before the coming of the Portuguese is cursory. Castanheda did not always give much explanation of the Asian conditions which helped to determine the policy and actions of the Portuguese: his version of relations with Java in the 1520s exemplifies this defect. Castanheda was essentially a faithful chronicler of the deeds of the Portuguese in the East: his outlook was narrower than Barros'.

Gaspar Correa (*c.* 1495–*c.* 1565) spent much longer in Asia than Castanheda. He reached India in 1512. Soon afterwards he became one of Albuquerque's secretaries. He remained in the East for nearly all the rest of his life. There is no evidence that he ever visited South East Asia, though a drawing of Malacca is attached to the manuscript of his work, *Lendas da Índia* or *Corónica dos feytos da Índia*. Correa had finished this book by 1551

[81] Ibid., iv, 149.   [82] E.g., ibid., i, 19, 50, 420.

but was still revising it in 1561 and 1563. It covers the history of the Portuguese in Asia down to 1550.

Correa asserted: 'In this my work I have wished to write only of the deeds of the Portuguese and not of countries.'[83] There are few descriptions of places. Most of the text relates quarrels, battles, and expeditions of the Portuguese. Despite Bell's praise, Correa's repute as an historian is not high. He is generally regarded as unreliable, except where he tells of events he witnessed. Certainly, his story of affairs in South East Asia is marred by errors of fact, omissions, and a strong tendency to muddle names. However much Correa may reveal the ideas of the Portuguese in the East—and here a good deal may be said in his favour—his narrative is of dubious worth.

Braz (Afonso) de Albuquerque (1500–80) was the son of the Portuguese conqueror of Malacca. He served as a royal counsellor in the reign of king John III and was a prominent citizen of Lisbon. He never went to Asia. In 1557 he published the *Comentários do grande Afonso de Albuquerque*: a second and revised edition appeared in 1576. Braz de Albuquerque dedicated both editions to dom Sebastian, who was crown prince in 1557 and king in 1576. The declared aim of the work was to remind the king of his obligations to the descendants of men who had done good service to earlier rulers. The *Commentaries'* second object was to give greater prominence to the feats of the elder Albuquerque. Braz de Albuquerque claimed that he based his book on originals of his father's letters to king Manuel.

The *Commentaries* deal almost exclusively with the career of the elder Albuquerque in India and more especially with his term as Governor of Portuguese India, 1509–15. The story of his visit to Malacca in 1511–12 has most of the references to South East Asia. They include a summary of the history of Malacca under the Malay sultanate, a description of the city's customs and trade and an account of its conquest. The *Commentaries* go on to say what happened in Malacca between the conquest and the Governor's departure. There are brief mentions of Siam, China, Sumatra, Java, and Pahang. Braz de Albuquerque's book is not always right and it may sometimes distort the truth, as any reader of Giovanni da Empoli knows. But its story of events in and near Malacca in 1511–12 is very valuable because the Governor's report on them has disappeared.

The *Commentaries* assume that the Muslims in Malacca were treacherous to the Portuguese in 1509. The Governor seized the city because of that treachery and because of Muslim pride in 1511.[84] He hoped that the conquest would check the spread of Islam and give the Portuguese control of the carriage of drugs and spices from South East Asia to the Red Sea.[85]

---

[83] Correa, *Lendas da Índia* (1858–66), iii, 66.
[84] Albuquerque, *Comentários* (1923), i, 38, 130.
[85] Ibid., ii, 96–7.

It is interesting to compare the writings of Tomé Pires with the words Braz de Albuquerque attributed to his father. All in all, the book is a notable contribution to the history of Malaya and to an understanding of the attitudes and policy of the Portuguese in South East Asia in the early part of the sixteenth century.

The extant works of António Galvão and Fernão Mendes Pinto fall within one class but vary much in character. António Galvão (*c.* 1490–1557) ended his service in the East as Captain of the fort at Ternate from 1536 to 1540. His manuscript of nine or ten 'books'[86] on affairs in the Moluccas and India was never printed and has disappeared. There remains the *Treatise* or *Livro dos Descobrimentos das Antilhas e Índias pollos Espanhões feytas* (sic), published posthumously in 1563.

Most of Galvão's *Treatise* is a summary of Spanish and Portuguese discoveries between 1492 and 1550, with short notes on peoples and curiosities in America and Asia. The references to South East Asia are brief and sometimes wrong. Moreover, Galvão, like Pires, overestimated the importance of the Moluccas, which he thought not less rich than India or New Spain.[87] It is unlikely that he saw many documents outside Ternate, but he did record Ruy Nunez da Cunha's embassy to Pegu. Barros, Castanheda and Braz de Albuquerque said nothing about it: even a modern editor of the *Treatise* has doubted Galvão's story.[88]

Fernão Mendes Pinto (*c.* 1510–83) travelled more widely than Galvão. Between 1538 and 1557 he sailed the seas from Aden to Japan. Of the countries of South East Asia, he claimed to have visited Malaya, Sumatra, Java, the Moluccas, Burma, Siam, and Indochina, to say nothing of the mythical kingdom of Calaminham. In 1562, a few years after his return to Portugal, he began to write his *Peregrinação*—the story of his adventures. He went on with the task till he died. The *Peregrination* was printed in 1614, after being edited by Francisco de Andrade.

Pinto began life in Asia as a soldier and trader, but he later became an associate of missionaries: for a time, he was a novice in the Society of Jesus. The tone of his book points to a change in Portuguese interests and ideals in the second half of the sixteenth century. Unlike Pires, Pinto was not confident that the Portuguese in Asia could serve God and Mammon simultaneously. He reflected adversely on the behaviour of Portuguese adventurers and on the assumption that 'it was enough to be a Christian, for God's mercy was great'.[89] He did not have Barros' and Castanheda's faith in the righteousness of the expansion of Portuguese power in the Orient.

Critics have differed about the value of the *Peregrination* as history. It is

---

[86] Galvão, *Tratado dos descobrimentos*, edited by Visconde de Lagôa (1944), p. 69.
[87] Ibid., p. 168.   [88] Ibid., p. 167.
[89] M. Collis, *The Grand Peregrination* (1949), p. 256.

not always easy to name the places its author really went to. He certainly reached Malacca and Burma: he may have been to Siam: his visits to Sumatra, Java, and the Moluccas are either less likely or improbable. Pinto lied about his travels and about others matters too. He so mixed fiction with truth that it is often hard to say where the *Peregrination* even approaches a moderately sober record of events that its writer witnessed or heard about. Good judges have suspected many of Pinto's stories and have damned them as untrustworthy.

The book (Fr. Schurhammer has said) is a romance of adventures, auto-biographical and brilliantly written. Not only are all the speeches and letters and all the voyages to the mysterious interior of Africa and Asia invented, but also almost all the descriptions of his adventures, though they may often contain some historical basis. We also consider the voyage to the Moluccas and the captivity in Arabia . . . as pure inventions.

But even on occasions when Pinto was indubitably present, as, for example, during the residence of Xavier at Bungo and his return from Japan, the happenings are romantically adorned by unrestrained fantasy, so great that no historian could ever base himself on him alone. The dates are completely mixed. They are sometimes in direct contradiction to those from contemporary and reliable sources and even to one another. For instance, if we follow the dates of Mendes Pinto and add up the months and years that he gives for the time between 1542 and 1551, we find ourselves with thirteen years instead of ten.[90]

Fr. Schurhammer is a great authority, but historians of Malaya, Sumatra, and Java are sometimes hard pressed. When they lack much other evidence, they may think it foolish not to make cautious use of the *Peregrination*. Thus, they can begin by assuming that Pinto got to know Malacca fairly well between 1539 and 1556. They can go on to say that his account of the position of the sultan of Johore between 1539 and 1547 is not impossible. Without finally accepting Pinto's story, they can point out that it may throw added light on conditions which then existed on both sides of the Malacca Strait.

Writers have occasionally asserted or implied that the *Peregrination* is untrustworthy in details, but shows a grasp of important factors in the history of the western part of the Malay Archipelago. Such a use of Pinto is hardly dangerous, for it merely brings him in to confirm an impression gained from other evidence. Only exaggerated trust betrays the user of the *Peregrination*. It would be unwise to make it the chief evidence for 'essential facts': it would be risky to follow its details closely. Yet, it has become

---

[90] G. Schurhammer, S.J., '1543–1943—Descobrimento do Japão pelos Portugueses no ano de 1543', *Anais da Academia Portuguesa da História*, II serie (1946), i, 144.

customary to accept Pinto's word that an Achinese attack on Johore Lama took place in 1564.

Pinto mentioned the date in what was virtually a footnote. Modern historians have seized upon it partly because of a shortage of printed histories of Portuguese activities in South East Asia in the second half of the sixteenth century. Thirteen works written by 1651 and printed by 1844 tell all or part of the story for the years before 1550: few of them go much further. Only Couto and Faria e Sousa tried to cover all the rest of the century and they both leave the gap between 1575 and 1580. Consequently, the small group of writings on some events in South East Asia between 1574 and 1588 is important. [91]

Two works in the group are printed. One is the *Hystória dos cercos que em tempo de António Moniz Barreto, Governador que foi dos estados da Índia, os Achens e Iaos puserão a fortaleza de Malaca, sendo Tristão Vaz da Veiga capitão della*, written by Jorge de Lemos and published in 1585. According to Innocêncio da Silva, there exist only three printed copies of this book, together with two manuscript versions: [92] at least one of the latter has a slightly variant title. [93] Lemos was born in Goa, where he served as secretary of Viceroys and Governors of India. He spent some time in Portugal, but returned to India and was clerk of the Portuguese Exchequer there for over six years. He died in Asia after September 1593. Judging from the Évora manuscript, his book describes the sieges of Malacca in 1574 and 1575 and adds details about the aftermath of the death of the sultan of Acheh in 1579. It makes reference to Johore and Java and ends with a description of Sumatra and a plea for the conquest of Acheh. Lemos apparently took some care to get exact information about the story he told. The *History* has few philosophical reflections.

The other printed work is João dos Santos' *Ethiópia Oriental*, first published in 1609. Santos served in the East as a missionary from 1586 to 1600: he went back later and died there in 1622. His book includes an account of the capture of Johore Lama in 1587: he founded it on the evidence of a brother friar who was present.

Five chapters of the *Vida de Mathias de Albuquerque* refer to earlier events in Malayan waters: so do several pages of Eredia's short *História dos servicos com martírio de Luís Monteiro Coutinho*, which also alludes briefly to Solor. [94] Cunha Rivara [95] dated the manuscript of the *Vida* in the seven-

[91] To this group should probably be added Bocarro's *History of the Moluccas*, which I have not yet been able to consult in detail.

[92] Innocêncio F. da Silva, *Diccionário bibliographico português* (1858–1923), iv, 172.

[93] *Descripçam dos cercos de Malaca, sendo capitão Tristão Vaz da Veiga e'de huma vitória naval que teve da armada do Achem*. Codex CXVI/1–26 in Évora Public Library and District Archives.

[94] The MS. of the *Vida de Mathias de Albuquerque* is Codex CXV/1–13 in Évora Public Library and District Archives; the MS. of Eredia's History is Fundo Geral No. 414 in the National Library at Lisbon.

[95] J. H. da Cunha Rivara, *Catálogo dos Manuscriptos da Bibliotheca Pública Eborense* (1850), i, 315.

teenth century and its composition in the lifetime of its subject: it would therefore seem to have been written well before 1650. Eredia dedicated his *History* to the archbishop of Goa in 1615: he based it partly on attested documents which related experiences of Coutinho. Both biographies tell of things which occurred in Couto's blank period of 1575–80: they throw light on the history of Johore and Acheh during those years. As noted earlier, the *History* has mistakes.

In 1616 António de Ataíde, the first count of Castro Daire finished a life of dom Paulo de Lima, his relative by marriage. Most of it reproduces Couto's biography of the same man. [96]

Another work ought to be associated with those in this section. It is Padre Manuel Xavier's *Vitórias do Governador da Índia Nuno Alvares Botelho* (1633), which narrates Portuguese successes in Malayan waters in 1629 and 1630. The book is contemporary rather than considered history.

The last group of secular historians is in many ways the least valuable. Manuel de Faria e Sousa (1590–1649) was born in Portugal, but lived in Spain and wrote in Spanish. His *Ásia Portuguesa* appeared posthumously in 1666: it traces the history of the Portuguese in the East from 1498 to 1640. Faria e Sousa relied most on printed materials, not always of the best type. He was the first chronicler to think Pinto 'very truthful': [97] he inserted long extracts from the *Peregrination* in the *Portuguese Asia*. Faria e Sousa usually wrote history by abridging the work of authors he trusted: the first part of his book was merely an abstract of some of Barros' *Decades*. He copied and summarized the writings of other men, adding speeches and dogmatic assertions that were sometimes at variance with the facts. He accepted earlier historians' ideas of the praiseworthy nature of Portuguese expansion.

Jacinto Freire de Andrade (1597–1657) wrote a *Vida de dom João de Castro* after repeated requests to do so from dom Francisco de Castro, a descendant of the hero. The *Life* adds little to earlier chronicles, save for a 'mixture of Tacitean phrases, conceits and rhetorical affectation'. [98] It was printed in 1651.

3. *Ecclesiastical Histories*

From the time St. Francis Xavier reached India in 1542, Portuguese in the East became more concerned with missionary activity. The increased interest eventually had the by-product of biographies of the saint and histories of the Jesuits in Asia. Portuguese had written four such works by 1614.

The first was a short life of Xavier and a commentary on Indian affairs, which were put together by Manuel Acosta and published in 1568. Acosta

[96] The MS. is Codex CXVI/1–24 in Évora Public Library and District Archives.
[97] The statement occurs in Faria e Sousa's discussion of his sources at the beginning of his *Ásia Portuguesa*.
[98] A. F. G. Bell, *Portuguese Literature* (1922), p. 266.

wrote in Europe, but the next author, Padre Manuel Teixeira, was in Asia from 1551 till his death in 1590: in the 1560s he accompanied an embassy to China. He completed a life of Xavier in 1579. Teixeira's book was not printed till 1912, but a life of Xavier by João de Lucena was published in Lisbon in 1600. Lucena's book has been called a panegyric rather than a biography: it drew heavily on Pinto for an account of Xavier in Malaya. Sebastião Gonçalves finished the first part of his *Hist. Soc. in Indiis Orientalibus* in 1614. The greater part of it is an abstract of Lucena's work. The ecclesiastical histories all follow St. Francis' travels from India to Japan and Teixeira, Lucena, and Gonçalves give descriptions of parts of South East Asia, sometimes taken from the saint's letters. Yet these works cannot compare with the histories that laymen wrote. They cover a narrower field of Portuguese activities and were based largely on secular writings and letters from priests: most of the first and many of the second can still be consulted. Exhaustive modern research into the life of St. Francis and the recent publication of letters from Jesuit missionaries in the East by the Society has further lessened the importance of the ecclesiastical chronicles. [99]

4. *Conclusion*

By 1650 the Portuguese government had lost nearly all its possessions in South East Asia. It retained only precarious footholds on the islands of Solor and Timor. Missionaries and merchants still stayed in or visited other parts of the region, but their activities were generally unspectacular and without effective support from the Crown. Not surprisingly, no monumental works recorded their endeavours. In addition, the wish to write fresh histories of earlier periods seems to have lessened. For South East Asia, the streams of Portuguese historical writing were drying up.

There were exceptions. In the late seventeenth and early eighteenth centuries reports were sent home from India on the history of missions in the East: they included references to South East Asia. In 1710 Francisco de Sousa published his *O Oriente conquistado á Jesú Christo pelos padres da Companhia de Jesús*: it had lengthy accounts of Jesuit efforts in the Malay Archipelago in the sixteenth century and also mentioned secular affairs. In 1718 or 1719 a relation of António de Albuquerque Coelho's voyage from Madras to Macao was printed at Heungshan.

In the eighteenth century attention came to concentrate on the republication of old histories rather than the writing of new ones. The process may be said to start with the issue of part of Couto's *Decades* in 1736. Other major works were reprinted in the next seventy years. Their reappearance, together with the destruction of the India House archives in 1755, may have

[99] For a commentary on these works see G. Schurhammer, S.J., 'Historical Research into the life of St. Francis Xavier in the sixteenth century', *Revista da História* (Portugal) (1923), xii, 192–223.

fostered the inclination to accept and copy. When they touched on South East Asia, some prominent writers of the nineteenth century, such as Francisco de Santo Luiz, Manuel Pinheiro Chagas, and E. A. Bettencourt[100] did little better than echo in abridged form the words of historians of the sixteenth and seventeenth centuries. But matters have improved gradually and more especially in recent years, with the work of scholars like Armando Cortesão, Humberto Leitão, Panduronga S. S. Pissurlencar, and the Visconde de Lagôa. Among other things, modern scholarship can correct errors of the old historians: in doing so, it may make it possible to define the qualities of their writings with more precision.

Even now, certain characteristics stand out. The old histories concentrate on the first half of the sixteenth century, though fresh discoveries of manuscripts may yet fill in some later gaps. In many works there is a strong patriotic and religious bias, a sense of Portuguese mission in Asia, a note of pride, an intolerance and suspicion of Muslims and a disregard for rights of Asians. In Barros' *Decades* there is also a marked moral purpose which tended to hide the significance of some developments in South East Asia. The chronicles are tales of Portuguese rather than Asians, but some show considerable interest in Asian history and circumstances: this is yet more pronounced in one or two reports. Even the best histories deal mainly with wars, voyages and intrigues and have little 'profounder study of law and government' or trade: again, it is reports that remedy some of the lack of information on economic matters. A few authors are notably inaccurate: others hide things. People who went to Asia were in no way exempt from these defects. The nature of Portuguese enterprise in the East meant that it tended to be best recorded by men with careful judgements and access to royal archives. By the second half of the sixteenth century there were already topics which were probably better documented at home than in India. Most Portuguese writers regarded South East Asia— *as partes do Sul*—as a region apart from India and gave it separate treatment. Occasionally they exaggerated the importance of parts of the area. On the whole, Portuguese historical writings of the sixteenth century include a rich mine of information for historians of South East Asia. The pity is that two of the poorest histories have gained fairly wide circulation in English. Faria e Sousa and Jacinto Freire de Andrade are at the end of a literary and historical epoch. In front of them are greater writers and better historians, whose labours have kept a good deal from the holocaust which destroyed the archives of India House. These earlier works contain, often in much detail, a not unworthy memorial to Portuguese interest in South East Asia in the sixteenth and seventeenth centuries.

---

[100] Francisco de Santo Luiz, *Os portugueses na Africa, Ásia, America e Oceania* (1835), eight volumes; Manuel Pinheiro Chagas, *História de Portugal* (1867); E. A. Bettencourt, *Descobrimentos, guerras e conquistas dos portugueses em terras ultramares nos seculos xv e xvi* (1881–2).

14. SOME ASPECTS OF SPANISH HISTORICAL WRITING ON THE PHILIPPINES

C. R. BOXER

Camoens Professor of Portuguese in the University of London

Spanish historical writing on the Philippines before 1887 has two out-standing characteristics. Firstly, virtually all of it was written by members of the Religious Orders, chiefly by missionaries of many years service in the islands, who had a good knowledge of the languages and the people. Secondly, it is inseparably connected with the historiography of their missions in the Moluccas, Indochina, China, and Japan, and can only be considered in conjunction therewith. After 1887 several important secular historians enter the lists; but even so, the missionary influence has re-mained a very strong one down to the present day. The historical works written by the missionaries naturally have a strong religious bias, but nevertheless they contain more interesting and varied material than is often realized.

When the Spaniards occupied the Philippines in 1565–75, they found that the Filipinos had no written historical records of any kind, but relied exclusively on oral tradition. Such at least is the version given by the con-temporary chroniclers, one of whom, Padre Pedro Chirino, S.J., writes in his *Relacion de las islas Filipinas* (Rome, 1604), as follows: 'For none of these three things, religion, idolatry, and superstition, nor for matters appertain-ing to government and polity do they make use of their written characters; for they have never made any use of these latter save only for writing letters to each other. The whole of their government and religion is based on oral tradition . . . which is handed down in songs which they learn from memory when children, hearing them sung when they go sailing, when they work, and when they rejoice and make merry, and still more when they mourn the dead. In these barbarous songs they sing of the fabulous genealogies and the vain deeds of their gods.' Chirino further explains that although the great majority of the Tagalogs and Visayas were literate, their written characters (which he reproduces in his book) were of Tagalog origin, the Visayas having adopted them only very recently.

Some doubt may be cast on Chirino's statement by another passage in his *Relacion* of 1604, where he recounts (p. 47) that the Jesuits had con-fiscated and burnt a 'book of certain very pernicious poems which they call *Golo*', on the grounds that it contained an 'express pact with the devil'. Moreover, it seems very improbable that in a region where the literacy rate was admittedly far higher than that in contemporary Europe, no attempt should have been made to record the deeds of past generations save in traditional oral ballads. On the other hand, Chirino's observation is confirmed by other ecclesiastical chroniclers, including Fr. Gaspar de San Agustín, O.E.S.A., and Padre Juan Delgado, S.J., who are dealt with below; and I know of no reliable evidence that the Spanish *conquistadores* and missionaries systematically destroyed all existing written records, as they did to some extent in Mexico.

The Philippines were the remotest of all the far-flung Spanish dominions, and the soldiers of the Cross who gravitated to this colony were, like those of the Crown, of two main types. Either they were self-sacrificing and energetic characters who sought new spiritual (or temporal) fields to conquer, or else they were apt to be irresponsible ne'er-do-wells, of whom Spain, Mexico, and Peru were glad to be rid. The chroniclers and historians naturally belonged to the former class, but the presence and activities of their weaker brethren are very evident in their writings. The historiography of Spanish rule in the Philippines reflects the struggle for justice which was taking place both there and in America.[1] The struggle between the followers of Las Casas and Bishop Palafox[2] on the one side, and the *conquistadores* and *encomenderos* who sought to exploit the Amerindians and the Filipinos on the other. Not, of course, that the line between the just and the unjust necessarily coincided with the division between the missionaries and the *conquistadores*. Many of the former were truculent, arrogant, and avaricious; while there were men among the soldiery and the laity who were conspicuous for their humane and reasonable views. But it can be said as a broad generalization that it was the representatives of the Cross rather than those of the Crown who showed a greater concern for the inhabitants of the islands until the second half of the eighteenth century.

Before considering the missionary historians in more detail, it may be as well to get the only secular writer of this period out of the way. This is the celebrated Dr. Antonio de Morga (1559–1636), a judge of the local High Court, whose *Sucesos de las Islas Filipinas* (Mexico, 1609), is one of the most interesting books ever written about the Philippines, and was the only lay history published before 1887. The scope of this work is more accurately indicated by the original manuscript title which it bore in

---

[1] L. Hanke, *The Spanish struggle for Justice in the conquest of America* (Philadelphia, 1949), affords the best introduction to the subject in English. Comparative Philippine and American material will be found in *Cuerpo de documentos del siglo XVI sobre los derechos de España en las Indias y las Filipinas*, ed. L. Hanke and A. Millares Carlo (Mexico, 1943).

[2] Bartolomé de Las Casas, O. P. (1474–1566), Bishop of Chiapa, famous champion of the liberty of the Amerindians and author of the *Brevissima Relación de la Destrucción de Las Indias*, and other works highly critical of various aspects of Spanish colonization. Juan de Palafox y Mendoza (1600–59), Bishop of Puebla de los Angeles and later of Osma, author of numerous historical, judicial, and theological works, including a treatise entitled *Virtudes del Indio*.

1607: 'Descubrimiento, conquista, pacificacion, y poblacion de las Islas Philipinas.'[3] The book was evidently written partly in justification of Morga's conduct in his disastrous naval action with Olivier Van Noort in Manila Bay (14 December 1601). Its publication at Mexico in 1609 was apparently inspired by the idea of forestalling Bartolomé Leonardo de Argensola's *Conquista de las islas Moluccas*, which appeared at Madrid in the same year and covers much the same ground. Being published in a very limited edition, Morga's book did not, for nearly 300 years, achieve the renown of Argensola's work which is one of the classics of Spanish literature. Since the publication of W. E. Retana's definitive edition of the *Sucesos de las Islas Filipinas* at Madrid in 1909, there is no longer any excuse for historians ignoring this magnificent work.

Morga was a devout Catholic, but his religion did not blind him to the folly of the friars who meddled in matters which were not their concern, nor to the laxity which often pervaded the Religious Orders in the enervating physical and moral climate of colonial Manila.[4] He gives a very full account of Spanish intervention in Cambodia in 1596–9, printing copious extracts from the relevant official correspondence; but he indicates quite clearly that he was opposed to the enterprise from the start. He also realized that the Chinese rebellion of 1603, which was suppressed with such savagery and loss of life, was largely if not entirely provoked by the Spaniards' own truculent behaviour.[5] This admission is the more creditable since Morga, in common with the great majority of his countrymen, regarded the *Sangeleyes*, or Chinese mercantile community at Manila, with dislike and suspicion. As might be expected, that part of his work which deals with the period prior to his own arrival in Luzon is nothing like so full and detailed as the section covering the years 1595–1603. His description of the Filipino tribes is, according to Retana, 'sufficient of itself to make this book one of the most interesting which is registered in any colonial bibliography'. This may be so, but since Morga never left the immediate vicinity of Manila during his eight years in the colony, his account is mainly derived from earlier writers and more particularly from a description written by the Franciscan friar, Juan de Plasencia, in 1589.[6]

[3] 'Discovery, conquest, pacification, and colonisation of the Philippine Islands.' Cf. *Sucesos de las islas Filipinas por el Dr. Antonio de Morga. Nueva edición enriquecida con los escritos inéditos del mismo autor ilustrada con numerosas notas que amplian el texto y prologada extensamente por W. E. Retana* (Madrid, 1909), hereafter cited as Morga-Retana, *Sucesos*.

[4] His report of 8 June 1598, printed in Morga-Retana, *Sucesos*, pp. 247–50, may be compared with the letter of Fr. Alonso de Vico, dated ten days later and printed on pp. 436–7 of the same work, and with the allegations of the English Dominican renegade, Thomas Gage, *The English-American. A new survey of the West Indies, 1648*, ed. A. P. Newton (The Broadway Travellers, 1946), pp. 5–12, 33–34, 40–43, 90, 110–17, 256.

[5] '. . . que solo esto, les fue bastante motivo, para hallarse necesitados, de hazer lo que no pensauan' (Morga-Retana, *Sucesos*, p. 149).

[6] First published in 1886. Cf. R. Streit, *Bibliotheca Missionum* (Aachen, 1928), iv, 332–3.

Morga proved himself a just and upright judge during his tour of duty in the Philippines, and his work bears the impress of a judicious and impartial mind; but he never came to regard the Islands and their inhabitants with the sympathy and affection that some of the missionary writers showed.

By way of contrast to Morga's moderation and relative impartiality, we may consider the work of his contemporary, Fray Diego Aduarte, O.P. (1570–1636), whose *Historia* of his Order in the Philippines and the Far East was published posthumously at Manila in 1640.[7] The famous Filipino patriot and writer, Dr. José Rizal (1861–96), characterized this doughty Dominican as follows: 'Fr. Diego Aduarte is the typical adventurous friar of that period, half warrior and half priest, brave and stoical, confessing, baptizing and killing, full of faith and without any scruples . . . not forgetting to confess his companions before launching them to kill people who were sleeping peacefully and to burn their houses.'[8] This judgement is obviously influenced by Rizal's understandable anti-clericalism, although it is not altogether unfounded. Fr. Diego Aduarte certainly did advocate the conquest of Cambodia, and he reproached the Portuguese for their lack of the *conquistador* spirit and missionary élan; but a careful perusal of his *Historia* shows that he was something more than a fanatical crusader with a cross in one hand and a sword in the other. He criticized the theories of those who argued that the spiritual power must always be closely supported by the temporal power in the mission-field, pointing out that peaceful penetration by the missionaries was usually more effective. He claimed that the Christian converts made in China were particularly admirable, since they had no temporal inducements to embrace the new faith, and did so only from genuine conviction. He defends the Chinese against the accusation of xenophobia which is so often brought against them. Although he was on one occasion imprisoned and tortured at Canton, he explained (correctly enough) that the Chinese laws regarding the treatment of foreign castaways were remarkably humane and enlightened.[9] He denounces the view that mediocre missionaries were good enough for the Filipinos, and states that on the contrary, learned and zealous men were essential. He professed a great admiration for the Koreans, rating them higher than their two famous neighbours for the following reasons: 'They share the good understanding and sharpness of the Chinese, but are not so deceitful since they are mostly peasants, while they have something

[7] *Historia de la provincia del Sancto Rosario de la Orden de Predicadores en Philippinas, Iapon, y China* (Manila, 1640). After Aduarte's death in August 1636, the work was concluded by Fr. Domingo González, O.P. A second edition was published at Saragossa, 1693.

[8] *Sucesos de las Islas Filipinas por el Doctor Antonio de Morga*, ed. J. Rizal (Paris, 1890), p. 95. The Spanish colonial government destroyed all copies of this book which they could find, so this edition is a distinctly rare one.

[9] Aduarte, *Historia* (ed. 1640), pt. I, p. 406.

of the courage of the Japanese without their ferocity. In this way they form a happy and laudable mean, and are far more fitted to receive and keep our holy faith.'[10]

Aduarte's *Historia* was avowedly published mainly to stimulate friars in Spain to volunteer for missionary work in the Far East, and particularly for the dangerous field of Japan. It is therefore filled with edifying anecdotes about exemplary converts, with gory details of martyrdoms, and with hagiographical biographies of Dominican friars who died in those missions. These characteristics are shared by all mission histories to a greater or lesser extent; but Aduarte's work also (like them) contains matter of greater interest to present-day readers. These topics include his own experiences in Cambodia and Canton, the introduction of printing into the Philippines, and a vivid description of Japanese prison economy. Like most of the friars in the Philippines, Aduarte was no admirer of the Jesuits, and his outspoken criticism of some of their doings apparently delayed the publication of his book for a time.

Much more of a firebrand than Fr. Diego Aduarte, was the Jesuit Padre Alonso Sánchez (1547–93), who is chiefly famous (or infamous) for his persistent advocacy of the conquest and forcible conversion of China, preferably with the aid of an auxiliary force of Japanese Christians.[11] In the upshot, Sánchez' views were not accepted by the government at Madrid any more than were the schemes of Aduarte and his colleagues for the conquest of Indochina. But although the Jesuit's crackpot plans make one smile today, he was taken very seriously at the time. He was a most prolific memorialist, even if none of his bellicose effusions were printed in his lifetime, for his views were controverted by many of his own Society, including the famous Padre Joseph de Acosta.[12] But they also met with warm approval from many Spanish missionaries and officials, and others were found to champion them later. Sánchez' main thesis was that Christ had delegated full spiritual and temporal powers to the Pope as his Vicar on earth. His Holiness could, in turn, delegate as much of these as he chose to anyone he selected for preaching the gospel to the heathen, supported by whatever means were judged most suitable.[13] Sánchez argued that missionaries would never be allowed to preach freely in China unless they were protected by force of arms. From this it was a short and inevitable step to arguing that a Spanish conquest of China (or of any other

[10] Aduarte, *Historia* (ed. 1640), pt. II, p. 85.

[11] A bio-bibliographical sketch of Alonso Sánchez, S.J., and his writings in Streit, *Bibliotheca Missionum* (nr. 1217), iv, 326–31. For his projected conquest of China, cf. C. R. Boxer, *The Christian Century in Japan 1549–1650* (California University Press, 1951), pp. 257–60.

[12] L. Lopetegui, S.J., *El Padre José de Acosta S.J., y las missiones* (Madrid, 1942), pp. 461–85.

[13] 'Tratado de la potestad espiritual y temporal de Christo en la tierra, y de la que dexó á su Vicario el Pontifice Romano, y de como la puede comunicar, y cometar á quien le pareciere convenir, para que en su nombre predique el Evangelio en todas las partes del mundo, y con los medios, y ayudas que fuere menester', written at Manila about 1582.

non-Christian country for that matter) would be a 'just war' if ever there was one.

It must be reiterated that Sánchez was not typical of his Society, and that most of the Jesuit historians of the Philippines (Chirino, Combés, Colin, etc.) were men of more moderate views. Their historical writing is, of course, like that of their colleagues in the Mendicant Orders, heavily biassed by their religious convictions. Their histories and chronicles were written mainly to edify and encourage their supporters in Roman Catholic Europe, particularly in Spain. Like Aduarte's *Historia*, they therefore tend to be too full of edifying anecdotes and miracle-mongering for the taste of the modern reader, although not for that of their contemporaries. But they all contain some interesting chapters devoted to the description of the Philippines and their inhabitants as they knew them, and these sections are still of interest to the historian today.

One inevitable defect which these mission histories have in common, is that being written exclusively from the standpoint of one particular Religious Order, they minimize or omit to mention what others were doing in the same field. To get the whole picture, it is therefore necessary to plough through most of the mission histories published by the different Orders between the appearance of Fr. Marcello de Ribadeneyra, O.F.M.'s *Historia* at Barcelona in 1601, and that of Fr. Joaquín Martínez de Zúñiga, O.E.S.A., *Historia* at Sampaloc in 1803.[14] The best of these histories is undoubtedly that by Fr. Juan de la Concepción, O.E.S.A., *Historia general de Filipinas* (14 vols., Sampaloc, 1788–92). This really is a general history, and not just a missionary history, for the worthy Augustinian ranges both wider and deeper than any of his predecessors, but it ends with the year 1758. Luckily for those who know no Spanish, copious and representative selections from all these histories, together with a great mass of supporting documentation will be found translated in Blair and Robertson's truly monumental compilation.[15] Lack of space precludes discussion of all but a few representative missionary historians, and I will confine myself to outlining some of the ideas which influenced the writing of them.

Fr. Gaspar de San Agustín, O.E.S.A. (1650–1724), spent most of his life in the Philippines, dying at Manila at the age of seventy-four.[16] He was a poet as well as a historian, and became a good Tagalog scholar, but

[14] Full bibliographical descriptions in Streit-Dindinger, *Bibliotheca Missionum*, iv–vi (Aachen, 1928–31).

[15] *The Philippine Islands 1493–1898. Explorations by early navigators, descriptions of the Islands and, their peoples, their history and records of the Catholic missions, as related in contemporaneous books and manuscripts, showing the political, economic, commercial and religious conditions of those Islands from their earliest relations with European nations to the close of the nineteenth century* (55 vols., Cleveland, Ohio, 1903–9).

[16] Bio-bibliographical details in Streit, *Bibliotheca Missionum*, v, 319–24.

he never acquired much sympathy for the people among whom he worked. Fr. Gaspar's bias is strikingly demonstrated in a letter which he wrote in the year 1720, and which had a wide circulation in manuscript.[17] In this he takes the usual attitude of racial superiority which the white man in the East affected for so long. Superficial writers often allege that the Iberian or Latin races had no colour-bar in comparison with (say) the Dutch or the English, but this assertion is much exaggerated when it is not altogether false. Stringent rules against the admission of half-breeds existed in the Religious Orders working in the colonial mission-fields, and although they were not always strictly applied, they usually were so. Spanish historical writing teems with sneering and deprecatory allusions to Creoles, Mestizos, and Mulattoes, who were nearly always discriminated against, both legally and socially.[18] Fr. Gaspar's attitude is very like that of the old hand in George Orwell's *Burmese Days*, who said to the newcomer: 'Remember, laddie, always remember, we are sahiblog and they are dirrt.' At the risk of giving Mr. Krushchev some more material for anti-colonial propaganda, I cannot refrain from drawing attention to the Augustinian historian's views, which were shared by many of his colleagues.

Fr. Gaspar de San Agustín squarely took issue with Fr. Bartolomé de Las Casas and Bishop Palafox, those redoubtable champions of the natural virtues of the Amerindians and other coloured races. He claimed that the Filipinos were basically inferior, as indeed were all Asian peoples with the sole exception of the Japanese, 'who, as Gracián wisely remarked, are the Spaniards of Asia'.[19] The Chinese, who were considered to be a highly civilized race by many Europeans, in view of their age-old culture, wise government, and love of learning, were, in Fr. Gaspar's view, fundamentally no better than the Filipinos. He considered that the basic defects of these islanders were ingratitude, inconstancy, impertinence, sly malice, laziness, love of gossip, and an extraordinary fondness for frequently bathing themselves and keeping their bodies clean. He added, apparently for good measure, that they were likewise litigious, revengeful, cowardly, and prone to drunkenness and debauchery. He alleged that the chastity of their women left a great deal to be desired, although he admitted that the Pampango and Tagalog (unlike the Visaya and the Amerindian) women would rather die than have anything to do with a Negro or a Mulatto. Last not least, he complained that the Filipino only copied the Spaniard's vices but never his virtues.

[17] Printed in 1892, on pp. 273–93 of Delgado's *Historia general*. Cf. note 21, below.

[18] Bailey W. Diffie, *Latin American civilization. Colonial Period* (Harrisburg, 1947), pp. 207–10, 460–91; C. H. Haring, *The Spanish Empire in America* (Oxford University Press, 1947), pp. 209–24. Creoles were not discriminated against in law, but in practice they were almost invariably subordinated to Peninsular Spaniards.

[19] Balthasar Gracián (1601–58), celebrated Spanish Jesuit and writer, was never in Asia himself.

Fr. Gaspar de San Agustín's admitted dislike of Asians and all their ways, perhaps explains why in his *Conquistas de las Islas Filipinas* he deliberately falsified an incident connected with the abortive effort of Fr. Martín de Rada, O.E.S.A., to return to China in 1576. Fr. Gaspar alleges that Rada and his companion, Fr. Agustín de Albuquerque, were savagely beaten and nearly killed by the occupants of the junk in which they had embarked. From Rada's own account of the incident (which Fr. Gaspar admittedly used) it is crystal clear that the two Europeans were not man-handled in any way, although their native interpreter was brutally flogged.[20]

Fr. Gaspar's sweeping strictures on the Filipinos did not go unchallenged. The cudgels on their behalf were taken up by a Jesuit historian in the Philippines, Padre Juan Delgado (1697–1765), whose valuable history was written in 1751–2, but first published over a century later.[21] Padre Delgado states that Fr. Gaspar's denunciation had attained such a wide circulation that he feared it might put off many Religious in Europe who would otherwise volunteer for work in the Philippine mission-field. He therefore refuted his Augustinian colleague point by point. He stated that Fr. Gaspar and those who thought like him,[22] had spent most of their time in high ecclesiastical offices, and hence had only come into close contact with the urbanized Filipinos of Manila and its vicinity. These latter had been corrupted by their association with beggarly low-class Spaniards and vicious Sangleyes, whereas the Filipinos of the rural mission-stations were very different. Writing as a missionary of thirty years' experience in the interior, Padre Delgado unhesitatingly affirmed that the Filipinos had been grossly maligned by their critics. He pointed out that the lazy and improvident Spaniards depended entirely on the Filipinos for the donkey-work of the colony, and that even the Manila galleons which maintained communications with Mexico were manned mainly by native seamen. The scanty Spanish garrison could never have maintained Spain's rule in the Philippines without the loyalty and courage of the far more numerous Pampango and other auxiliaries. Refuting Fr. Gaspar's allegation that the natives would never give up their vices even if they were made bishops, he pointed out that there were several pure-blooded Filipino (secular) Clergy who led irreproachable lives and 'pueden ser ejemplo y confusión de los europeos'. Far from being lazy, improvident, and inefficient, the Filipinos worked like slaves to support the Spaniards, and they produced artists, musicians, and craftsmen of no mean abilities. All three printing-presses in Manila were operated by Filipinos, and there was no trade,

[20] C. R. Boxer, *South China in the sixteenth century* (London, 1953), p. lxxiv.

[21] Juan J. Delgado, S.J., *Historia general sacro-profana, política y natural de las islas del poniente llamadas Filipinas* (ed. Manila, 1892).

[22] Including two other historians of the Philippines, the Jesuit Pedro Murillo Velarde (1696–1753), and the Franciscan Juan Franciso de San Antonio (1682–1744).

craft, or industry in which they were not well represented. There were, of course, idle, dissolute, and litigious individuals among them, as there were in every nation in the world, but they were the exception and not the rule. The missionaries were particularly indebted to their Filipino parishioners, for without them they would starve. 'And they serve us and take us through the islands with such love and security, that they would all die rather than imperil a Padre on any occasion whatsoever'.[23]

From this it will be seen that Delgado was a historian in the tradition of Las Casas and Bishop Palafox, and the same thing may be said, to a certain extent, of his Augustinian colleague, Fr. Casimiro Diaz (1693–1746). This friar was the continuator of Fr. Gaspar de San Agustín's *Conquistas*,[24] and the author of an interesting handbook for parish priests on the treatment of the islanders.[25] As in the preceding two centuries, the missionaries were still deeply divided over the problem of how the Faith should be preached to heathen peoples who were unwilling to receive it, and how far the use of force was necessary to protect the missionaries and their converts. This problem crops up in all the historical writing of the period, wherein 'the two Spains' are represented by varying shades of two schools of thought, neither of which lacked vociferous and influential champions. Fr. Casimiro Diaz, O.E.S.A., who came out to the Philippines in 1712, strongly disagreed with the widely-held view that pioneer missionaries must have soldiers to protect them, since otherwise they might be killed or driven away without having had a chance to deliver the Gospel message. He admitted that though the support of soldiers might be necessary in dealing with the savage races of America and Africa, yet in Asia, at any rate,

the heathen seldom oppose our preaching, and if they do oppose it, it is not because they disbelieve it, nor out of zeal for their own rites, but for motives which are purely temporal and political; either because they fear that they will be subjugated by the Spaniards, or that they will be made to pay an onerous tribute, or that they may be enslaved or killed . . . And thus experience has taught us that when the missionaries have ventured among them entirely deprived of temporal support, and armed only with zeal for God's honour, they have gathered more fruit than in those regions where they have been protected by the King's weapons. And what is more, the only missions which have achieved permanence and stability are those where the missionaries have delivered themselves into the hands of the heathen, trusting in the divine help.[26]

[23] Delgado, *Historia general* (ed. 1892), pp. 293–322.
[24] Bio-bibliographical details in Streit, *Bibliotheca Missionum*, vi, 251–2.
[25] *Parrocho de Indios instruido* (Manila, 1745).
[26] C. Diaz, *Parrocho de Indios instruido*, p. 238 *verso*.

If the Filipinos found warm-hearted and influential defenders as well as acidulous critics among the Spanish missionary historians, the same can hardly be said of the Sangleyes.[27] Although the existence of the colony depended as much on the China trade as it did upon the labour of the Filipinos, the Spaniards were virtually unanimous in their dislike for the hated if indispensable Chinese traders. The panegyrics of the Peking Jesuits on the admirable features of Confucian morality and Chinese civilization aroused only faint echoes at Manila. Fr. Martín de Rada had brought back with him from Fukien in 1575 a wide selection of Chinese books, including a number of historical works. With the aid of Sangley interpreters, he compiled the first historical sketch of China which was based entirely on Chinese sources, but this promising start was not followed up. His collection was dispersed immediately after his death, and it remained for Martin Martini, S.J., and the French Jesuits in China to continue and complete the work which he had begun. Many of the Dominican friars stationed at Manila learnt Chinese (probably Hokkien) after a fashion, but this was only with the object of ministering to their flock in the Parian or Chinese quarter, and not with the intention of engaging in historical research.[28]

Spanish historical writing on the Philippines from the time of Rada to that of Zúñiga was naturally based upon the premise that the King of Spain (or rather the Crown of Castile) had an irrefutable right to the possession of the islands, although the historians might and did differ on various aspects of the spiritual and the temporal conquest. Some chroniclers saw more clearly than others that rights involved duties; but even these did not advocate complete racial equality between the resident Spaniards and the bulk of the Christianized Filipinos. While recognizing that there were some of the latter who were the equal of Europeans and should be treated as such, they argued that most of the Filipinos were mentally equivalent to European children or adolescents, and must be ruled, or at least guided, by the missionaries for their own good.[29] They were prepared to protect and defend their converts against abuses by the civil and military powers, but they could not envisage the time when their own tutelage might no longer be required.

The upheavals, mental and otherwise, caused in Spain by the successive repercussions of the French Revolution, the Napoleonic Wars, the revolt of the American colonies, and the growth of militant anti-clericalism, naturally had important if belated influences on historical writing con-

[27] For the position of the Chinese traders in the Philippines under Spanish rule see W. L. Schurz, *The Manila Galleon* (New York, 1939), pp. 63–98. For the origin of the term *Sangley*,
[28] C. R. Boxer, *South China in the sixteenth century*, p. 260.
cf. B. Biermann, O.P., 'Chinesische Sprachstudien in Manila', *Neue Zeitschrift für Missionswissenschaft* (1951), pp. 18–23.
[29] C. Diaz, *Parrocho de Indios instruido*, p. 163.

nected with the Philippines. At the end of the eighteenth century, the Augustianian friar, Joaquín Martínez de Zúñiga, severely criticized the chronicles of his clerical predecessors (including those of his own Order), for being too concerned with the minutiae of missionary and ecclesiastical history, to the neglect of more important secular matters.[30] Zúñiga's *Historia*, though published in 1803, only came down to the year 1764, and the gap was not filled until the publication of the second lay History since Morga's *Sucesos* of 1609, a three-volume work by D. José Montero y Vidal which appeared in 1887–95.[31] Montero y Vidal, a civilian official who had served for some time in the Philippines, was very critical of the missionary historians, although his first volume, covering the period down to 1759, adds nothing to what the friars and the Jesuits had previously recorded. But at least his was a new approach; and he takes the clerical chroniclers severely to task for ascribing most Spanish victories to the miraculous intervention of some saint connected with their Order, instead of giving due credit to the soldiers or sailors who really did the fighting.[32]

Montero y Vidal wrote with the avowed intention of arousing the interest of his lethargic countrymen in the value and potentialities of their colonial possessions in the Pacific, but he was already too late. Nationalist feeling was rapidly growing among the educated Filipinos, and the repressive measures of the Spanish government only hastened its progress. The Mendicant Orders no longer served as a buffer between the rural Filipinos and their oppressors; but on the contrary, the friars were now the most embittered and reactionary enemies of all forms of political progress. In 1886, Dr. José Rizal, 'El gran Filipino', published at Berlin his famous novel, *Noli me tangere*, in which he exposed the defects of Spanish misrule and strongly criticized the behaviour of the friars. Rizal was a singularly talented man who tried his hand at history as well as poetry, sculpture, philosophy, medicine, agriculture, and politics, achieving distinction in all these varied fields. Using a British Museum copy of Morga's *Sucesos*, he published the second edition of this work with copious notes and annotations at Paris in 1890.[33] Strongly anti-clerical, and making insufficient allowance for the ideas and assumptions of earlier centuries, Rizal's notes are nevertheless full of penetrating observations, and his edition is still worth consulting. The work is also interesting as being the first history of

---

[30] J. Martínez de Zúñiga, O.E.S.A., *Historia de las islas Filipinas* (Sampaloc, 1803).

[31] *Historia general de Filipinas desde el discubrimiento hasta nuestros días* (3 vols., Madrid, 1887–95). The same author also wrote a *Historia de la piratería malaya-mahometano en Mindanao, Joló y Borneo* (Madrid, 1888), as well as other works on the Philippines.

[32] Montero y Vidal, *Historia general*, i, 279 n.

[33] With a very interesting foreword by the Austrian scholar, F. Blumentritt (Leitmeritz, 9 November 1889), denouncing European colonial racialism, and prophesying that Spain would not be able to hold down the Islands by repressive measures much longer.

the Philippines written from the viewpoint of the ruled and not of the rulers. Rizal fell before a Spanish firing-party on 30 December 1896, but his work was done. The Philippine Revolution had broken out four months previously, and two years later Spanish rule in the Islands was a thing of the past.

An interesting contrast to Rizal is the Spanish historian, W. E. Retana (1862–192?), whose enormous output on all aspects of the history, literature, and bibliography of the Philippines is distinguished by immense industry and scholarly accuracy.[34] Apart from his definitive and copiously documented edition of Morga's *Sucesos*, Retana inaugurated a new approach in Spanish historical writing on the Islands. He frankly admitted that the Spaniards were guilty of numerous crimes and misdemeanours in the Philippines; but he argued that their rule was, relatively speaking, better than that of the Muslim chiefs from Jolo, Mindanao and Borneo, who would have conquered the island-group entirely but for the arrival of Legazpi in 1565. In support of this argument he pointed out, as Rizal had done before him, that right from Legazpi's day there were always far more Filipinos than Spaniards fighting on the Spanish side.[35] According to him, the pacification and the preservation of the Islands were primarily achieved neither by the force of Spanish arms nor by the blandishments of Spanish missionaries, but because so many Filipinos spontaneously joined with the Europeans against their Muslim enemies and oppressors. The thesis was not an entirely original one, for in 1751 Padre Juan Delgado had claimed that if the Spaniards had not occupied the Philippines, these islands would inevitably have been conquered by either Muslims, Chinese, or Japanese, any or all of whom would have proved harsher masters than the *conquistadores* and the friars.[36] This is obviously arguable, but a survey of Philippine history does seem to indicate that the bulk of the population were on the side of their Iberian rulers until the second half of the nineteenth century.

The last great name in Spanish historical writing on the Philippines is that of the Jesuit Padre Pablo Pastells (1846–1932). His magnificent edition of Colin's *Labor Evangelica*, and his *Catalogue* of documents connected with the Philippines in the colonial archives at Seville, provide a wealth of printed documentation on the first century of Philippine history which is

---

[34] *Archivo del Bibliófilo Filipino* (5 vols., Madrid, 1895–1905); a new edition of F. Combes, *Historia de Mindanao y Joló* (Madrid, 1897); *Aparato bibliográfico de la Historia general de Filipinas* (3 vols., Madrid, 1906); *Vida y escritos del Dr. José Rizal* (Madrid, 1907); *Noticias histórico-biblograficas del Teatro en Filipinas* (Madrid, 1910); *Orígenes de la Imprenta Filipina* (Madrid, 1911), to mention only a few of the important works by this prolific writer.

[35] 'Con España y por España pelearon siempre más gente filipina que española' (Morga-Retana, *Sucesos*, p. 366).

[36] Delgado, *Historia general* (ed. 1892), p. 311. Cf. also the quotations from F. Blumentritt and V. M. Concas y Palau in Morga-Retana, *Sucesos*, pp. 378–81.

unlikely ever to be surpassed.[37] His outlook was naturally conditioned by that of the Society to which he belonged, but there can be nothing but admiration for the ant-like industry with which he assembled his materials in print.

Rizal, Retana, and Pastells. Three very different historians but three of whom any nation might be proud. All three treat in different ways that theme which runs through Spanish colonial historiography from the early sixteenth century to the present day. The struggle for justice, and the balance between the spiritual and the temporal power, which preoccupied Fr. Bartolomé de Las Casas and Dr. Ginés de Sepúlveda, Padre Alonso Sánchez, and Padre Joseph de Acosta, Dr. Antonio de Morga and Fr. Diego Aduarte, Padre Juan Delgado, and Fr. Gaspar de San Agustín, is still the chief concern of many Spanish colonial historians today.[38] On the one side are those who realize the suspicion that attaches to a European missionary in the East as the representative of an alien culture and an Occidental power. They advocate the complete separation of church and state in the Oriental mission-field.[39] On the other side are those who decline to separate the spiritual from the temporal power, either now or in the past. They claim that the spiritual conquest of overseas territories was (and is) impossible without the armed support of the temporal power. 'Only thus was realised the true ideal of a missionary race: one cross, one empire, and one sword!'[40]

[37] *Labor Evangélica de los obreros de la Compañía de Jesús en las islas Filipinas por el Padre Francisco Colín de la misma compañía. Nueva edición ilustrada con copia de notas y documentos para la crítica de la historia general de la soberanía de España en Filipinas por el Padre Pablo Pastells, S.J.* (3 vols., Barcelona, 1900–3); *Catálogo de los documentos relativos á las islas Filipinas existentes en el Archivo de Indias de Sevilla por D. Pedro Torres y Lanzas, precedido de una historia general de Filipinas por el P. Pablo Pastells, S.J.* (10 vols., Barcelona, 1925–34).

[38] Not only Spanish, but Spanish-American, of whom it will be sufficient to mention E. O'Gorman, *Fundamentos de la historia de América* (Mexico, 1942), and S. Zavala, *Servidumbre natural y libertad cristiana según los tratadistas españoles de los siglos XVI y XVII* (Buenos Aires, 1944).

[39] R. P. A. Gallego, O.P., 'Por qué el Oriente no se convierte', *Missionalia Hispanica*, Año IV (1947), pp. 209–47, especially pp. 235–8. The writer is a missionary with twenty-six years' service in Tongking.

[40] Introduction of P. Felix Garcia, O.S.A., to his edition of *Fr. Juan González de Mendoza. Historia de las cosas mas notables, ritos y costumbres del gran reyno de la China, 1585* (Madrid, 1944), pp. xvii–xxiii. Other prominent historians who are unrepentant advocates of the Church Militant include the two Spanish Jesuits, Constantino Bayle and Egina Ruíz, and the Argentine Jesuit, Guillermo Furlong Cardiff.

15. ASPECTS OF DUTCH HISTORICAL WRITINGS ON COLONIAL ACTIVITIES IN SOUTH EAST ASIA WITH SPECIAL REFERENCE TO THE INDIGENOUS PEOPLES DURING THE SIXTEENTH AND SEVENTEENTH CENTURIES

H. J. DE GRAAF

Privaat-docent in de nieuwere geschiedenis der Indonesische volkeren aan de Rijks-Universiteit te Leiden

Even before Dutch ships began to trade to the Indies there appeared, already in the year 1595/6 at Amsterdam, a description of the Eastern quarters: the *Itinerario naer Oost ofte Portugaels Indien* (Itinerary to East or Portuguese India) of Jan Huygen van Linschoten (±1563–1611). Being in Portuguese service this merchant of enterprise stayed at Goa from 1583 till 1589, and there he not only made notes of the situation of the Portuguese in the East, but he also collected the data which came from other fellow-country men. His description of the East excels in sober honesty and reliable fulness of detail. It opened the eyes of his countrymen to the weakness and the defects of the Portuguese colonial empire, so that it is no wonder that it rendered great services to his countrymen who traded to the Indies on their own for the first time (1595–7). Without this enlightenment the long expedition would probably not have come off so smoothly. It was also read abroad. Translations into French, German, English, and Latin were published. Moreover, the eagerness of the author of spreading the knowledge of the far regions is so great that he also calls pictures to his aid. Contrary to the earlier and contemporary Portuguese works about these subjects, his work is illustrated richly, lively, and expertly, although the drawings do not show a master's hand. Portuguese works of the present-day about the expansion of the Portuguese avail themselves of Van Linschoten's illustrations and maps. Illustrating such works was to become a Dutch tradition, so that the outward image of colonization has not been present in the minds of any people as clearly as in that of the Dutch.

About the voyages during the so-called Wilde Vaart (1596–1602) and from the first years of the Verenigde Oost-Indische Compagnie (United East India Company, V.O.C.), there appeared a series of illustrated journals and descriptions, which are carefully and scientifically published again by the Linschoten society, following the steps of the Hakluyt Society. It was the great interest of the Dutch public in the far voyages to the East which called forth these popular books, often the journals of skippers. Sometimes there appeared several descriptions of a voyage. The *Journalen van de Gedenckwaerdige Reijsen van Willem IJsbrantsz Bontekoe*

(Journals of the Memorable Voyages of Willem IJsbrantsz Bontekoe) (1618–25), enjoyed a wide popularity, which preference, as appears from the numerous publications, lasts down to the present day. It can be said that after a shorter or longer time, of nearly all the important expeditions of the early period, journals were published embellished with simple wood-cuts. Some were rendered into foreign languages. All this is history to a limited degree, as the authors only recorded their own experiences. A compilation of these favourite journals, which appeared at Amsterdam in 1646 under the collective title of *Begin ende Voortgangh van de Vereenigde Nederlandsche Geoctroyeerde Oost-Indische Compagnie* (Beginning and Progress of the United Dutch Chartered East India Company) might be considered to be somewhat more of a historical work. Itineraries like *Wouter Schouten, Oost-Indische Voyagie* (Voyage to the East Indies); J. Nieuhof, *Zee- en Lant-Reize* (Voyage and Journey); A. Bogaert, *Historische Reizen door d'Oostersche deelen van Asia* (Historical expeditions through the Oriental parts of Asia); Nicolaus de Graeff, *Reisen . . . naar alle gewesten des werelds* (Journeys to all regions of the world) which do not intend to give a report of one voyage, but render the experiences and adventures of one person, the author, are of a slightly different nature. They also contain important historical material from time to time.

Closely connected with this kind of works are the itineraries of German officials and soldiers in the service of the East India Company. They are not Dutchmen, it is true, but they feel in many respects in sympathy with their employers. They deserve special mention because they report much that Dutchmen omit as they are too much accustomed to it, at the same time describing a later epoch than the said journals. Part of these itineraries was published by the publisher M. Nijhoff between 1930 and 1932.

However important this kind of works may be, it is not yet historiography in the real sense of the word. True historical works from the time of the Company are rather rare.

Remarkable to say these few works exclusively deal with the Molucca Islands, the territory with which the V.O.C. was first intensively concerned and where, on account of the long period of time, one could speak of history for the first time. Livinus Bor (±1620–69), of patrician origin, under the severe superintendent Arnold de Vlaming van Oudshoorn, took part in the latter's campaigns against the rebel Amboynese, which he committed to paper immediately after the end of the conflict in 1656. In 1663 his *Amboinse oorlogen, door Arnold de Vlaming van Oudshoorn als superintendent over d'Oosterse gewesten Oorloghaftig ten eind gebracht* (Amboynese wars, martially brought off by Arnold de Vlaming van Oudshoorn as Superintendent of the Eastern regions) appeared. Written in the style of the Dutch poet-historian P. Cornz. Hooft, this work contains a fervent glorification of his chief, the said Arnold de Vlaming. A serious drawback is the scarcity of dates, whilst the tone is more or less dithyrambic.

Much more sober was the *Plinius Indicus*, the famous German Georg Rumph, known as Rumphius (1628–1702), the blind seer of Ambon. Attracted by the fame of oriental nature he had gone to the Indies in 1652. In the Molucca Islands, the only station he had during his stay of nearly half a century in the East Indies, he especially occupied himself, besides his official occupations, with the investigation of nature, to which he chiefly owes his fame. The loss of his eyesight in the year 1670 interfered, it is true, with these investigations, but did not stop them. Besides he wrote a thorough *Ambonsche Historie* (Amboyna History), up to 1664, strictly chronological in construction, sober and businesslike. The company, which for the rest appreciated and favoured Rumphius' studies, kept this Amboynese history to itself as a 'secreet en seer dienstig document' (secret and very useful document) and made a secret of it. Only in 1910 was it published in the *Bijdragen van het Koninklijk Instituut*. It may be remarked here that in some degree Rumphius also tries to describe the history of Amboyna before the arrival of the Dutch.

It was, for that matter, the custom of the Company, which considered itself to be in the first place a commercial corporation, to hide its documents carefully from the view of the outer world. What important commercial organization would not do this! and this whilst the letters and reports of its subjects contained so many important things, also in the historical field. In 1687 the 'Court of Committees' of the English East India Company declared, that 'the wize Dutch, in all their general advices, which we have seen, write ten paragraphs concerning their government, their civil and military policy, warfare, and the increase of their revenue, for one paragraph they write concerning trade'. The records of the Dutch East India Company, housed in the Colonial Record Office at The Hague, therefore contain a hardly explored mine of wealth of the most precious data about the history of South and East Asia during the seventeenth and eighteenth centuries. Many Asiatic investigators like those of Japan, India, Pakistan, and Ceylon, realize the importance of these records and take the trouble to learn the Dutch language of the seventeenth century.

When, already at a high age, the counsel of the company, Piet van Dam, LL.D. (1621–1706), at the request of his superiors, composed a *Beschrijvinge van de Oost-Indische Compagnie* (Description of the East India Company (from 1693 till 1701), he could draw on the rich and copious data from the records, besides his experience of many years concerning the business of the company. Besides a descriptive character this giant work in eight volumes also bears a historical character, as it had to contain 'een pertinente en naeukeurige beschrijving . . . van de constitutie, regeering en handel der Compagnie, van haer begin en geboorte af' (A pertinent and exact description . . . of the constitution, administration and commerce of the Company, from its beginning and origin). In consequence of the understandable system of secrecy of the Company this work was carefully preserved in the Company's Records and it was only published lately in the *Rijks Geschiedkundige Publicatiën* (The Hague, 1927–41) thanks to the good care of Dr. F. W. Stapel. Only one volume, dealing with the relations with the British, appears to have been lost.

Since this work was only printed rather a short time ago, its influence on colonial historiography before its appearance could only be a limited one. Nevertheless, it was the basis for the work of G. C. Klerk de Reus, *Geschichtlichen Ueberblick der administrativen, rechtlichen und finanziellen Entwicklung der N.O.I. Compagnie* (Verhandelingen Bataviaasch Genootschap XLVII, 1894). This impressive work owes its value in the first place to the large quantity of facts, which are mentioned concerning the organization of the East India Company. Naturally Van Dam's office with the company carried with it the obligation of being very sparing of comments. Lyrical utterances do not occur at all. Moreover, the already voluminous work is further enriched by numerous annexes. How highly this publication is valued may appear from the fact that already now it can only be obtained secondhand.

Whilst Van Dam's work, which was kept a secret, was of an official nature, in his *Oud en Nieuw Oost-Indiën* (The Old and New East Indies) (8 vols., Dordrecht, 1724–6) Dr François Valentijn (1666–1727) clearly shows himself to be the more outspoken private person. During the two periods he stayed in the Indies as a clergyman (1685–94 and 1705–13) he saw and noticed much and especially collected a lot of things, and also after his final repatriation further data were sent to him, which is evident from his work. It is for the greater part an enormous compilation of information, extracts, documents, lists, etc., mingled with personal reminiscencies told with relish, for instance about his two voyages to and from the Indies or about the campaign against Surapati in 1706. More than once fragments of works of others occur in it without the original author being mentioned, but at the time this happened now and again. Thus he tremendously ransacked Rumphius's Amboynese history without mentioning the source. His critics wrote much about his self-complacent and vain character, perhaps somewhat too much, but connected with it is a great interest in and love for his subject, about which he was able to tell so much. Of course, in the first place all the doings of the gentlemen of the company had his attention, but his interest is far from unilateral. As already the title shows, his magnum opus is not only a description of the Indies of those days, to which he adds that of the Cape of Good Hope and Japan, but it is at the same time of a historical nature, as is sometimes obvious from the titles of the chapters. After the *Beschrijvinge* (Description) of the Molucca Islands in Volume I the *Zaaken* (Affairs) of the Molucca Islands follow. Many chapters bear a purely historical character, like the 'Levens der Opperlandvoogden' (Lives of the Chief Governors) or 'Batavia's Grondvestingen' (Batavia's foundations) in volume IV, borrowing the latter from the Governor-General J. Camphuis. Although conversant with the shortcomings of the Company's rule, he never doubted the lawfulness of its actions, he even made a show of it. As he takes whatever he can lay his hands on, he publishes Dutch data beside Portuguese ones without preference, sometimes mentioning the authors in order to give his work more importance. In this way we know from him the original traditions of the Molucca Islands (still wanting in Rumphius), the first data from the Sadjarah Melaju, and even fragments from the Javanese historical tradition, which sometimes differ from the tradition now accepted. The Javanese babads proper (chronicles) were still unknown to him.

Notwithstanding its many striking shortcomings, we must be very grateful to Dr Valentijn for this gigantic work with its 1050 illustrations and maps, to which he devoted a considerable part of his last years. In point of fact, his work is a large, illustrated encyclopaedia of the Netherlands Indies of those days and adjacent territories and the most correct estimate may be formed about him when we imagine what we would know about the East, if we did not have him. In the nineteenth century the work was even partly reprinted (The Hague, 1856–8) and even then it was a very useful handbook of the Molucca Islands.

The later Governor-General Rijklof van Goens (1619–81) heard of the existence of Javanese chronicles for the first time on his travels to Mataram as ambassador (1648–54) but it would still take more than a century before they would seriously draw the attention of Dutch investigators. The Javanese language, less generally known than the lingua franca of the Archipelago, Malay, was an impediment, but also the curious and unusual contents, which struck the Dutch sometimes as being so queer that it aroused their inclination to laugh more than their desire to study, discouraged them still more. Nevertheless, in the long run something of the contents of these Javanese writings penetrated into the outside public, especially after the foundation of the 'Bataviaasch Genootschap voor Kunsten en Wetenschappen (Batavian Society for Arts and Sciences) at Batavia in 1778.

The first part of a Javanese *babad* appeared in the first treatise of said society. Probably about 1807 the Governor of Java's East Coast, Nicolaas Engelhardt (1761–1831), had another form of the chronicle of the Javanese principalities, the Serat Kanda, translated into Dutch, but nearly a century had still to pass before this remarkable manuscript drew the attention of a scholar like Dr. J. Brandes (Notulen Kon. Bat. Gen.— Minutes of the Royal Batavian Society, 1904).

It is reasonable to suppose that during the last years of the East India Company more about the history of Old Java was known than the public became aware of. Particularly Javanese pedigrees and lists of court-dignitaries were present in the Batavian Records. Moreover, under the influence of the enlightenment and inspired by J. J. Rousseau, people had begun to consider the natives with other eyes than was the case till then. Therefore, the British Lieutenant-Governor, T. S. Raffles, who ruled the conquered Java from 1811–16, must have followed in the steps of less brilliant anonymous Dutch predecessors. Also he had Javanese *babads* translated, this time into English, and from this a great part of the *History of Java* (London, 1817) was composed. He availed himself little, and if so with bias, of Valentijn, who was not unknown to Raffles, so that this history of Java has a rather unilateral outlook. That does not alter the fact that, on account of the wider interest of the author for the natives, his work opens up new ways and in this way brings to the fore much that is valuable in the old and new Javanese civilization. For instance, how great a part do the Hindu-Javanese monuments play in it, or the Javanese gamelan, the wayang, Javanese literature, etc. About the Dutch and their colonial government he cannot say much good, especially about his predecessor Daendels.

Although Raffles was not very critical of his Javanese sources, parts of his work, nevertheless, especially those dealing with the fifteenth and sixteenth century, would serve as a provisional history of Java over that period for many years to come.

The ex-soldier and civil servant, J. Hageman (1817–71), may be considered the successor of Raffles and even overdid some peculiarities of his predecessor, and that in such a way that he severely brought discredit on the indigenous historical sources for the time being. As a consequence, not only were these sources neglected, but it also encouraged a historical practice which only incidentally fixed its attention on the indigenous part of the population.

Just as in the middle of the nineteenth century many old governmental records in Europe came open to scientific historical investigation, in the same way the records of the Dutch East India Company were unclosed. In 1862 the keeper of the national records, J. K. J. de Jonge, LL.D. (1828–78?), since 1854 connected with the records, began to publish a series of sources under the title of *De Opkomst van het Nederlandsch Gezag in Oost-Indië* (The Rise of Dutch Power in the East Indies) (The Hague-Amsterdam, 1862–88), which he provided with extensive historical prefaces. After his death M. L. van Deventer and L. W. G. de Roo carried his work on. By doing so Valentijn did not loose his importance, it is true, but his monopoly, and our colonial historians obtained the disposal of a treasure of new data. Now more reports and stories of eye-witnesses and even originators of the important events are mentioned, than Valentijn had ever been able to give.

It was only after this publication that Coen's famous words: 'Dispereert nooit' (Never Despair) became known and popular. It was through De Jonge that we became more acquainted with the cruel sunan Mangku-Rat I (1646–78), that the infamous deed of Commander Govert Cnol and his complicity in the murder of the Javanese governor of Surabaya came to light (1709), and that the Batavian hero Pieter van den Broucke was exposed (1619). For the first time the motives and the course of the vast revolt of Raden Truna-Djaja (1674–82) became quite clear. This work marked a new era in the study of Indian history, as the choice of his fragments deserve all praise on the whole.

In view of the nature of these fragments this publication bears, as also the title indicates, a highly colonialistic character, so that the indigenous population is only discussed more or less incidentally. Nevertheless, it is peculiar that in the preface of the first of his ten volumes, as a kind of farewell, De Jonge salutes the ideal cherished by Raffles and Hageman to write 'a complete general history of the Netherlands Indies'. He states not to be able to compose a 'narrative of the adventures of the indigenous peoples' from the very varied native sources, which moreover contradict each other, and leaves this to more competent pens.

'But there is', he continues, 'still a second requirement to be met, and that is knowledge of that which the Dutch have done and achieved in the Indies as dominant European nation.' As we may conclude from these passages, he considers his own publication of sources only *part* of a larger work on history to be completed one day and which would have to comprise the whole history of Insulinde.

De Jonge's wise self-restraint exercised a fatal influence on his subsequent colonial historians in so far as most of them did not see the work of their great predecessor as a fragment, but as a completed and well-rounded whole, namely, as the history of Indonesia during the V.O.C. (1602–1799). In this way a practically pure colonial history took the place of a national one, although one cannot say this was deliberately intended.

What De Jonge had done for Java in the seventeenth and eighteenth centuries, P. A. Tiele tried to accomplish for the Moluccas (East-Indonesia) in the same period. From 1886 to 1895 there appeared three volumes of: *Bouwstoffen voor de geschiedenis der Nederlanders in den Maleischen Archipel* (Materials for the history of the Dutchmen in the Malay Archipelago). Only the years between 1612 and 1647 were finished, when death brought his activity to an end. From 1877 to 1887 this solid and industrious scholar had published in the Bijdragen of the Koninklijke Instituut nine excellent articles called: De Europeërs in den Maleischen Archipel (The Europeans in the Malay Archipelago). Those articles contain the history of the discoveries and conquests of the Europeans between 1509 and 1623 and are principally based upon Portuguese, Spanish, and English sources.

Now the peculiar fact arises that, although some realized that it was inevitable to write, beside the history of the colonizing Dutch, also that of the autochthonous population, hardly anybody set himself to this task, let alone succeeded.

A few frankly admitted actual ignorance of the adventures of the indigenous principalities, as H. T. Colenbrander, who simply calls his handbook in three volumes *Koloniale Geschiedenis* (Colonial History) (The Hague, 1925–6).

Somebody else, Professor P. J. Veth, in his *Java, Geographisch Ethnologisch, Historisch* (Java, geographical, ethnological, and historical) (Haarlem, 1875–84) intended to write the history of all the inhabitants of Java, it is true, but he could only make a beginning with it. His work, written in a smooth style, is a summary of the available works on Java namely those of Raffles, De Jonge, and others, supplemented with what the archaeological research just started had yielded about the Hindu-Javanese past, which was still very little. The discredit from which native sources suffered since Hageman's exaggeration, hampered him in making a serious study of it. He is even glad he can leave them alone as soon as Western sources are at his service. As regards the sixteenth century and before, however, he feels himself obliged to use these blind guides. For the rest his enthusiasm for Java's history is very slight. The native princes are arbitrary tyrants, the V.O.C. a scraping commercial corporation. Only in the nineteenth century light begins to dawn over Java, in his opinion, under the influence of liberal politics. This gloomy view of Java's history, however, is connected with the fact that he had never been there and did not know any tropical country, nor did De Jonge for that matter. For it is striking that the opinion of M. L. van Deventer, who wrote a *Geschiedenis der Nederlanders op Java, 1600–1800* (History of the Dutch in Java, 1600–1800) in two volumes and who had been in the tropics (Brazil) is so much more favourable concerning the results of colonization, much in contrast with his predecessors De Jonge and Veth, with whom he carries on a continuous controversy.

Also the second keeper of the national records, Dr. F. de Haan, had provided us with work which contrasts with liberal historians in so far as his *Priangan, de Preanger-Regentchappen onder het Nederlandsch Bestuur tot 1811* (Priangan, The Preanger Regencies under Dutch government till *1811*) (4 vols., Batavia-The Hague, 1910–12) as well as his *Oud Batavia* (Old Batavia) (2 vols., with illustrated book) clearly show that in consequence of the author's long stay at Batavia he thoroughly knows colonial society. His brilliant style and biting wit, which sometimes assumes a personal character, make one forget sometimes that some of his conclusions have to be compared with the sources. The success of his work, especially of his

Oud Batavia, has been enormous, so that the latter was even reprinted, which is exceptional for a book on colonial history.

The so-called Utrecht school objected to the pessimism in respect of the Dutch colonial past, which exercised a fatal influence on the enthusiasm of the Dutch for the colonies and put a weapon into the hands of young native nationalism. This school, grouping themselves round the eminent Professor C. Gerretson, took exception to the, according to them, too lax attitude which the Leiden professors assumed regarding coming nationalism, also in the historical field. From this school some twenty theses resulted, of which only one or two deal with the history of the seventeenth century. The point at issue here is the person of the founder of the Dutch colonial empire, Jan Pietersz. Coen, about whose character opinions were very different. Professor Gerretson stood up for him in his *Coens eerherstel* (Coen's rehabilitation) (Amsterdam, 1944), in which, *inter alia* he tries to justify the latter's way of acting in Banda.

Beside these historical works numerous other historical sources were published, coming from the rich colonial records of The Hague and Batavia. Of these publications of sources I only mention the *Dagregister* (Journal) and the *Plakaatboek van Batavia*, for which J. A. van der Chijs, LL.D., took the initiative, the *Corpus Diplomaticum Neerlando-Indicum*, started by J. E. Heeres, LL.D., continued by F. W. Stapel, finished by Ph. Coolhaas, the *Bescheiden omtrent Coen's beleid in Indië* (Documents about Coen's policy in the Indies), by H. T. Colenbrander and Coolhaas, the *Bouwstoffen voor de Geschiedenis der Protestantsche Kerk in Ned.-Indië* (Materials for the History of the Protestant Church in the Netherlands Indies), by Dr. J. Mooij.

Now we are waiting for the first part of the edition of the 'Generale missiven' (General missives), the annual reports which the 'Hoge Regering' (Supreme Management) of Batavia sent to the 'Heren XVII' (seventeen directors) in the Netherlands, under the supervision of Dr. W. Ph. Coolhaas.

Until a short time ago historians had to get along principally with the Raffles version of the *Babads*. J. Brandes, G. P. Rouffaer, and especially Hoesein Djajadingrat devoted their efforts to the study of the Moslem kingdoms, but except for the kingdom of Bantam it does not seem that they greatly altered our historical conception of this period. Temporarily it remained for the historian a dim and confused age, which, despite its possible importance, did not receive the attention it deserved.

In the meantime the picture that we were endeavouring to form of Javanese history in its entirety gained a still more inharmonious character, and precisely because of the vigorous growth of the Hindu-Javanese studies during the last half century. The connecting link that would fill the gap between the Hindu period and the time of the Dutch East India

Company was only rarely, if ever, discussed. Lines of connection which could join older with newer history of Java are scarce and tenuous. Moreover, the transition period, the sixteenth century, is rather poorly known, and with the coming of the Westerners we enter the colonial period, of which the historical image is such that one can only seldom find traces of a previous age.

This disharmony emerges clearly in the mammoth five-volume work, the *Geschiedenis van Nederlandsch-Indië* (Amsterdam, 1938–40), a compilation achieved under the leadership of F. W. Stapel, which, despite the excellence of some sections, in general hangs together like dry sand, with the disastrous result that the founder of the kingdom of Mataram, panembahan Senapati, disappears entirely, having been lost between the first and second volumes.

In order to bind Hindu-Javanese history, through the time of religious conversion, to the colonial period, one ought to begin with a more serious study of the native kingdoms, including the time of the coming and the settling of the Dutch in the Archipelago, and to pay particular attention to whatever concerns the internal history of these kingdoms.

The possibilities for such a study have indeed increased. Following the first printing, eighty years ago, of an extract from the Javanese imperial chronicle, the so-called *Babad Tanah Djawi* ('s-Grav., 1874–7), for the convenience of prospective civil officers, and of an alphabetical index based on it by J. Brandes, there appeared in 1941 a Dutch translation by W. L. Olthoff, with a very useful index by Dr. A. Teeuw.

Among the recent publications of other Javanese chronicles, I might mention the *Babad Gijanti*, which deals with the so-called third Javanese war of succession (with a first-rate index), and the complete *Babad Tanah Djawi* (unfortunately without index) by Volkslectuur (Balai Poestaka) of Djakarta, both in Javanese with Javanese characters.

In the last few years certain people, namely Professor C. C. Berg and the present writer, have tried to describe the history of the native kingdoms, including the time of the Dutch East India Company, with the help of native sources.

These two researchers undertook the work in diametrically opposite ways. Professor Berg, a Java scholar by origin, began with King Airlangga (eleventh century) and gradually worked up to Sultan Agung (1613–45); the undersigned, historian by origin, began his study with the great revolt of radèn Truna Djaja (1674–82) and gradually worked back, stopping for the time being at about the so-called fall of Madja-Pait (*c.* 1478). In this research our paths were bound to cross, though our meeting has not resulted in complete agreement on all points. Differences of opinion can be traced to our widely divergent conceptions of the character of the royal chronicles of Java, the *Babad Tanah Djawi*, concerning which the final word has no doubt not yet been said. Both authors, however, concur on the date of an earlier edition of this Javanese work, namely the second half of the reign of the above-mentioned Sultan Agung.

Leaving it to Professor Berg to explain his own position, I beg leave to put forth my own view of the Javanese *babad*. First, let it be assumed that the Javanese possess much the same feeling for history as Westerners. Moreover, they realize that a story must be true if one wants to place his faith in it. Nevertheless, the historical material reaches the Javanese historiographer in the very imperfect form of a legend distorted by the passage of time and by political influences. Nor can he apply to this material the tools of critical historical research. His rather different ideas as to what is physically possible or probable, his desire to schematize, his imitation of classical examples, do not make the historical image any more trustworthy. It is consequently not always simple to distinguish truth from invention, and information from outside sources, either Chinese or Western, are very welcome. Still these *babads* are most trustworthy whenever they accidentally permit the reader to peek into the time of the authors themselves.

Nonetheless, no matter how difficult they are to use as research materials, these native sources of history have great significance for the Western historian, since for once they enable the 'other party' to have the floor. As time goes by they will assume ever-increasing importance in the composition of a history of the Indonesian peoples.

One may well ask, however, who in the future will address himself to the history of this so remote segment of mankind.

In the first place our hope is of course with the Indonesians themselves, whenever the desire should awake in them to possess a true knowledge of their ancestors.

Moreover, I do not think it entirely out of the question that Westerners also will devote increasing efforts to this study. Not primarily because of the abundance of their present written and printed sources, manuscripts, and archival documents, but for the simple reason that historical research must no longer be restricted to the countries on this side of Suez. The ever-increasing internationalism of our society compels historians to reflect on the experience of the Eastern peoples.

It is still the custom to regard someone as a learned historian who has made himself somewhat familiar with the old Europe west of the Iron Curtain and with the United States of America, though at the same time he has left the rest of the world to the various literary scholars. Ethnology, on the other hand, does not impose these limitations on itself; on the contrary, it is most strongly attracted by the strangest sorts of foreign peoples. It is ethnology, too, which more than once has expressed the wish to possess more knowledge of the history of its objects of study.

Therefore, it seems reasonable to me that the field of general history also might shatter its isolation, and step across the borders which it has thus far painfully respected, in order to concern itself more closely with the experience of the peoples of the East. In my opinion it will broaden the outlook of inquirers, when they discover that even in these out-of-the-way places people have lived, whose history is worth learning. Considering the entirely different mentality, and the unfamiliar geographical environment of these foreign peoples, a certain amount of ethnological study should be included in one's preparation for such historical investigation.

In this way the history of South East Asia, and especially of Indonesia, would attain a more important and more fitting place in the history of mankind, than has so far been the case.

16. DUTCH CONTRIBUTIONS TO THE HISTORIOGRAPHY OF COLONIAL ACTIVITY IN THE EIGHTEENTH AND NINETEENTH CENTURIES

W. PH. COOLHAAS

Professor of Dutch History, University of Utrecht

Eighteenth Century

Of the two great encyclopaedic works on the East India Company which, *inter alia*, also contain detailed historical information, the first was written between 1693 and 1701. Pieter van Dam, who had already served the Company as Advocaat (i.e. what would now be called director of trade) for forty-one years at the beginning of this undertaking, had an unparalleled knowledge of everything existing in writing about the Company's affairs and of the decisions taken concerning them after full consideration by the Heren XVII (the governing body, similar to a modern Board of Directors). He set down his knowledge in his extremely detailed *Beschrijvinge van de Oostindische Compagnie*, a work, which is a treasure-house of information, concerning both the organization and working of the Company, in the Netherlands and beyond Europe, and the conditions and relations in his own day and the past, in all parts of the world where she carried on her trade, and not by a long way only in the economic sphere, though that was what in the first place interested her. During the Company's existence the work was kept strictly secret; even the Directors might consult it only in the presence of one or more colleagues; in the following century it was seen by only a few individual researchers (among whom G. C. Klerk de Reus in particular made use of it for his *Geschichtlicher Ueberblick der Administrativen, Rechtlichen und Finanziellen Entwicklung der Niederländisch Ostindischen Compagnie*, published in 1894), while (with the exception of the fifth part dealing with the struggles with the English which was lost round about 1820) it was first published in our own days in seven thick volumes (1927–54, six volumes edited by F. W. Stapel, the seventh by C. W. Th. Baron van Boetzelaer van Asperen en Dubbeldam). It is an indispensable work for anyone working on the history of South and East Asia in the seventeenth and eighteenth centuries.

Far better known is the other encyclopaedia of olden days, Dr. François Valentijn's *Oud en Nieuw Oost-Indien*, which appeared between 1724 and 1726 in eight heavy folio volumes. Valentijn made no study of official archives, but from his arrival at Batavia in 1685 he assiduously devoted himself to the collection of material for his work. He was best acquainted with the three easterly governments of the Indian Archipelago, Amboina, Banda, and Ternate (the Moluccas), where he long remained as a padre and was able to make use of the manuscripts of the naturalist Rumphius, but material also poured in to him from all the other parts of that area, where the Company's activities extended, so that he was able to put together a compilation that was a first hand source for the history of the Company and of the peoples with whom he came into contact. Valentijn is very diffuse, he often repeats what others have said (some indeed better, as for instance Rumphius), his critical sense was not always strong enough to judge the quality of the evidence he collected, but nevertheless in his immense book he presents us with a wealth of knowledge; moreover, Valentijn has still constantly to be consulted today.

With these two compilations the scientific productivity of the Company's servants, which earlier had so often provided important contributions to the knowledge of South and East Asia and its history, appears to have been exhausted. I, at any rate, know of no later eighteenth-century work of great or even moderate importance to the historian. Stavorinus's *Reis* (1768–71) has little value, the Batavian Society of Arts and Sciences, founded in 1778, was only later to become of great scientific importance; its first flowering-time was under Raffles, while thereafter it was important especially from the last quarter of the nineteenth century, not least for historical science.

The nineteenth- and twentieth-century Dutch historians have always shown deep interest in the sixteenth and seventeenth centuries, which were so glorious and important for their own people; later also in the fifteenth and nineteenth centuries; the eighteenth century was long neglected, and to some extent is so still; today even the editorial board of the 12-volume *General History of the Netherlands* are finding it extremely difficult to recruit competent contributors for the two volumes covering this century. Moreover, when it is borne in mind that the number of historians who have worked on colonial history has always been few—a fact that is not entirely counterbalanced by the astounding energy of some of them—it can then be realized that many portions, and important ones at that, of eighteenth-century Dutch colonial history in South and East Asia have been studied either not at all or incompletely, and indeed that we have not yet reached a position from which an exact assessment of its problems is possible. For example, no single study puts us in a position to get to understand so central a problem as that of the attitude of the Netherlands E.I. Co. to the expansion of French and English power in those regions. J. van Kan's brochure, *De Rechtstitels der Compagnie* (1942) deals with only a small fragment of this theme.

If we inquire what sources for the history of the eighteenth century have been made available (in print) from the wealth lying in the Public Record

Office at The Hague and, for the Indian Archipelago, in the Arsip Negara at Djakarta, besides the archives at Madras and Nuwara Elya, we find that in reality these afford us a firm basis for the study of the Company's history in Java only. The four volumes of de Jonge's well-known *Opkomst van het Nederlandsch Gezag in Oost-Indië*, which gives eighteenth-century sources, deals only with Java. In the same way F. de Haan's four-volume *Priangan* (1910–12) gives us a wealth of material about West Java, including much also about the country and people. Most other great source publications, such as the *Dagregisters* of Batavia, do not come up to the eighteenth century. On the other hand the *Plakaatboek*, a collection of the orders issued by the Governor-General and Council, edited by van der Chijs, covers the eighteenth century in volumes III–XII (1886–94). This work again for that matter is of special interest for Java. Also the recently completed volumes IV–VI (1935–55) of the *Corpus Diplomaticum Neerlando-Indicum*, the collection of contracts made by the Company with Asian rulers and peoples, edited by F. W. Stapel, contain those for the eighteenth century. But this little is inadequate for dealing with the general history of the Company as well as that of most of the territories where it was active. The present writer is by order of the Government engaged upon the preparation of a ten-volume selection from the *Generale Missiven*, the reports regularly despatched by the Governor-General and Council to the Company's authorities in the Netherlands. The first volume, the completion of which may soon be expected, covers only the period from 1610 to 1640.

For Java some fairly old historical works are available: Veth's *Java* (second edition, 1897–1905), and van Deventer's *Geschiedenis van de Nederlanders op Java* (second volume, 1887). Besides these come studies of particular subjects such as P. J. F. Louw, *De Derde Javaansche Successieoorlog, 1746–1756* (The Third Javanese Succession War) (1889), P. J. B. C. Robidé van de Aa, *De Groote Bantamsche Opstand van 1751* (The Great Bantam Rebellion of 1751) (1881), J. Th. Vermeulen, *De Chineezen te Batavia en de Troebelen van 1740* (The Chinese in Batavia and the Troubles of 1740) (1938). F. de Haan's *Oud-Batavia* (2 vols., 1922) is an interesting history of the city though somewhat too much infected with the author's love of scoffing. Even the sole biography of an eighteenth-century Governor-General (1743–50), which we possess, N. J. Krom's *G. W. van Imhoff* (1941) is strongly Java-centric. Van Imhoff's own *Consideratiën*, plans for the recovery of the Company's business, dating from 1740, were published by J. E. Heeres in 1912 in *Bijdragen tot de Taal-, Land-en Volkenkunde*. As regards his more important—in my opinion—successor Mossel (1750–61), he is no better known to us than the rest of the eighteenth-century rulers.

For other parts of the Indian Archipelago there is a single work on South Borneo: J. C. Noorlander, *Bandjarmasin and the Company in the Second Half of the 18th Century* (1935), and Netscher's *De Nederlanders in Djohor en*

Siak (pp. 50–243 on the eighteenth century) (1870). Also pp. 94–155 of E. C. Godée Molsbergen's *Geschiedenis van de Minahassa tot 1829* (1929) may still be mentioned.

There is fairly good information on the discovery and subsequent history of New Guinea in A. Haga, *Nederlandsch Nieuw-Guinea en de Papoesche Eilanden* (1884, i, 149–385), P. A. Leupe, *De Reizen der Nederlanders naar Nieuw-Guinee en de Papoesche Eilanden in de . . . 18de eeuw* (Bijdr. T.L. en V., 1875, pp. 188–311), and A. Wichmann, *Entdeckungsgeschichte von Neu-Guinea* (Nova Guinea, Band I, 1909).

Several works are also available on contacts with Ceylon and India. The government of Ceylon has had memorials printed, with English translation, of a number of outgoing governors (Simons 1707, Becker 1716, Pielat 1734, van Imhoff 1740, Loten 1757, Schreuder 1762, Mooyaart 1766). We have besides W. Zwier, *Het verdrag van 1776 tussen de O.I.C. en den Vorst van Kandi* (The treaty of 1766 between the E.I. Co. and the King of Kandy) (1927), and G. Nijpels, *Hoe Nederland Ceilon verloor* (How the Netherlands lost Ceylon) (1908). The Government of Madras published, in most cases with English translations, a number of memorials of retiring governors, who are of importance for the history of the Malabar Coast. A. Galetti, A. J. van den Burg and P. de Groot, *The Dutch in Malabar* (1911) is useful as an introduction to this series. J. Ph. Vogel edited for the Linschoten Vereniging (the too little-known—to the outside world—sister of the Hakluyt Society) the beautifully produced and important *Journaal van J. J. Ketelaar's Hofreis naar den Groot Mogol te Lahore 1711–1713*. Kalikinkar Datta used for his *The Dutch in Bengal and Bihar (1740–1825)* (1948) neither Dutch sources, nor Dutch books, save for a translation of Stavorinus. G. C. Klerk de Reus wrote *De Vermeestering van Chinsura in 1781 en 1795*.

This review may be further augmented by a number of articles of A. K. A. Gijsberti Hodenpijl in the *Bijdragen T.L. en V.* and in *Bijdragen voor Vaderlandsche Geschiedenis*, wherein points of detail from the history of the Company in Java, Ceylon, and India are dealt with: 'Dezwerftocht van Sultan Pakoeboewana II na 1742' (B.T.L.V. 74, 1918, pp. 562–615), 'Van Imhoff als gouverneur van Ceylon (B.T.L.V. 75, 1919, pp. 481–626), 'Het Ontslag van den G. G. Durven in 1731' (B.T.L.V. 73, 1917, pp. 178–219), 'De Gouverneurs van Koromandel van Teylingen, 1761–1765 en Haksteen, 1765–1771' (B.V.G.V. 10, 1923, pp. 134–57, 257–77; VI, 11, 1925, pp. 109–23, 281–300).

E. C. Godée Molsbergen has by no means succeeded in giving a comprehensive picture of Dutch history in the East in the eighteenth century in volume IV of the *Geschiedenis van Nederlandsch Indië* (1939), edited by F. W. Stapel. Although the number of preparatory studies was actually not very great, he has either not known of them or not consulted them; he gives in particular information taken from his own publications in detail (for example, the burial ceremony of G. G. van Riebeeck runs to twenty-one pages!), while far more important points are dealt with in a single word or overlooked; any attempt at synthesis is lacking, so that everything has the consistency of dry sand. In justice to the author it must be said that he wrote his work during a severe illness which led to his death.

Nineteenth Century

The historiography of the nineteenth century presents quite a different picture. A great number of works deal with particular subjects of this history; they are often of an exhaustive nature. Political history especially, but also economic, military, and ecclesiastical history attracted attention; education, the development of land and people, social welfare, nature study and art all had their historians. A comprehensive work has not yet appeared. In this connection it may be observed:

1. The area, which was investigated, shrank considerably; for historians could no longer speak of the Dutch possessions on the mainland of Asia the last remainder of which disappeared in 1824, after contact with them had been broken between 1795 and 1816 or in some cases later. With one single exception no Dutch historian has any longer dealt with South and South East Asia outside the Indian archipelago in the nineteenth century.

2. Knowledge of the area within the limits of the archipelago increased considerably in both breadth and depth; various islands or parts of islands, with which earlier there had been little or no intercourse and of which almost nothing was known, now came within the field of vision of the Dutch and thus aroused the interest of the historian; local officials, missionaries, and soldiers did pioneer work in the realm of history, while knowledge of the areas previously more regularly visited or continuously settled by the Dutch became much more profound. There is, moreover, still a marked difference between Java, so important economically in the nineteenth century, and the other islands (the so-called 'outer possessions', later the outer provinces), which partly from about 1870, and mainly from the beginning of the twentieth century, became of great importance.

3. After the fall of the Republic of the United Netherlands in 1795 and the establishment of the Batavian Republic in its place on modern French lines, after the decision in 1798 that the existence of the East India Company should cease as from 1 January 1800 and the state itself should assume the government of the Asian settlements, it was inevitable that interest should become more widespread in the question 'how to manage a colony'. In the Company's time only the (sixty) Directors and their staff were engaged in the business (to use this word in a very wide sense); now, however, it was the state's affair. The ordinary citizens, however, who took over the direction, found the task, in view of their previous ignorance of it,

so great that only a few developed a real interest in colonial questions, and this tendency became all the stronger because contact with the Asian possessions had become practically impossible. After the period of the Batavian Republic (1795–1806) interest dried up still more, partly because the government of the settlements came into the hands of King Louis Napoleon (1806–10), partly because they were all lost to England (1810–16), while thereafter in the restoration period there was no opportunity for the citizen body to interfere, since the supreme rule was vested exclusively in the king. This lasted until 1848, while up to 1830 the Netherlands-Indies appeared to be only a dead loss. It was wholly otherwise, when from the last-named date the Culture System began to yield great profits, and in this connection the Constitution of 1848 transferred to the States General an important share in the colonial task. As a result interest (in the Netherlands-Indies) became greater than ever before among the upper classes, who alone, in consequence of the limited franchise, exercised influence on political affairs. The powerful liberal group in this class was strong in its advocacy of the abolition of the Culture System and the freedom of agriculture. During the years of struggle over this matter in the States General there appeared in 1860 a novel, *Max Havelaar* by Multatuli (pseudonym of the ex-government official Douwes Dekker), which was one of the best books of nineteenth-century Netherlands literature. Douwes Dekker had left the service because of a conflict with the Government of the Indies, and in his work he brilliantly described the failings of that government in Java. The influence of his work may be compared with that of Mrs. Beecher Stowe's *Uncle Tom's Cabin*, with this qualification, however, that slavery in America was already a matter of great concern to the humanitarians while no interest had been aroused in the subject about which Dekker wrote. It was the literary quality of the work (which was not specially directed against the abuses of the Culture System, so that the conservative members of the Chamber saw in Dekker an ally), which brought it about that a great interest in Indonesian questions was aroused both in the broad strata of the petite bourgeoisie and, in the long run, in those of the proletariat. *Max Havelaar* is a book that right up to the present day is read by practically every young (man or woman) with anything more than elementary education, and thus at a time of life when they are susceptible to the pathos of the subject. In many cases the influence of the book persisted into later life when they became personally acquainted with the Indian Archipelago.

Meanwhile, about 1870 the struggle over the Culture System was decided in favour of the ideas of the liberals. Moreover, not only did all the interest in the history of the Dutch in Indonesia come into being in this way, but history-writing showed the strong impress of the struggle against the Culture System. In the eyes of the liberals there was nothing good in the system; the treatises written about it were in reality controversial pamphlets, in which only the faults of the system were emphasized, because they could contribute to its fall. And the preponderance on the side of the liberals was so great, that the rather caricatured picture of the system, which had thus come into existence, and was central to our historiography concerning colonial affairs in the nineteenth century, persists right up to today in our text—and school—books. The article on the Culture System in the *Encyclopaedie van Nederlandsch-Indië* (1917, i, 545–52), the treatment in H. T. Colenbrander's *Koloniale Geschiedenis* (1926, iii, 34–62), and in G. Gonggrijp's *Schets eener Economische Geschiedenis van Nederlandsch-Indië* (first edition, 1928, pp. 115–67) are based upon these controversial writings. The statements about the Culture System made in these works are usually found in simplified and abbreviated form in the school textbooks. The defence of the conservative side was not strong; a biography of the conservative Governor-General and Minister of Colonies Baud by his supporter and colleague Mijer (1878) may be mentioned. Only in our own time has a more powerful defence of the Culture System come from the neo-conservative side. The Utrecht professor Gerretson, very well known also as a poet and politician, dealt with it in the course of his observations concerning political unity and in a sharp controversy with Colenbrander. He went so far as to declare to a student congress at Wageningen that 'the Culture System has been the greatest blessing that the Netherlands has conferred upon the Indies' (*De sociaal-economische invloed van Ned. Indië op Nederland*, Wageningen, 1938). Still more than in his own writings is the defence of the system to be found in the academic theses of a number of his pupils who came strongly under his influence (A. Alberts, *Baud en Thorbecke, 1847–1851* (1939); W. A. Knibbe, *De Vestiging der Monarchie* (The establishment of the monarchy) (1935). Other pupils of his have dealt with other parts of the history of nineteenth-century colonial policy, often in the same spirit of support for the opinions of their teacher. At almost the same time as the balance was thus shifted powerfully to the other side by the so-called Utrecht school attempts were now being made outside Utrecht, *sine ira et studio*, at a more scientific treatment of the Culture System than those of the liberals. W. M. F. Mansvelt, the writer of a very important *Geschiedenis van de Nederlandsche Handel-Maatschappij* (1924), the body that brought the products of the Indies to the Netherlands for the Government, and continued also to play a very important role in the economic development of the Netherlands Indies, came in this work to conclusions quite different from those of the liberals. Later as head of the Central Office of Statistics at Batavia he put together (1937–9) a number of economic-historical-statistical publications, which were intended as preliminary studies for a scientific work on the Culture System; before he could carry out that work Mansvelt was murdered in 1945 by Indonesian extremists at Batavia. From quite a different angle J. J. Westendorp Boerma, from an examination of the records of J. van den Bosch, the man who projected the Culture System and in 1831–3 introduced it, managed to gain some insight into the aims of this remarkable man with such a deep interest in social questions. After his thesis, which describes in particular the earlier years of van den Bosch, he issued in 1950 a short biography: *Een Geestdriftig Nederlander, Johannes van den Bosch*, that in anticipation of a hoped-for more extensive work serves in some degree to satisfy expectations. The recent dissertation by J. Reinsma, *Het Verval van het Cultuurstelsel* (1955) is the meritorious work of a beginner.

In view of the great influence of the liberals upon the historical writings on the Culture System, it may be noted here that the rather unfavourable judgement on the East India Company also originates from them. They regarded it as a precursor of the hated Culture System, a monopolist body in any case, and hence, almost unconsciously they laid too much emphasis upon its bad side. Veth, van der Chijs, Colenbrander exposed especially the dark side; M. L. van Deventer alone tried in his *Geschiedenis der Nederlanders op Java* (1887) to bring out clearly the good side also. In this field also there are disciples of Gerretson but this is not the place to go into the matter.

The liberal historians were happier in their attempts to throw light upon the forerunners for their persuasion, and in this they have been followed by others. The life and work of the remarkable Dirk van Hogendorp, who in one period of his life (1795–1805) stood out for the economic deliverance of the European and the Asian from the bonds in which the Company's system held them, is hence well known (Biography by J. A. Sillem, 1890; P. J. Platteel, *De Grondslagen der Constitutie van Nederlandsch-Indië* (1936); E. du Perron-de Roos, *Correspondentie van Dirk van Hogendorp met zijn broeder Gijsbert Karel*, in *Bijdr. tot de Taal- Land-en Volkenkunde van Ned. Indië*, vol. 102, 1943). M. L. van Deventer continued de Jonge's *Opkomst* in a thirteenth volume up to the English conquest of Java, while L. W. G. de Roo, as a reaction to this, compiled two further supplementary volumes. Although these publications of source-material shed a good deal of light on the work of the revolutionary general H. W. Daendels, who was Governor-General from 1806 to 1810, a comprehensive work from the Dutch side dealing with his government in the Indies is still lacking; it is, however, being worked into a biography, intended as a sequel to that by Mendels, which only goes up to 1806.

The figure of Raffles is for Dutch historians a difficult lump to digest. There is agreement only in admiration for the man's scientific labour. For one part of the liberals he was a forerunner, for another part a man 'of great words' (van Vollenhoven). Non-liberals are even more averse to him. His anti-Dutch attitude makes an objective judgement difficult for us. Moreover, the English biographies are not very helpful in this respect. Boulger and Egerton wrote round about 1900 at the time of the Boer War, and hence they emphasized strongly the 'inferiority' of the Dutch. Wurtzburg in his biography (1954) shows no knowledge—or too little—of the Dutch writings. It is possible that the Australian J. Bastin, whose Leiden dissertation *Raffles's Ideas on the Land Rent System in Java* appeared in 1954, may be able to give us a biography of Raffles based upon knowledge of the existing economic data. The best account of Raffles's activities in Java is still the one given by H. D. Levysohn Norman in his dissertation (of 1857!), *De Britsche Heerschappij over Java en Onderhoorigheden, 1811–1816*. Van der Kemp, who is mentioned immediately below, collected much material about Raffles's activities in Sumatra and in connection with the founding of Singapore. It is, however, obvious that the above-mentioned works of Boulger and Egerton strongly irritated him.

Concerning the years 1816 to 1830 (especially up to 1825) an exceptionally large number of works have been published. This is partly accounted for by the numerous and bulky publications of source-material by P. H. van der Kemp, who aimed at carrying on the de Jonge-van Deventer *Opkomst* to include the period after 1815, but who in twenty-three years (1897–1920) got no further than 1818 in a large number of independent books, and then 1825 in very lengthy articles to journals. (These have been listed in the bibliography at the end of volume 5 of the *Geschiedenis van Nederlandsch-Indië*, edited by F. W. Stapel, 1940).

The central theme of the nineteenth century, the Culture System, has already been dealt with. Besides what is to be found in a number of dissertations by van Gerretson's pupils, there is also much concerning later political questions in works dealing with the general parliamentary history of the Netherlands. Among biographies there are still to be mentioned that of *Duymaer van Twist* (Governor-General from 1851 to 1856), by J. Zwart (1939), that of *J. W. van Lansberge* (or, more strictly, the account of his period of office as Governor-General 1875–80), by M. Boon (1943), while J. C. Lamster produced in 1942 the most recent biography of J. B. van Heutsz, and later a more specialized study of his period of office (1904–9). There are also among others biographies of the biologist *Junghuhn*, the Islamic scholar and government adviser *Snouck Hurgronje* (with special reference to the Acheh war, by K. van der Maaten, 2 volumes, 1948, and in the *Koloniaal Tijdschrift*, 1937–8, by H. T. Damste), the writer *Douwes Dekker* (numerous, varying from strongly-pro to strongly-anti), of the 'ethical' statesman C. T. van Deventer (3 volumes by H. T. Colenbrander and J. E. Stokviss, 1916), of the archaeologist *van Stein Callenfels* (very anecdotal, by B. D. Swanenburg, 1951), of the historian G. P. *Rouffaer* (by N. J. Krom in *Bijdr. Taal-, Land-, en Volkenkunde*, 84, 1928)

of the jurist *Cornelius van Vollenhoven* (a very sensitive work by Mrs.
H. L. T. de Beaufort, 1954). These, however, bring us partly into the
twentieth century.

A great number of works deal with portions of the military history,
often very detailed and containing also much information about the native
community; there are also many works dealing with the history of geographical or ethnic divisions of Indonesia. It is unnecessary to enumerate
them here.

Among the many books of records published by the great economic
bodies some are of outstanding standard. Mansvelt's excellent *Handel-
maatschappij* has already been mentioned, Gerretson's *Geschiedenis der
Koninklijke* (Royal Dutch Petroleum, 3 volumes, 1932–42, uncompleted)
is delightfully written; important also are J. C. Mollema, *De Ontwikkeling
van het eiland Billiton en van de Billiton-Maatschappij* (1932, with a supplement
by F. W. Stapel, 1939), and L. de Bree, *Gedenkboek van de Javasche Bank*
(2 volumes, 1928–30). Another subject of economic history is dealt with
by D. H. Burger in his thesis *De Ontsluiting van Java's Binnenland voor het
Wereldverkeer* (1939).

Finally, a few more titles of works in which completely different historical subjects are dealt with. U. J. Brugmans, *Geschiedenis van het Onderwijs
in Nederlandsch Indië* (1938, excellent), C. W. Th. baron van Boetzelaer
van Asperen en Dubbeldam, *De Protestantsche Kerk in Nederlandsch-Indië*
(1947, pp. 137–262 on the eighteenth, pp. 262–460 on the nineteenth and
twentieth centuries), M. J. Sirks, *Indisch Natuuronderzoek* (1915, pp. 62–86
on the eighteenth, pp. 86–284 on the nineteenth century), D. Schoute,
De Geneeskunde in Nederlandsch Indië gedurende de negentiende eeuw (1935?).

17. FRENCH HISTORIOGRAPHY AND THE EVOLUTION OF COLONIAL VIETNAM

JEAN CHESNEAUX

Directeur d'Études, Sciences Économiques et Sociales, École Pratique des Hautes Études, Paris

The colonial period in Vietnam opens in 1858, with the landing of Rigault de Genouilly's squadron. One may consider that it concludes with the peace of Geneva, even if the disintegration of the colonial régime had begun in Vietnam well before that date.

This interval of almost exactly a century saw, in France as in most of the other occidental countries, decisive progress in the historical sciences. Whereas history under Louis Philippe had hardly begun to free itself from chronicles, compilations, and academic statements, it becomes, in the second part of the nineteenth century, a true science: by its own method, which obeys strict rules of internal and external criticism, makes use of a great number of 'auxiliary sciences' and which seeks, above all, to base itself on *facts*. Also by its object, which is to penetrate beyond the superficial descriptions to a knowledge of the evolutionary laws of societies. By its compass, too, and its field of activity, which cover not only political, diplomatic, and military history, but 'the history of civilizations', economic and social history, the history of migrations, or that of literary currents. In the twentieth century this evolution towards a scientific conception of history has continued, particularly in the economic and social sphere. This is not the place to discuss their limitations or inadequacies, but there is no doubt that the works of the French historical school on the society of the Middle Ages, on the Revolution of 1789, and on contemporary diplomatic relations mark a serious scientific advance upon those of former times.

This brief reminder was necessary in order to assign their place to those historical works relating to colonial Vietnam which were accomplished during the same period. Is it not indeed a paradox that the list of works conceived according to the standards of University scientific history is extremely short in this sphere? A chair of Colonial History, given to the historian Cultru, existed for some years at the University of Paris at the end of the nineteenth and beginning of the twentieth century; but its incumbent had no successor. The work which Cultru devoted in 1910 to the beginnings of French Cochin-China may still, today, be consulted with interest; it affords a fairly broad picture both of the conquest of Cochin-China and of the beginnings of colonial rule in that region. But that is only the exception which proves the rule; until a very recent date, there practically does not exist any French work presenting a picture of the history of Vietnam as a whole during the colonial period, and putting into the foreground the evolution of administrative systems, Vietnamese political life, the activities of colonial financial group, political, and economic relations with the metropolis and the transformation of Vietnamese society. It is significant that a work such as Maybon's *Histoire moderne du Pays d'Annam*, which has the merit of existence, even if it adopts a very narrow point of view, and even if, at the time, it had been the object of severe criticism by Paul Pillot on account of his many negligences, ends with the advent of Gialong; its author had, however, announced his intention of bringing the work up to date.

What then was the powerful force which prevented French historians from carrying out scientifically a study of modern Vietnam? The question is the more interesting inasmuch as it appears in almost the same terms with regard to the other French colonial territories—African in particular. It is only, for example, very recently that Professor Emerit's work or that of Professor Julien on Maghreb during the colonial period has begun to clarify that history.

Is the great scarcity of works of synthesis relating to the colonial period in Vietnam the result of a lack of materials and monographs? To assert this would merely shelve the problem. There is, as a matter of fact, a large number of works worthy of consideration as materials or preliminary studies. But their common characteristic is precisely that which brings one back to the same problem, that of not being, or only very rarely being the work of qualified historians, whether professional or amateur. These works may be classified into four principal categories.

(1) *Memoirs and recollections of political agents, military chiefs of staff and statesmen:* such are those of Francis Garnier, J. Dupuis, E. Millot, Ch. Gosselin, and J. Silvestre on the conquest, or those by Le Myre de Villers, Lanessan, Paul Doumer, and Paul Beau on the beginnings of French administration.

(2) *Economic monographs*, which à propos of some given economic problem often provide important historical material: these monographs are often the work of civil service administrators (such as those of Morel on the finances of Tongking, or on land concessions in Tongking) often also of businessmen, or clerks in the big banks and colonial companies (such as the works of Paul Bernard); they were sometimes the work of professional geographers, such as, recently, Professors Gourou and Robequain.

(3) *Reports and Essays* of which there is a long series from *Indochine, erreurs et dangers* by Colonel F. Bernard, and *Nuages sur l'Indochine* by Jean Ajalbert, to *Indochine S.O.S.* by Andrée Viollis and *Vietnam* by Roubaud, passing over *La route mandarine* by Roland Dorgelès, *Les Jauniers* by Yvonne

Schultz, *Les Forceries humaines* by G. Garros, and so many analagous works by L. Werth, Barthel, Captain Monet, Dorsenne, Vanlande, E. Brieux, etc. These factual reports, each one of which tried to explain the data of 'the problem of Indo-China' and to propose a solution, more or less brutal or more or less utopian, contained information, present or retrospective, of great historical interest. Not one was an historical work, properly speaking.

(4) *Compilations of military or police origin.* There are several of these works which keep close to military communiqués or reports by the political police; although their authors have only a very imperfect idea of the criteria of a work of genuine historical interpretation, their interest is great, because of the unusual or inaccessible nature of the material which they utilize: such is *L'Histoire militaire de l'Inde-chine française*, compiled by officers of the General Staff which gives a very detailed picture of the campaign against the 'rebels' from the conquest to the Great War, or the *Contribution à l'histoire des mouvements politiques en Indochine française*, drawn up by the chef de la Sureté, Marty, after the disturbances of 1930.

The diversity of 'genres' which this attempt at classification brings to light, in its turn demonstrates clearly the scarcity of truly historical works, to which none of these four categories can, for obvious reasons, be assigned entirely.

What are the guiding principles and the fundamental tendencies of these different works and different authors? It would be better to consider this question here and now than to draw up a list from these works which would be tedious. And, perhaps, in this way it will be possible to clarify the question posed at the beginning of this report, that is to say, the delay in French historical writing relative to Vietnam.

Here the most important criterion, since it concerns a colonial country, is the attitude of the various authors towards colonialism itself, towards the problem of dependence and independence, towards the continuity which exists, or no longer exists between colonial Vietnam and the independent Vietnam of former times. It is in the working out of this principal problem that one can judge the intentions and abilities of each one, and that one can see how each of the works in question reflects the preoccupations of such a group at such a time. Five examples may here be studied from the historiographical point of view: the conquest of Vietnam, the political régime of the colonization, the evolution of colonial economy and of traditional economy during the colonial period, the transformation of Vietnamese society and the stages of the Vietnamese national movement during the colonial period.

The study of *colonial conquest* has not made any serious advance since the time when this conquest, because it occupied the forefront of contemporary events, had given rise to a goodly number of historical or para-historical works. This touch of actuality marks for example studies correctly termed historical such as those of Pallu de la Barrière on the Cochin-China expedition or that of Romanet du Caillaux on the abortive conquest of Tongking in 1873; furthermore, it is evident in other works of a personal character such as those of Dupuis, Millot, or Captain Gosselin. In these works and in the very numerous analagous volumes which appeared between 1860 and 1890, the same postulates appear with some faint differences: that of the legitimacy of conquest first of all, although it is generally assumed as a matter of course, something one scarcely pauses to justify; that of 'Asiatic treachery' which justifies beforehand all the 'preventive' violations of past agreements with the government of Hué, whether it be La Grandière's occupation of western Cochin-China in 1867, Francis Garnier's attack on Tongking in 1873, or the Hué affair in 1885; and finally that of the episodic and illusory character of Vietnamese resistance.

These postulates are equally adopted by the few general surveys of the conquest published rather later; such as the *Histoire militaire* cited above, which is an official publication of the General Staff or the interesting series of articles published 1895–8 by J. Silvestre in the *Annales de l'Ecole des Sciences politiques*. Which brings one back to the point that many problems relating to the conquest still await their historian. It is significant that not one author has published a work drawing upon the archives of the Quai d'Orsay although they are so rich for the whole period of the conquest. The rôle of the Catholic Missions awaits clarification, because a certain anti-clerical tradition, represented at the end of the nineteenth century by men like Cultru or Lanessan (although favourable to the conquest) thereafter gave place on this point to a much more conformist attitude on the part of the authors. No less discreet are the greater number of those on the rôle of big private interests, in the opening up and unfolding of the conquest; even the Press has hardly been utilized, and it is only very recently that an article has appeared in Paris, making a study, for example, of the reactions of the French Chambers of Commerce to the conquest of Tongking.

The evolution of French governmental and administrative methods in Indo-China constitutes another fundamental problem in the evolution of modern Vietnam. For the most part, such works as have appeared on this question have only a quasi-official character; they are confined like Alberti's big manual to describing colonial institutions from the outside, without analysing their real functions. It was only in times of crisis, as in 1907 or 1930 that this was inquired into, but with the sole object of finding out the 'mistakes' which had been made: the works published in these circumstances are not deficient in additional interest, such as Colonel Bernard's *Indochine; erreurs et dangers*, and also those memoirs in which the heads of the administration criticized the proconsulships of their predecessors in order to exalt their own work: Le Myre de Villers, the first civil governor is very interesting to read on the period of 'the admirals', and in the same way Lanessan on Le Myre de Villers, and Paul Doumer on Lanessan.

It is a trait common to all these authors that they were, indeed, convinced of the fundamental viability of the colonial system as such; they all agreed in refusing, systematically, to admit the fact of Vietnamese nationalism, in refusing to admit Vietnamese unity although so clearly demonstrated in the history of even ancient Vietnam, and which, moreover, the naval officers of Napoleon III had faithfully noted; Doumer's system, by which Vietnam was divided into three, Cochin-China, Annam and Tongking, themselves linked to Cambodia and Laos to form Indo-China, an entity without any historical basis, was to them an article of faith. Even the word Vietnam had disappeared from all French manuals of instruction whether Secondary or Higher before 1945. Let us note, in passing, that these French authors tried to project this negatory attitude into the past, and to prove that this tripartite division dominated the whole history of Vietnam throughout the ages.

But it was a matter of making this system work well; it was not a question of giving it a trial. At this point the famous discussion as between 'assimilation' and 'association' takes place. The adherents of the first system wanted to modify traditional forms of Vietnamese society as little as possible, and on the contrary to rely upon the 'native aristocracy'; this was the position of men like the first admirals (Bonnard and his collaborators Aubaret and Philastre, all of them eminent orientalists), or like those University men Paul Bert, and Lanessan, who in their passage to the position of head of the administration attempted—in vain—to rally the scholars, all these men, moreover tended—as is normal—to idealize ancient Vietnamese society, to extol the charms of the 'Annamite commune' and to cast into the background the true nature of the power of the Vietnamese feudal magnates and landed proprietors, on whom they definitely intended to rely. For the others, on the contrary, such as Le Myre de Villers, Doumer, and Alexandre Varenne, it was a question of overturning the old Vietnamese institutions and substituting for them forms of organization approximating to those of the metropolis: a trend which was usually accompanied by a disparaging attitude towards Vietnamese political traditions and national past.

There is no doubt that all these authors closely connected for the most part with the machinery of colonial administration, could only with difficulty stand back and analyse realistically from an historical and interpretative viewpoint the actual working of colonial administration. They were not in a position to show how, because of the opposition it encountered, the administration could never escape from the very arbitrary methods from which there was practically no deviation between 1860 and 1945; nor why, at the same time, in order to satisfy both Vietnamese opinion which they nevertheless took into consideration, and metropolitan opinion, this colonial administration had to agree to a façade of apparent reforms, an unceasing succession of which is characteristic of this period (the 'reforms' of Paul Bert, Lanessan, Doumer, Sarraut, Varenne, Pasquier, etc.).

What were the economic changes in Vietnam during the colonial period? This question, at first sight, ought not to prove a difficulty for the French writers of this period. It is a fact that a large number of works has been devoted to drawing up an economic balance sheet for the colonization or to studying some particular aspect: such is Professor Robequain's work, or the huge year books of Teston and Percheron, in which is found a reasonably adequate statement of progress in the production of rice and rubber, of road, rail, and harbour equipment and the development of external trade.

But it is not enough to state and describe this development of a modern section of the Vietnamese economy. Really to study it as an historical phenomenon, it is essential to define precisely the relation between this modern economic section and the metropolitan financial groups, and at the same time to pinpoint the way in which this modern section dovetails into the whole layout of the economic life of Vietnam. Now there is no doubt that the great majority of writers have systematically abstained from engaging in research in this sense.

There is the metropolitan capital which has 'improved' Indo-China. The first question which arises then is to assess the full value of these investments.

But that is a hard task and one which the interested parties have not made any easier. Thus according to an inquiry at Vichy, capital invested in Indo-China represented 39 milliards of francs in 1940, and according to an inquiry by the issuing Bank 34 milliards only—an appreciable difference already. But a close review, based on the legal coefficients of a revision of the balance sheets, has recently enabled M. Henri Lanoue to reduce this figure by at least a third of this amount—say $11\frac{1}{2}$ milliards. Why this enormous magnification of the investments in the official statistics and by official writers? Doubtless to obtain higher compensation from the metropolitan government in case of withdrawal. That is only one example. Many of the total estimates furnished by specialists in colonial economics should be received with the utmost reserve; for example, the economist Paul Bernard, in a work published in 1934, estimates the sum total of the costs of public works affected since 1900 at 650 millions; in another work published in 1937 he finds no difficulty in reducing this figure to 522, although for a longer period. Philippe Devillers, in his *Histoire de Vietnam*, estimates the proportion of Indo-Chinese rubber bought by France before the war at 95 per cent.; a simple calculation based on the official year books results, however, in a somewhat lower figure, that of 30·5 per cent.; the remainder went principally to the United States, Japan, and Singapore.

These examples enable one to understand how difficult it is to resolve the essential question that of the *return* on metropolitan investments in Vietnam. This question is not even raised in the majority of those works of an economic character. And when it is, it is only to receive an answer devoid of all semblance of truth; during the recent war a minister gave the opinion that this colonial profit never reached 2 per cent. during the whole colonial period!

This metropolitan capital, these plantations and railways were not established in a vacuum; on the contrary they were inserted into the Vietnamese economy which was already complex, and from the middle of the nineteenth century had got beyond the stage of a local economy of consumption; one in which there already existed the elements of commercial production and inter-regional trade. Did not the brusque intrusion of colonial financial concerns, with their very different preoccupations which sought above all to develop those branches of production which were certain to find markets outside Vietnam, did it not pervert the internal evolution of Vietnamese economy? Colonial production developed hardly taking into account the needs and possibilities of the national Vietnamese market. In the same way the railways were constructed under colonial rule primarily in response to either strategic mobility or export needs (the Saigon–Locninh railway); these railways have hardly any connection with the ancient traffic axes of pre-colonial Vietnam. There are so many problems which one only mentions here as a memorandum, but which illustrate very well the summary nature of the balance sheets of colonial undertakings so often presented in so many books relating to colonial Vietnam.

What were the internal changes in Vietnamese society during the colonial period? This other question is one of equal importance for a true understanding of colonial Vietnam. Here again the apparently considerable mass of writings devoted to modern Vietnamese history is only an illusion and sham. Most certainly a study of this subject implies the existence already of a detailed analysis of pre-colonial Vietnamese society, of the nature of social relations inside villages, of the extent of the development of a commercial bourgeoisie in the ports, of the position of artisans, of social recruitment and the links between the literary and the mandarin class. This analysis is still lacking today, and it is well known that the work of the 'École Française d'Extrême Orient' in respect of social and economic history is far behind its ethnographical and archaeological work.

This tardiness, however, does not sufficiently explain the considerable lacunae revealed by an examination of those works relating to modern Vietnamese society. It is on the subject of the peasantry that the best work is available: such are the analyses of Yves Henry, an official of the Agricultural Service between the wars, or the geographical investigations of Professors Gourou and Robequain into peasant life of the Tongking Delta and on the Thanh-hoa; these works provide valuable data on such facts as rural overpopulation, the parcelling out of land holdings, or the numerical importance of farmers (ta-dien). But their great blank is the fact that they refrain entirely from any historical presentation, and give no information whatever on the evolution of the phenomena they are studying (such for example as the concentration of landed property).

An inquiry of the same kind on the subject of industrial workers by Goudal is due to the initiative of the International Labour Bureau at Geneva. But it presents the same lacunae. As for the Vietnamese bourgeoisie, that is very much a *terra incognita* of modern Vietnamese history. Not even one article has been devoted to it, in all the available literature.

The historical analysis of social conditions as a whole, has progressed as little as the study of this or that particular social stratum. No author, in fact, asks himself this primordial question: was the standard of living of the Vietnamese population raised or lowered during the eighty years of colonial rule? It was not until 1949 that M. H. Lanoue calculated the fall of the average consumption of rice *per capita* from figures which anyone could have obtained, namely those of the total population and those for the production of unexported rice: it had fallen from 262 kg. in 1900 to 182 kg. in 1937.

What were the principal stages in the Vietnamese nationalist movement during the Colonial period? This question in spite of its obvious interest has not proved any more tempting to those historians and other authors examined here. It is significant that no correctly termed historical work has sought to study this phenomenon, to put it into perspective with economic evolution, the emergence of new social classes, such as the bourgeoisie or industrial workers, and also the general transformation of Asia. With the exception of a short but interesting chapter by Philippe Devillers, who has the merit of regarding the question from this definitely historical angle, the only works concerned with the Nationalist movement are either short summaries in journalists' reports (like those of Roubaud, Dorsenne, and Vanlande), or studies emanating from the very specialists in repression—military and police which have been cited above. These works, in spite of the interest of the materials they offer, suffer from the extreme narrowness of the point of view they adopt; for them the nationalist movements are only the doings of grumblers and agents without any real weight in the population; they like to explain them away as 'foreign agents': from China and Japan before 1914, Germany 1914–18, China and the Soviet Union 1920–30, Japan 1935–45, and the Soviet Union again after 1945. Whereas on the contrary, the really impressive fact is the absolute continuity of a movement which, in diverse forms and with diverse political objectives, has never ceased from the time of the landing of Napoleon III's admirals to Dien-Bien Phu (cf. J. Cheneaux, *Stages in the development of the Vietnam national movement, Past and Present,* April, 1955).

The same conclusion emerges then from an examination of the five fundamental questions which have just been chosen to serve as touch-stones: with very rare exceptions French historical or para-historical production relating to colonial Vietnam has but very inadequately approached an examination of those points which are, from a scientific point of view, the most interesting. One is indeed obliged to see here a fear of facing reality, a fear which is in great part responsible for all the lacunae and all the weaknesses we have remarked above.

When it is a question of the conquest, or political organization or economic evolution or social changes or the nationalist movement, the attitude of those authors whom we have here studied is basically the same: they practically reduce the history of Vietnam to the history of the French machinery, political, military, and economic in Vietnam; they do not think, they do not manage or else they do not try to picture Vietnam as a subject of knowledge in its own right, as a complete entity in time and space; thus they separate Vietnam (which they no longer know except under the name of Indo-China, whose extent is very different) from its pre-colonial past; they allow themselves to be hemmed in by that artificial division invented by the French in the course of the conquest (Tongking, Annam, Cochin-China, these three terms were moreover completely foreign to the political tradition of ancient Vietnam). The historical perspective is completely inverted: the succession of governors-general takes precedence over the evolution of the resistance movement, and the progress of rice exports is put in the foreground, at the expense of the fall in internal consumption.

French historical production relating to colonial Vietnam has here only been considered globally in regard to its general characteristics. It yet remains to define the rhythm in which it developed formerly. One can, it appears, distinguish four periods here from the point of view of historical writing.

About up to the time of Paul Doumer, that is to say, up to the end of the nineteenth century, this production is relatively rich. The conquest is quite recent and still keenly interests the French public. People believe in the future of French colonization in Indo-China and do not fear to express themselves relatively frankly on the subjects of errors committed and difficulties to be encountered. The period 1900–30 is, on the contrary, a period of calm, and Indo-China rarely occupies the forefront of events in France; besides neither 'assimilation' nor 'association' have proved practicable, and the political system in the colony maintains that same arbitrary character which, at the beginning, was represented as only a temporary necessity; one would prefer to leave this régime in the background, and similarly those rapid fortunes which were built up under its protection; serious works are rare. The approach of the economic crisis of 1929 on the other hand, and the swift renewal of political agitation which accompanied it in 1930 provokes a recrudescence of interest in the affairs of Vietnam: as much from the political point of view (it is the epoch of great newspaper reports) as from the economic standpoint (the works of Gouron, Robequain, Goudal, and Paul Bernard, etc.); for people are disturbed anew about the 'future of Indo-China'. At length the World War, and then the Franco-Vietnam war of 1946–54, gave rise to new works; the problem of the unity and independence of Vietnam which by common consent everyone had shunned for the last eighty years was raised irrevocably by events themselves, and it is not surprising that there then appear, for the first time, French books or books in the French language which approach the history of modern Vietnam from the point of view of Vietnamese national continuity, not from the point of view of colonial machinery: such are the numerous historical and economic articles by Henri Lahoue, the *Contribution à l'histoire de la nation vietnamienne* by Jean Chesneaux, *Vietnam* by Le Thanh-Khoi, and up to a point *Vietnam* by Paul Mus, and *l'Histoire du Vietnam* by Philippe Devillers. The establishment of new political relations between France and Vietnam such as they entered upon at the Peace of Geneva, will doubtless be the source of a complete renewal of French historical works on modern Vietnam.

18. ENGLISH HISTORIANS OF 'THE INDIAN ARCHIPELAGO': CRAWFURD AND ST. JOHN

B. HARRISON

Professor of History, University of Hong Kong

'Indian Archipelago' was in vogue as a geographical expression among English writers during the first half of the nineteenth century. It appeared in the title of a number of publications of historical interest: in Crawfurd's *History* (1820) and later in St. John's (1853), in the *Notices* of J. H. Moor (1837), and in Logan's *Journal* (1847–62), as well as in various works of travel.[1] The use of the term partly reflected, no doubt, the inherited 'India-centric' viewpoint of the English in their approach to what we now call South East Asia. But it also marked what may be seen as a stage in the search for a satisfactory term to describe an area that included the Malay Peninsula, the 'East Indian' islands, and the Philippines. To Crawfurd and others who used the term, 'Indian Archipelago' may well have seemed an improvement on those in earlier usage, such as 'India beyond the Ganges' (or Ultra-Gangetic India!)—apparently inherited from Ptolemy[2]—or even 'East India'. After Crawfurd, 'Indian Archipelago' seems to have established itself firmly in use, until it in turn gave way to 'Malay Archipelago' (the title of A. R. Wallace's work published in 1869), or 'Malaysian Archipelago'—terms which were free, at last, of Indian associations.

The interesting question of nomenclature cannot be pursued further here, but it may be worth adding that, having chosen the term 'Indian Archipelago', Crawfurd was consistent enough to describe the inhabitants of the archipelago as a whole as 'Indians'. There was no danger of confusion in this, as might appear, for when referring to the inhabitants of India (or 'Hindustan') Crawfurd described those as Hindus.[3]

Crawfurd published his *History of the Indian Archipelago* in 1820 at the age

---

[1] John Crawfurd, *History of the Indian Archipelago* (3 vols., Edinburgh, 1820). Horace St. John. *The Indian Archipelago, Its History and Present State* (2 vols., London, 1853). J. H. Moor, *Notices of the Indian Archipelago and Adjacent Countries* (Singapore, 1837). (Moor was for some time editor of the *Malacca Observer*, the *Singapore Chronicle*, and the *Singapore Free Press*. His *Notices* contains miscellaneous articles by himself, John Leyden, T. J. Newbold, etc.). *Journal of the Indian Archipelago and East India*, ed. J. R. Logan (12 vols., Singapore, 1847–62).

[2] H. Yule and A. C. Burnell, *Hobson-Jobson* (London, 1903), p. 434.

[3] This usage continued. Yule and Burnell, in *Hobson-Jobson*, declared: 'We use the adjective *Indian*, but no modern Englishman who has had to do with India ever speaks of a man of that country as 'an Indian'. See also *The Shorter Oxford English Dictionary* (*S.V.*), 'Indian': 'A native of India or the East Indies: an East Indian. Now *rare*: usu. repl. by *Hindoo*.'

of thirty-seven. His qualifications for writing a work of this description were his seventeen years' experience of service as a scholar-surgeon-administrator in India, Penang and Java; his official visits to Bali and Celebes; and his knowledge of Malay and Javanese life, language, and literature.[4]

Crawfurd's book is not 'straight' history in our sense. Marsden, Raffles, and Crawfurd all used the title 'History' in something like the original Greek sense of *inquiry*; it meant to them 'a comprehensive view' (a phrase dear to Crawfurd) or a general descriptive account of a country or region. In their works the strictly historical chapters therefore form only a comparatively small proportion of the whole. This 'comprehensive' or 'extensive' aim is well conveyed in Marsden's full title: *The History of Sumatra, Containing an Account of the Government, Laws, Customs, and Manners of the Native Inhabitants, with a Description of the Natural Productions, and a Relation of the Ancient Political State of that Island.*[5] All this was, somehow, indivisibly 'history', and in Marsden's *History* there is no Table of Contents—nor could there well be, for neither are there chapter-divisions.

In Raffles's *History of Java*[6] there *is* a Table of Contents; and it shows that the first volume deals successively with geographical situation, inhabitants, agriculture, manufactures, commerce, political, and social institutions, language, literature, and art. The second volume opens with chapters on religion, etc., and it is not until page sixty-five of the second volume that we come to the strictly historical part of the work. This consists of two chapters (pages 65 to 230) covering the history of Java 'from the earliest traditions . . . till the arrival of the British forces in A.D. 1811'. Raffles's work, like Marsden's, is therefore not so much a history as a descriptive account.

Similarly, Crawfurd's specifically historical treatment of his subject does not commence until Book VII in the second volume is reached. He then devotes six chapters to the 'native' history of the archipelago and three to the 'European' period. He forewarns the reader, however, that both periods 'are too obviously defective in interest and dignity to demand the solemn and continuous narrative of regular history'. There was little of real interest in the archipelago's history, mainly because of 'the paucity of great events, and the absence of great characters'. The native peoples of the region have shown a 'feebleness of intellect'—a result of the state of society and the climate; the Asian immigrants have been 'petty traders';

[4] John Crawfurd (1783–1868), after studying medicine at Edinburgh, was appointed in 1803 to the East India Company's medical service in India; was transferred after five years to Penang; was a member of the British expedition which conquered Java in 1811; held various administrative posts in that island during the British occupation, 1811–16, and went on a political mission to Bali and Celebes. See his *History*, i, pp. v, vi, and the *Dictionary of National Biography*, where details of his later career and publications are given.

[5] First edition (1783).   [6] 2 vols. (1817).

and although the Portuguese can furnish a list of distinguished characters in the history of the archipelago, the most outstanding of the Dutch 'do not seem to have risen much beyond the level of ordinary educated Europeans of their own day'; and among the Spanish 'it would be difficult to produce one name of distinction, except that of Legaspi . . .'[7]

Crawfurd's writing shows a complacent and condescending attitude towards the Asian peoples of his time. He does not hesitate to pronounce the most sweeping judgements on the civilization of the 'Indian islanders', their art, and literature. He contrasts the 'generous and manly genius of the European nations' with the 'feebleness, incapacity, and puerility which has ever characterized those of Asia'. In the literature of Java, he asserts, the European scholar will find only 'bombast, puerility, or utter inanity'. Here is the 'Europe-centric' viewpoint in all its original confidence. 'Whatever is ennobling, or bears the marks of genius and enterprise in the civilization of the Asiatic nations', Crawfurd wrote, 'may be fairly traced to the European race'.[8]

Yet, when it comes to detail, Crawfurd makes what is on the whole a favourable assessment of the qualities and characteristics of the 'native' people of the archipelago, especially the Javanese; and he remarks that 'every man of sense who has visited the Indian islands and dealt temperately and honestly with the natives, comes off with a favourable impression of their character'.[9] Moreover, one significant assumption underlies the whole of Crawfurd's *History* (as also those of Marsden and Raffles)—the basic assumption that the people of the Indian archipelago, their manners, customs, arts, science, and agriculture, are worthy of scientific study. But Crawfurd remains contemptuous of their historical literature. If Javanese accounts of their early history are 'less monstrously extravagant and impudent than those of the Hindus, they are fully more childish and incongruous', he roundly asserts.

We are not here directly concerned with Crawfurd's account of the pre-European period in the history of the archipelago. But his attitude to the past history of European colonial activities was that it was only less unimportant, in its details, than that of the earlier period, even though it had 'produced a most important influence on the fortune and character of the native races'.[10] Clearly Crawfurd's interest—and knowledge—extended less to the history of the archipelago, in our sense, than to its 'present state' considered against the background of a 'sketch' of its history. Consequently the interest which his work holds for the modern historian lies less in the historical narrative itself, sketchy and uneven as it is, than in the incidental observations, the asides, with which the historico-sociological treatment of the whole subject is interspersed, revealing as they

[7] ii, 285-92.
[9] iii, 241 (footnote).
[8] ii, 16, 21; iii, 205.
[10] ii, 285.

do his approach, his assumptions, and his attitudes towards the people of the archipelago and their history.

Before considering some aspects of his historical treatment of the period of colonial activities in the archipelago, it may be worth adding that Crawfurd's main interest lay not merely in the existing conditions in the archipelago but also in the possibilities of their future development. Here his favourite theme is 'improvement'. The word has a utilitarian overtone; improvement could be brought by European nations to the archipelago, in something of the sense in which the eighteenth-century English landlord 'improved'; it applied particularly to labour. As workers and artisans, Crawfurd observed, the islanders were persevering and adaptable, so that 'with this nation at least, we might therefore expect, under favourable circumstances, a progressive improvement in the mechanical arts'.[11] There had already been some progress in this respect in the western parts of the archipelago: 'Man is there most improved', Crawfurd writes, but 'his improvement decreases, in geographical ratio, as we go eastward'.[12]

But if the west could bring improvement to the East in the future, it had failed to do so in the past. Perhaps the most striking feature of Crawfurd's treatment of the history of colonial activities in the archipelago is what appears to be its anti-colonial bias. He writes of 'colonial intrigue and depravity',[13] 'the revolting and disgusting scenes of colonial intrigue',[14] 'the plunder of the East',[15] 'coercion and virtual spoliation'.[16] But what Crawfurd was really condemning so wholeheartedly was not colonial activity as such but 'the evil genius of monopoly'.[17] 'The principle [of monopoly] . . . has actuated the conduct of the Companies and their servants, without interruption, down to the latest times.'[18] 'The independence of most of the natives of the Archipelago was subverted, and their commerce and industry subjected to the will of the monopolists.'[19] The Philippines alone had improved in civilization, wealth, and populousness, Crawfurd argued, partly because 'private industry and wholesome competition have been allowed'.[20] Crawfurd quotes with approval Adam Smith and Ricardo, and concludes that the duty of the legislator 'lies solely in seeing justice done to all parties, and taking care that the natural and wholesome influence of competition be not obstructed by the impertinence of restriction, or pretended regulation'.[21] This 'liberal', free-trade, view colours Crawfurd's whole treatment of the history of colonial activities in the archipelago.

Crawfurd advocated not only free trade but also direct European colonization. He believed that the success of Spanish colonial activity in

[11] i, 204. [12] i, 16. [13] ii, 285.
[14] ii, 392. [15] ii, 340. [16] iii, 220.
[17] ii, 420. [18] iii, 239. [19] iii, 220.
[20] ii, 447–8. [21] iii, 199.

the Philippines was due, above all, to 'the freedom given to European colonization', with its consequence that 'the influence of the genius and manners of Europe has been felt by the natives',[22] and he deplored the 'unwise restraints imposed on European colonization' elsewhere.[23] 'A perfect freedom of colonization and settlement to Europeans, an equality of rights to every denomination of inhabitants, and an unlimited and un-restricted freedom of commercial intercourse, will prove the certain, but the only means of disseminating *civilization* and *Christianity*.'[24] For Craw-furd, then, free trade principles were not incompatible with colonial expansion. The free, independent trader of the future would still need, for convenience and for security, an intermediary between himself and the native trader. 'A colonial establishment becomes the only means of effec-ting this object.' And besides the commercial considerations, there was a moral duty involved. 'Innumerable islands of the vast Archipelago are still unappropriated, and to colonize them is, therefore, not only consistent with natural justice, but, in the existing state of the European world, might almost be urged as a moral duty.' And Crawfurd went on to make the specific proposal for a colony on the island of Banka (Raffles had chosen Singapore, however, before Crawfurd's book came out).[25]

As a historian of Western colonial activities in the archipelago, Crawfurd felt called upon to pass large and definite judgements, mostly of con-demnation. One feels that he approached his subject with his mind already made up. And, it is hardly necessary to add, he wrote for English readers, not for 'Indians'. It is not surprising, given his viewpoint, that he has nothing good to say of the Dutch: their 'formation of a joint-stock com-pany . . . has since, by its example, had so pernicious an influence upon the commercial history of the East'.[26] For the Portuguese, conquest and religious conversion were primary objects, and commerce only a secondary one, with the result that 'more monuments of their arts, their religion, and their language, exist (in the archipelago) than of those who succeeded them'. This, again, was a consequence of 'the unfettered influence of European manners and institutions'.[27] The Spanish administration in the Philippines won Crawfurd's approval, as has already been noticed, because of what appeared to him to have been an enlightened commercial and colonizing policy. It compared favourably, he considered, with the British administration in India. Judged by 'the attachment of the great body of its subjects, the Spanish administration of the Philippines stands higher than any other that was ever established in the Archipelago, and probably higher than that of the British government of India'.[28] In the Archipelago,

[22] ii, 448-9.
[24] ii, 279.
[26] ii, 413.
[28] ii. 479.

[23] iii, 73.
[25] iii, 263.
[27] iii, 216.

the English, like the Dutch, had 'entered upon a system of coercion and virtual spoliation'.[29]

Raffles, who reviewed Crawfurd's book in the *Quarterly Review*, commented that 'the English company are not, we think, very fairly included in the same censure with the Dutch'. He also criticized Crawfurd's 'extraordinary admiration and preference bestowed on the Spaniards, for the enlightened system they are said to have introduced in the Philippines. We believe this is the first time they have received such a tribute of applause, and we fear . . . it is likely to be the last.'[30]

The further comments of Raffles, whose *History of Java* had been published three years before Crawfurd's work, are of some interest. Crawfurd had earlier reviewed Raffles's *History* in the *Edinburgh Review*, and had 'thrown a cloud', as Raffles himself remarked, over his treatment of 'the literature, history and antiquities of Java'. Raffles therefore expected from Crawfurd 'a somewhat new view' of these subjects,[31] but after reading his copy of Crawfurd's *History* in Bencoolen, he wrote (to a cousin): 'It does not contain one fact that is new to me, and most of the reasoning and conclusions are founded on partial views . . .'[32]

There were two major points of criticism in Raffles's review in the *Quarterly*. The first was that since 'ample details' had already been published concerning Java, it was expected that Crawfurd would give an account of other portions of the archipelago. 'In this particular . . .' Raffles wrote, 'we have been disappointed; the author has not gone beyond those civilized portions which have already been so fully treated.'[33] This was, on the whole, a fair criticism. Crawfurd's work does not live up to the expectations raised by its comprehensive title. The principal defects of the work were, in the words of Raffles, 'a rage for generalizing on partial and insufficient data, and the substitution of bold speculation for the patient investigation of facts. With materials sufficient, perhaps, for an account of one of these islands, the author has attempted to grasp the whole.'[34]

With Crawfurd, Java certainly assumes a disproportionately large place in what purports to be a history of the whole archipelago, and no doubt he was himself concious of this. When he writes, as a medical man, of the physical constitution of the islanders, he warns that as the subject 'is one which peculiarly demands precision, my observations will chiefly refer to the Javanese, of whose conditions alone, on matters so much in detail, I can speak confidently',[35] and it is really with Java, Sumatra, and the

---

[29] iii, 220.

[30] *The Quarterly Review* (October, 1822), pp. 126–7. The review is unsigned, but see C. Wurtzburg, *Raffles of the Eastern Isles*, p. 591.

[31] Wurtzburg, op. cit., p. 563.

[32] Op. cit., p. 591.

[33] *The Quarterly Review*, loc. cit., p. 112.

[34] Ibid., p. 122.   [35] Crawfurd, i, 30.

Malay Peninsula that he is mainly concerned in the work as a whole. Yet he does include some treatment, limited though it is, of other parts of the archipelago, including the Philippines; and perhaps the peculiarly significant aspect of Crawfurd's *History* for South East Asian historiography is its effort to widen the scope of inquiry, its gallant, if hopeless (or at any rate premature), attempt to establish the 'Indian Archipelago' as an intelligible field of historical study. The charge of generalizing upon insufficient data is, of course, one which might be brought against many who have attempted, then and since, to produce work in South East Asian history; many, desperately trying to make bricks with very little straw, have offended. As has been said, let him who is without offence throw the first footnote. Crawfurd was himself critical of the 'indistinct and imperfect accounts' available for many parts of the archipelago, including eyewitness accounts of travellers; when referring to the people of New Guinea he remarks that 'Forrest, who had good opportunities of observing them, is as usual most unsatisfactory'.[36]

The other major point of criticism in Raffles's review in the *Quarterly* was that Crawfurd had not given sufficient acknowledgement of his sources.[37] There are only occasional footnote references to sources in the chapters that Crawfurd devotes specifically to the history of the archipelago, and those are anything but precise; page references are never given. His sole reference to sources for his four chapters on the history of Java is contained in a footnote: 'The materials of the history of Java have been chiefly collected from a variety of Javanese historical compositions in the author's possession, which have been duly collated with such European authorities as have fallen in his way.'[38] Nothing could be more evasive—and no mention of Raffles! For the history of the Malays, Crawfurd refers to Van der Worm, Valentyn, Marsden, and the *Hang Tuah* ('a most absurd and puerile production').[39] His sources for the history of the Celebes consisted of 'the manuscript memoir of a Governor Blok, written in 1759, a judicious performance; and of several native writings, both in the Bugis and Macassar language, of which translations were made into the Malay for the author's use'.[40] For the chapters on the history of European activities in the archipelago Crawfurd's references to sources are neither numerous nor precise.[41]

---

[36] Ibid., i, 26.   [37] *The Quarterly Review*, loc. cit., p. 125.
[38] Crawfurd, ii, 370.   [39] Ibid., ii, 373, 377–8.   [40] Ibid., ii, 390.
[41] For the history of the Portuguese in the archipelago Crawfurd's references are to 'Maffaei, *Historia Indica*; Latfiau, *Histoires des découvertes et conquêtes des Portugais dans le nouveau monde*; *Histoire General des Voyages*; *Modern Universal History*'. His chapter on the Dutch contains only two references: to Alexander Hamilton's *New Account of the East Indies*, and Harris's *Collection of Voyages and Travels*. For the Spanish in the archipelago, he gives his main authorities as 'An historical view of the Philippine Islands by Martinez de Zuniga. Relations des Isles Philippines, in the collection of Thevenot, vol. i. Voyage dans les Mers de l'Inde, par M. Le Gentil, Tom. II.'

The value of Crawfurd's work as history cannot, however, fairly be judged on the historical section (Book VII, Volume II) alone. There it is only with 'political' history that he is concerned, but historical treatment of social and economic matters runs through the three volumes of the whole work, the section on Commerce in the third volume being especially valuable in this respect.

Despite its limitations, Crawfurd's *History* remains, in the words of the *Dictionary of National Biography*, 'a work of sterling value and great interest'. But the work makes instructive reading for the historian mainly for its revelation of personal viewpoints and attitudes, and for the interesting questions that arise therefrom: whence were these attitudes derived, and how far were they shared or reflected in contemporary or in later writing? Reading Crawfurd one notes as prominent features of his writing a strong sense of the moral superiority of Europeans, coupled with a high opinion of the potentialities of the native peoples provided they are 'improved' by European influence; a readiness to embark upon Toynbee-like generalizations, for example as to 'the influence of food in forming the character of the different races', and yet a close attention to detail in treating of such matters as agriculture and music; the breadth of scope of the whole survey—in the tradition of Condorcet; a censorious attitude towards the morals of Europeans in the East; a comparatively high opinion of the Spanish achievement in the Philippines; an extensive treatment of the economic history of the archipelago; the attitude of *laissez-faire* liberalism as applied to trade; and the advocacy of European colonization partly as a moral duty—the White Man's Burden of later days.

This last feature of Crawfurd's writing—what may perhaps be termed the imperialist spirit—appears also, with some added emphasis, in Horace St. John's *The Indian Archipelago*, published in 1853. The age of complacency had not passed. 'It is not easy', writes St. John, 'to disbelieve, and it is ridiculous to deride the theory, that it is the destiny of the West to spread its dominion over the East, through the length and breadth of Asia. I put faith in the fortunes of Great Britain, which may lead her to possess, if not the whole, at least most of that region which she has proved herself, of all others, the most capable to rule . . .'[42] Even the Dutch, monopolists though they had been, were now, it appeared, reformed imperialists. No one should hold it against them that they had striven to build an empire in Asia. 'That Holland invaded the Indian islands to found an empire among them, is no charge upon her national reputation. . . . It is in the details, not in the object, of their policy, that the guilt of the Dutch lies.'[43]

The history of Dutch colonial activities occupies a large place in St. John's work. He goes so far as to assert that from the date of the foundation

[42] i, 274.   [43] i, 262.

of Batavia, when the merchants of Amsterdam were become the founders
of an empire, 'the history of the archipelago is the history of their progress'.[44]

St. John's attitude to the record of Dutch colonial activities is interesting
and revealing. Like Crawfurd, he condemns the restrictive trade policies
of the past; Dutch restrictions, he asserts, destroyed the native trade, and
'it is humiliating to the civilization of Europe to confess that the establishment of its influence in Java broke up a free and thriving commerce'.[45]
But with St. John this attitude is tempered by a qualified—and somewhat
patronizing—approval of the record of the Dutch in the East Indies since
Crawfurd's day, and by a belief in an enlightened—and inevitable—
Western imperialism. St. John concedes that after the Dutch had been
restored in 1816 they 'devised several plans in emulation of the British
policy . . . The liberty of trade, though still restrained by rigid enactments,
was slightly extended, and other beneficial regulations were enacted.'
These measures, it is true, 'were all conceived to promote in politics and
commerce the interests of Holland; but', he continues, 'it is a characteristic
of wise and benevolent rule, when the happiness of the people is increased
by laws which provide for the aggrandisement of the governors'.[46] Here a
theory of identity of interests between 'colonizers' and 'colonized' is associated with the concept of general happiness.

St. John points to an increase of over three million in the population of
Java since 1824 under 'a comparatively good administration'. Although
'the peasant is undeniably in a state of serfdom . . . he may be said to
enjoy under Dutch government at least as much happiness as he ever
enjoyed before'. 'The islands have become reconciled to their loss of
independence; the hopes of the native princes have fortunately been ex-
tinguished; tranquillity has long reigned . . .'[47] But for all that, St. John
believed the British would have done better as colonial rulers; had they
not restored Java and other islands to the Dutch the results would have
been 'the trade of England enlarged, the prosperity of the Archipelago
increased, and Christendom graced with a new dominion'.[48]

The nineteenth-century concept of inevitability—common to liberal
progressives, Darwinians, and Marxists—partly underlay St. John's enthusiasm for empire. 'If we reflect on the history of European intercourse
with the East,' he observes, 'we find that states once subdued by the arms
of the white races seldom or never recover the dignity of independence.
Sooner or later their inevitable fate is to be absorbed by the conquering
civilisation which has spared them for the day . . . Some may pass more
fleetly, some more slowly, down the decline of their existence; all will in
the end yield even the name of independence, and recognize the authority

[44] i, 284.   [45] i, 301.   [46] ii, 57.
[47] ii, 355.   [48] ii, 54.

of the ascendent power. On the continent of India Great Britain is developing this beneficent process; in the Archipelago Holland is illustrating it.'[49]

Although St. John, like Crawfurd, tends to pronounce large judgements, his book provides much more of a continuous and detailed narrative than Crawfurd's; it is more a history in our sense and less an encyclopedia. St. John's aim was more restricted than Crawfurd's; it was simply to describe 'the progress of European trade and conquest in the Asiatic Archipelago'.[50] 'The origin and spread of the Malayan race', and 'the periods intervening between that remote and problematical era and the arrival of the Portuguese', are summarily disposed of in the first fifty pages or so of his first volume. But throughout his work St. John is much more careful than Crawfurd in acknowledging sources. There are footnote references to earlier works on almost every page. Besides a multitude of other works, St. John had consulted 'those of Crawfurd, Raffles, Marsden, Temminck, Keppel, Mundy, Earl, Forrest, Dampier, Newbold, Faria y Sousa, Zuniga, Walton's Discourse, Hugh Low, and Belcher, with the contributions of Mr. Logan and several other writers to that valuable publication the *Journal of the Indian Archipelago*. *The Singapore Free Press*, also, has been exceedingly useful.'[51] St. John does not claim, as did Crawfurd, to have consulted vernacular sources.

However it may be with other fields of history today, there can be little doubt that in the writing of South East Asian history there is much scope and urgent need for specialized studies. But a larger view of history, however blurred it may be, can serve to bring out the deeper significance of such studies and thereby to stimulate them anew. Something of that larger view Crawfurd and St. John, in their day and within their limitations, succeeded in revealing by their writings on the Indian Archipelago.

[49] i, 392.
[50] i, Preface, v. He had already published, in 1852, a *History of the British Conquests in India* (2 vols.). St. John was by profession a journalist; he frequently acted as special correspondent of *The Times* and other newspapers (D.N.B.). His 'studies had for a long time been directed to the East' (*The Indian Archipelago*, i, Preface, v).
[51] i, Preface, x.

19. BRITISH WRITERS OF BURMESE HISTORY FROM DALRYMPLE TO BAYFIELD

D. G. E. HALL

Professor Emeritus of the History of South East Asia, University of London

Although English intercourse with Burma may be said to have begun in 1587 with the visit of the Elizabethan prospector Ralph Fitch, whose journal was included by Richard Hakluyt in his *Principall Navigations* and by Samuel Purchas in his *Pilgrimes*, it was a long time before the East India Company developed relations with the country, and a far longer one before any Englishman had anything to say about its history. The earliest publication of a historical nature was the collection of papers relating to the English settlement on the island of Negrais (1753–9) and the East India Company's relations with King Alaungpaya which was included by Alexander Dalrymple in the first volume of his *Oriental Repertory* (London, 1791–7).[1] The papers, mainly journals of the envoys deputed to negotiate with the Court of Ava, contain hardly any references to the history of the country before the rise of Alaungpaya in 1752, but an introductory one, composed by Dalrymple himself in June 1759, and entitled 'Letter concerning the *Negrais Expedition* and concerning the adjacent countries'[2] traces in outline the story of English intercourse with Burma up to the foundation of the settlement, and offers an estimate of the causes of failure of the East India Company's relations with Burma, and, in particular, of the Negrais factory.[3]

In 1759 Dalrymple had spent seven years in the East India Company's service at Fort St. George, Madras. During this period he had devoted all his leisure to examining the old records there. From them he had learnt of the spice trade and of the Company's earlier interest in the island world, then inappropriately referred to as the East Indies, from which the monopolizing Dutch had successfully squeezed out all European competitors in the seventeenth century. He had become fired with an intense desire to direct British commerce once again into the area.

In his book *The Founding of the Second British Empire* (1952) Professor V. T. Harlow describes Dalrymple as the propagator of a new type of

---

[1] A reprint of the portions of the *Oriental Repertory* relating to Burma was issued by the Superintendent, Government Printing and Stationery, Burma, Rangoon, in 1926. It retains the original pagination, title pages and contents tables of the 1808 edition.

[2] i, 97–128.

[3] When he wrote, the evacuation of the settlement was in progress. A few months later, on 6 October 1759, the Burmese massacred those who remained and destroyed the buildings.

imperialist doctrine, which was anti-colonial, i.e. opposed to the planting of colonies.[4] The everlasting discontent in the American colonies was for him an object-lesson in the futility of colonization. Britain, he urged, should proceed to the discovery of new lands 'not with a view to colonizing; nor with a view to conquest: but of an amicable intercourse for mutual benefit'. It was along these lines that he sought to further the eastwards expansion of the British Empire from India to the Pacific. The empire of his dreams was a chain of trading posts protected by naval bases at strategic points. Thus it is easy to see how the Negrais settlement and the history of British relations with Burma should have aroused his special interest. For it was founded in the year after his arrival at Madras and was intended as a naval repair station and a harbour for the protection of British commerce in the Bay of Bengal.[5]

Dalrymple's account of the history of English relations with Burma is extremely slight. The Madras records, upon which he relied, have little to say about Burma before 1680, and what he says about the earlier period is little more than guesswork. There were English factories in Burma from 1647 to 1657, planted and managed by Fort St. George, but for information about them one has to go to the Original Correspondence of the East India Company. Of the period after 1680 Dalrymple wrote: 'There is hardly any information to be obtained from Public Records during this Period, so that I have scarce been able to collect anything worthy Attention, from the Records of almost a Century.'[6] But he was not concerned with history for its own sake, and his search cannot have been a very thorough one, for the Fort St. George records from 1680 contain much material relating to Burma. Many years later, when compiling the second volume of the *Oriental Repertory* he made up some of the deficiency by including documents concerning the mission of Edward Fleetwood in 1695 and that of Thomas Bowyear in 1698.[7] But in any case before 1750, partly through deficiencies in the records, and partly through the East India Company's unwillingness to commit itself deeply in Burma, the story is patchy.

Then suddenly, soon after the conclusion of the Treaty of Aix-la-Chapelle in 1748, a dramatic change occurs in the situation. The East India Company becomes aware that its resourceful adversary Dupleix is contemplating Burma as a field for French expansion, and the records relating to that country become plentiful. Nevertheless, with the exception

[4] See especially pp. 37–8 and 62.

[5] We are not concerned here with the further development of Dalrymple's schemes. But it is noteworthy that between 1759 and 1764 he undertook on behalf of the Fort St. George authorities a series of prospective voyages to Borneo, the Sulu Archipelago and the Philippines. These, however, were only by way of being a preliminary canter. His great ambition, never realized, was to explore the southern Pacific, and he was to become the foremost exponent of the case for an undiscovered continent in the South Seas.

[6] Op. cit., i, 105.

[7] pp. 337–404.

of a brief paper of anonymous authorship recommending the planting of a settlement on the island of Negrais, Dalrymple's valuable collection of documents dealing with British relations with King Alaungpaya and his successor Naungdawgyi begins only with the year 1755. His explanation of this is as follows: 'In the year 1753 an Expedition to settle at Negrais was undertaken; as the particular Motives, for this Scheme, were communicated only to a Secret Committee, of these, or the plan laid down, if there was any, I can therefore say nothing.'[8]

Thus, the story which can be pieced together from Dalrymple's materials is seriously truncated; and not only is its beginning completely missing, but its ending also. For the story of the East India Company's final withdrawal from Burma in 1762 is contained in the Calcutta records, to which Dalrymple, working in Madras, had no access. This point must be stressed because his collection has been the principle source used by writers for the story of British relations with Alaungpaya from Michael Symes[9] to Mr. G. E. Harvey.[10]

Soon after Dalrymple published his first volume of documents, there appeared the first comprehensive account of Burma to be written in a European language. It was Michael Symes's *An Account of an Embassy to the Kingdom of Ava sent by the Governor-General of India in the year 1795.*[11] It begins with an 'Historical Memoir of the Ava Empire' occupying no less than 123 pages, which itself represents the first attempt by a European to write Burmese history. The writer's main object, of course, was to provide a background against which his account of Burma and of his experiences there could be viewed. In his Preface he writes: 'The rise and fortunes of Alompra and the establishment of the present Birman dynasty supply a short, but highly interesting, period of oriental history.' His narrative is graphic and there can be no doubt that the subject fascinated him. He has obviously been at great trouble to collect as much information as possible, and he tells the story for its own sake.

His sources, apart from Dalrymple's 'most useful and judicious compilation', were, he tells us, the accounts given him orally by 'individuals who themselves bore a part in the transactions'. Thus he obtained the story of the Chinese invasions of Burma in the reign of Hsinbyushin (1763–76), and that of the subsequent Burmese invasion of Manipur, from 'an old Mussulman soldier who bore arms in both'. 'He could have no inducement to deceive,' Symes comments, 'and the leading circumstances of his narrative were confirmed from other quarters.' Apparently he found it easy to obtain information, for the events 'were so generally known', and although

---

[8] Op. cit., i, 97. The records he was unable to consult are in the Madras Military Consultations.
[9] 'Historical Memoir of the Ava Empire'; in *An Account of an Embassy . . . 1795.*
[10] *History of Burma* (London, 1926).
[11] London, 1800.

the accounts of them were 'liable to that bias which is inseparable from the human mind', the leading facts were such as did not admit of misrepresentation.

For the earlier history before the rise of Alaungpaya Symes had to make what he could of the bits and pieces he was able to cull from European writers. His knowledge of Burmese was unfortunately inadequate for him to utilize the Burmese chronicles. Hence in describing his visit to Pagan he can say nothing cogent about its history. He records that it had been abandoned five hundred years earlier 'in consequence of a divine admonition'[12] but makes no mention of the Mongol conquest of 1287, which was the decisive factor. He begins his story with references to Ptolemy's account of 'the Eastern Peninsula'. Thereafter, he tells us, a period of almost total darkness obscured the area until the coming of the Portuguese. Then with the aid of Faria y Souza[13] and Mendes Pinto,[14] 'the prince of fiction, though an intelligent traveller', he constructs a picture of the states of Arakan, Ava, Pegu, and Siam, which forms a useful background to the big issues with which he was concerned, namely, the Burmese conquest of the Mons and Arakan and the struggles between Burma and Siam. Incidentally, he makes some use of the accounts of Siam compiled by the seventeenth-century French writers, de Choisy[15] and de la Loubère,[16] and mentions Louis XIV's relations with that country.

The first full-scale history of Burma based upon Burmese materials was not to appear until 1883 when Sir Arthur Phayre's pioneer work was published. In his introduction[17] Phayre mentions Symes's historical memoir, which, he says, 'gives a trustworthy account of events commencing from the re-establishment of the kingdom of Pegu under Binya Dala in A.D. 1740 until the time of his own embassy in 1795'. Such an estimate, coming from one who had a remarkable knowledge of the period from the Burmese chronicles themselves, is significant.

After Symes's book no further detailed treatises on Burmese history appeared until the publication in 1835 of G. T. Bayfield's *Historical Review of the Political Relations between the British Government in India and the Empire of Ava.*[18] In the meantime, however, John Crawfurd in his *Journal of an Embassy from the Governor-General of India to the Court of Ava*, published in 1829, included a chapter on Burmese history, which, though short, represented a distinct advance upon what Symes had to say about the earlier

[12] Op. cit., p. 269.
[13] *Asia Portugueza*, 3 vols. (Lisbon, 1666–75). English trans. by J. Stevens (London, 1695).
[14] Fernand Mendez Pinto, *The Voyages and Adventures of* . . . (London, 1653).
[15] F. T. de Choisy, *Journal du Voyage de Siam fait en* 1685 *et* 1686 (Paris, 1687).
[16] de La Loubère, *Description du Royaume de Siam* (Paris, 1691), English edition (London, 1693).
[17] p. vii.
[18] Published as a Supplement to Captain R. Boileau Pemberton's valuable *Report on the Eastern Frontier of British India* (Calcutta, 1835).

period. Apparently he was the first British writer, strange as it may seem, to realize that the Burmese had historical writings, for he says at the beginning of his chapter: 'The Burmese, as will hereafter be more fully explained, are not absolutely destitute of historical compositions; and I am indebted to translations of some of their narratives for a few of the details about to be given.' What especially aroused his interest was a Burmese parabeik,[19] which had been found in one of the stockades captured by the British army during the war of 1824–6. It contained a Burmese chronological table of kings with dates according to the Buddhist, Saka, and Burmese eras respectively. In an appendix to his book he published a translation of it made for him by the American Baptist missionary, Dr. Adoniram Judson, with the addition of the equivalent dates in the Christian era. In this way there came for the first time into English writings some mention of the dynasties of Prome, Pagan, Pinya, Sagaing and Ava, together with the Buddhaghosa legend telling of the introduction of Buddhism to Burma from Ceylon.

More important still, however, is the fact that Crawfurd explored the magnificent remains of ancient Pagan and wrote the first description of them on record.[20] Yet it is noteworthy that though vastly impressed by them, he repudiated the idea that they might be taken as 'proofs of considerable civilization and wealth among the Ancient Burmans'. 'The building of a temple among the Burmans', he writes, 'is not only a work of piety, but the chief species of luxury and ostentation, in which those who have become possessed of wealth either by industry or extortion are permitted to indulge.'[21] In the second volume of his *History of the Indian Archipelago*, published in 1820, Crawfurd had included a scholarly chapter dealing with the ancient monuments, statuary and inscriptions of Java, together with a number of excellent illustrations, including one of Chandi Borobudur itself. It is therefore disappointing that he offers nothing on the same scale in the case of Pagan. The reason of course is that his stay in Burma was too short for him to explore that country's antiquities and historical writings.[22] And, unfortunately, he was not a success with the Burmese; in the extremely difficult circumstances in which he was placed, with the Court of Ava suffering acutely from the shock of defeat in the war with the British, Crawfurd was too stiff and uncompromising to establish reasonable relations with them.

The opportunity to undertake serious research into Burmese history came with the appointment of Major Henry Burney as British Resident at the Court of Ava in December 1829. A grandson of the famous musician,

---

[19] He describes it as 'a long scroll of paper, folded zig-zag'.
[20] *Journal* (second edition), i, 108–25.
[21] Ibid., i, 125.
[22] He was in Java from 1811 to 1816.

Dr. Charles Burney,[23] Henry was a soldier who had been seconded to the East India Company's political service. As an officer of the Bengal native infantry he had taken part in the conquest of Java in 1811. Later, as a member of the staff of the Governor of Prince of Wales Island (Penang), he had been employed on missions to the Malay States connected with Siam. In 1825 he had gone to Bangkok as the Envoy of the Government of India, and in the following year had concluded a treaty, which regulated Anglo-Siamese relations until the Bowring Treaty of 1855. Thereafter he had spent several years as assistant to A. D. Maingy, the first Commissioner of the Province of Tenasserim, annexed from Burma at the end of the Anglo-Burmese War of 1824–6. In the course of these various activities he had acquired a considerable linguistic equipment, which included Urdu, Malay, Siamese and Burmese, and a scholarly interest in the culture and history of the South East Asian regions with which he had become acquainted. But although the East India Company's records contain a great amount of valuable material, especially on the subject of Siam, from his pen, dating from the earlier period, he had published nothing before his arrival at the Court of Ava.[24]

It was Burney's achievement to discover the historical literature of Burma. Crawfurd's somewhat supercilious reference to the existence of Burmese 'historical compositions' indicates the limitations of his knowledge. And, of course, he knew no Burmese and was too short a time in the country to make any close study of its writings. Burney, on the other hand, held office as British Resident for eight years. No British official had previously had so long and continuous a connection with the country, or had been able to develop such intimate relations with its government. Besides, he had a special reason for seeking out and examining its historical records, and an opportunity to do so under somewhat unusual circumstances.

In the first place a serious dispute was in progress between the Court of Ava and the Government of India because in adjusting the frontier between India and Burma in consequence of the Treaty of Yandabo (1826) the British authorities had handed over the Kabaw Valley, running between the Manipur mountains and the River Chindwin, to the raja of Manipur. One of Burney's most urgent tasks, therefore, was to look into the Burmese claim that the valley had been within the jurisdiction of the Ava monarchy almost since its foundation in the thirteenth century. For

---

[23] See Percy A. Scholes, *The Great Dr Burney*, 2 vols. (London, 1948). Henry's father was Richard Thomas Burney (1768–1808), Master of the East India Company's Military Orphan School, Kidderpore, Calcutta, and half-brother of Fanny Burney, Madame d'Arblay, the novelist.

[24] His *Siam Journal* and other papers were printed *in extenso* for private circulation in 1910–11 on behalf of the Vajiranana National Library, Bangkok. He himself had intended to publish them, and in 1841 received the permission of the Court of Directors of the East India Company to do so, but died before completing the work of preparing them for the press.

this purpose the chronicles provided his most useful source-material. In the second place he arrived at the Court at a moment when it had become history-minded in a rather big way. A committee of 'learned monks, learned brahmans, and learned ministers',[25] appointed by King Bagyidaw, was compiling what later came to be known as the *Hmannan Yazawin*, or *Glass Palace Chronicle*. For this purpose a complete survey of all the known sources of Burmese history was in progress, and it was a simple matter for Burney to obtain not only all the materials he required, but also expert guidance in consulting them. Indeed, every possible assistance in pursuing his researches was afforded him by the ministers.

The extent of Burney's researches into Burmese historical sources was far greater than one might imagine from his published work.[26] Although an active member of the Asiatic Society of Bengal and a frequent contributor to the early numbers of its Journal, he never produced a magnum opus. Nevertheless, the wealth of his unpublished work in the East India Company's records, and his unfinished work in the Royal Empire Society's Burney Collection, give some idea of what he might have produced had his health not broken down under the strain of the palace revolution at Ava in 1837.[27] His scholarly report on the Kabaw Valley question, in which he showed that according to the *Mahayazawin*[28] the valley had been in the possession of the Ava monarchy since 1370, can be read in the *Bengal Secret and Political Consultations*.[29] The *India Political Consultations*[30] contain another report from him dated Rangoon, 17 September 1834, entitled 'Account of the Burmese Mission which resided in Bengal from December 1830 to July 1833, compiled from the reports made by the Envoys to the Court of Ava and other Burmese documents.' It runs to no less than 124 large folio pages. The Burmese materials, which Burney used in compiling it, are now to be found, with much annotation and translation in his own handwriting, in the splendid collection of Burmese manuscripts, presented by him to the East India Company's Library, now the India Office Library. His papers in the Royal Empire Society's collection include extensive studies of Buddhism besides a profusion of historical notes.

[25] Pe Maung Tin's Introduction to *The Glass Palace Chronicle of the Kings of Burma* (London, 1923), p. ix.

[26] In 'Henry Burney, Diplomat and Orientalist', a paper read at the XXIV International Congress of Orientalists, Munich, Aug./Sept. 1957, I have indicated the scope of his work as an orientalist.

[27] The story is told by W. S. Desai in his valuable *History of the British Residency in Burma, 1826–1840* (Rangoon, 1939), pp. 251–302. Burney was censured by Governor-General Lord Auckland for removing the Residency to Rangoon as a result of what he believed to be the threatening attitude of King Tharrawaddy. He went home on sick leave, and although his health recovered sufficiently for him to return to India, it soon broke down again, and he died at sea on his way home.

[28] The Burmese *Great Chronicle*, an eighteenth century compilation.

[29] Vol. 367; in a dispatch dated Rangoon, 5 July 1832.

[30] Range 193, vol. 79, Consultation of 6 July 1835, doc. no. 18.

His published work based upon Burmese sources is for the most part to be found in volumes IV, V, and VI of the *Journal of the Asiatic Society of Bengal*. Its most important item is entitled 'Some Account of the Wars between Burmah and China' and is 94 pages in length.[31] The earlier part is based upon the *Mahayazawin*, the later upon copies or abstracts of official documents supplied to him by the Ministers of the Court of Ava. Its treatment of the Chinese invasions of Burma during the reign of Hsinbyushin (1763–76), and of the important treaty of Kaungton of December 1769, is of special interest today. It tallies exactly with the account given many years later by Sir Arthur Phayre in his *History of Burma*.[32] And it is clearly a more authentic record than the story told in recent times from Chinese sources by T'eng Tch'ong in his *Ming-te*, the French translation of which is in J. Siguret's *Territoires et Populations des Confins du Yunnan*.[33]

Even more valuable are Burney's detailed accounts of the missions that had passed between the two countries between the Kaungton Conference and his own day. His translations of the record in 'the 33rd volume of the Burmese chronicles' of King Bodawpaya's reception of a Chinese embassy on 3 April 1787,[34] and of the journals and routes of the Burmese missions to Peking in 1787, 1823, and 1833, together with the official correspondence that passed between the two monarchs, provide an effective antidote to the fantastic claims of the Chinese a century later, when Britain annexed Upper Burma.

The extent of Burney's influence in stimulating others to study the culture and antiquities of Burma has never been examined, even if suspected. How much, for instance, did Phayre owe to it? There is an intriguing entry in the record of a meeting of the Asiatic Society of Bengal on 6 April 1836, at which some Buddhist images and inscriptions, discovered at Tagaung by Captain S. F. Hannay, the officer commanding the Resident's escort, were received together with a paper by Burney giving the *Maha Yazawin* version of the early history of Tagaung. It runs: 'A drawing of the full size of the sculptured impression of Gautama's foot in Ava was presented by Ensign Phayre, with a description of the several compartments.'[35] Years later the *Mahayazawin* was to be the main source used by Phayre for his *History of Burma*. In his introduction he mentions Burney's work on it and his view that the Burmese chronicles bore 'strong internal marks of authenticity'.[36]

It was at Burney's suggestion, and with his active help, that his assistant, Dr. G. T. Bayfield, compiled his *Historical Review of the Political Relations between the British Government in India and the Empire of Ava* up to the year

[31] vi, 121–49, 405–51, 542–59.
[33] Peiping, 1937, ii, 144–52.
[35] Ibid., v, 157–64 and 190.

[32] London, 1883, p. 202.
[34] J. A. S. Bengal, vi, 408–13.
[36] Op. cit., pp. v–vi.

1834,[37] which for the best part of the next century was to be the main source used by students of the subject. Bayfield was an Assistant-Surgeon on the East India Company's Madras Establishment, and thus belonged to a class of men who once made important contributions to Western knowledge of the East.[38] For South East Asia there was first and foremost John Crawfurd himself. George Finlayson, who accompanied him as medical officer on his missions to Siam and Cochin China, published an independent account of them.[39] Dr. Buchanan, the medical officer with Symes's first mission to Ava in 1795, became a distinguished orientalist. Dr. Richardson, who was for a time attached to the Ava Residency, explored routes into China from Burma and published valuable accounts of his expeditions.[40] Dr. Thomas Oldham, who accompanied Phayre's well-known mission to Ava in 1855, carried out important geographical surveys, the results of which were published by Colonel (Sir) Henry Yule in his delightful volume telling the story of the mission.[41]

The greater part of Bayfield's *Historical Review* is devoted to an account of Burney's work as Resident, and is based upon his journals and despatches. His survey of the earlier history of British relations with Burma, though less detailed, uses the manuscript records of the East India Company. This is particularly true of the period from 1794 onwards, for which his main sources were the *Bengal Political Proceedings* and the *Bengal Secret and Political Proceedings*. As he was in Ava and the documents were in Calcutta, the donkey-work of copying must have been done for him by a clerk, and, indeed, one who was unpardonably careless, for this part of his book abounds in copyist's errors. There are both misspellings of names[42] and even bad mistakes of fact, which seem to have their origin in misreadings of the original. But he himself is guilty of worse mistakes. For instance, he cites William Hunter's *Concise Account of the Kingdom of Pegu*[43] as his authority for saying that in 1782 the English East India Company possessed a factory in Rangoon, surrounded by a brick wall on which its colours were hoisted.[44] What Hunter actually wrote was that in 1782, when he visited Rangoon, the Imperial Company (i.e. the Imperial Company of Trieste) possessed a factory there surrounded by a brick

---

[37] Published as a Supplement to Captain R. Boileau Pemberton's *Report on the Eastern Frontier of British India* (Calcutta, 1835).

[38] Probably because at a station or on a mission the doctor was the only man with a scientific training. Hence he was often employed as a sort of 'station adjutant' entrusted with the task of collecting information.

[39] *The Mission to Siam and Hué in the years 1821–2* (London, 1826).

[40] See his contributions to J.A.S.B., vols. v, vi, viii, ix.

[41] *Narrative of the Mission sent by the Governor-General of India to the Court of Ava in 1855* (London, 1858).

[42] E.g. Sealey for Lesly, an error repeated by Sir George Scott, *History of Burma* (London, 1924), p. 150, and G. E. Harvey, op. cit., p. 203.

[43] Originally published in Calcutta, subsequently in 1789 in London by J. Sewell, Cornhill, and J. Debrett, Piccadilly.   [44] Op. cit., p. xi.

wall on which its colours were hoisted.[45] This is bad enough, but Bayfield then proceeds to add, gratuitously, that the English company's
agent 'had no authority or weight in the Burmese Councils, and in this
state affairs continued until the year 1794'. The truth is that after the East
India Company's withdrawal from Burma in consequence of the massacre
of Negrais (1759), it never reopened a factory there.

Worse still, there are occasions on which Bayfield appears to be deliberately misleading. One glaring instance occurs in his treatment of
Michael Symes's second mission to Ava in 1802. He writes that on arrival
up the Irrawaddy at the Burmese capital Symes and his suite were
forced to halt at an island off Mingun on which corpses were burned and
criminals executed, and had to remain on it for forty days.[46] The true
story, as given by Symes himself in the very document from which Bayfield
took his account, was that the flotilla bearing the mission arrived at an
island close to the one on which King Bodawpaya was living while
superintending the erection of the Mingun Pagoda, and it was decided to
anchor there for the night. Early the next morning, however, the Burmese
officer in charge of the arrangements for the mission hurried over to tell
Symes that they must move away immediately because it 'was unclean',
through being a place where corpses were burned and malefactors executed; and they accordingly went to another island which he indicated.[47]
The wording of the document shows conclusively that Bayfield's story must
have been a deliberate fabrication. It has had a wide currency.[48]

The work is full of instances of Bayfield's cavalier treatment of his
source-material. In his hands it becomes a polemical pamphlet aiming at
exposing Burmese perfidy. He writes in a spirit of high moral indignation,
and takes every opportunity to display his contempt for the Burmese.
Needless to say, Michael Symes, whose sympathetic account of the Burmese in his book fired the American preacher Adoniram Judson to carry
the gospel to their country, comes in for very rough treatment at his
hands. On his book Bayfield writes:

'It is not within the limits of this paper to discuss the correctness and
fidelity of Captain Symes's picture of Ava as published by himself; but it
may not be irrelevant to observe, that his description of the Court of Ava,
and of men and manners, differs as much from what they were a year
afterwards, as related by Captain Cox,[49] and from what they now are, as
a polished European differs from an Andamanese.'[50] 'An assembly of

---

[45] Hunter, op. cit., p. 61.   [46] Op. cit., pp. xxiii, xxiv.

[47] D. G. E. Hall (ed.), Michael Symes, *Journal of his Second Embassy to the Court of Ava in 1802*
(London, 1955), pp. 142–3.

[48] It is not mentioned by Yule or Phayre. But see Harvey, op. cit., p. 286, and Hall, *Europe
and Burma*, p. 95.

[49] Captain Hiram Cox, *Journal of a Residence in the Burmhan Empire* (London, 1821). Bayfield,
however, used Cox's MS. letters, etc., in the Calcutta records.   [50] p. xii.

clowns' had been Captain Hiram Cox's description of the Court of Ava, but Bayfield's gibe is more unpleasant. He strives to present Symes as a combination of a simpleton, who hardly realized the studied insults, with which he was systematically treated by the Court of Ava, and a weakling who tamely pocketed them. And in order to heighten the effect he resorts to the expedient of falsifying the record, though at the same time giving copious references to his sources. This is the height of dishonesty, for it gives his reader a false sense of security in accepting his statements, and trades upon the fact that hardly anyone would ever be in a position to go through his archival material. Indeed students of Burmese history have found Bayfield's *Historical Review* of special value for the very reason that it has appeared to be a faithful summary of original records. Even his caustic comments have been swallowed, for the Symes 'legend', which he accepted with such evident relish, was given even greater force by Colonel Henry Yule's reference to his rose-coloured spectacles, in what is perhaps the most delightful book that has ever been written on Burma.[51]

Perhaps the most telling example of the spirit in which Bayfield wrote is his comment upon the Treaty of Yandabo, which marked the end of the Anglo-Burmese War of 1824–6. It runs: 'It is difficult to discover why our Government omitted to instruct our negotiators at Yandabo to insist upon the cession of Negrais Island, and to give that territory an important place in any treaty of peace. Such an act would have taught a great moral lesson to the Burmese and other Indo-Chinese nations, showing them that treachery and assassination could never be forgotten, or allowed to pass with impunity.'[52]

We must of course bear in mind that the Burma Bayfield knew had suffered the biggest military disaster in her history at British hands, losing Assam and Manipur, countries she had held by conquest, and her maritime provinces of Arakan and Tenasserim. The shock had driven her king insane, and he could not bear to see at his court the representative of the power which had inflicted on him so terrible a humiliation. His low-born queen and her brother, the Minthagyi, who controlled the government, were well known to dislike all westerners, and under their influence the Court of Ava had become more haughty and intransigent than ever before in its dealings with the British. Thus the conditions of his own day must have influenced Bayfield's interpretation of the past. But, when all is said, nothing can excuse the deliberate dishonesty to which he has descended in order to blacken the character of the Burmese. The extraordinary thing is that Henry Burney, who collaborated with Bayfield should have allowed the latter's version of the pre-1830 story to be published. He can only have checked over the part of the work dealing with

[51] *Mission to the Court of Ava in 1855* (London, 1858), p. 211.
[52] Op cit., p. ix.

his own tenure of the Residency. It is a pity, for mistaken views of history long accepted have amazing powers of persistence, and Bayfield's contemptuous treatment of the Burmese, supplementing Captain Hiram Cox's libellous utterances regarding Michael Symes, has wrought much harm.

20. ARTHUR PHAYRE AND HENRY YULE:
TWO SOLDIER-ADMINISTRATOR HISTORIANS

HUGH TINKER

Reader in Oriental History in the University of London

Professor Gordon Luce once remarked to the writer: 'The British are good at pioneering but poor at carrying out the detailed work that should be built up from the pioneer's discoveries.' It may be that the work of Phayre and Yule amply substantiate the first part of Luce's proposition: to what extent the second part is true is only incidentally touched upon in this paper.

Both these men came from very similar circumstances, and the scope of their work, although not identical, was broadly similar: the hum-drum but heroic activity of the British-Indian administrator in the days when he had to be a more forceful Pooh-Bah. Both men were inspired by the nature of their work to study the history and culture of the peoples among whom they moved. Both enjoyed long years of retirement, and maintained their output of writing and research up to their deaths. Here, perhaps, the similarity ends, and it becomes more interesting to observe how the two men differed in their response to a similar environment. Phayre worked largely in isolation, and from his long years as a district official in Burma he identified himself with the Burmese outlook, so that his *History of Burma* is not a history of Burma through British eyes, or a history of European contacts with Burma, but an account of the rise and fall of the monarchies of Burma, much as it is depicted in the Burmese chronicles. Yule, by contrast, lived and worked in close contact with the world of European scholarship, with English men of affairs, and with colleagues of the Government of India. His writings have a European rather than a British outlook; he presents the European impact upon Asia; and to the limited extent that he touches upon British rule in Asia, he writes with the sense of purpose and achievement which characterizes his Anglo-Indian contemporaries. Phayre was a single-minded scholar, concerned to perfect one great study of Burmese history, not much interested in fame or the agreeable pleasures of success. Yule was a man of ambition (one might apply to him a phrase used by Lord Beveridge about Sir William Hunter in his youth: 'almost a caricature of the young Scot on the make, with achieving greatness as his avowed aim and with complete confidence that he would succeed'). The list of his published works is stupendous (see Yule, *Marco Polo*, third edition (1903), complete bibliography, pp. lxxv–lxxxii).

He chased into print, and almost every experience was exploited to produce an article or book; he was remarkably perceptive in anticipating a field of interest (e.g. India's Eastern borders in the 1840s and '50s, Central Asia from the 1860s onwards). He was a popularizer, in the best sense, but (as we shall see) he too was a real pioneer. Phayre and Yule first met in 1853; they remained firm friends until Phayre's death in 1885 (probably the best short account of Phayre's life is that contained in the obituary notice composed by Yule, *Proceedings of the Royal Geographical Society* (1886), vii, 103–12). Their friendship must have been fostered, in a strange way, by the utterly disparate characters of the two men. Phayre, retiring and aloof, felt no jealousy of his more thrusting friend, but found in him a channel of communication with the London world of politics, the clubs and literature. Yule's regard for Phayre (as with many of the latter's friends) had an element of hero-worship towards this enigmatic and noble personality, a giant among men who consistently refused to play the part of a giant. Each was generous in acknowledging the work of the other in his publications, but the two only collaborated in the *Narrative of the Mission sent by the Governor-General of India to the Court of Ava in 1855* (hereinafter called *Mission to Ava*), published in London in 1858. It will be the purpose of this paper to survey the work of Phayre and Yule separately, and in a final section, appraise their respective shares in the *Mission to Ava*.

Phayre's Life

Arthur Purves Phayre was born at Shrewsbury in 1812. His family were not Anglo-Irish, as is usually stated, but were hereditary freemen of Shrewsbury. His father was a member of HEICo's civil service, in which he attained no particular distinction. Arthur had two brothers, Richard, who became a clergyman, and Robert, later General Sir Robert Phayre, G.C.B., an officer in the Bombay Army, who commanded in Baluchistan during the Second Afghan War, a great friend of Lord Roberts (he figures, anonymously, as the central figure in the incident described in CHI, vi, 499). Arthur's father secured for him one of the coveted nominations to a direct commission in HEICo's army and, soon after his sixteenth birthday, the lad embarked on the *Lady McNaughton* for India (August 1828). He did not see his native land again for twenty-nine years. He was posted to the 7th Bengal Native Infantry, stationed at Gorakhpur (U.P.), and during the following years was with a detachment at Azamgarh. Here his life was solitary and spartan; he filled out his inadequate education with copious reading, being assisted by two young Civilians. One was later to be Sir Robert Montgomery, Lieutenant-Governor of Punjab, and the other, Edward Thornton, was later Judicial Commissioner for Punjab and author of a *History of the British Empire in India* (1842–5) and other works.

Phayre received his first chance when his C.O. was asked to nominate a young officer for duty in Tenasserim with a 'Talaing Corps' which was to be raised for local defence. Phayre spent a few months in 1835 at Moulmein; the Corps was not a success, and on disbandment Phayre was returned to his regiment; but not before he had gained favourable notice from Blundell, the Commissioner, and others. He served briefly with the Assam Light Infantry; then in May 1837, while at Almorah (U.P.), Phayre was informed that he was appointed Senior Assistant to the Commissioner of Arakan. A Senior Assistant ranked as a District Officer, so it seems probable that Phayre must have undergone some training 'in the civil line' at Almorah: he was still an Ensign, but in 1838 he was promoted Lieutenant, with seniority from 1835. Phayre served as D.O. at Akyab, Kyaukpyu, and Sandoway: the only notable event of this period was a punitive expedition into the Kaladan Valley (somewhat egotistically recorded by Fytche in his *Burma Past and Present*). In 1846, Phayre was appointed Principal Assistant to the Commissioner of Tenasserim; two years later, he was briefly recalled to his regiment at Lahore, following the outbreak of the Second Sikh War, but he saw no fighting (under the curious rules applicable to army officers in civil employment before the Mutiny, Phayre remained on the active list and received promotion up to the rank of Lieutenant-General, although he never commanded any force larger than an infantry company).

In March 1849, Phayre succeeded his former chief, Bogle, as 'Commissioner in Araccan': unusually early promotion to such a senior position, but Phayre had caught the eye of the Governor-General, Dalhousie, and in October 1852 he was selected 'for the important post of organising and developing a local government' in the newly annexed province of Pegu. He was ordered by Dalhousie to correspond directly with him in 'demi-official' form, and this correspondence, edited by Professor Hall (O.U.P., 1932), provides the most connected picture of Phayre's working-life. As Agent to the Governor-General, Phayre was in diplomatic contact with the Burmese Court, and he led missions to the Court of Mindon for the purpose of establishing treaty-relations with Ava in 1855, 1862, and 1866. The three provinces of Arakan, Tenasserim, and Pegu were amalgamated into 'British Burmah' in 1862, and Phayre was appointed first Chief Commissioner (governor, but, as Mr. Harvey observes, 'the title [of governor] was as sacrosanct in the Indian as it is common in the colonial empire'). Ill-health compelled Phayre to relinquish his post in 1867. The following year, Sir John Lawrence offered him the appointment of Resident at Hyderabad, the premier political post in the Indian Empire, but Phayre declined, writing to Yule 'I should make a mess of an entirely new Court and people.'

In retirement, Phayre was restless; he travelled incessantly, in India, the

Far East, and America. He was frequently pressed to undertake missions to the Burmese Court, but he steadily refused: he never returned to Burma: perhaps he realized that his name was still so powerful, that his presence would make other people's work impossible. Unexpectedly offered the post of Governor of Mauritius in September 1874, Phayre accepted and left at once. He spent four useful years in the island: on relinquishing his post, he travelled in Africa, and then settled (if such a word can be used of such a restless man) near Dublin. He died quite suddenly in December 1885. He left no will, and as his brother Richard died immediately afterwards, his effects were disposed of hastily and his papers were scattered and many lost.

His Character

Phayre might have served as the original for the 'strong silent Englishman'. He was withdrawn and aloof, but extraordinarily courteous, and possessed of an almost unattainable concept of honour. His way of living was simple and austere: he was severely meticulous and methodical. W. H. Ridgeway wrote, 'I don't think I ever met so retiring and unpretending a public man.' His attitude towards religion was, for his day and sphere of society, heterogeneous: he attended every form of worship from the Roman Catholic to the Unitarian. His attitude to Buddhism was therefore unusually dispassionate: he afforded it the same respect as he gave to other religious views, occasioning some Burmans to think that he was himself a Buddhist. As Commissioner, and later Chief Commissioner, he was continually on tour and on the march: there was none of the Moghul pomp assumed by many British senior officials on tour, and whenever he halted, Phayre would be surrounded by the ordinary people of Burma. To the Burmese, as to the British, he was an enigma, but a friendly one; understanding their beliefs and sharing their ideas of humour and social intercourse. The high regard in which he was held by all from King Mindon downwards was, of course, vital to the exceptional knowledge of Burmese traditions, legends, and institutions which he brought to his study of the Burmese chronicles and to his own view of Burmese history.

It seems fair to suggest that Phayre's simple, methodical life and the intimate relations which he established with the Burmese (in contrast to the reserved, withdrawn face he showed to Englishmen) were all characteristics which his military training brought out. In the early nineteenth century, relations between officers and men in the Indian army were almost paternal or tribal (a relationship which was greatly modified after the Mutiny). Officers were accustomed to spend much of their time off-duty in the company of their men, who frequently went with them on leave. All this suggests the background to Phayre's easy intimacy with villagers, phongyis, and other Burmans; an intimacy which he never achieved amongst his own folk.

His Work

The whole of Phayre's literary work may be regarded as a series of preliminary studies for his final full-length *History of Burma* (1883). Yule included what he called a 'tolerably complete' bibliography of Phayre's published work in his obituary, previously cited. Almost all Phayre's work was given publication through the Journal of the Asiatic Society of Bengal: it is clear that this Society exercised a great influence in his development. It is remarkable that such a development ever occurred. Phayre left school soon after he was sixteen, having been to Shrewsbury School, whose headmaster was the then celebrated Dr. Samuel Butler, but he always insisted that he did not have much education. Charles Darwin, Phayre's contemporary at Shrewsbury, condemns the teaching in his *Autobiography*: it 'was strictly classical, nothing else being taught except a little ancient geography and history'. Thereafter, Phayre's life was passed in the backwaters of the Indian Empire, entirely cut off from any intellectual stimuli, a situation in which many of his contemporaries simply stagnated. Phayre was saved by the intense interest which he at once established in the topography, geology, and history of Burma. His first publication, *An Account of Arakan*, appeared in JASB, x, 679–711 (1841). A general survey, it included consideration of archaeological material, an inscription or so, coins and other raw material of history. Discussing the reaction of the Arakanese to British rule, Phayre quietly accepts that despite material benefits, the fierce national feeling of the people leads them to long—and to fight—for independence. There followed a study *On the History of Arakan*, JASB (1844), xiii, 23–52. This was a translation of an historical compilation by U Mi based upon the Arakan chronicles. It is a straight translation of a record which was both legend and national myth (in the Sorel-ian sense). Phayre's editorial work was confined to elucidating names of places and personages. Nevertheless, certain major events in Burma's history began to emerge, and he concluded with a chronological table of the Kings of Arakan. In establishing his chronology, he took issue with a preceding table produced by Paton: it appears that Phayre was able to a limited extent to draw upon the evidence of coins and inscriptions. In any event, this list published in 1844 is still accepted (with only minor changes later made by Phayre himself) as the standard chronology for the Arakan kings.

During the following twenty years, Phayre was fully occupied with administrative and diplomatic activities; JASB received only an occasional note upon some limited topic. Then, in 1865, publication begins of the series, *On the History of the Burmah Race*, a record from earliest times up to

Bayinnaung's day, completed in 1869. This history was (in Phayre's phrase) an 'epitome' of the *Maha Yazawin*, the Burmese royal chronicle, a copy of which was specially presented to Phayre by Mindon. Phayre's treatment is now substantially different from that adopted in his apprentice Arakan history. He begins with a respect for the *Yazawin* as an essentially reliable source, compiled by scholars working from original inscriptions, but he rejects the motivations and presuppositions which have shaped the Burmese scholars' presentation of their matter. What does Phayre wish to produce? A history of kings and dynasties, of wars external and internal: only to a very limited extent a study of government and administration, and not at all a study of society and economic life. Presumably Phayre must have gained his conception of what constitutes 'history' in his reading in the 1830s and '40s: lacking a formal academic training, and isolated from other scholars he must have felt diffident in introducing any concept of history other than the accepted 'political' history of the West which, he would feel, he was not qualified to challenge. The 'Burmah' series was followed by three papers *On the History of Pegu*, JASB, 1873–4. This was based upon a narrative written by Sayadaw Athwā in Mon, compiled from ancient Mon chronicles, translated into Burmese by U Shwe Kya. Phayre informs us that 'the chronology . . . is very confused' and 'neither the author nor the translator has attempted to correct the manifest errors'. Phayre checked his main source against an historical essay in Burmese by U Byan, a Mon, and against the Burmese *Yazawin*. His study ends with Bayinnaung, and it becomes apparent that in dealing with the sixteenth century, Phayre is not happy in handling the accounts of Europeans (who now appear in Lower Burma) in relation to the indigenous chronicles. He seems to be aware that they offer a different species of historical evidence, and one that does not fit easily into the pattern which has been forming out of the histories of Arakan, the Burmese, and the Mons. Once again, the 'Burmah' and the 'Pegu' series included chronological lists of rulers which have been adopted without revision by later scholars.[1]

In 1882 appeared the study of *Coins of Arakan, of Pegu and of Burma*, and in the following year, the *History*. This is based upon the sources used in the preliminary studies, with particular reference to the *Yazawin*. At this stage, it may be worth considering Phayre's linguistic equipment. He had, of course, a first-class knowledge of colloquial Burmese; of literary Burmese, his mastery may not have been so complete. He appears to have had no acquaintance with Mon, and almost no knowledge of Pali. Among the European languages, he may have had a smattering of French and Italian, but certainly no German. His real strength was not in formal academic

[1] Recently Mr. G. H. Luce has revised the list of rulers of Pagan, 1044–1287, using the evidence of contemporary inscriptions.

equipment, but in his wide knowledge and real respect for Burmese culture and tradition.

The broad picture of Burma's history which Phayre evolved has never been substantially modified. He is responsible for the periodization which we still accept: 'The Pagan Period', 'The Shan Period', 'The Konbaung Period', and the other divisions. The nomenclature for the kings which Phayre employed (particularly of the Konbaung line) has become standard among Western writers, although not perhaps acceptable to some Burmans. The character of 'history' in the Burmese setting is still largely as Phayre left it: a story of struggles between peoples and princes, with virtually no consideration of economic, cultural, or other aspects. Phayre was well acquainted with Burmese governmental and social institutions, and he appreciated the importance of Buddhism in the Burmese environment: yet almost nothing of this emerges in his *History* (half a page is allotted to Bodawpaya's revenue inquest). Phayre appears to have lacked the confidence to break away from the '1066, William the Conqueror' type of history. The scope of this paper does not permit a detailed analysis of the *History*, but certain points have particularly interested this writer. In his opening pages, Phayre considers the tradition of the Indian origin of the Burmese race: he concludes that 'The tradition, therefore, as to the building of cities and the first commencement of the Burmese monarchy by Indian settlers, whether Kshatriya princes or others, may be accepted as probably true' (p. 5). It is noticeable that modern Burmese scholars continue to subscribe to this view. But in one of his previous studies (JASB (1865), xxxiii, 1–30), Phayre had reviewed this problem and flatly rejected the Indian origin (apart from the influx of a few Buddhist missionaries), deciding that the races of Burma originated in Central Asia. He also rejected the Burmese tradition of the early introduction of Buddhism from India. Why did he reverse his views? Presumably because, on reflection, he decided he could not over-rule the version given in the *Yazawin*. Only on one occasion is Phayre unhappy about the chronicles; discussing the rise of Alaungpaya, he remarks, 'No Burmese history now to be found contains what can be accepted as trustworthy information concerning the descent and early life of this national hero. . . . It is from European authors alone that the plain facts can now be gathered' (pp. 149–50). To this writer, this aside seems to illuminate Phayre's whole treatment of the chronicles: what is essentially an epic has been regarded as a rational record with certain magical and non-rational accretions. And this approach has persisted in almost all subsequent Western investigators. In conclusion, Phayre's treatment of the European impact upon Burma is unusual. The Europeans are isolated from the main narrative and relegated to the final chapter which is virtually an appendix. The first Anglo-Burmese War is treated in some detail, but thereafter Phayre cuts short his

story with the deposition of Bagiydaw in 1837, an event of minor importance. Is it significant that this event coincided with Phayre's arrival in
Arakan? Phayre might have found a suitable terminal date with the
Second Burmese War and the annexation of Pegu; or, if he had wished to
illustrate the best side of Burmese history, he could have carried the narrative forward to cover the reign of good king Mindon. But any such arrange-
ment must have brought Phayre himself into the picture, and so his story
ends half a century before the time at which he was writing. Apart from
his official reports, Phayre has left nothing in print with regard to British
rule in Burma (in marked contrast to almost every other pro-consul of his
time). This provides yet another illustration of Phayre's character and of
his view of history; and perhaps of his view of the British record in Burma.

Yule's Life

Henry Yule was born at Inveresk in Midlothian in 1820 of mixed low-
land and highland descent. He was the youngest son of Major William
Yule of the Bengal Army, who had been Assistant Resident at the courts
of Lucknow and Delhi, and was reputed a good Persian and Arabic scholar.
Henry's two elder brothers also served in India; Robert in the 16th
Lancers, and George in the Bengal Civil Service, finishing his career as
Chief Commissioner of Oudh, Resident at Hyderabad, and Member of
the Viceroy's Council. Henry was 'intended' for Cambridge and the Bar:
he studied under two clerical tutors, both of whom became Cambridge
professors, and for his age he received a good education, excelling in
German and Greek. Plans for the Bar fell through; Yule spent what he
called 'a most dreary time' at University College, London, and then in
February 1837 joined the HEICo's Military College at Addiscombe. At
the end of two years, he passed out—first—and, being posted to the Bengal
Engineers, was attached to the R.E. Headquarters at Chatham for further
training. At the end of 1840 he arrived in India. It was the prudent custom
of the HEICo to place its military engineers in civil employ except when
they were actually required for sapper duties in time of war. Yule was
employed in a very diverse series of occupations. His first task (in Assam)
was to devise a means of transporting coal from Cherrapunji down to the
plains. Then, in 1842, he was set to work upon the construction of the
Ganges Canal, the first great British irrigation work in northern India.
In 1843, Yule came home to get married; his wife returned with him to
India, but after a year she underwent a serious illness and was forbidden
to live in India. The compulsory separation from his family which was now
Yule's lot must have influenced his attitude to Indian service. Canal work
alternated with war-experiences, including the First and Second Sikh
Wars, after which he took three years home furlough, returning in January
1853; he was at once ordered to make a survey of the passes over the

Arakan Yomas. He travelled many hundreds of miles on foot to complete this survey, emerging at Prome in March 1853, where he first encountered Phayre. The second half of this year was spent at Singapore, where Yule was required to improve the fortifications. Back in India, his next post was that of Deputy Consulting Engineer for Railways, at the time when the first railway schemes were being drafted. In 1854, Dalhousie proposed the creation of a new all-India Department of Public Works. The following year, Yule was appointed the first Deputy Secretary for Public Works in the Government of India, but within his first year in the new post he was called upon to accompany Phayre on his first mission to Ava, acting as Secretary and second in command of the Mission. It is clear from various expressions in his writings that Yule often looked back upon his experiences in Burma with nostalgia as to an enchanted interlude from the Indian grind. His time in South East Asia was brief: two tours in Burma, a few months in Singapore, and a holiday in Java (1860), but he appears to have developed a feeling for South East Asia as a lighter, brighter world than that of India.

Back in Calcutta, Yule's P.W.D. responsibilities greatly increased with the onset of the Mutiny: he was required to strengthen the defences of Allahabad Fort and to improvize accommodation for the thousands of British reinforcements pouring up the Ganges plains. In 1858, after officiating as head of the P.W.D., Yule was formally appointed Secretary to Government. This steady rise to the heights was disastrously checked in 1862. Both Dalhousie and Canning had shown Yule great favour, and his intimacy with the latter was particularly close. Yule could confidently look forward to advancement to a governorship or a seat upon the Viceroy's Council, achievement comparable to that of those other brilliant sappers, Sir Henry Durand and Sir Richard Strachey. But when Canning retired in 1862, Yule, who was utterly weary of India, accompanied him home and, upon assurances of Canning's influence in securing him advantageous employment in England, sent in his resignation. Then quite suddenly Canning died, and Yule was left (still in his early forties) with no hope of further advancement. With his family, Yule travelled in Germany and Italy where he settled for some years at Palermo, devoting himself to writing and research. In 1875 he was appointed a member of the Council of India in London (it is not clear how the ten-year rule was evaded, Yule having been over thirteen years away from India). He was regarded as the Council's expert upon Central Asia, and when his term of office was about to expire, this was renewed for life by special Act of Parliament. Other appointments and honours came to him (membership of Florence Nightingale's Army Sanitary Committee, and of the Board of the Indian Engineering College, Cooper's Hill; the Presidency of the Hakluyt and Royal Asiatic Societies, Vice-Presidency of the Royal Geographical Society, membership of the Institute of France). He died in December 1889, four years after Phayre.

His Character

Ambition is ever-present: first, for high rank in his service, then, when this proved vain, for scholarly pre-eminence. He was capable of sustained, concentrated hard work: indeed, his long life was filled with work. Like many Scots intellectuals he had a great respect for facts and their collection: but this accumulative attitude to knowledge was tempered by a vein of Highland imagination. He had a hasty temper, and a harsh, irritable side to his character which, according to his daughter, was ascendant after the disastrous disappointments of 1862. In politics he was a Tory, and his outlook was, on the whole, that of the conventional Anglo-Indian of his day. In Burma he would not enter a Buddhist monastery because he would be required to remove his shoes, thereby losing dignity; such a consideration had no weight with Phayre, who was prepared to conform to all proper Burmese conventions: he only took exception when *according to Burmese standards* he was asked to do something humiliating. Unlike most Anglo-Indians, however, Yule had a European outlook. To the German, Greek, and Latin of his youth he added a good knowledge of medieval French and Italian (among Asian languages, Yule claimed only 'a fair familiarity with Hindustani and some reminiscences of elementary Persian'; he much deplored his own shortcomings). He was one of the earliest British Orientalists to draw upon the new methods and new materials of nineteenth-century Continental scholarship, and he entered into correspondence with many European Orientalists. In his own work he blended the European inheritance with his own massive research.

His Work

Like Phayre, Yule first found an opening for his writings in JASB. His two earliest articles were concerned with the Khasis of the Shillong plateau: slight as these articles were, they exhibited two prominent features of Yule's future style: his power of observation and his use of graphic illustration. Both these features were undoubtedly sharpened by his sapper training and by the duties which came the way of the military engineer in British-Asia, such as his survey of the Arakan passes. There followed a steady stream of writing in journals and reviews, almost all illustrated by Yule's ready pencil. The first full-length product of Yule's retirement was *Cathay and the Way Thither* (Hakluyt Society, 1866). This is an anthology of the writings of medieval travellers of the trade routes of Asia, including the account of Ibn Batuta. Yule's editorial work was upon a Teutonic scale, erudite, and weighty, and in voluminous footnotes he reviewed many problems of linguistics, geography, archaeology, and other studies. It is noticeable that all Yule's material comes from European sources (he employed a French translation of Ibn Batuta), but the greatest part of these sources had not before been available to English readers. Yule repeated this exercise on an even more elaborate scale with his *Book of Ser Marco Polo* (1871). This represents the climax of his technique of marshalling whole libraries of facts and opinions; his words richly illustrated by splendid drawings, photographs, diagrams, and maps. Was there an element of propaganda in Yule's work, a hint that the road to China might be now taken by more powerful European travellers with more profit than by their lonely forerunners? Something of this may be read in the Preface to *Cathay and the Way Thither*, but by the time that *Marco Polo* was launched, Yule appears to have lost any ulterior motive in the fascination of his subject. It is interesting to compare the way Yule handles his travellers with the method of Pelliot in his *Deux Itineraires de Chine en Inde à la fin du VIIIe Siècle*.

Pre-eminent among the later works is *Hobson-Jobson*, first published in 1886. This work, which advertises itself as a 'Glossary of Colloquial Anglo-Indian Words and Phrases' is in fact much more: it is invaluable source-material for the social and economic history of South and East Asia, a guide to the commerce in commodities, customs, and ideas which has been carried across the Indian Ocean and the West Pacific from the sixteenth to the nineteenth century. About threequarters of the material is Indian or Anglo-Indian, but in addition there is much from Malaya and Java, and a little from China, Burma, Persia and Arabia. Like all Yule's later works, it is the outcome of the most voracious and rare reading, all systematically noted and classified; it is also based upon the researches of a wide circle of associates, so that Yule's contribution is that of editor as well as author. Yule has accepted the name of another man (A. C. Burnell) on the title-page with his own, but there is something slightly ignoble in the manner in which he plays down his co-author's share in the work, while drawing attention to his own generosity in acknowledging him as co-author. Right to the end, Yule thirsted for success, and he did not wish to share his glory with others.

However, Yule's work is self-sufficient. He played a large part in the development of Central Asian studies, and in *Hobson-Jobson* he pioneered a linguistic approach to the history and culture of South and East Asia. It is noticeable that apart from a Second Edition of *Hobson-Jobson* in 1903 after Yule's death, there has been no systematic development of comparative linguistic exploration of the history and culture of this area in succeeding years.

Mission to Ava

The present writer's reference to this work as a 'collaboration' between Yule and Phayre does not, of course, have any bibliographical warrant:

Yule's name stands alone upon the title-page. The observant reader of the *Mission to Ava* will, however, notice the number of footnotes supplied by Phayre, and the passages describing interviews at Court which are stated in the text to have been taken from Phayre: but he supplied a good deal more. The present writer has been able to transcribe the private diary kept by Phayre during the stay of the Mission at Amarapura. It is clear that Yule used this diary as the main source for his entire account of the activities of the Mission as such. Images and expressions are frequently reproduced, employing the actual words of the diary. Elsewhere in the book, where the subject-matter is not the actual Mission, Yule appears to have worked alone or with other assistance: for instance, the historical chapters are exclusively about European relations with Burma, an emphasis directly contrary to Phayre's approach. But much of the information about manners and society throughout is derived from Phayre; so that the book is almost a partnership towards which Phayre contributed his unrivalled knowledge of Burma, while Yule developed for the first time the technique employed later in *Cathay* and *Marco Polo* of accumulating a mass of inter-related information to create a total picture of the subject; transforming this accumulation into a work of art by his talent for presentation and in particular his flair for illustration.

Out of this fruitful partnership emerged a work which is probably the finest single British contribution to Burmese studies. Despite the one hundred years which have since passed, its picture of Burma and Burmese society has an enduring quality. Probably one of the most valuable features of the book is its account of the ancient ruined city of Pagan. With nine full plates and a number of smaller illustrations, the reader is provided with a series of pictures, elevations, plans, and studies of architectural detail which surpass every other work on the subject. In his still unpublished 'Old Burma', Professor Luce cites the *Mission to Ava* as a leading work of reference. And yet, the Mission halted a mere three and a half days while ascending the Irrawaddy, and less than two days while descending, at Pagan. During this while, Yule was incapacitated by an attack of fever one day, while yet another day was devoted to his Secretarial duties. Out of a visit of three and a half days, Yule has created this unsurpassed picture of Pagan. His effort may be partly ascribed to early Victorian energy, but partly also to sapper training which enabled him to make detailed, true to scale studies with such facility and accuracy.

A by-product of the everyday work of a military engineer and a military administrator, *Mission to Ava* challenges comparison with the best literary work of the early nineteenth century British soldier-administrators in Asia.

21. IDEAS OF HISTORY IN THE JOURNAL OF THE MALAYAN (STRAITS) BRANCH OF THE ROYAL ASIATIC SOCIETY, 1878–1941

C. D. COWAN

Lecturer in the History of South East Asia, School of Oriental and African Studies

The Straits Branch of the Royal Asiatic Society was founded in Singapore in 1878, and published the first number of its Journal in the same year. Except for the interruption caused by the Japanese occupation of Singapore the Journal has appeared regularly since. In 1923 it was renamed the *Journal of the Malayan Branch of the Royal Asiatic Society*.

Until the end of the nineteenth century the Journal contained little of note from the historical point of view. The Society had been founded in the first place as a result of the interest in the Malay States aroused in the Straits Settlements by British political intervention there in the years after 1873. Most of the contributors were officials. They were the first generation of Englishmen working in the Malay States or in North Borneo, and the papers they submitted represented their early discoveries in what was then a completely unexplored field. Naturally as Residents and Assistant Residents surveying and opening up large areas their day-to-day activities brought them into contact with the geology, flora, and fauna of the Malay lands, and the day-to-day life of their peoples. It was natural therefore that the major part of these early Journals should have been devoted to such topics.

Those few who found the time and inclination to be interested in the history of the areas in which they worked turned to the only bodies of history writing available—Malay chronicles and genealogies on the one hand, and on the other earlier European accounts of travels and European relations with the Malay States. Most of the papers on historical themes in the early numbers of the Journal are translations from chronicles, or from Portuguese and Dutch accounts. The first contributor was Hugh Low, then Resident of Perak but previously employed in Labuan, who published five papers on the dynastic history of Brunei based on local chronicles and inscriptions in the Journal for 1880. The most regular contributor in these years, however, was W. E. Maxwell, who from 1882 published a series of translations from Malay and Dutch sources. The most important of these were 'The History of Perak from Native Sources' (1882 and 1884), 'The Dutch in Perak' (1882), and 'Valentijn's Description of Malacca' (1884 and 1885). Of these technically the most interesting is 'The Dutch in Perak', because it makes use of both Dutch and Malay materials in the same paper, in addition to drawing on the English accounts of Dampier and Hamilton.[1] Maxwell's translations of Valentijn stimulated E. Koek to produce in 1886 'The Portuguese History of Malacca', composed mainly of translated excerpts from y Souza's *Asia Portugueza*, and in 1890 Maxwell himself for the first time not only brought Malay and Dutch materials together, but used one source to elucidate the other. This was in 'The Poem of Raja Haji and the Siege of Malacca of 1784'. This was a major work of translation, but beyond explaining the circumstances of the events referred to in the text of the poem it does little to relate the incidents described to the history of the period.

Though a number of these papers were published in the Journal during the 1880's the topics with which they dealt were only incidentally related to each other, so that they do not collectively add up to a coherent body of historical writing. All have the same self-contained but isolated character. The contributors to the Journal were gradually acquiring the linguistic equipment to grapple with the materials which came to their attention. But they lacked a framework of history which would have enabled them to relate to each other the scraps of material they thus acquired. This was true not only of the early history of the Archipelago and of the Malays, but also of the history of European activities in the area. That there was a conscious awareness of this is shown by the attempt made by a young official, A. M. Skinner, to fill part of the gap with 'An Outline History of the British Connection with Malaya' (1882). Apart from some notes on the nineteenth-century development of the three Straits Settlements and the Malay States brought under British control in 1874, this paper is almost wholly confined to the dates of foundation of the seventeenth- and eighteenth-century Dutch and English factories in the Archipelago, and to a series of misleading and ill-founded generalizations on the nature of the British connection with the area. Nevertheless, it merits closer attention because of the light it throws on contemporary knowledge of the subject.

Skinner divides British activities in Malaya and the Archipelago into three periods:

First, the period 1602–84, styled the period of individual trading.
Second, the period 1684–1762, that of trading connected with the East India Company.
Third, the period after 1762, that of direct political and military intervention.

This last period he again divides into four, i.e.,

(i) from 1762, the date of the Manila expedition, to 1805, when Penang became a separate Presidency of India.

[1] William Dampier, *A New Voyage Round the World*, various editions (London, 1697–1729). Alexander Hamilton, *A New Account of the East Indies* (Edinburgh, 1727).

(ii) from 1805 to 1827, when the three Straits Settlements were formed into one administrative unit.

(iii) from 1827 to 1867, when the Straits Settlements were transferred from the control of the Government of India to that of the Colonial Office.

(iv) after 1867.

We should now be inclined to reverse the descriptions of the first and second periods. We can react only with incredulity to the author's description of British trading activities in the Archipelago before 1684.

> This period consists exclusively of individual enterprises of a non-political character. These enterprises were almost wholly concerned with the pepper trade in Bantam and the spice trade in Banda, Amboyna, Ternate and Tidore. . . .
>
> The English East India Company, though it did not promote them and before long began to oppose them, took advantage of these enterprises in some cases. For instance, after Lancaster's visit to Bantam in 1602, the Company established a factory there.

Our present knowledge of the facts makes it quite clear that the first half of the seventeenth century was precisely the period when the East India Company planned and launched their campaign to establish themselves in the Archipelago; Lancaster was a servant of the Company. It was the period after the foundation of Benkulen in 1684 when it was left to the private trader to push British enterprises in the Archipelago.

On the basis of Skinner's paper we can make two points about the contributors to the Straits Branch Journal and their background at this period. One is the prominence given to administrative developments in the nineteenth century, a continuing characteristic in writing on the history of the Straits Settlements. Second, that Skinner could have committed himself to such opinions on the earlier British connection with the Archipelago without challenge argues a scarcity of works of reference in Singapore at the time, coupled with a lack of interest in the theme amongst his fellow contributors. With all its faults and limitations his paper would have made a good starting point for criticism and discussion, and the use of such works as Horace St. John's *Indian Archipelago* (published 1853) or even Crawfurd's *History of the Indian Archipelago* (published 1820) would have exposed his errors and shed fresh light on the subject. As it was his paper was not followed up, and perhaps happily interest in Malayan history amongst the officials and traders there developed along different lines.

Most of the articles in the earlier numbers of the Journal came naturally from the efforts of officials to make themselves at home in their new Malayan environment. Their study of Malay led to the discovery of local chronicles, which when translated yielded vivid though disjointed pictures of early Malay history and society in the states where these officials were serving. Recourse to what material was available in the Straits Settlements provided equally disjointed and fragmentary pictures of life in Malacca and surrounding areas from the point of view of Europeans, and yielded some comparative material for the points where Malay stories described contacts with Europeans. But it did not provide a European framework into which the Malay material could be fitted, so that no 'colonial' history of Malaya grew up at this stage. Instead the classical form of historical contribution to the Journal became the state (or later settlement) history. The treatment was local, and tended to follow the same lines as the chronicles and to be Malay in type, although the writers were Englishmen. The chronicles were mainly concerned with the history of one state or dynasty, and the officials who studied them, being stationed in and concerned with one state at the time they wrote, tended to accept this fact in framing their interests. Most important, this tendency was reinforced by practical considerations. Officials attempting to govern by advice and to act as far as possible according to Malay custom, like the early Residents, needed to know what the precedents were. In matters of disputed successions, for instance, they needed to check for themselves the genealogical and political facts supplied to them by interested parties. This, and the emphasis on administrative factors which we have already noticed in Skinner's paper on the British connection with Malaya, produced a distinct form of history writing. It was basically practical history, undertaken to serve the needs of the present and the demands of European officials for facts. It was a narrow form of history, because it confined itself to individual states, and addressed itself largely to tracing the antecedents of political and administrative questions of contemporary importance. But it stimulated and gave scope for the study of Malay language, literature, history, and culture generally. Its earliest example to be published in the Journal, Martin Lister's 'Origin and Constitution of Negri Sembilan' (1887) was confessedly adapted from an official report. So were W. E. Maxwell's 'The Ruling Family of Selangor' (1890), and R. N. Bland's 'Aturan Sungei Ujong' (Regulations or traditional organization of Sungai Ujong) (1895).

Though for fifteen years after the publication of Bland's paper no historical articles were published in the Journal, this line of what might be called Malay Studies, spurred on at first by the needs of administrative inquiry, eventually bore rich fruit in the field of history. It was the background to the early years in Malaya of a small group of officials who in those fallow years after 1890 created a tradition of systematized Malay scholarship in the Malayan Civil Service. Two names stand out, those of R. J. Wilkinson and R. O. (now Sir Richard) Winstedt. From 1906 onwards these two took the lead in the production of a series of *Papers on*

Malay Subjects (first series, 1907–1911; second series, 1912–21), of which Wilkinson was General Editor. These papers were intended by the Government Committee for Malay Studies, which sponsored them, to serve as text-books for civil service cadets, and as works of reference. Apart from papers devoted to Malay life and customs, law, literature and industries, they included semi-historical accounts of some of the Negri Sembilan states in the now established tradition of state historiography, and some notes on Malay history prior to the British ascendancy.

The *Papers on Malay Subjects*, though they were not published in the Journal of the Straits Branch, make up a generation in Malayan history writing, and must be mentioned here. After the long gap after 1895 the first significant contribution to appear in the Journal itself was Parr and Mackray's 'Rembau . . . its History, Constitution and Customs' (1910). This seems to have been a production which in some way escaped the net of Wilkinson's series, though it was prompted by the same factors. Its authors confessedly wrote under orders 'to prepare a summary of the Rembau customs' and later to add 'historical and constitutional sketches of the State'. Winstedt's 'History of the Peninsula in Folk Tales' (1911), the first hint that this writer was to turn his developing mastery of Malay studies to the service of history, appears to have sprung directly from his pamphlet in Wilkinson's series (*The Literature of Malay Folk Lore*, by R. O. Winstedt, 1907). Wilkinson's own papers in the Journal, the 'Malacca Sultanate' and 'The Capture of Malacca' (1912) are fragments supplementing the historical papers which he wrote for the government series. There is little else of historical note in the Journals of this period except for W. G. Maxwell's translation of 'Barreto de Resende's Account of Malacca' (1911) and a collection of documents extracted by A. C. Baker from the Singapore and Malacca records, and entitled 'Anglo-Dutch Relations in the East at the beginning of the 19th Century' (1913). After the appearance of Baker's paper there is another gap of some ten years before the next major historical contribution to the Journal. This is presumably in one way or another the result of the First World War and its aftermath.

The first major contribution to appear in the Journal after the war was a monograph, L. A. Mills's 'British Malaya, 1824–1867' (1925). The first work on the subject by a professional historian, it was originally written as a doctoral thesis. It is in fact a history of the Straits Settlements in the period of the East India Company, with introductory chapters on the English and Dutch in the East Indies in the seventeenth and eighteenth centuries. There is also a chapter on the early nineteenth-century history of Sarawak and North Borneo. The introductory chapters are based on secondary accounts, and on the printed papers of the East India Company, but the main body of the book is a very closely documented study from the manuscript records of the Straits Settlements in the India Office collection.

Mills's work is not, as its title suggests, a general history of Malaya in this period. Events in the peninsular states are dealt with only in so far as they involved relations with the Straits Settlements, or affected British relations with Holland or Siam, and the author makes no use of Malay sources. His themes are those of colonial history—the development of the British position on the China trade route, Anglo-Dutch rivalry in the Archipelago, the administrative problems of the Straits Settlements themselves. But in the event the appearance of Mills's monograph in the Journal seems to have been as important for history writing on the Malay States as it was for the history of the Straits Settlements. This was partly because it provided a model of a large-scale scholarly monograph, partly because it drew attention to sources which for the most part were equally available to people working in Malaya (for the India Office records on which Mills worked were to a great extent duplicates of materials preserved in the Straits Settlements records in Singapore). These materials had not up till then been exploited; Wilkinson's 'History of the Peninsular Malays' (published separately in various editions, 1921–3), which may be regarded as a summary of the results achieved up to that time by the officials whose work in the context of the *Papers on Malay Subjects* we have already discussed, owes very little to them.

Whatever the reasons, the 1930's saw the appearance in the Journal of a mass of history writing on Malaya which, for its range and volume, coming from so few hands in so short a period, must be unique in the Asian field. It falls broadly into two categories; on the one hand full-scale state histories, the logical outcome of the tradition of Malay scholarship which we have described, and mainly the work of officials; on the other—a new development—a series of papers from non-officials, reflecting a growth of interest in the ancient history and pre-history of the area.

The first of the full-scale state histories, Winstedt's 'History of Johore' appeared in 1932. Then came the 'History of Perak', by Winstedt and Wilkinson, the 'History of Kelantan, Part I', by Anker Rentse, the 'History of Selangor' and the 'History, Polity and Beliefs of the Nine States' (Negri Sembilan), both by Winstedt. All these were published in 1934. Two years later, in 1936, appeared W. Linehan's 'History of Pahang', and Winstedt's 'Notes on the History of Kedah'. And in between, in 1935, Winstedt published in the Journal the first and so far the only attempt at a general synthesis and summary, the 'History of Malaya'. Almost all these were published as monograph numbers of the Journal. Their virtues and limitations arose from their background, which we have already examined. They are irreplaceable mines of information on Malay history, custom, and genealogy, and though their authors have drawn freely on the colonial records of the Straits Settlements for material they are in no sense 'colonial history'. But though their interest in Malay history for its own sake prevents it from being presented as a mere prelude to the period of British administration, it also confines the text to the narrow themes of the Malay chronicles and the British official reports. Thus Winstedt, in his 'History of Selangor', was led into telling the story of the Selangor civil war without mentioning Yap Ah Loy and his Chinese tin miners.

The work on the ancient history of the area was mainly produced by R. St. J. (now Dato' Sir Roland) Braddell, who published five long papers in various issues of the Journal between 1935 and 1941, entitled 'An Introduction to the Study of Ancient Times in the Malay Peninsula and the Straits of Malacca' (JRASMB, 1935, 1936, 1937, 1939, 1941). A lawyer and a member of an old-established Straits family, Braddell set out to awaken interest in the study of the early history of the area because of his dissatisfaction with the handling of the pre-Muslim period by Winstedt and the Malay school. Instead of starting from the traditions of the Malay chronicles he began with the accounts of the classical geographers like Ptolemy, and with the Indian and Chinese materials. His papers are an important part of history writing in the Journal in this period, not only for their intrinsic worth, but because of the other contributions which they stimulated. His attempts to identify place-names from the navigational data of the early materials was supported by studies of early charts by J. V. Mills, whose most important paper, 'Malaya in the Wu-Pei-Chih Charts' appeared in the Journal for 1937. On the archaeological side a number of papers were directly related to his studies, the most considerable, Quaritch Wales's 'Archeological Researches on Ancient Indian Colonization in the Malay Peninsula', a monograph number of the Journal which appeared in 1940. Braddell's papers also provoked comments from Winstedt, Wilkinson, Linehan, and many others, some of them published as addenda to various parts of his study, some, like Winstedt's 'Mr. R. Braddell's Ancient Times' (1937), as separate papers.

L. A. MILLS

Professor of Political Science, University of Minnesota

The number of American writers on South East Asia has been limited, and few of them dealt with events prior to the twentieth century. This situation was even more marked before 1941, for since that date interest in the area has become decidedly more widespread. The explanation is that until the Japanese conquests the United States was hardly aware of its existence. Attention was concentrated upon China and Japan, and Far Eastern studies were well established in the universities. India was regarded with more sympathy than knowledge, and the situation there was oversimplified into a struggle between Gandhi and British imperialism. Only a handful concerned themselves with South East Asia, and this indifference was almost as marked towards the Philippines as the rest of the area. Both before and since World War II the majority of the writers have been intellectuals, usually liberals, and a large number have been university professors. The principal exception was that a few American officials in the Philippines wrote accounts of the American period of rule there.

Of the small number of historical works two deserve mention, Miss Emily Hahn's *Raffles of Singapore* and Professor John Cady's *The Roots of French Imperialism in Eastern Asia*. Miss Hahn studied her sources carefully, and paid more attention to Dutch material than earlier English writers had done. She obviously admired her subject but neither over praised him or unduly depreciated him. Apart from her impartiality and her painstaking thoroughness her strongest point was her ability to make Raffles live. Too often the victim of a biography is embedded so deeply in excerpts from state papers that he appears more dead than when he was newly placed in his coffin. With Miss Hahn Raffles emerged as a living figure, a man who made mistakes and achieved successes—altogether a human and understandable mixture. The book would have gained, however, if the authoress had given less detail and curtailed the lively commentary of praise and blame which played the role of a Greek chorus to the principal actors of the story.

Professor Cady gave a very detailed and heavily documented account of the motives and actions of French imperialism in China and Indochina from 1840 to 1861. The quarter century 1861–85 was condensed into a single chapter, since the author was unable to consult the archives of the French Ministry of Marine and Colonies, which were especially needed for this period. Professor Cady studied carefully the available French, British, and American source-material, as well as the small number of Chinese documents that had been translated. He was accurate and impartial, and he took great pains to avoid all bias in setting forth conflicting policies and interests. In contrast with Miss Hahn he refrained from any expression of personal opinion, and rigidly restricted himself to a statement of the facts.

The majority of American authors described the contemporary situation in one or another country of South East Asia, or occasionally in the area as a whole. Some concentrated upon political and others upon economic developments, and very often gave a combination of the two. Their works were frequently prefaced by a somewhat sketchy historical account. Roughly during the past decade anthropologists, geographers, and sociologists also entered the field; but their writings lie outside the scope of this paper. Naturally enough more books have been written about the Philippines than any other country in the area.

American authors share the national prejudice against imperialism, and this attitude is about as marked among those who hold research degrees as those who do not. This is an interesting commentary on the effectiveness of graduate studies in inculcating impartial scholarship. Sometimes this bias shows itself in an editing of the facts, but more often it is an unconscious emotional prejudice which reveals itself in an occasional turn of phrase or an impalpable but all pervasive attitude of mind. An example was Dr. Virginia Thompson's (later Mrs. Virginia Thompson Adloff) *French Indochina* which was published in 1937. The authoress carried on investigations in the dependency and diligently studied all the material available in French or English. As a compendium of information on every phase of Indochinese affairs her book had real value as a work of reference. Her appraisal of French policy and administration was one of almost unrelieved blundering and occasional misdeeds. The indictment was so sweeping that the reader came to feel that it was unbelievable that the French never did the right thing even by accident. The idea grew that sometime, somewhere, there must be something which could be said in defence of French officialdom. Dr. Thompson showed the same industry in research and the same power of interpreting it in the light of preconceived prejudices in her *Post Mortem on Malaya*, published in 1943. She assumed that a dependency was a synonym for political domination and economic exploitation. Every instance of blundering, treasury parsimony or deference to the Anglo-Chinese tin and rubber industries was emphasized. Whenever the government did a good deed it was either ignored or it was stated that the motive was the reverse of praiseworthy. The result was a one-sided and distorted picture of pre-war Malaya. The same impression was produced by Miss Ellen Hammer's *Struggle for Indochina*. Her history was very detailed, particularly for the period since 1941. She quoted extensively from everything that was available in Western languages, though not the vernaculars. One can agree that the government made very serious mistakes, but it seems unnecessary to exaggerate this by omitting an account of its accomplishments, e.g., the extension of drainage and irrigation works.

Professor George McT. Kahin wrote his *Nationalism and Revolution in Indonesia* in 1949, basing it partly upon printed material but largely on the information he collected from personal interviews while in Indonesia in 1948–9. He showed great industry in the collection of facts, and his book was a mine of detailed information on Indonesian politics. Frequent references were made to the source from which the information was obtained. Professor Kahin was markedly prejudiced against the Dutch and sometimes this influenced his presentation. In the account of the relations between Holland and the Indonesian Republic between 1945 and 1950 all the charges of the Republic against the Dutch were given at length, while those of the latter against the Indonesians were omitted or passed over lightly. For example, Professor Kahin minimized the terrorist tactics of the badly controlled Javanese guerilla soldiery against the Dutch and pro-Dutch Indonesians. When there was conflict between the Dutch and Indonesian accounts of an incident, the latter was accepted as true without any careful examination of the evidence. On occasion a very complicated situation was over-simplified and presented in such a fashion that the Indonesian version was sustained. One example was the repeated assertion that the Indonesians of the Outer Islands had no local patriotism and fear of Javanese control, and that the federation set up by van Mook was a purely artificial creation forcibly imposed to perpetuate Dutch control. Sukarno's overthrow of the federal system does not seem to have been as democratic an exhibition of the will of the majority as the author contended. In East Sumatra, for example, high handed methods were apparently used, and the action taken appears to have been that of a small minority of politically conscious nationalists—many of them from other parts of the island—and not a spontaneous exhibition of the popular will, which was not consulted. Other examples could be cited, and the general impression left by this book was that while it shed much light on Indonesian politics it must be checked against other writers on any question involving the Dutch. In some respects Charles Wolf's *Indonesian Story*, published in 1948, was more impartial than Professor Kahin's book. He was American Vice-Consul at Batavia in 1946–7, and knew much less than Kahin about the pre-war government. This sometimes resulted in surprising statements, e.g. the assertion that prior to 1941 Holland had not granted any degree of self-government. Wolf was strongly prepossessed in favour of the Indonesian Republic but he tried to be fair to both sides.

He was frank about the 'unbridled terror' practised by Javanese guerillas in 1945, and he detailed the breaches of the Linggadjati Agreement by the Indonesians as well as the Dutch.

American hostility towards imperialism had its origin in the American revolution, and at first was directed primarily against British colonial rule. The ghost of King George III still agitates the subconscious minds of many American authors, and its influence is reinforced by a failure fully to understand the intricacies of many problems of tropical government. A frequent criticism, for example, has been that the social services were not as good as those of Western industrialized nations. Thus Professor Emerson in his *Malaysia, A Study in Direct and Indirect Rule*, blamed the pre-1939 governments of Malaya and the East Indies because the social services were far inferior to those of Britain and Holland. Practically never, however, did the critic examine the problem of finance, and the impossibility of obtaining from a predominantly agricultural economy the large sums needed to pay for adequate health, education, and other services. Nor was allowance made for the refusal prior to World War II of every colonial power (including the United States in the Philippines) to subsidize tropical social services from its own resources. Hostility towards the British Empire spread to those of other European nations.

The anti-imperialist attitude was strengthened by the failure to realize that during the nineteenth century the United States had its own periods of expansion in North America as well as in the Philippines. Canadians and Mexicans take a less charitable view of the growth of the continental United States. Canada's opinion is that whenever there was a boundary dispute she paid up like a gentleman. The explanation of the Americans' attitude is that the contemporary phrase for their advance to the Pacific was 'manifest destiny'. The term 'imperialism' was coined in the later nineteenth century to characterize European expansion in Africa and Asia. Americans failed to realize that it described the same phenomenon as their own manifest destiny. The exception should be noted that the conquest of the Philippines was acknowledged subsequently to be imperialism. It was felt, however, that this was counterbalanced by the policy of preparing the islands for ultimate independence, whereas the European empires all intended to maintain control over their colonies. Especially before the war there was sometimes the belief that motives and accomplishments were superior to those of other colonial powers. W. C. Forbes, *The Philippine Islands*, wrote a fair-minded and on the whole accurate account of American rule from the conquest of 1898 to 1925. But when he had occasion to draw comparisons he claimed for the United States a more altrustic intention. He supported this by the curious statement that by contrast Britain and Holland paid little attention to public health and opposed mass education in their colonies. It is only fair to add that authors of other nationalities have shown an equal ignorance of conditions in the Philippines.

Another factor which influenced many American intellectuals was the Marxist argument that political control was established over subject peoples in order to carry out a policy of capitalist exploitation. Bruno Lasker, for example, wrote a very detailed study in *Human Bondage in Southeast Asia* in which he supported his statements by frequent citations from government reports and the works of other authors. He tried to be truthful and impartial and showed no trace of national bias, e.g. his frank avowal of the failure of the American government to eradicate debt slavery and *caciquism* in the Philippines. Occasionally, however, the pre-conceived bias intruded itself. An accurate and on the whole favourable description of the Malayan government's policy for the protection of labour was followed by the statement that the fundamental cause of Communism in Malaya was that 'a long history of oppression has . . . kept alive the embers of a discontent, ranging from a mild pining for the recognition of man's worth to sullen defiance'. It was 'a social movement . . . made up of many rivulets of human desire . . . the uprising of Malay and Proto-Malay population groups, long held in subjection by invading usurpers of their heritage, former plantation labourers and their offspring with vivid memories of insufferable exploitation and indignities, wage earners forcibly prevented . . . from organising effectively'.

Professor Rupert Emerson's writings, e.g. *Malaysia, A Study in Direct and Indirect Rule*, were the product of painstaking documentary research and investigation in South East Asia. They were accurate and detailed, and the author tried to be scrupulously just to the colonial governments. On the whole they were reliable and impartial; but every now and again an emotional hostility to imperialism coloured his presentation. Thus he described the Crown Colony government in the pre-war Straits Settlements, and came to the conclusion that practically no one was seriously dissatisfied or wanted democratic reforms. This was followed by the somewhat contradictory statement that the government was controlled by those who had won wealth and power in order to exploit under-privileged Asians, and that it was doubtful if Britain would ever introduce democracy. He admitted that neither the British government in Malaya nor the Dutch in the East Indies regarded itself merely as the agent of national capital, and that individual officials championed the interests of the local inhabitants. But since it was an article of faith that the prime purpose of every colonial government was to assist exploitation by national business interests, any reform was attributed purely to expediency or enlightened selfishness. Thus the Malayan Code for the protection of Chinese and Indian labourers was due to the realization that they must not be 'ruthlessly exterminated . . . nor driven to revolt', and that 'the contented cow produces more and better milk'. Education was necessary because modern industry required skilled workers and clerks, and medical and health services were needed since disease did not operate on the principle of racial discrimination. The purpose of roads and railways was not to open a larger market to the Asian smallholder, but to enable the output of European mines and plantations to reach the seaports. No one would argue that the social services were established from pure altriusm. Their history in Great Britain and other self-governing countries showed that the causes were usually a nice combination of self-interest and benevolence. But to deny all humanitarian motive in the tropics was simply not in accordance with the facts.

The Marxist interpretation of imperialism was also responsible for the belief of many American authors that the colonial governments prevented the industrialization of their colonies. It was true that France at least discouraged this; but the attitude of the other colonial powers was one of neutrality. It could scarcely be otherwise since before the war all of them represented capitalist societies. None of them could require their nationals to establish factories in their colonies; and with a few exceptions private corporations did not consider that the profits would justify the expense. It was believed that greater gain could be made from mines and plantations that produced raw materials for export, or from selling manufactures to the colonies. The record of American investment in the Philippines was the same, and it was remarkable that American intellectuals blamed the European colonial powers for not following a policy which was not practised in their own dependency. An additional reason in the British and Dutch empires was the system of free trade. The development of manufacturing in the colonies would have required protective tariffs, and it was not politically possible to impose them until markets shrank during the Great Depression and Japanese competition began to make heavy inroads into the colonial markets. Thereafter industry, especially textiles, made significant advances in Java, under the protection of a quota system. Professor Warren Thompson's *Population and Peace in the Pacific* illustrated this particular prejudice. His work was authoritative, judicious, and well argued when he was writing about his own subject of demography. But when he dealt with less familiar topics he assumed as a truism that all the colonial powers discouraged industrialization (except in the Philippines) in order to retain the colonial market, and that health and education services were set up because they were necessary for more profitable exploitation. An exception to the usual attitude was found in J. R. Andrus' *Burmese Economic Life*. Unlike most of the other authors he was a professor of economics, and his opinion was that Western firms followed the policy which promised the most profits. Some authors carried the argument a stage further and argued that the colonial governments ought to have assisted the local population to establish factories which would have supplanted those owned by Europeans, e.g. Emerson's *Malaysia*. This was decidedly not practised by the American administration in the Philippines. This point of view seemed to resolve itself into a demand that colonial governments should conform to an ideal which was not followed anywhere in the Western world.

American—and a good many British—authors were horrified by the low standard of living in the tropics compared with that of the United States or Western Europe. They paid no attention to the prevalence of the same situation in Latin America, which had been independent for over a century. Instead they over-simplified the case by ascribing it solely to colonial exploitation. While European imperialism was not blameless, other factors were involved of which no notice was taken. Erich Jacoby's *Agrarian Unrest in Southeast Asia* was a typical expression of this point of view. No cognizance was taken of e.g. the preference of most South East Asians for subsistence farming, their lack of thrift, and what may vaguely be called a money sense, the large amount of unnecessary borrowing from moneylenders, the effect of overpopulation in e.g. Java, the desire of the educated to become government officials rather than executives in business firms, and the curious circumstance that penniless Chinese and sometimes Indian immigrants rose to affluence while the people of the country did not. The similarity of conditions in Thailand was explained by saying that it was in semi-colonial status and too weak to resist exploitation by the European powers. A practice frequently censured was the drain of profits from Western enterprises to the investing countries. None of the authors except Andrus in his *Burmese Economic Life* pointed out that by the same criteria Canada and South America are in semi-colonial status towards the United States, and that the latter was in the same position towards Europe in general and Great Britain in particular during the nineteenth century. One of the principal problems of Canada at the present time is that about 25 per cent. of its industries are controlled from the United States, and that the drain of their profits into America is a principal problem of Canadian finance. A country in an early stage of development does not have the native capital to hasten the process and thus achieve the attainment of a higher standard of living through its own efforts. Either it must postpone the attainment of these aims or it must borrow the capital from abroad. Colonial or dependent status is not peculiar to imperialism, but is a mark of any underdeveloped country whether it is politically independent or not. The principal difference between a colony and an independent state is that the former has no choice whether it will accept or reject outside capital.

Most American authors believed instinctively that every people wanted independence, and that this was the same as democracy. It seemed never to be considered that a subject people might want self-government, and yet think that this might be based upon an élite of its own race and not the whole population. No attention was paid to the significant fact that the revolt of the Latin American colonies from Spain led to dictatorships and not democracy. One root of this belief went back to the American Revolution, and another cause was the lack of the European experience in governing many peoples in different stages of development. Prior to World War II particularly the American lack of contact with other races —apart from the Filipinos in whom most of them took no interest—deprived them of this opportunity for education. Theodore Roosevelt, Governor General of the Philippines a quarter of a century ago, pointed out in his *Colonial Policies of the United States* that most Americans were confident that all people were much the same. 'The people of Vermont, let us say, were convinced that if you once established on the island of Jolo among the Moros a democratic form of government with the requisite laws, provisions, etc., that those Moros would make it work and that Jolo would, *ipso facto*, become an operating republic.'

This attitude accounted in part for the critical attitude of Americans towards European imperialism. Believing it to be morally wrong for one race to govern another, colonial rule was condemned *ab initio* as a fundamental denial of freedom. Professor Emerson's account of the pre-war governments of Malaya and the Dutch East Indies in his *Malaysia* was strongly coloured by this point of view, though he was more realistic than most in his appreciation of the difficulty of rapid progress towards democracy. In his recent work, *Representative Government in Southeast Asia*, he somewhat modified his earlier optimism. His instinctive hostility towards imperialism still influenced his writing, but he was no longer so sure that the abolition of colonialism and the drafting of a democratic constitution was a guarantee of political democracy and economic prosperity. He felt that democracy was an alien importation that was contrary to the peasants' traditional idea of government from above, and his earlier optimism was shaken by the course of developments in Thailand and the Philippines. Professor Emerson's dispassionate appraisal of the Filipino oligarchy in this book was a reversal of the pre-war attitude, when most American authors took it for granted that the experiment in the Philippines was a triumphant success. Among recent writers who have given a realistic appraisal of the situation in the Philippines are Professors C. A. Buss and R. H. Fifield and W. H. Elsbree.

The American belief that everybody wanted democracy found typical expression when Japan conquered Malaya and the Dutch East Indies. Dr. Virginia Thompson's *Post Mortem on Malaya* was a good example of this school of thought. There was hardly a mention of the weakness of the British armed forces in Malaya, or of the inability of Great Britain to spare enough men and equipment owing to the urgent need of them in other theatres of war. Instead the authoress insisted that they were defeated because they had not 'given the resident peoples enough of a stake in the country to make it worth their while to defend British rule'. Dr. Thompson's complete confidence in the military efficacy of the vote was not shaken by the fall of the French republic, or the resistance of the Russians in spite of the undemocratic character of their government. Precisely what she believed the British should have done was not altogether clear. She remarked that grievances should have been removed, e.g. Malay hostility to the Chinese, that the British should have persuaded Malays, Chinese, and Indians to work together and that they should have been given a wide measure of democratic government. Professor Raymond Kennedy set forth the same thesis that free, democratic peoples would defend themselves in *The Ageless Indies*, written in 1942. He lamented that Britain and Holland had scorned 'a bright eyed newcomer to the field', the United States, which in a generation had made the Filipinos into 'champions of democracy because they know what it means in their own lives'. Actually the Philippines of 1941 were a quasi dictatorship that operated under the forms of democracy, and judging by the election returns with the full approval of 69 per cent. of the voters. By a further act of faith Professor Kennedy portrayed the Chinese as fighting to defend the democracy of Chiang Kai-shek.

A characteristic shown by some American authors was the failure to see that the letter of the law might differ from its practice. These writers usually showed great thoroughness in collecting information from written sources, and their books tended to be heavily footnoted and copiously enriched with excerpts from authorities. They did not appear to realize that documents might not give the whole truth. Quite often these writers did not visit the areas about which they wrote. The result was books which had a resemblance to reality but at the same time distorted it. The explanation was that the authors drew a misleading analogy from the rigidity of the American constitution. In some respects the actual operation of government departed from constitutional theory, but on the whole they coincided more closely in the United States than in any other country which had a written constitution. By contrast no Frenchman would confuse the two, and any Englishman was well aware that if constitutional law said one thing practice was likely to do the opposite.

This was one criticism that could perhaps be made against Miss Hammer's *Struggle for Indochina*. Developments were minutely described and heavily footnoted, but the impression persisted that the writer was working at long range and had no personal knowledge of the country. Otherwise, to cite one instance, it was hard to see why she could have believed that Bao Dai in 1954 was the man best fitted to rally Vietnam in a fight for independence against Ho Chi Minh. As a second example Professor T. E. Ennis, *French Policy and Developments in Indochina*, conscientiously studied all information printed in Western languages, but did not visit Indochina. The result was that his work impressed one as not quite in accord with actuality. Dr. Virginia Thompson's *Thailand, the New Siam*, written in 1941, showed this writer's accustomed diligence in accumulating an encyclopaedic range of information on every aspect of Thai affairs published in Western languages. She seemed in her preface to claim little or no personal acquaintance with Thailand. This perhaps explained a number of incorrect statements, and the faulty explanations given for some of the political events of the nineteen thirties.

Erich Jacoby, *Agrarian Unrest in Southeast Asia* (1949), gave a detailed description of the agrarian situation in the six countries of South East Asia. As regards the Philippines it was based on the author's own observations during four years' residence there, and was a reliable and impartial account. For the other parts of the area he relied upon government reports and books by other authors, and this sometimes misled him into making statements of questionable accuracy. For instance the facts did not support his assertion that the development of the tin and rubber industries in the Federated Malay States 'pushed' the Malays into the Unfederated Malay States, because they felt safer there from Western penetration.

Several of the best books about the Philippines have been by American officials. The first in point of time was *The Philippines Past and Present*, written in 1914 by Dean C. Worcester, a member of the Governor General's Cabinet. He described with great accuracy and detail the political and economic history of the American regime from 1898 to 1913. This was the most reliable and fullest account of the early American period. Cameron Forbes, a former Governor General, wrote about the period down to 1925 in his *The Philippine Islands*, though the latest edition had a brief final chapter on events from 1925 to 1941. He gave a temperate and fair account of American accomplishments in the development of self-government and the establishment of the social services. Little attention was paid to the economic situation and its politico-economic consequence *caciquism*. The author was unusually just to the Spanish regime, pointing out its accomplishments. The principal weakness was that Forbes said little about the American failure to reform the system of land tenures and abolish debt slavery. He asserted that the attempt to give freeholders secure title to their lands was on the whole a success; but between 1909 and 1937 the registration of land titles through cadastral surveys had covered only 3,354,000 hectares, while 25,708,000 hectares had still to be dealt with. The American government also tried through the Homesteading Act to enable landless peasants to obtain land, and Forbes was silent as to its comparative failure. The figures showed that between 1904 and

1936 212,094 Filipinos applied for farms and only 34,821 received them. The best account of the agrarian problem down to 1941 and the attempts at reform was in Professor Karl J. Pelzer's *Pioneer Settlement in the Asiatic Tropics*. Pelzer's account was based upon a careful study of official reports and first-hand observation. His facts were reliable; but the judgements which he based upon them were biased. The facts as he set them forth showed the not over-successful attempts of the American and Filipino governments to resettle surplus peasants in Mindanao, and the rather more successful efforts of the Dutch to lessen the overpopulation of Java by colonizing the Outer Islands. From all this Pelzer drew the conclusion that the Filipino experiment was the more commendable because its avoidable blunders arose from 'establishing democratic procedures'. The Dutch method was more efficient but was criticized as paternalistic.

By far the best book on the Philippines in the twentieth century was the late Professor J. R. Hayden's *The Philippines, A Study in National Development*, which appeared in 1942. The first half gave a penetrating and very understanding study of the historical evolution of the Philippine government and its existing structure, in theory and also in actuality. This was followed by a full discussion of education, public health, defence, foreign policy, the Chinese, and the political implications of agrarian discontent. The author lived for many years in the islands, and was by turns a newspaper correspondent, an official, a member of the Governor General's Cabinet, and a university professor. He combined an intimate personal knowledge of every phase of Filipino life with a monumental amount of thorough and scholarly research. His book was very detailed, meticulously accurate, impartial, and notably free from the prejudices which were discussed previously. One of its best features was that Hayden never restricted himself to describing the machinery of government as laid down in the constitution but went on to emphasize how differently it operated in practice. There was a very realistic explanation of why the Philippines had a single party government and the party leader, who was also the elected President, was a quasi dictator. He did not write an uncritical eulogy of a successful democratic experiment in Asia, but a careful study of how an American style democracy was in process of transformation into something which better expressed the national characteristics of the Filipinos themselves. The book was completed just before the Japanese invasion, and a useful continuation for the post-war period to 1950 was given by George A. Malcolm, *First Malayan Republic*: *The Story of the Philippines*. The author, a former justice of the Supreme Court, served in the islands from 1906 to 1940, and revisited them in 1948–9. Most of the book described the constitution and political history since 1945. It was well documented though less detailed and scholarly than Hayden. The most valuable features were that the actual operation of government was explained as well as its theory, and the author drew on his personal knowledge as well as written sources. He was frank and temperate in pointing out the serious shortcomings in the government of the Republic, and like Hayden he argued that it was as democratic as could reasonably be expected.

Another book which deserves mention was Professor Grayson Kirk's *Philippine Independence*, published in 1936. He described it as 'a case study in the motivation of national policy', and covered the period from the conquest in 1898 to the establishment of the Commonwealth in 1935. It was based upon a study of the archives in Washington, and in its complete impartiality and lack of bias it could serve as a model for anyone writing about his own country. Kirk traced for instance the economic motives for the annexation, and how they were presented for public consumption not as imperialism but as manifest destiny 'to educate the Filipinos, and uplift and civilize and Christianize them'. The book was particularly valuable for its analysis of how at the time of the Great Depression the farm bloc's representatives in Congress granted independence as the only way in which to shut out competing Philippine products from the American market.

The most outstanding American book on Indonesia was Professor Amry Vandenbosch's *The Dutch East Indies*, a description of the pre-war Dutch government and of the political and economic problems of the dependency. It was based upon a very thorough study of Dutch publications, supplemented by personal investigation in Indonesia. Each topic was analysed in great detail, and enough of a historical background was given to make the contemporary situation intelligible. Vandenbosch was completely free from prejudice, and was scrupulously just and impartial. On occasion he praised or criticized; but he was invariably careful to give the reasons for his attitude and also the arguments which were advanced against his position. It was rare, however, for him to intrude his own views, and his usual practice was to give the reader all the facts on both sides so that he could form his own opinion.

Three American writers on Burma deserve special attention. On the whole the most comprehensive though not the most detailed description of the pre-war political and economic situation was in Professor John L. Christian's *Modern Burma*. His death in action in 1944 was a serious loss. He had lived in Burma for eight years, and used government reports and works in English and Burmese. The account of Burmese nationalism and political parties and the development of self-government was completely free from anti-British prejudice; and Christian was fully aware of the distinction between the form of the constitution and its practical operation. He was sympathetic to the Burmans, but frankly admitted the factionalism and corruption of their political parties. At the same time Christian was not an apologist for British rule. He dealt justly and accurately with the problem of rural debt and the loss of lands to the *chettyars*, though he tended to underestimate the magnitude of the British blunder in failing to remedy the situation.

J. Russell Andrus, who published his *Burmese Economic Life* in 1947, was a former professor of economics at the University of Rangoon who made a study of rural life and welfare. He also used official reports and the writings of previous authors. His book was a detailed description of every phase of Burma's economy with emphasis on agriculture, of which he gave a fuller account than Christian. Like him he showed great impartiality and freedom from the usual prejudices against imperialism. Andrus was scrupulously fair in appraising the benefits and shortcomings of British rule. Writing as an economist he dealt cogently with many of the charges of exploitation, and pointed out that Burma's economic evolution was very similar to that of any other region which had been newly opened to capitalist development, e.g. the United States between 1800 and 1850.

Professor John Cady wrote part of *The Development of Self-Rule and Independence in Burma, Malaya and the Philippines*, and contributed a chapter to *The New World of Southeast Asia*, by L. A. Mills and Associates. He compressed a great deal of information into the restricted space to which he was confined, and for this reason his writings were briefer and less comprehensive than Christian's. The writings were impartial and deliberately impersonal. On some phases the account was fuller than Christian's, e.g. the agrarian situation, the ineffectiveness of village government and the reasons for the Burman hostility to the Indians and the British. Professor Cady lived in Burma both before and after the war, and his work was based upon personal knowledge and a study of government reports and the books of previous writers.

Kenneth P. Landon was a missionary in Thailand before the war, and is now an official in the American Department of State. He spoke the vernacular, and in addition to personal knowledge he studied the written material available in Thai as well as English and French. His two books, *Siam in Transition* and *The Chinese in Thailand* were authentic and scholarly. The book on the Chinese was very fair both to them and the Thai government, and the same characteristic was shown in his *Siam in Transition*. This described the revolution of the 1930's, and also had chapters on the social services, economics and religion.

Among works on South East Asia in general one of the most important was *The Rice Economy of Monsoon Asia* by V. D. Wickizer and M. K. Bennett, published in 1941. The book covered the whole of Southern and Eastern Asia, and the chapters on South East Asia were a valuable and reliable study of the cultivation, consumption and export of rice during the inter-war period. The reader was almost overwhelmed with quotations from authorities and statistical tables in massed formation. The treatment was severely factual, thorough, and studiously impartial. The facts were stated with scientific detachment, and the authors never intruded their own opinions. *Foreign Capital in Southeast Asia* was published by Helmut G. Callis in 1942. For each country Dr. Callis tried to ascertain the amount of capital invested in government bonds and business enterprises of all kinds. So far as possible he traced the nationality of ownership of the investments. One of the most important features of the book was the attempt to discover the extent of Chinese investments and the amount of the annual remittances to China. The book was based upon an exhaustive study of government reports and books in English, French, and German, and Dr. Callis wrote with scientific detachment. He frankly admitted that many of his figures were estimates, and later research has shown that in some instances they were incorrect. He set himself a difficult task in which absolute accuracy was often impossible.

Summing up what has been written most American writers were trained in methods of research. They were at great pains to collect information and tried to set it down accurately. Usually their statement of facts could be relied upon. Where some of them fell short of scholarly standards was in the interpretation they placed upon their material and the inferences they drew from it. Some but by no means all of them were biased by preconceived prejudices which affected their understanding of a way of life very different from that to which they were accustomed.

BOOKS CITED

Andrus, J. Russell, *Burmese Economic Life* (Stanford, 1947).

Cady, John F., *The Development of Self-Rule and Independence in Burma, Malay and the Philippines* (New York, 1948), pp. 1–50.

Cady, John F., *The New World of Southeast Asia*, by L. A. Mills and Associates (Minneapolis, 1949), pp. 126–73.

Cady, John F., *The Roots of French Imperialism in Eastern Asia* (Ithaca, N.Y., 1954).

Callis, Helmut G., *Foreign Capital in Southeast Asia* (New York, 1942).

Christian, John L., *Modern Burma* (Berkeley, 1942).

Emerson, Rupert, *Malaysia, A Study in Direct and Indirect Rule* (New York, 1937).

Emerson, Rupert, *Representative Government in Southeast Asia* (Cambridge, 1955).

Ennis, Thomas E., *French Policy and Development in Indochina* (Chicago, 1936).

Forbes, W. Cameron, *The Philippine Islands* (Cambridge, 1945).

Hahn, Emily, *Raffles of Singapore, A Biography* (Garden City, N.Y., 1948).

Hammer, Ellen, *The Struggle for Indochina* (Stanford, 1954).

Hayden, Joseph R., *The Philippines, A Study in National Development* (New York, 1942).

Jacoby, Erich H., *Agrarian Unrest in Southeast Asia* (New York, 1949).

Kahin, George McT., *Nationalism and Revolution in Indonesia* (Ithaca, 1952).

Kennedy, Raymond, *The Ageless Indies* (New York, 1942).

Kirk, Grayson, *Philippine Independence* (New York, 1936).

Landon, Kenneth P., *Siam in Transition* (Shanghai, 1939).

— *The Chinese in Thailand* (London and New York, 1941).

Lasker, Bruno, *Human Bondage in Southeast Asia* (Chapel Hill, N.C., 1950).

Malcolm, George A., *First Malayan Republic: The Story of the Philippines* (Boston, 1951).

Pelzer, Karl J., *Pioneer Settlement in the Asiatic Tropics* (New York, 1945).

Roosevelt, Theodore, *Colonial Policies of the United States* (Garden City, N.Y., 1937).

Thompson, Virginia, *French Indochina* (New York, 1937).

— *Thailand, The New Siam* (New York, 1941).

— *Post Mortem on Malaya* (New York, 1943).

Thompson, Warren S., *Population and Peace in the Pacific* (Chicago, 1946).

Vandenbosch, Amry, *The Dutch East Indies*, second edition (Berkeley, 1941).

Wickizer, V. D., and Bennett, M. K., *The Rice Economy of Monsoon Asia* (Stanford, 1941).

Wolf, Charles, *The Indonesian Story: The Birth, Growth and Structure of the Indonesian Republic* (New York, 1948).

Worcester, Dean C., *The Philippines Past and Present* (New York, 1914).

23. THE POSITION OF HISTORICAL STUDIES IN THE COUNTRIES OF FORMER FRENCH INDO-CHINA IN 1956

L. MALLERET

Ancien Directeur de l'École Française d'Extrême Orient

The development of historical studies and of their ancillary sciences covers less than a century in the countries of former French Indo-China. In other words, it has coincided with the continuous progress of research methods and objective statement during the same period. These investigations have not been without their hesitations, generally as a result of the inadequacy of written sources, or, again, of the incorrect interpretation of texts.[1] The structure was built upon uncertain foundations because of a lack of information which extended to any degree in space or time, for the peoples of Indo-China often lacked a true historical tradition, either because the notion of time was hardly familiar to them, or because they had not taken the trouble to record events or to assess their relative importance as causes or consequences of other facts. The definite idea of an evolutionary movement of civilizations seems in fact, to be a western concept which forms part of the system of scientific tenets elaborated in Europe in recent times. This should be considered among the importations into non-European countries. Secondly, it has not been definitely established that the conscious acceptance of peoples as distinct units endowed with a true collectvei personality is of long standing, at least in the full sense of our usage. These two propositions must be kept in mind in any attempt to appreciate the extension and consolidation of historical knowledge from the moment when it is freed from the traditional conception of official historiography.

It cannot be denied that the territorial concept which has been labelled 'Indo-China' has been no more than a fortuitous construct, created as much in accordance with a political programme, with its concomitant economic data, as upon a diversity of peoples grouped together by the simplification of common features. But the concept has also demonstrated the persistence of convenient generalizations in the geographer's vocabulary.[2] It has also permitted the continued historical significance of intermediate regions between territories which have been drawn, through the ages, by the force of divergent attractions. Before 1860, the date at which

---

[1] For example, the great inscription of Sdok Kak Thom in Cambodia.

[2] It will be remembered here that the term is due to the geographer Malte-Brun, and that for a long time those countries situated between India and China were designated by the terms '*Inde ultragangetique*' or 'pays au delà du Gange'.

the mass penetration of people, ideas, and methods of western, mainly French origin, began, the countries of Indo-China were still poorly differentiated in the eyes of Europeans, either because these countries were tied by vassal bonds to neighbouring countries or because they had not clearly attracted attention to themselves by distinct and positive characteristics.

From the seventeenth century there has existed an immense literature, accounts of journeys or of sojourns, by navigators or by missionaries. Certain of these accounts contain historical chapters which could sometimes have provided a framework for research. Although their information was generally obtained at secondhand, they do not deserve the degree of disdain which has generally been their lot. In the light of knowledge acquired from other sources, these accounts deserve to be the object of a general critical study. They constituted the first source which was available and readily accessible at the beginning of the colonial era. Of very unequal interest and value, they could provide no more than a patchy account of events which occurred in privileged localities, and their information related principally to the most readily accessible of the coastal regions. So it is that the pages consecrated to Tonkin occupy a disproportionate space by contrast with that on the regions of Laos which could be reached only by the river route of the Mekong with its rapids, or with Cambodia which has never been so strongly subject to missionary penetration.

In each of the countries under consideration, written documents were rare, and the obstacle of a mosaic of languages impeded their being understood or co-ordinated. These documents were annals or chronicles much more concerned, like those of Cambodia, with dynastic affairs or palace intrigues than with the social and political evolution of the peoples. Remembering the fact that the Indo-China peninsula presents an extraordinary diversity of dialects and peoples, the first operation necessary was a stocktaking of documents, whether historical or other. To this general mission was dedicated L'École Française d'Extrême-Orient (EFEO), whose foundation in 1901 was the determining factor throughout Indo-China in the progress of humane studies. A considerable quantity of texts has been collected, which, on account of its very size, it has not yet proved possible fully to work through, to translate, to use. This fundamental inventory has not yet been fully completed, and it is only in recent years that, for instance, the School's investigators have recovered in Laos the Annals of Champassac or of the principality of Chieng Khuang: the same is true of the versions of the *Phongsavadan* in use on the Lao-Burmese border.

Among the texts it is proper to accord a particular importance to the stone inscriptions, the only ones which in some countries like Cambodia furnish information about the early periods. It was urgent to collect, to translate and to interpret them, when no other source was available. In this way it was possible, through a combined programme of work in the various countries of Indo-China, to assemble a corpus of rubbings of Chinese, Vietnamese, Cham, Khmer, and Cambodian inscriptions. The publication of *Stèles royales de Lam-so'n* by M. Emile Gaspardone[3] should be accompanied by the same author's study of their contents, and there can be no doubt that a comprehensive publication of the inscriptions of Viet-nam would be most desirable. The Cham inscriptions, from the same country, have mostly been published, mainly in translations and inter-pretations by Louis Finot. From the beginning of the century Barth and Bergaigne began the study of the Khmer inscriptions.[4] The publication of six facsimile volumes,[5] and that of six volumes of translations by M. George Coedès[6] have contributed greatly to the provision of material for a history of Cambodia which is now freed of fictions.

A parallel cataloguing of monuments, as much in the interest of in-creasing our knowledge as of preserving the buildings, has been carried out, as well as of sculpture and, in general, of all the evidence for cultural history. This has constituted another source of information, both on account of the chronological conclusions derived from the evolution of the architecture and decoration and of the evidence of material culture to be found in the bas-reliefs. The establishment of major museum collections has supplied the historian with other topics of study, providing a docu-mentary series with at once local and national significance. It has also brought home the need to emphasize the influence exerted by the civiliza-tion of neighbouring countries. It is this concept which has given rise to museums of homogeneous, one might say specialized type, like that at Tourane for Cham antiquities or at Phnom Penh for Khmer archaeology, and the great concentrations of *objets d'art* which have been set up in Viet-nam which show the complex influences which this country has experienced and the divers civilizations which it has supported.

In the course of recounting the development of primary documentation, attention will here be drawn especially to the setting up of archives. This idea was not unknown to Viet-nam before the French penetration, because archives existed at Hué. But the very idea of written documents considered as evidence which might be subjected to criticism and scientific use for their historical content does not seem to have been widespread at least until recently. The prestige which surrounded imperial decrees and the writings of the mandarinate has reduced to secondary importance, or even, on occasion, jealously inhibited direct access to, the sources. Enclosed in

[3] Paris (1935). [4] *Les inscriptions sanskrites du Cambodge et du Champa.*
[5] *Inscriptions de Cambodge*, published under the auspices of the *Académie des Inscriptions et Belles-Lettres* (Paris).
[6] G. Coedès *Inscriptions du Cambodge*, I and II Hanoi 1937 and 1942, III, IV, V and VI (Paris, 1951 to 1954).

heavy bureaux, or in lacquered coffers from the shelter of which they were periodically extracted in accordance with a rigorously prescribed ritual, the archives were virtually inaccessible.[7] Consideration of their inestimable historical value was relegated to a position of minor importance, and it is not inconceivable, paradoxically, that they could thus have been exposed to the risk of destruction through indifference or carelessness. Thus can be explained no doubt the fact that they have undergone vicissitudes, either by being expurgated before the French period, or because they have by no means received all the care which is desirable since the war. On several occasions EFEO has made copies of texts for its own collections which have been set up at Hanoi. Léopold Cadière and Paul Pelliot have given an outline of the most important of these collections.[8] Paul Boudet has been privileged to have direct access to the archives and has been able to arrange the public donation of items of unusual interest to Hanoi and Saigon. Since 1950, EFEO has sent to Hué two of its collaborators to undertake an enormous programme of microfilming what remains of the former archives, grievously ravaged by the events of the war since 1945. One of them, M. Búi-quang-Tung, has resolutely applied himself to this effort of preservation and he has reported, without much success both to the responsible authorities and in a printed account[9] the wretched conditions which have obtained for some years in the former Imperial Archives of Annam.[10]

In Cambodia, as in Laos, it does not appear that any official care had been given to the conservation of documents written upon perishable materials before the introduction of modern ideas upon the preservation of historical sources. At Luang Prabang, for example, it is the temples which serve as repositories for manuscripts.[11] Those infrequent Cambodian chronicles translated by Francis Garnier and Etienne Aymonier[12] are but vaguely explicit and are of decisive value only when they can be collated, where this is possible, with European texts. The picture of Cambodian history reconstructed with the help of inscriptions on stone has proved, when all considerations are taken into account, far more significant for the early periods, especially when it has been possible to compare the monuments with the rare Chinese texts, of which one at least, that of Chu Ta

[7] See particularly Paul Boudet, *Les Archives des Empereurs d'Annam et L'Histoire annamite. Bulletin des Amis du Vieux Hué* (1942), xxix, 229–259.

[8] See L. Caddière and P. Pelliot, *Première étude sur les sources annamites de l'Histoire d'Annam*, BEFEO (1904), iv, 617–71.

[9] See Paul Boudet, *l'Indochine dans le Passé* (1941). G. Taboulet and L. Malleret, La Cochinchine dans le Passé (Saigon), *Bulletin de la Société des Etudes Indochinoises* (1942), xviii, No. 3, 7–133.

[10] Búi-quang-Tung, Pour un meilleure conservation des Archives vietnamiennes (*France-Asie*, Saigon), No. 109–110, June–July 1955, pp. 742–6.

[11] See Louis Finot, Recherche sur la litterature laotienne, BEFEO (1917), xvii (5), 1–218.

[12] Francis Garnier, Chronique Royale du Cambodge, *J. Asiatique* (1871), pp. 336–85; 1872, pp. 124–44. Etienne Aymonier, Chronique des anciens rois du Cambodge, Excursions et Reconnaissances (Saigon II, 1880), No. 4, pp. 149–90.

Kuan, is of inestimable interest for the twelfth century.[13] There is no instance in these countries, as there is in Viet-nam, of great scholars or compilers who have left precise accounts of the state of early archives. The setting up of the protectorate had no effect upon the élan of an indigenous culture which had already fallen back upon fiction, to the extent that they attributed the construction of the Angkor monuments to the gods, and allowed the names of great kings like Jayavarman II or Jayavarman VII to be buried in oblivion. But Cambodia, within its straitened frontiers of today, has not wholly forgotten the memories of its ancient expansion. Its geographic homogeneity has maintained the impression of a powerful monarchical concentration despite dynastic crises and internal rivalries. Laos, on the other hand, so far as its present frontiers are concerned, is an artificial political construct which does not embody any historical reality of definite validity. Divided into reaches between the rapids and narrows of the Mekong, this territory has given birth to principalities which lie in echelon along the main valley, its tributaries or the adjacent areas of neighbouring plateaux. On account of this one finds different historical traditions in southern Champassac, for instance, which has directly profited from Khmer influences; in the principality of Luang Prabang in the north, which is in contact with China and which does not seem to have received Indian influences (except by the bye-ways of Central Asia); or, yet again, in the Tranninh plateau whose history is recounted in the Annals of Chieng Khuang.

The constitution of French archives operated in a truly systematic manner only after the time when a federative system came into force. Each official department or each local government continued to operate its own private archives, while, under the notably fruitful drive of a professional archivist, Paul Boudet, there was set up at Hanoi a central archives which is notable especially for the papers that recount the activities in Cochin-china of the Admirals-Governor. The breaking up of the federal system which began in 1945–50 inevitably involved the division of the archives into national lots. This operation set in train a colossal process of spoliation and necessitated a considerable time for its proper execution. To our knowledge, it remains uncompleted, and this relic of a federal past will weigh heavily upon the development of local research if the necessary measures are not taken. A considerable body of documents relating to the French period remains in each country at the disposal of the national archives. It is in Europe, however, that the best-documented sources for the periods prior to the colonial regime and the protectorate are to be found. Victor Tantet has given an account of the contents of the files which used to be housed at the Ministère de la France d'Outre-Mer and

[13] Paul Pelliot, *Mémoire sur les coutumes du Cambodge*, BEFEO, ii, 123–77. A new and copiously annotated edition, unfortunately left unfinished on account of Paul Palliot's death, appeared in Paris, 1951.

which have now been transferred to the Archives Nationales.[14] Several of them have been published, thanks to Henri Cordier. But there exist numerous other collections where methodical investigation can disclose the most unexpected discoveries, those of the Ministère de la Marine, des Affaires Etrangères, and of the Société des Missions Etrangères and the Muséum d'Histoire Naturelle, to instance only the main ones and to say nothing of special collections in provincial towns and private archives. Finally one must not omit to mention the national archives of other European powers which have been interested in Indo-China, those of Holland, for example, or of Portugal and of Spain.

This, then, is the indispensable assemblage of documents which the French historians of the countries of Indo-China have striven to establish. This prospector's task presumed linguistic specialization which should normally be accompanied by translations and comparisons with the infrequent syntheses by indigenous writers. During their work the research workers of EFEO have explored extensively the texts which they have collected, but have generally recoiled before the enormous enterprise which is implicit in a general edition, with translations and critical commentaries. To those who may be tempted to wonder that traditional knowledge has not had the benefit of a wider publication, the reply will be that a start has been made from more or less nothing on a task which demanded the effort of several generations of scholars. From the first the Cambodian chronicles were translated, and Paul Pelliot, Henri Maspéro, Edouard Huber, Léonard Aurousseau, Paul Demiéville, Léopold Cadière, Emile Gaspardone, to mention only the oldest, accomplished a vast exploration of Chinese texts relating to Indo-China and neighbouring countries. The School has begun the publication of the Vietnamese *Cu'o'ng muc*, at the hands of M. Maurice Durand who has elsewhere dedicated a study to the dynasty of the Former Lý from another text.[15] But the School has primarily devoted itself to making clear the main aspects of the history of South East Asia, beginning with those of the peninsula of Indo-China.

It is in the light of this that one should consider, as being fundamental the work of among others Paul Pelliot and of Father Léopold Cadière on Annamite sources for the history of Viet-nam, in an article published in 1904, after research carried out in the Archives and Royal Libraries of Hué;[16] the paper of the latter, *Le Mur de Dông-hoí*, published in 1906;[17]

[14] Victor Tantet, *Inventaire sommaire de la correspondance générale de la Cochinchine* (1686–1863) (Paris, 1905).

[15] Maurice Durand, *Texte et commentaire du miroir complet de l'Histoire du Viêt* (1950); and *Cu'o'ng-Muc (II)*, BEFEO (1955), xlvii, 2, 369–434; *La dynastie des Ly antérieurs d'après le 'Viêt-diên u linh tâp*, BEFEO (1947–50), xliv, 437–52.

[16] L. Cadière and P. Pelliot, *Première étude sur les sources annamites de l'Histoire d'Annam*, BEFEO (1904), iv, 617–71.

[17] L. Cadière, *Le Mur de Dong hot. Etude sur l'établissement des Nguyên en Cochinchine*, BEFEO (1906), vi, 87–254.

that of the former, *Deux itinéraires de Chine en Inde*, which was based not only upon local documents but also on Chinese, Sanskrit, and Pali sources and appeared in 1904;[18] that of Henri Maspéro on *Le protectorat général d'Annam*, which was published in 1910;[19] finally Léonard Aurousseau's paper on the first Chinese conquest of Annamite countries in the third century B.C., which appeared in 1923.[20]

In a general survey of sources to which French historians have devoted their efforts, it will be no surprise that the part occupied by bibliographical research into the resources of oriental and European language libraries is appreciable, notably in the activities of EFEO. It is scarcely necessary to recall the *Bibliotheca Indosinica* of Henri Cordier with an index by Mme Rolland Cabaton.[21] Unfortunately the work stops at 1912. It has been continued by the *Bibliographie de l'Indochine Française*, by Paul Boudet and Remy Bourgeois, of which the coverage, up to 1945, does not extend beyond 1935.[22] The first of these two works includes references relevant to all the countries of South East Asia, but the second meets a more limited need. It is the writer's belief that it is vital that this effort be extended for all the headings in European and Oriental languages. These bibliographies, however, fall short of being general in character. They would merit being continued as historical studies taking in not only epigraphy, texts in local and European languages drawn from archives, chronicles, compilations, specialized monographs, but also the great mass of recollections, memoirs, and accounts of events which have multiplied, in the first case between 1860 and 1900, and in the other since 1945. Finally, they should include a ransacking of periodicals not generally accessible, such as *Bulletin de l'École française d'Extrême-Orient*, that of the *Société des Etudes Indochinoises*, that of the *Amis de Vieux Hué*, now no more, or again of the former *Revue Indochinoise*.

Libraries meeting varied requirements, general or specialized have been set up. Their catalogues have, in some cases been published in part, like that of the European collections of EFEO, or of the Chinese collections in the same establishment.[23] But it is above all the catalogues of manuscripts which deserve to be printed. That of the Khmer manuscripts in

[18] P. Pelliot, *Deux itinéraires de Chine en Inde à la fin du VIIIe siècle*, BEFEO (1904), iv, 131–413.

[19] H. Maspéro, *Le Protectorat Général d'Annam sous les T'ang*, BEFEO (1910), x, 539–84 and 665–82. See also by the same author *Etudes d'histoire d'Annam*, BEFEO, xvi (1), 1–55, and xviii (3), 1–364.

[20] L. Aurousseau, *La premeère conquête chinoises des pays annamites* (Illes. avant notre ère). BEFEO (1923), xxiii, 137–264.

[21] Henri Cordier, *Bibliotheca Indosinica, Dictionnaire bibliographique des ouvrages relatifs à la peninsule indochinoise* (Paris, 1912–15 and 1932).

[22] P. Boudet and R. Bourgeois, *Bibliographie de l'Indochine française* (1913–26; Hanoi, 1929; 1927–9; Hanoi, 1932, 1931–5; Hanoi, 1943).

[23] *Inventaire alphabétique de la Bibliothèque du l'Ecole Française d'Extreme-Orient* (Hanoi, 1929–51), three tomes in six volumes (publication broken off at letter M).

the Bibliothèque Nationale, Paris, appeared in 1953.[24] But two considerable collections exist at Phnom Penh, that of the Institut Bouddhique and of EFEO. In Laos, two important collections are to be found, at Vientiane and Luang Prabang, for which catalogues, properly arranged with a view to publication, are essential. For Viet-nam EFEO envisages the publication of its Vietnamese collections, comprising about four thousand titles. But this country has already benefitted from the efforts of great scholars like Le-quy-Dôn and Phan-huy-Chú, from whom M. Emile Gaspardone has derived a substantial bibliography[25] completed by an important article by M. Trân-van Giáp.[26] Nothing of this sort, so far as we are aware, existed for Cambodia and Laos, countries in which the book occurs in a palm-leaf format of less circulation than works produced by the wood-block process. Finally, mention should be made of historical iconography of which there exists, at present, but one pioneer effort, that of Paul Boudet and André Masson.[27] This is scarcely possible, save from European documents.

This systematic enumeration of sources enables one to grasp the general position of historical studies at the moment when the peoples of Indo-China enter upon a new phase of their national existence. French historians have exhibited a marked distaste for elaborating grand syntheses for which they lacked a fundamental and firmly established documentation. Faced by the obstacle of diversity of languages, they preferred to go to European sources to which they had direct access, and it cannot be denied that the work of Ch. B. Maybon, *Historie Moderne du Pays d'Annam*, whatever may be its merits, errs through insufficient use of native documentation. The specialists of EFEO did not fail to underline this fact on its appearance.[28, 29] Works of general history have been thought premature in contrast with monographs or publications of stone inscriptions, documents, archives, memoirs, letters, and first-hand accounts of events. However, some outlines have been attempted for Vietnam, those of Pétrus Ky or Adrien Launa, today superseded.[30] The utilization of native sources has led M. George Coedès, former Director of EFEO, to write his *Histoire ancienne des Etats hindouisés d'Extrême-Orient* which, at the present state of our knowledge is by far the most considerable synthesis for a period prior to the sixteenth

[24] Au Chhieng, Catalogue *du fonds khmāt de la Bibliotheque Nationale* (Paris, 1953).

[25] E. Gaspardone, *Bibliographie annamite*, BEFEO (1934), xxxiv, 1–173.

[26] Trân-van-Giáp, *Les Chaitres bibliographiques de Lê-quoi-Don et Phanhuy-Chú, Bulletin Soc. Etudes Indochinoises* (Saigon, 1938), xiii, No. 1, 9–217.

[27] P. Boudet et A. Masson, *Iconographie historique de l'Indochine française* (Paris, 1931).

[28] Charles B. Maybon, *Histoire moderne du Pays d'Annam* (1592–1820) (Paris, 1920).

[29] L. Aurousseau, *Compe-rendu de l'ouvrage de Ch. B. Maybon*, BEFEO (1820), xx, 73–120.

[30] P. Troung-vinh-Ky, *Cours d'histoire annamite* (Saigon, 1875–7), 2 vols. A. Launay, *Histoire ancienne et moderne de l'Annam, Tong-King et Cochinchine* (Paris, 1884). Only the principal works in French are mentioned here, although there are other works, not without merit, written in Vietnamese.

century.[31] Certain periods in Cambodia, notably in regard to its relations with Champa, have been studied in a penetrating manner by Pierre Dupont, who died too soon to extend his researches to the whole of Khmer history.[32] For Laos there is only one work, based for the most part on European documents, that of Paul Le Boulanger.[33] On the countries of Indo-China taken as a whole the first volume of a collection of documents of astonishing richness has been published in the form of an anthology: this is *La geste française en Indochine*, by M. Georges Taboulet who has methodically prospected in the collections of archives in France and Indo-China and who publishes in this volume no more than a minute fraction of the immense documentation which he has garnered.[34] Over and above the general histories there are some specialized studies which form distinct aspects of future synthesis. Such, for example, are the works of art history, now more or less established,[35] or military[36] or economic[37] history, or of religious history begun over a wide field by Father Adrien Launay and intensively and in detail by Mgr. Chappoulie.[38, 39]

For Vietnam, where however the wealth of written documents is much greater than elsewhere, the oldest evidence goes back no further than the twelfth and thirteenth centuries, whether in the case of inscriptions or of printed works. Up to the nineteenth century this country's archives have experienced endless vicissitudes. This is why the development of historical studies in this country will necessarily be bound up with the progress of archaeological work, as it is in Cambodia, through lack of documents other than inscriptions. There were, it is true, historians of importance in the former Viet-nam, but their works, of unequal interest, are not always utilizable through lack of method and of a critical spirit. Few have been translated into French beyond *Gia-dinh thông chi*: 'History and Description

[31] G. Coedès, *Histoire ancienne des Etats hindouisés d'Extrême Orient*, second edition (Paris, 1948),

[32] Dupont, *La dislocation du Tchen-la et la formation de Cambodge angkorien*, BEFEO (1943–57). xliii, 17–55; *Le Sud-Indochinois aux VIe et VIIe siècles: Tchen-la et Panduranga*, Bull Soc. Etudes Indochinoises (Saigon, 1924), xxiv, 9–25; *Les debuts de la royauté angkorienne*, BEFEO (1952), xlvi, 119–76.

[33] P. Le Boulanger, *Histoire du Laos français* (Paris, 1930).

[34] G. Taboulet, *La geste française en Indochine*, first vol. (Paris, 1955).

[35] H. Parmentier, *L'Art du Laos*, 2 vols. (Paris, 1954). J. Boisselier, *La statuaire khmère et son évolution*, 2 vols. (Paris, 1955). P. Dupont, *La statuaire préangkorienne*, 1 vol. (Ascona, 1955). P. L. Stern, *L'Art du Champa et son évolution* (Paris, 1942). L. Bezacier, *L'Art vietnamien* (Paris, 1955).

[36] *Histoire militaire de l'Indochine de 1664 a nos jours*, établie par des officiers de l'Etat-Major sous la direction du Général Puypéroux.

[37] R. Deloustal, *Ressources économiques et financières de l'Etat dans l'ancien Annam, Revue Indochinoise*, 1924 and 1925), *Bulletin des Amis du Vieux Hué* (1932). Cf. also A. Schreiner, *Les institutions annamites en Basse-Cochinchine avant la conquete francaise*, 3 vols. (Saigon, 1900–2).

[38] A. Launay, *Histoire Générale de la Société des Missions Etrangerès*, 3 vols. (Paris, 1894). *Histoire de la Mission de Cochinchine* (3 vols. of historical documents) (Paris, 1923–5). *Histoire de la mission du Tonkin* (historical documents), 1 vol. (Paris, 1927).

[39] Mgr. Chappoulie, *Rome et les missions d'Indochine au XVIIe siècle*, 2 vols. (Paris, 1943–8).

of Lower Cochin-China' by the mandarin Trinh-hoài-Duc, published by G. Aubaret in 1863, which anyway is of regional interest only.

It is essential that new teams of Vietnamese historians take the place of their elders, not in scorn for the achievements of their predecessors who have often helped to restore a national individuality to the peoples of Indo-China, but in a desire to base new research upon the direct and critical exploitation of native sources. It is no paradox to claim that the tradition handed on by Lê-quy-Don and Phan-huy-Chu found, during the French period, one who would carry it on in the person of Father Léopold Cadière. M. Nguyên-van-Huyên, Membre de l'EFEO, published an excellent little book entitled *La civilisation annamite* in 1944.[40] Designed for use in schools it was no more than a summary text-book, but full of promise and valuable for long periods of the past. Since then other books by Vietnamese writers have appeared which present a new version of historical knowledge or add to it unpublished chapters. Among these there is one, that of M. Lê-thành-Khôi, *Le Viet-nam*, of which the first volume has appeared, which marks a stage of some importance in the presentation of the facts.[41] It would be rash to state that the work has drawn extensively upon original texts, and it makes free use of the greater part of the knowledge gained over the last fifty years. But we must be grateful to him for having set the history of Viet-nam in the field of South East Asia where main streams of civilization meet, such as those of India and China. Another merit of the first volume is to have battered down a certain number of false concepts which found credence in the flaccid ignorance of so-called scholars. The author admits to certain imperfections in his work, due to insufficient reliance upon indigenous sources. To this one would add the lack of balance which is apparent between the ancient period and the recent which occupies about a third of the book. A certain Marxist point of view inspires its factual interpretation. But this tendency is much more definite still in *Contribution a l'histoire de la nation viêtnamienne* published by M. Jean Chesneaux in 1955.[42] The period which runs from antiquity to the end of the eighteenth century is there represented by two chapters at the most, or an eighth, approximately, of the whole. One might as well say that this book is a work of contemporary history, even that it deals with a period so recent that it will no doubt be agreed that historians have not yet achieved either enough perspective or tranquillity to tackle it. Finally, it can be asked to what extent Marxist concepts elaborated in the nineteenth century are of value for the retrospective application which can be made of them for the understanding and explanation of social movements in periods of antiquity.

[40] Nguyên-van-Huyên, *La civilisation annamite* (Hanoi, 1944).
[41] Lê-thành-Khôi, *Le Viet-Nam. Histoire et Civilisation* (Paris, 1955).
[42] J. Chesneaux, *Contribution à l'histoire de la nation viêtnamienne* (Paris, 1955).

These considerations give rise to a general question which it is convenient to state clearly at this point: has the fact of colonialism weighed upon the concepts of History so as to falsify its orientation to such a point that it may be necessary to reverse the tendency and to revise fundamentally the results so far? In truth, even if such a disgrace had really formed part of the system of ideas which prevailed during the French period, historical research would have been preserved by the spirit of objective research which animated EFEO in the persistent inquiry which it has conducted towards the enumeration of native sources and towards their preservation. This enterprise has been conceived in a spirit which we believe to have been sufficiently free to avoid preconceptions and *arrière-pensées*, without excluding the desire for a sympathetic understanding of the true personality of the peoples and to restore to them a historical culture which, it must be admitted, they had sometimes forgotten.

In our view the advance of the peoples of what was formerly Indo-China to a new national existence should not lead to ends other than those of objective research, free from all contingencies and subject only to the dictates of science. Modernism, of which the totality of scientific concepts forms a part, was introduced wholesale into the countries of Indo-China by colonialism. It has not been proved that, without western political impetus, the same disequilibrium would not have been produced. It has led to the disappearance of the former intellectual training of the scholar class to the profit of a new élite, and one may regret that no compromise has been found between traditional culture and modern education. It may equally be asked whether the often criticized fact of a division of Viet-nam into three regional units was not imposed by geographical considerations deriving from the enormous length of the country and from economic factors which concentrated facilities in two deltas separated by 1,500 kilometres of coast line. Finally, the conception of 'Indo-China' as a federal system was not so artificial as people were pleased to assert, for it rested largely upon complementary financial and economic factors. The point which makes it much more debatable is the concentration of Hanoi, in an outlying situation, of the powers of the Governors-General and above all of an immense concentration of documents which were available for use only to those few who were within reach.

At the dawn of a new phase of research into the past, it is right to emphasize that the work accomplished as a result of about a century's western impetus has allowed us to distinguish not only the national personality of existing peoples, but also to restore one to minorities without written traditions, whether these live in the interior of Viet-nam or on its coasts. Historical entities which had been almost entirely destroyed like the Dông-són culture, those of Funan, Lin I, or early Champa have re-arisen with a significance which is no longer purely nominal. At least seven cultures have left traces on the soil of Viet-nam, and it will be proper to investigate in the future the exact causes and method of Vietnamese expansion towards the south. Incontestably, this prolific and dynamic nation represents the most active and considerable element, demographically speaking, in the whole of Indo-China. But if its culture has covered up that of others, one should not lose sight of the previous territorial expansion of neighbouring peoples like those of Cambodia. The history of this country and its forerunners, notably Funan and Chen-la, still calls for further intensive research. The gropings which have characterized the reconstruction of its past have been marked for long enough by the provisional idea of a pre-Angkorian period which preceded the setting up of political power in the Angkor region. It is only quite recently that the discovery of Oc-Eo has conferred a renewed authority upon the Chinese references on Funan gathered together by Paul Pelliot.[43] Thus a great challenge presents itself to scholars of all nationalities to lead historical research to a new stage. It is our belief that the future of historical studies lies not in the indiscriminate repudiation of our predecessors but in the adjustment of our knowledge to the exact truth.

[43] P. Pelliot, *Le Fou-nan*, BEFEO (1803), iii, 248–303.

24. A CRITICAL STAGE IN THE STUDY OF INDONESIA'S PAST

C. HOOYKAAS

Reader in Old Javanese in the University of London

This paper, by a non-historian, will mainly deal with the following questions:

1. Is 'Indonesia' a workable term for historians?
2. Why 'past' and not 'history' and 'historiography'?
3. Why should studies be said to be in a critical stage?

Answering these questions separately and strictly in this order proves difficult; this statement at the outset may help the reader.

1. *Is 'Indonesia' a Workable Term for Historians?*

To begin with: the term has existed for nearly six and a half years as the name of a *de jure* acknowledged Republic; it is nearly eleven years since the proclamation of Indonesia's political independence, and roughly a century since the cultural unity of the islands as a whole was envisaged. 'The Islands' are meant as they appear in the name of one of the departments of the S.O.A.S.: South East Asia and the Islands.

Here the Philippines are excluded. The Indonesian and Philippine peoples are related, the languages are related, and the Indonesian and Philippine islands taken together form a geographical unit between the continent of Asia and that of Australia and New Guinea. But Indonesia has for many centuries undergone strong influences from India, at first Buddhism and Hinduism, and then, shortly before the arrival of the Europeans, from Islam, whereas these influences left fewer traces in the Philippines; this fact taken by itself perhaps offers a sufficient reason for the historian to deal separately with the two archipelagos. Moreover, apart from the Portuguese period, for the last four centuries Indonesia has felt gradually increasing influence from the Protestant North-European 'expatriates', whereas the Philippines were influenced by the Roman Catholic South-European 'settlers'. These two causes taken together are a sufficient reason to leave the Philippines out of the picture here.

In the cultural sense of the word, as is usual in this paper, the name Indonesia includes Portuguese Timor, British North Borneo, and the Malay Peninsula. Large cities such as Benares and Saigon are built exclusively on one side of a big river, and the other side is flat country and seems to play no role. But the Malacca Straits offer the opposite aspect: both sides are populated with Malays. Control of the Straits was the preponderant economical and political issue for the successive harbour-cities. Malacca on the Peninsula ruled the waves at one time, and was succeeded by Acheh at the extreme North point of Sumatra. The earliest known rulers of the Straits were the kings of Srivijaya, who seem to have had their basis in Palembang and Jambi, midway between present day Singapore and Jakarta. Buginese adventurers from Makassar in Sulawesi/Celebes exercised their power from the island of Riau near Singapore. The Peninsula's chief historiographical work, the *Sĕjarah Mĕlayu*, makes the Malacca dynasty come from Palembang, and the inhabitants of Negeri Sembilan actually originate from the Padang Highlands on Sumatra's west coast. True, Singapore has been important for more than a century, but this British settlement with its numerous Chinese immigrants was completely marginal as regards the Malay population of the Peninsula. True, for some decades British power has made itself increasingly felt, and Indians and Chinese have contributed considerably to the total population of the Peninsula and have created problems unknown in the Republic of Indonesia. The twentieth-century development of the Malay Peninsula certainly deserves a chapter apart in the book of Indonesia's development, but the preceding ten centuries of the more or less known past can best be dealt with together with Sumatra and the rest of Indonesia, culturally, politically, and perhaps economically.

On the one hand the Hindu vestiges in the Peninsula are brought into relief by being dealt with together with those in Sumatra and Java; on the other hand the proto-Malays of Sumatra can better be adequately dealt with when envisaged together with their more numerous brethren of the Peninsula, where they still form a not-to-be-neglected percentage of the population.

The boundaries with Thailand/Siam in the extreme North-West seem to have been in a continuous state of change; geography does not help here, but the contestable regions are so small in comparison with the whole area, so relatively few people and interests are involved, that this circumstance is not detrimental to the conception 'Indonesia'. Acheh's language has peculiarities in common with Cham, but this interesting feature is also no hindrance at all.

Somewhere in the extreme South-East a line of racial and cultural demarcation must be drawn, the line of political demarcation if not yet *sub judice*, is a point of bitter contest.

The Indonesian standard has the Old Javanese inscription: *Bhinneka tunggal ika*, i.e. 'One notwithstanding differences'. Actually nearly all the 250 or more languages of Indonesia belong to the same family, and for many Indonesians it is no unsurmountable difficulty to acquire a certain degree of mastery over the new official language, which is based on Malay.

But it must be learned, and experience has taught that rural upheaval, the extirpation of illiteracy and the learning of the unifying language cannot be combined. In the next paragraph but one we will revert to this new official language, Bahasa Indonesia, the language for Indonesia.

Small islands like Bali and Lombok, which we cross by car in an hour or two, are practically speaking linguistic entities, even if recent investigation in Lombok by Teeuw brought to light a considerable amount of dialectical diversity. 'One island, one language' is not the case with the other Lesser Sunda Islands, more to the East. Indonesia's central and principal island, Java, is inhabited in the first place by Javanese, then by Sundanese and by Madurese, populations with separate languages and their own voluminous literature. Especially in the towns, moreover, one has to know bazaar-Malay, and Bahasa Indonesia for all contacts with the administration. Sumatra, apart from the small adjacent islands, is divided into some ten language-areas. Kalimantan/Borneo and Sulawesi/Celebes are the home of numerous languages.

These numerous languages, however, are not to be thought of as causing so many watertight compartments. To begin with numberless people have learned to help themselves by mastering neighbouring languages, even where no school education helped them and where often they even got no education at all along standard lines. Moreover trade and shipping throughout the Indonesian archipelago, perhaps since the days of Sri Vijaya, has largely used bazaar-Malay. This language was learned by the immigrating Chinese in their wake, and Malay was the administrative language for the lower levels of the former Dutch administration. It also gained popularity in those regions where the indigenous languages, in order to express the difference in birth, age, rank of the persons involved, use different words in speaking and in writing. Malay practically ignores these differentiations and proved to be a convenient auxiliary. Missionaries, apart from their excellent and indispensable work in a number of smaller languages, also helped in the propagation of Malay. The nationalist movement gave it a much wider horizon, for in the course of the last decades youth enriched it with all those terms which were not available in the languages of the Muslim merchants, who were still rather medieval in their outlook. Since the majority of nationalist leaders had visited Dutch schools, the modern Malay as developed in the Republic of Indonesia uses numerous Dutch words and some Dutch constructions—just as modern Malay in the Peninsula is strongly influenced by English. Bahasa Indonesia, though energetically propagated for good reasons, will be, at least during the next few decades, rather the language *for* Indonesia than the language *of* Indonesia.

Of more consequence perhaps are the great differences in education. Nearly a thousand years ago a Javanese king ordered that a précis should be made of the eighteen books of the Sanskrit Mahābhārata, and from the parts which have reached us we may conclude that at the Javanese court this straightforward epic material was well understood. A considerable amount of Sanskrit literature, mainly philosophical and theological treatises, was in those days translated and adapted into Old Javanese. Among the texts there was one which has just been introduced as a set book for the London University B.A. degree in Sanskrit, the Bhaṭṭikāvya, which in India also is still a standard text. On the one hand this formal Sanskrit was studied, understood, and adapted in Old Javanese poetry, as much as ten centuries ago, and the larger Javanese courts have continued to favour the arts ever since. On the other hand, the illiteracy of the population, even of that of Java and especially of the Principalities, was as bad as in so many other Asian countries, whether colonial or independent.

To take another example—Marco Polo tells us about Islam in Acheh, and from Snouck Hurgronje in his 'Mekka' and his 'The Achehnese' we learn how firm the roots of Islam are in this country and how much learning existed here. But more to the East, in Lombok, which in the seventeenth and eighteenth centuries appears to have been Javanized and Islamized to a considerable extent, Islam has by no means yet penetrated so deeply. Bousquet and Goris have written most enlightening articles on this subject. In 1941 I visited the village of Bayan where the population did not yet understand that the Friday service had to be attended by the community in the mosque: the villagers had it done for them by a functionary, who in this way proved to be rather the heir of the pre-Muslim village priest and witch-doctor than an imām.

I think I can take another example from the same island, the investigation of the culture of which was entrusted to me a few years before the war. The Sasak population of Lombok has been Muslim since the Javanese days, and a century and a half of Balinese colonization (1744–1894) has not converted it to Balinese Hinduism. Pre-Hindu and Pre-Muslim was the conception that the water from the lake on the slope of Mount Rinjani was the fertilizing power for Sasak agriculture, on which their welfare and even their life depended. Self-evidently the ruling king, being the intermediary power between Destiny and mankind, had to bring the propitiatory offerings. The Balinese kings had no objection to performing this role, and when the Dutch took over in 1894 these offerings became part of their responsibility. They gave some trouble in the Dutch Lower House about 1900, when an ultra-Protestant cabinet was in power (Holland's political life was and is still largely organized along religious lines), but I was a witness in 1941 to the fact that the Dutch Government still maintained the ceremony, continuing the tradition that the *de facto* Government is the mediator between Heavenly Powers and frail mankind. This conception, however, is nowadays losing its foothold in Indonesia.

It will not be necessary to dwell upon that remarkable enclave in the world of Islam, the matrilineal Menangkabau community (about which De Jong recently wrote a Leiden thesis in English), which has maintained itself for the centuries with great tenacity; but when discussing the diversity of the Indonesian population, this people, exceptional in the world of Islam, should be mentioned in passing.

It is easy enough to point to fundamental differences between the islands and populations of Indonesia, but the major question is whether they can still be envisaged as a workable entity. The arguments in favour are the common origin of the Indonesians in Indo-China, the common pattern of languages and other cultural manifestations, the considerable amount of Indian influence which they gradually absorbed, and their common subordination to the North-European Protestant colonizing Powers. Much remains to be investigated; Raffles, over a century ago, drew attention to Java's Hindu past, but knowledge about that of Sumatra and the Peninsula only dates from the last few decades. Bali still shows its Hinduism on the surface, in Java it is permeated and overgrown with Islam, elsewhere it is scarcely recognizable or has never even existed. Islam was in the process of spreading in Marco Polo's days; it expanded with the establishment of centres of trade and power, and is still spreading, both in breadth and in depth. Western power and education, initially confined to pinpoints in Java and the Spice Islands, first penetrated into Java, mainly during the nineteenth century in the 'outer territories', but only in the twentieth century with its new possibilities did it gain definite influence throughout Indonesia. Neither the colonial period, nor Islam nor previous Indian contacts by themselves are perhaps strong enough to form an entity, but taken together with the common continental heritage of prehistoric times they have formed that entity-in-diversity of which the Indonesian Republic is proud, which exists at the present day, and which may perhaps persist, provided entity and diversity are well balanced in practical politics as well as in historical speculations.

'South East Asia and the Islands' is not so very large in comparison with Africa; but its extent is roughly that of India. It falls clearly into two parts: the continental countries—Burma, Thailand/Siam, and Vietnam with their subdivisions—and Indonesia. The latter has the widest boundaries, the largest population, and as yet perhaps the strongest solidarity, in common blood and culture as well as in common development.

2. The second question to be dealt with is this: why the words 'historiography' and even 'history' have been avoided, and 'past' has been used instead? We are of the opinion that 'historiography'—at least in the Indonesian field—is at present very unsatisfactory and disproportionate, and consequently the term should only be used with the utmost care. But a wealth of material exists and is easily available from which an immense

amount of knowledge can be derived for the drawing of a picture of the past in Indonesia.

The 'historiography' of the principal Indonesian peoples has already been dealt with in several papers: that of the Javanese by Berg, of the Buginese and Makassarese by Noorduyn, that of the Malays by Winstedt. Though the Balinese have produced a considerable amount of historiography, generally concerning the rise and fall of their petty kingdoms, no special reason was felt to deal with them separately in connection with the congress. Attention might have been drawn to an early work by Snouck Hurgronje's most brilliant Indonesian pupil Husein Djajadiningrat's 'Critical Survey of Dates concerning the History of the Achehnese Sultanate in so far as found in Malay Works', but though the Achehnese field had not yet been covered, the Malay historiography has. The same author's 'Critical View of the Sejarah Banten' (West Java) has helped Berg to develop his conception of Javanese historiography, and in so far has been incorporated. For such a large archipelago, so many monuments of the past, and such a numerous population, the harvest is far from abundant; most parts are not covered at all, and, where historiography exists, it only rarely dates from before the Muslim period. One would be completely at a loss for a picture of the past if one had to confine oneself to Indonesian 'historiography'.

Coolhaas and De Graaf devoted their papers to the Dutch historiography on Indonesia, where the British, the Danes and the Portuguese were also active. Though the archives still contain much material as yet unpublished, the printed treatises on the activities of the merchants and conquerors already by far outnumber the indigenous historiography. Even their seventeenth- and eighteenth-century Dutch is more intelligible than the Indonesian languages, which frequently offer philological difficulties, most of all because the European writings generally call a spade a spade. The danger inherent in using these Dutch materials is their often one-sided character, caused by the authors' ignorance of Indonesian languages, beliefs, institutions, motives, etc. Not every historian had the wisdom to call his book: 'Rise of the Dutch Power', or 'Colonial History'; too many books appeared with the title 'History of the Netherlands East Indies', in which Dutch actors stood in the foreground and Indonesians in the background. Historiography of this type should be classed under some limited heading such as 'Activities of the Dutch (British, etc.) overseas'; seen from this point of view Dutch writings are a most important source of information on Indonesia's past. It appears that the Dutch were not the only colonial power who tended to draw such a distorted picture, and thereby to make a scientific and a politic mistake at the same time. In their exculpation it must be recognized that the drawing of the real picture is an immense task of great difficulty.

We must explain why the term 'history' has been avoided before we can give content to the term 'past'. *The History of Sumatra* by Marsden, in its time was a useful encyclopaedic handbook concerning everything known about Sumatra, with precious little history in it, for the simple reason that a century and a half ago the history of Sumatra was still more inadequately known than it is today. *The History of Java* by Raffles, written some years later, was in its day the remarkable achievement of a brilliant mind; it endeavoured to trace Java's history, but one hesitates to decide whether this was Javanese or European historiography. The book deals with various topics unconnected with history. These books give no history in the present-day sense of the word, partly because this was as yet unknown to the authors, partly also because the available material did not admit it (and still does not admit it). *A History of Malay Literature* by Winstedt (1940) is an excellent book, but it deals with genres more than with periods, again for the simple reason that through the lack of dates this systematic division was the only workable one. A history of, say, English literature looks quite different. In the Old Javanese field Krom felt himself in a position to write his *Hindu-Javanese History*, but it looks as if, for the time being, this will remain the exception in the Indonesian field. Students will be aware that his book on the monuments is called *Introduction to Hindu-Javanese Art*, not 'History of idem'. A considerable number of facts are known, but their chronology is so uncertain that it seems wiser not to raise expectations by using the word 'history' and to content ourselves with the more modest term of 'past'.

We must be well aware of the fact that perhaps the richest single mine of information on Java's past, and even on her history, is the Nāgara-krĕtâgama. It describes the royal capital, but in such lofty terms that they awakened too great expectations in Maclaine Pont, who tried to rediscover its site near Trawulan (Modjokerto). When in his posthumous book, *The Kraton of Majapahit*, Stutterheim set himself the same task, he took a considerably broader basis and came to a much more modest and acceptable result. He took into account the necessarily laudatory character of the *Nāgarakrĕtâgama*, compared the present Javanese kratons of Jogjakarta and Surakarta, and used what information he could get concerning the demolished puri of Klungkung, Bali, since a Balinese puri strove to be a faithful replica of its Javanese model of Majapahit.

The divine character of kingship in S.E. Asia becomes gradually clearer, but additional evidence is always welcome. In connection with this subject a piece of information is to be found in the *Arjunavivāha*, another court poem in Indian metres like the *Nāgarakrĕtâgama*, but some three centuries older. Berg has shown not only that the poem was composed during king Erlanggha's reign, but also that it was definitely written in his honour, and that the king in his exploits was represented as equal to the divine hero Arjuna. Now Arjuna at the moment of his glory, of his temporary kingship over the whole universe, was clad in a multi-coloured garment. Such a garment was worn at state ceremonies in the Principalities by several rulers until the beginning of this century, and, whether still understood or not, continued to embody the old conception of universal kingship.

In the above-mentioned case, necessarily told too briefly, a court poem contributed to our understanding of Old Javanese kingship. Next a case will be mentioned, where the *Sĕjarah Mĕlayu*, the chronicle of Malacca, sheds light on the *Babad Buleleng*, the chronicle (although, again, without dates and years) of a tiny kingdom occupying most of the north coast of Bali. We learn there in a very laconic statement that Panji Sakti, the founder of the dynasty, shortly after having murdered the local ruler and having assumed independent power, had a gong (*gamĕlan*, orchestra) made for his use. In a country where nowadays a thousand orchestras are estimated to exist to a population of not so much more than a million, this statement only acquires significance if we are aware of the fact that Malacca considered a full orchestra as a prerogative of the Malaccan overlord, and smaller orchestras as the due of the vassal kings. The possession of an orchestra was the attribute of royalty, perhaps according to a pre-Hindu conception. Therefore it is all the more interesting to read subsequently in our chronicle that Panji Sakti imported an elephant, the royal conveyance according to Indian ideas.

Whether one studies the Java war of a century and a quarter ago, or the recent Japanese invasion, one will find the presence of expectations of the Messiah still persisting among the Javanese population. Dipánĕgrá and other 'insurgents' were led by an unshakable belief in the *pralambangs* (prophecies) ascribed to the Old Javanese king Jayabhaya. Drewes has studied this aspect of mysticism and its written sources in his thesis on 'Three Javanese gurus, their doctrines, preaching and expectations from future'. The very recent thesis by Kalma deals with similar religious phenomena in West-Irian/New Guinea, on the fringe of or just outside the Indonesian world, but this belief in its depth and breadth in Indonesia and its significance in known historical events has not yet been dealt with exhaustively.

The famous Chandi Bàràbudur in Middle Java is a historical monument of the Buddhist period. Economists rightly test their powers in attempting to make an estimate of the labour involved in constructing it, or of the density of population postulated for such a work. Sociologists who compute the numbers of present-day Indonesians who travel towards their holy places of pilgrimage make guesses concerning its importance in Java's past. Historians moreover wish to know whether Hīnayāna or Mahāyāna Buddhism was involved in the construction of the stūpa with its many statues and miles of panels. The iconography of Greater India has helped here; the texts could be read partly from still existing Indian sources, e.g. the *Lalita-vistara*, partly from a Greater-Indian source, the *Gandavyuha*, forgotten in India, found in Nepal by the late Sylvain Lévi, and recognized as throwing much light on the reliefs of Bàràbudur on the occasion of his visiting the monument. The late Dr. Stutterheim in his book *Chandi Bàràbudur, its name, form and meaning*, endeavouring to explain the structure of the monument, found his material in the Old Javanese mahāyānistic treatise *Sang Hyang Kamahāyānikan*. Paul Mus in his enormous but still incomplete book tapped additional Buddhist literary sources.

Summing up the last four paragraphs we see that the divine character of Javanese kingship found support in a literary text; a Malay chronicle shed light upon the explanation of a Balinese one; for the Messianic expectations we find material in literature; the meaning of the great monuments finds elucidation in written treatises.

It is not sufficiently known that literature in Indonesian languages numbers thousands of MSS. The catalogues, lists, short descriptions of contents, etc., put together fill a shelf of at least one yard. In some ten different languages has developed a many-sided literature, taken here not only as belles-lettres but as anything which has been confided to script on perishable material such as palm-leaf and paper. It includes legislation and moral precepts, geography, astrology and physics, divination, divine knowledge and metaphysics, grammar, lexicography and metrics, and many more such subjects.

Thanks to missionaries, civil servants and other interested persons several dozens of 'lesser languages' and cultures are documented to a certain extent. Nowadays we are less bold than our predecessors a century ago in deriving complete cosmologies and pantheons from folk tales and litanies. During the last decades, apart from the well-known work of Kruyt and Adriani, long litanies have been noted down by or for Steinhart in Nias, and by Scharer and Dunselman in Kalimantan/Borneo, amongst peoples who knew no writing or were of the first generation to have learned it. The student of pre-Western and pre-Indian culture in Indonesia, let us cautiously say Dongson, finds here a rich mine of records of the past, besides his material remains.

We have at our disposal a few hundred Javanese inscriptions and a few hundred Balinese ones; they are presumably the subject of De Casparis' paper. Here it should only be mentioned that the not too numerous stone-inscriptions generally appertain to historiography, in that they commemorate an event of dynastic interest and were therefore erected and considered important for the population. The more numerous copper-plates, found in the ground, are generally contracts, judge's decisions, freedoms given by the ruler. In the preamble they may contain particulars of the king's motives, and so become real sources of information for us, extremely useful for historiography and even a direct historical source, but they were intended as legal or notarial documents. Not only does the script and language of these inscriptions offer difficulties, but the contents often provide more problems than they solve. The old indigenous law-books (not all of which have been published yet) shed some light here, as do the numerous printed collections on customary law throughout the archipelago (Adatrechtbundels).

As for objects, it will perhaps be sufficient to remember the kris for the near past, the kettledrum for the more distant past (and the vast subject of textiles of both periods). These objects are undated, and will not be of help to reconstruct 'history', but their existence and function shed some light on a country's past. Their decorative motifs help us to understand religious conceptions. Ceramics, a field in itself, can contribute to a picture of the past, since great frequency of potsherds may testify to a former well-populated settlement of some wealth. And Chinese porcelain in many cases can be dated fairly precisely, or at any rate offer a date *post quem*.

These few remarks and examples only emphasize the point that Indonesian 'historiography' is bound to be unsatisfactory for the reconstruction of what we nowadays call 'history', but such a large number of documents and diverse objects has been collected that—as far as material is concerned—by making full use of them a fairly coherent picture of several peoples of Indonesia in their past can be drawn.

3. *Why should Studies be said to be in a Critical Stage?*

Three reasons of a rather disconnected character, which may be briefly formulated here as follows:

  (*a*) the new demands made on historiography;
  (*b*) the new outlook on historiography;
  (*c*) Indonesia's preoccupation with the future.

(*a*) In order to be up-to-date, a good historian must nowadays necessarily be at home in more fields than his predecessor of one or two generations back. He must have an open eye for the economic causes which so often underlie diplomatic steps and formal wars, not to mention migrations. He must moreover have absorbed the rudiments of sociology and, especially in underdeveloped countries, of social anthropology. The premature deaths of Van Leur and Schrieke, before they could make known the full amount of their knowledge and opinions in books and in teaching, is felt all the more seriously since their method was scarcely represented at all.

(*b*) De Casparis and De Graaf, the latter before and the former after the war, pointed out that historical studies in the Indonesian field were strongly centred on Europe, instead of being centred on the Indonesian people and soil, and on their beliefs, words, and deeds. In politics the Westerners at the top gradually wrought complete changes, which only in the course of time more or less influenced the lower levels of society. In the field of economics the impact was considerable; but an agrarian population remained agrarian, as in China or Thailand. One per cent became Christian, but it is of more importance that most people now in power have had a Western education and are revolutionizing their country mainly according to Western ideas and slogans. Up to a few decades ago Western religion, law, language, literature, and arts had scarcely touched more than a fringe of the population. In view of the long past of Indonesia as well as of the paucity of contact and influence of Europeans it seems dangerous to overestimate European influence before the twentieth century. Undoubtedly much useful work remains to be done by delving into European archives, but for a real understanding of Indonesia's past the attention must mainly be directed towards the manifold activities of the Indonesians themselves, notwithstanding the inherent difficulties of such a study.

Berg has for twenty years been examining Javanese literature in great detail. He finds evidence which has escaped his predecessors, reads behind the lines, ventures explanations of stories which hitherto either escaped efforts at explanation or even went by unnoticed. His method of interpretation is new and daring; if found sound it revolutionizes not only the traditional picture of Javanese history, but also that of Malaya, and may be expected to be of importance even for larger areas. Until recently an acknowledged method of research was one of comparison of Asian and European (*in casu*: Javanese and Dutch) records concerning certain happenings and periods. In case of concordance, the better; in case of discordance, the worse for the Javanese text, which was discarded and generally more or less disqualified. Now Berg is convinced that the Javanese author had his reasons for his method of presenting and 'misrepresenting' facts. The whole Javanese mental outlook is different and makes him ignore or stress matters in a method entirely different from ours. He is constantly writing and rewriting a state-myth, according to Berg's formula.

Berg's theories are not yet generally accepted and have recently met with controversy; it could scarcely be expected that all his results and the intricate reasoning by which he has obtained them would be universally approved of. But his conception of the state myth applies remarkably well to the *Salasilah Kutai* (Salasilah is Arabic and means 'chain', i.e. of reigning princes; Kutai is situated at a great river near the east coast of Kalimantan/Borneo, not far from the present oil-refinery Balik Papan). This Malay text of moderate size (150 pp. print) was first partially published, together with a summary, by Mees, and quite recently a posthumous commentary of W. Kern was published. The style of narrating, it may be said in passing, reminds us repeatedly of that of the rhapsodical Malay romances, the *pĕnglipur-lara* stories, and this in turn reminds us of the incantations of the village medicine-man. The contents of the beginning of the *Salasilah* were, until the war, consulted by the Master of Ceremonies, for here he found the description which he needed for the court-ceremony of installation. At one time these ceremonies must have been fixed and instituted, prescribed for the future and ascribed to the mythological past: the work is, in fact, a state-myth.

And the description of how the ruler of Kutai asks Majapahit to be taught its ceremonial is strongly reminiscent of the numerous literary works dealing with other aerial voyages by august travellers in order to get an initiation into the highest wisdom. This is again probably state-myth.

In Majapahit, so the *Salasilah* relates, the king has four queens, ranking as *Paramesvari, Mahadevi, Matuh*, and *Paduka Liku*—just as we find in the Panji-romances. This spiritual export-product from Java conquered the Malay coasts as well as Bali, and it will be difficult ever to decide whether this system of four unequal queens once really existed and has been propagated in those romances, or whether the romances helped in a number of cases to suggest that this institution ought to have existed. But here the description is, only to be evaluated rightly by that investigator of the past who is conversant with the Panji-myth.

The *Salasilah Kutai* has been commented upon in the philological sense, but the commentary on its meaning has still largely to be written, by a social anthropologist or a student of the phenomenology of religion, and only then a historian can use it for a picture of the past. That is the reason why so much old work must be reconsidered and partially redone; the conception of Indonesian historiography is in a latent crisis.

(*c*) Indonesia's preoccupation with the future. Perhaps the best method of explaining this difficulty is by comparison with (British) India. Hinduism, since the Moghul invasion, maintained itself in an antithetical position; it was not too much confronted by Europeanism. Hinduism in Indonesia was gradually superseded by Islam, and whatever culture existed in Indonesia, it was, at least in the twentieth century, confronted with ten times as much Europeanism as was Indian Hinduism, since the Dutch governmental system used ten times as many Europeans per million of Asians as did the British in India. The Nationalist movement in the twenties and non-co-operation in the thirties were not so extensive or so highly developed in Indonesia as in India, but the thirties were followed by the forties. More than three years of intense Japanese propaganda, and in their wake the struggle for independence, military actions, guerilla war, etc., for more than four years had disastrous results in many respects. The Indonesian state-machinery needs every capable man available to run the present affairs and prepare a brighter future. Moreover, by now for some thirty years, the past has been depicted as one long period of 360 years full of oppression and frustration, preceded by the glorious Hindu era. One should notice that this conception has taken root: not only Bhinneka Tunggal Ika and the five guiding state principles, the Pancha-sila, are clad in Old Javanese wordings, but in the names of guerilla-troops, regiments, etc., repeated reminiscencies of the pre-Muslim past can be found (e.g. barracks is *asrama*).

Bambang Utomo's paper stated that no historical writing at all is pursued now in Indonesia, no investigation of the past. This would be disastrous from our point of view, since the Dutch contribution is bound to shrivel. *Koloniaal Tijdschrift* and *Koloniale Studien* have ceased to be published; so has DJAWA and practically TBG; they are not yet replaced by Indonesian counterparts or by the new Dutch quarterly *Indonesië*.

However, some hopeful signs can be seen. The Archaeological Service, *Dinas* (Dutch 'dienst' survey) *Purbakala* surmounts its difficulties and works on, and at grammar school level a not negligible amount of Old Javanese is being taught. Every contribution to knowledge in the field of Java's past is important, and after the present slump something may be expected from the coming generation. Moreover, as soon as a somewhat forced unity is no longer felt so necessary against foreign enemies, there will be more opportunity for local patriotism and nationalism, less need for propaganda and information. But with the gradual disappearance of the Dutch efforts in the field of history and the expected, but scarcely visible, Indonesian contributions, one is reminded of the Javanese saying concerning the unorthodoxy of their adherence to Islam: *Budanipun sampun ichal, agamenipun dereng wontĕn* (the Hindu-beliefs have gone, Islam has not yet come).

In this critical stage something should be done.

25. THE APPLICATION OF A SOUTH EAST ASIA-CENTRIC CONCEPTION OF HISTORY TO MAINLAND SOUTH EAST ASIA

A. W. MACDONALD

Attaché de Recherches au Centre National de la Recherche Scientifique, Paris

Professor D. G. E. Hall in his recent work, *A History of South East Asia*, remarks that European scholars concerned with these regions feel today that their previous approach to their subject 'has been too much influenced by certain preoccupations inherent in their own training and outlook' (pp. vi–vii). He quotes with approval M. de Casparis' criticism of a 'Europe-centric' approach to these studies and notes that 'Indian writers who, largely through the work of the French and the Dutch have come to discover Greater India may be accused of an India-centric approach.' Professor Hall himself has sought 'first and foremost to present South East Asia historically as an area worthy of consideration in its own right, and not merely when brought into contact with China, India or the West'. I do not intend to discuss here the extent to which Professor Hall has succeeded in his task.[1] His book, despite its popular character, marks a date in our studies inasmuch as it is the first full-scale History of South East Asia in the English language. Nor shall I venture into the Indonesian field where authorities such as MM. Berg and Bosch still come into conflict. My intention is rather to discuss in general terms the methodological implications of the point raised by Professor Hall insofar as the field of Mainland South East Asian studies is concerned.

Those interested in the civilization of China, like those interested in present-day tribal cosmologies, know that self-centred conceptions of history are as common in the Far East as in the West and are certainly as ancient as these latter. Cultural superiority in all latitudes is defined primarily by disparaging comparisons with the habits of each civilization's barbarians. But the first point to be made is that the kind of overall vision of South East Asian history implicit in Professor Hall's book is itself a product of Western thinking, although not entirely based on results achieved by Western scholars. The scope of the book is even wider than that of M. Coedès who, concerned primarily with the *Etats hindouisés*, used more of his sources at first-hand but could leave out of account those regions of South East Asia which have come within the orbit of Chinese civilization or, for one reason or another, have been little touched by

---

[1] I must, however, note that Professor Hall has been accused in turn of an 'Anglo-centric' approach to his material by F. N. Trager in his review in the *Far Eastern Quarterly*.

Indian influences. It is interesting to note that Professor Hall, in his own words 'came to realise the need for some such book' as his 'through contacts with students and teachers in South East Asia'. In fact there exists no book by a South East Asian national, either in a local or a foreign language, which covers the field. This fact is obviously not the consequence of a lack of general education among South East Asians. But without taking into account the admitted competence of, for instance, many other Chinese and Vietnamese *lettrés,* one could cite the recent work of M. Le Thanh Khoi, *Vietnam, Histoire et Civilisation, I* (Paris, 1955), as an indication that historical thinking in these regions is, at the present day, primarily nationalist. There are social, political, and economic reasons in plenty to explain this state of affairs, and my remark is in no way intended as a criticism of what is in many respects a very able, useful, and above all well-written, book.

In the West we have certainly tended to write South East Asian history as we see our own. Perhaps I should say as we used to see our own. For we are still, in the South East Asian field, concerned primarily with the correct determination of genealogies in the ruling families, with the life of the court and the palace, the tenure of office and the policies of important ministers of state, the aesthetic or museum value of religious architecture and other works of art, the big battles, etc.[2] The structure of society, of the very many different societies in the past and present of South East Asia, has not yet been analysed. In this respect one must deplore the fact that the second volume of J. Auboyer, R. Grousset et J. Buhot, *L'Asie orientale des origines au XVe siècle* (Paris, 1941), has not been published. This second volume, as announced by Grousset in his Preface to the first volume, was to have studied 'the evolution of the society, the institutions and the beliefs of the peoples of Eastern Asia'. Henri Maspero died in a concentration camp in the last war, and M. P. Mus, his co-author in the project, has now other preoccupations and obligations, and has given up any idea of finishing the book. Archaeological interest having been centred mainly up to now on town-sites, we know deplorably little about life in the past of South East Asia, outside of its towns and large villages. And until we know more of present-day conditions in the country-areas all serious social or economic analysis, of mainland South East Asia as a whole, seems frankly impossible. It goes without saying that in the West only those who have written, whether on manuscript, fibre, wood, or stone, or have erected durable monuments, occupy an important place in the history books. Wide therefore as the scope of Professor Hall's book may seem to be, it still to all practical purposes leaves out of account considerable groups of population which have undoubtedly played an important role in the

---

[2] This viewpoint is naturally 'conditioned' to a certain extent by the present state of our sources.

succession of events in South East Asia for they still live and have their be-ing there today. Because, in the past, they have not made use of solid build-ing materials nor employed writing to extol their exploits or explain their political and religious systems, we tend to ignore their history. But the fact that it is very difficult for us to get to know their history does not mean that they have none. For instance, the historical role of the Karens, Kachins, Chins, Nagas, Kukis, and other groups of more or less illiterate inhabitants of North Burma was, during the 1939–45 war, of considerable importance. It is not mere supposition to state that the role of the mountain-dwellers in the past history of these regions has been underestimated. In this respect, it is encouraging to note that both M. Le Thanh Khoi and M. J. Chesneaux, in his book *Contribution à l'Histoire de la nation viet-namienne* (Paris, 1955) stress the importance of the part played by various mountain-groups at various stages in Vietnamese history. Of course we can only judge the importance of the mountaineers' activities by what we can infer from what others have written about them. And by 'others' in this context one almost always means the authors of Chinese texts. In this respect I may say that the *Notes* to the edition of the text of Marco Polo which Pelliot published in conjunction with Professor A. C. Moule shortly before the war are going to be published in English in Paris. I have so far read three or four hundred pages before they go to press. They take the form of an index arranged alphabetically. I have not yet got beyond the letter C, but can assure all interested that they represent, as one would expect, a capital contribution to our subject and, what is important in the present context, fully exploit the Chinese sources. To give only one example the note s.v. Cowry is seventy typewritten pages in length.

The Western overall historical perspective is, I have suggested, bound to remain incomplete; and Easterners have not yet felt the necessity of adopting it in their own writings. This is scarcely surprising. For South East Asia has little or no cultural unity. If the various Indian and Chinese politico-religious systems brought in from outside have given to far-flung regions a semblance of unity in techniques of worship and political organization, the theories advanced by Western scholars to explain the cultural formation of South East Asia, based as they are on the isolation of certain cultural factors such as language, tool-forms, folklore, methods of cultivation, etc., are remarkable for their ingeniousness rather than their solidity and are far from providing us with the picture of a unique culture-pattern. There are undoubted similarities in the ways of living of the many present-day Indonesian groups throughout the area but these groups are not yet sufficiently well known to enable us to generalize on the matter. Once the conclusions of the research-work undertaken by M. G. Condominas since 1948 among certain groups of Moi will have become public we shall have a better knowledge of some of the Indonesian facts.[3]

Anthropological research, which furnishes an indispensable complement to our historical sources has been considerably impeded by the political situation since 1939, and before that date it was never the strong point of the École Française d'Extrême-Orient's multiple activities. However, perhaps the most serious attempt to sketch the outlines of a certain cultural unity in South East Asia, has been made by a man who, although he has done several months field-work among the Chams, is primarily a philologist. I refer to the article of M. P. Mus, *L'Inde vue de l'Est* (Hanoi, 1934). This article, which is not mentioned in Professor Hall's book, has never to my knowledge been criticized by an anthropologist although it has been quoted extensively by M. H. G. Quaritch Wales in *The Making of Greater India* (London, 1951). M. Mus writes: 'Partout oú des conditions de navigabilité établissent l'unité des échanges, il n'est point paradoxal d'attendre une unité de culture, et évoquer une religion de l'aire des Moussons sera plus raisonnable que de parler de religion indienne, ou chinoise, antérieurement aux civilisations qui devaient donner un sens à ces mots. Si l'étude des rituels saisonniers, à laquelle resterent attachés les noms de M. Przyluski et de M. Granet tient à ce qu'elle promet, c'est même proprement d'une religion des Moussons qu'il nous faudra parler un jour.' We must await the work of the successors of Przyluski and Granet before judging the results achieved on the basis of M. Mus' hypothesis. The ritual activities of the mountain groups, and the economic aspects of these rituals will have to be considered much more seriously than they have been in the past. For we can no longer subscribe to the view that the only civilized areas worthy of attention are the plains and the coastal regions. Since we are concerned with various kinds of centrism I will limit myself here to putting the question: 'If one were to write an article entitled "China seen from the South" would one employ the same materials as M. Mus employed in his analysis?'

To say that historians, given their preoccupation with the written word and the durable monument, cannot hope to dominate the entire South East Asian field, is only to state part of the problem. For can they ever really hope to tell us what it meant to be an ancient South East Asian? Some lines of M. C. Lévi-Strauss, which refer to one particular culture, that of ancient Greece, seem to me in this respect worth quoting: 'Ce que nous savons aujourd'hui,' he writes, 'et ce qu'ignoraient encore les hommes du XVIIe siècle (qui pourtant possédaient déjà les pièces du precès) c'est qu'en dépit des monuments, des statues et des livres, nous ne saurons vraiment jamais ce qu'a été la culture grecque. Nous avons préservé des

---

[3] Since this was written *Nous avons mangé la forêt de la pierre-génie Gôo, Chronique de Sar Luk, village Mnong Gar* has been published in Paris (Editions Mercure de France, 1957).

membres disjoints; mais l'essentiel, c'est à dire la manière dont tout cela se combinait dans une expérience vécue ... a disparu, et disparu à jamais. Il en sera de même pour nous' (*Les Temps modernes*, Paris, March 1955, p. 1203). If it is impossible for the historian with the mass of documents at his disposal to portray what it was like to be an ancient South East Asian, it is certainly impossible for the anthropologist, with the meagre documents at his disposal, to say what it is like to be a modern mainland South East Asian.[4] Despite the willingness of anthropologists to draw up models of society in different parts of the world, none is likely to be so rash as to propose a model which englobes Mainland South East let alone South East Asia as a whole. Of course anthropologists differ amongst themselves, just as historians do, in their conception of their subject. Few professional anthropologists are in fact engaged in working over the South East Asian materials. And English social anthropologists are in disagreement with those of what one may call the Vienna school and those who publish in *Anthropos*, and, if they have been forced to read M. C. Lévi-Strauss' book *Les structures élémentaires de la parenté* (Paris, 1949), seem on the whole inclined to the view that Social Anthropology in France does not exist.

If anthropologists, of whatever persuasion they may be, are not prepared to subscribe to the view that South East Asia can stand alone as a cultural unit, can they help us to establish a hierarchy of cultures within the geographical limits of South East Asia? M. Lévi-Strauss has written: 'Nos idées sur la culture étant elles-mêmes partie intégrante d'une culture (celle de la société à laquelle nous appartenons) il nous est impossible de prendre la position d'observateurs extérieurs qui seule pouvait permettre d'établir une hiérarchie valable entre les diverses cultures; les jugements en cette matière sont nécessairement relatifs, affaire de point de vue, et tel Africain, Indien ou Océanien serait tout aussi fondé à juger sévèrement l'ignorance de la plupart d'entre nous en fait de généalogie que nous sa méconnaissance des lois de l'hérédité ou du principe d'Archimède' (*Race et civilisation*, Paris, 1952, p. 40). For him therefore all sections of South East Asian society would be equally worthy of consideration and we would not be entitled to envisage the whole area from the standpoint of any one privileged group. Marxists do not agree with this. M. Rodinson writes: 'Aucune fraction de l'humanité n'est inférieure à une autre par ses qualités humaines, par ses potentialités moyennes ... Mais il n'en est pas moins vrai que la société capitaliste est supérieure par la netteté des rapports sociaux qu'elle établit entre les classes, par le développement scientifique et technique que ses conditions de fonctionnement imposent (sauf à son stade de pourrissement) par la faculté que sa structure donne à la lutte des classes de poser (et de résoudre) la question fondamentale de l'exploita-

[4] G. C. Lévi-Strauss, *Anthropologie structurale* (Paris, 1958), pp. 357–8, and note 1 of p. 358.

tion définitive du régime des classes et de l'exploitation de l'homme par l'homme, du passage au socialisme. Cette supériorité prouvée par les faits d'une façon éclatante n'implique nullement une supériorité raciale des Européens occidentaux. Elle signifie seulement que l'Europe offrait et offrait seule, entre le XIIIe et XVIIIe siècles les conditions sociales qui permettaient la naissance de cette forme supérieure de société' (*La Pensée*, Paris, March–April 1956, pp. 9–10). If I have understood him correctly he would seem to reject the relativist viewpoint of many anthropologists, would subscribe to a thoroughgoing evolutionist conception of history and would, on the basis of Marxist criteria, be prepared to establish a hierarchy of South East Asian cultures. Whether we agree with this or not, we would do well not to ignore what Marxists think on this subject. For Marxist thinking seems destined to play an ever-increasing role in the formation of concepts of history in the minds of South East Asians themselves.[5] The interaction of Marxist thinking and local beliefs and forms of thought (in Vietnam) have been sketched out by M. P. Mus in some pages of his book, *Viet-Nam, Sociologie d'une guerre* (Paris, 1952). Marx's own work still awaits analysis by a competent anthropologist. This seems to me a pity. Because he constantly makes use of ways of thinking which from a methodological or analytical viewpoint we are accustomed to find in 'primitive' or mythological documents. The resurgence of this *pensée mythologique* in his writings, if proved, would go far to explain his appeal to those who live in what modern politicians call 'under- or insufficiently-developed areas' of the world.[6]

All this, it may be said, is not of much positive help in the problem of evaluating the multiple cultures of South East Asia. But if we can never fully free ourselves from the influences exercised on us by our own background and training, and if, despite all that anthropologists may say, we must persist in the West in subscribing to a linear, evolutionist concept of history, it is none the less possible, by studying our source materials in their particular cultural contexts to improve our understanding of their value. In any given historical situation the set of cultural influences involved varies. It is obvious that the same factors will not have to be

[5] This development is to be audited with the greatest interest; for up till recently Marxists have been noteworthy for their 'Europe-centric' attitude—M. Rodinson's phrase quoted above is fairly typical. Marxists are again usually condemned to a 'Capitalist-centric' attitude, the advantage of which is that it sometimes succeeds in hiding their essentially European preoccupations. I am not, of course, referring here to Chinese Marxists. History-writing in present-day China apart, one should note the advent of Marxist historians of India such as Walter Ruben, D. D. Kosambi, and Mohammad Habib. If Kosambi and other Marxists have to date been systematically ignored by the authors of the first five volumes the Bharatiya Vidya Bhavan's *History and Culture of the Indian People*, Professor Habib's *Introduction* to the 1952, Aligarh, reprint of Elliot and Dowson's *History of India*, vol. ii, does not seem to be known to Kosambi, at least in his *Introduction to the Study of Indian History* (Bombay, 1956).

[6] On the notion of economic inequality see recently A. Piatier, *Les inégalités du développement demographique et économique*, in l'Encyclopédie française, t. xi; *La vie internationale* (Paris, 1957), ch. 4.

considered if we study, say, the history of a group of Chinese resident in Singapore and that of the inhabitants of a Moi village. Anthropologists, of whatever persuasion they may be, are used to asking themselves: 'Why does this text, or this myth, or this ritual, say what it does say?' Historians, as Professor Hall seems to suggest, have until recently been much too inclined to take their sources, which are inevitably incomplete, at their face value. The best example of what can be achieved by a proper evaluation of source-material seems to me that provided by M. R. A. Stein in his long article, 'Le Lin-yi, sa localisation, sa contribution à la formation du Champa et ses liens avec la Chine', published in *Han-Hiue, Bulletin du Centre d'Etudes sinologiques de Pékin* (Pekin, 1947, ii, fasc. 1–3). In order to locate K'iu-sou, the early capital of the Lin-yi, one must use chapter 36 of the *Chouei-king thcou*. I think it best to give M. Stein's recapitulation of the problem in his own words:

Li Tao-yuan (the author of the text in question) était un administrateur. Il passa une partie de sa carrière chez les aborigènes de la Chine méridionale. De par ses fonctions il pouvait disposer de renseignements précis sur les routes et les distances. Mais sa description du Tonkin et de l'Annam ne repose que sur des lectures et peut-être sur quelques renseignements oraux. Il ne connaît point le pays pour y être allé. Les renseignements ainsi obtenus devaient s'inscrire dans l'image géographique du monde telle qu'il la concevait ou telle qu'elle pouvait lui apparaître sur une carte de son époque. C'est là qu'intervient sa formation de lettré. Il connaît les annales historiques officielles et notamment leurs chapitres géographiques. Mais il les subordonne dans son esprit à des vues qui lui viennent de deux cosmographies religieuses différentes. D'une part il s'inscrit notoirement et sciemment dans la ligne des folkloristes des Han et des Tsin qui relèvent du milieu taoiste. Plus que d'histoire il se soucie d'hagiographie; ce n'est pas la géographie réelle qui l'intéresse, mais la localisation des lieux-saints, des légendes, des faits miraculeux, des produits extraordinaires.

D'autre part, son premier chapitre surtout, et la mention d'Açoka au chap. 37, par exemple, montrent qu'il est versé dans la cosmographie bouddhique. La rédaction même du chapitre 36, si singulière par la suite adoptée pour l'exposé des faits, rappelle un itinéraire légendaire bouddhique tel que celui du *Smrtyopasthâna Sûtra* dont la traduction chinoise est un peu postérieure ou peut-être contemporaine de la rédaction du *Chouei-king-tchou*. Un certain nombre de thèmes legendaires sont communs au *Chouei-king-tchou*, aux itinéraires bouddhiques et aux Ancients (Ptolémée, Périple). A ces thèmes d'abord assez vaguement répartis sur une Chryse indivise, s'accolent des faits précis provenant de notes de voyageurs.

Dans un domaine restreint il en résulte pratiquement que, pour la localisation du site de K'iu-sou, il faut faire abstraction du *Sseu-houei-p'ou*, terme vague qui relève des notions géographiques générales de Li Tao-yuan sur la configuration de l'Indochine.

La légende de Ma Yuan met en scène l'érection de bornes-frontière près d'un passage difficile, point stratégique qui détermine la limite de l'expansion chinoise vers le Sud. La notion du Je-nan (au Sud du soleil) se rattache au thème du gnomon. L'analyse de ces conceptions et la discussion de la cammanderie Siang (éléphant) et de son folklore montrent que l'application de ces thèmes à des traits de la géographie réelle a déterminé un déplacement général de la nomenclature géographique vers le Sud.

Les itinéraires, l'observation du gnomon et le folklore local oblige à chercher K'iu-sou aux environs de l'actuelle ville de Badon sur le Song-Gianh, dans le Quang-Binh, Annam. Les distances données entre ce site et la capitale du Lin-yi ancien, l'observation du gnomon aussi, ainsi que le thème des colonnes de bronze et certains itinéraires, amènent à placer le noyau du Lin-yi primitif, et sa capitale, dans le pays de Hué. Le Lin-yi primitif et sa capitale, se sont formés aux dépens de Siang-lin, préfecture la plus méridionale de la commanderie Je-nan . . . (pp. 317–318).

I have quoted this passage at length because it seems to me one of the few examples of a method which would satisfy the requirements not only of Eastern and Western historians, but also those of anthropologists of any school. M. Stein is not frightened of using documents which at first sight would seem to be only remotely connected with the cultural context involved. But he only brings them into play once the context itself has been fully analysed from within. I need not insist on this author's well-known mastery of source-material.

I certainly do not for a moment think that we should abandon the study of South East Asian history, envisaged *en bloc*, 'in its own right'. We cannot have too many well-documented synthetic class-books, and I would like to see many more, written by South East Asians. For they would tell us more about what a South East Asian-centric conception of history really means. But if we are to make real scientific progress in this field, if we are to deepen our knowledge of particular problems in their cultural contexts in the light of the methods used by M. Stein, we must abandon any hope of covering the whole field. The range of knowledge required to use at first hand all the sources which concern South East Asian history is in any case beyond the ambition of the most gifted and laborious among us. The burden of a heavy teaching programme seems to leave less and less time for personal research and many a hard-pressed university lecturer, or perhaps even professor, must have said to himself: 'How on earth did Pelliot find the time to do all the work he did?' For there are other 'pre-occupations in our training and outlook' than those which result from our purely geographical position. If South East Asia was first divided between three main colonial powers, Britain, Holland, and France, it has suffered a further dismemberment at the hands of Historians, Anthropologists, Linguists, Philologists, Epigraphists, etc., which has not always resulted in a corresponding and manifest increase in our general knowledge of the whole area.[7] It is extraordinarily difficult for one man to master thoroughly in his lifetime more than one or two academic disciplines. But if we live in an age of specialization we also live in an age when seminars, when not obligatory, are fashionable. There does not therefore seem to me to be any real danger that, by concentrating more on the evaluation of our sources, and undertaking detailed research-work at first-hand, we shall (if the expression be allowed) lose sight of the wood because of the trees. After all, not only Pelliot and M. Mus, but many other of our illustrious predecessors in the field of South East Asian studies were far from being narrow specialists, although they never spent much time in seminars.[8] M. Coedès, besides being the admirable historian whose work we all admire, is an excellent epigraphist and Buddhologist, has a sound know-ledge of South East Asian architecture and ethnography, and, up till this year, taught Siamese at the Ecole des Langues orientales in Paris. Henri Maspero, a brilliant linguist and philologist, author of the admirable synthesis of ancient Chinese history, *La Chine antique* (Paris, 1927), a stickler for historical spadework if ever there was one, also gave us some of the best pages on T'ai society which we possess ('Moeurs et coutumes des populations sauvages', in *Un empire colonial francais*, t. I (Paris, 1929); 'La société et la religion des Chinois anciens et celles des T'ai modernes', and 'Les coutumes funéraires chez les T'ai noirs du Haut Tonkin', in *Les religions chinoises* (Paris, 1950), pp. 139–94 and 215–26). The multi-farious activities of Jean Przyluski, former Professor of Indochinese History and Philology at the Collège de France, an analytical bibliography of whose work I am preparing for the *Bibliographie bouddhique*, were not limited to purely historical research work.

When one looks back at the working lives of such men, one cannot help wondering whether the new Humanism which Oriental studies have sometimes been thought to represent, is not already in process of being destroyed by the requirements of the administrative machine. In the last resort, our conceptions of history and for that matter of anthropology,

[7] 'Social Anthropology' bibliographies, for instance, seldom show much knowledge of Buddhism See my note, *Buddhisme et Sociologie* in *Archives de Sociologie des Religious*, No. 2 (Paris, 1956).

[8] It could, of course, be argued that the seminar-method was practised at the Ecole pratique des Hautes Études in Paris before it developed elsewhere: the point is subsidiary.

will always derive from what we are; but what we are, I would suggest, byes not always depend on the job we hold. Rousseau was long ago worried do the kind of problems we have discussed in this paper, and what he had to say about it still seems worthy of consideration: 'I have here entered upon certain arguments, and risked some conjectures, less in the hope of solving the difficulty, than with a view to throwing some light upon it, and reducing the question to its proper form. Others may easily proceed farther on the same road, and yet no one find it very easy to get to the end. For it is by no means a light undertaking to distinguish properly between what is original and what is artificial in the actual nature of man, or to form a true idea of a state which no longer exists, perhaps never did exist, and probably never will exist; and of which it is, nevertheless, necessary to have true ideas, in order to form a proper judgment of our present state.[9] It requires, indeed, more philosophy than can be imagined to enable any one to determine exactly what precautions he ought to take, in order to make solid observations on this subject . . .' (Preface to *A Discourse on the Origin of Inequality* (Everyman edition, London, 1946), p. 155).

[9] Attention has recently been drawn to the importance of this phrase by C. Levi-Strauss in his *Tristes tropiques* (Paris, 1955), p. 423.

INDEX

Aa, P. J. B. C. Robidé van de, *De Groote Bantamsche Opstand van 1751*, 227

'Abd al-Karim al-Jīlī, *Insān al-Kāmil*, 41

'Abd al-Ra'ūf, *Daḳā'iḳ al-Ḥurūf*, 42–3

Abreu, António de, *Orcamento do Estado da India do que remde*, 173

Abū Shakūr al-Salimi, *al-Tamhīd fī bayān al-Tauḥīd*, 45

Acosta, Manuel (biographer of Xavier), 197–8

Aduarte, Diego, *Historia de la provincia del Sancto Rosario de la Orden de Predicatores en Philippinas, Iapon, y China* (1640), 203–5

Alaung Mintaragyi Ayedawpon, 57

Alberts, A., *Baud en Thorbecke, 1847–1851*, 231

Albuquerque, Braz (Afonso) de, *Comentários do grande Afonso de Albuquerque*, 190–1, 193–4

Albuquerque, Jorge de, 183

Al-Ranīrī, *Jawāhir al 'ulūm fī kashf al-ma'lūm*, 43; *Bustān al-Salātīn*, 44–5; *Nubdha fī da'wā'z-zillma'a ṣāḥibihi*, 45; *Tibyān fī ma'rifat al Adyān*, 45

Amerta, Annual Reports of the Archaeological Service of Indonesia, 153

Andrade, Francisco de, *Chrónica do muyto alto e muyto poderoso Rey destes Reinos de Portugal, Dom João o III deste Nome*, 190

Andrus, J. R., *Burmese Economic Life*, 291–2, 298

Angrok story, the, 18–22, 165

An-Nam Chi Lu'o'c (Brief History of Annam), 96

Anon., *Lembranças de cousas da India*, 173, 177

Argensola, Bartolomé Leonardo de, *Conquista de las islas Moluccas*, 202

Arjunavivāha, 17, 136, 141, 319–20

Aubaret, G., 310

Auboyer, J., Grousset, R., and Buhot, J., *L'Asie orientale des origines au XVe siècle*, 327

Aurousseau, Léonard, 306

Aymonier, Etienne, 'Chronique des anciens rois du Cambodge', 304 and n. 12

Babad Gijanti, 222

Babad Buleleng, 320

Babad Tanah Jawi, 8, 9, 16–17, 20–23, 159, 164, 166, 168–9, 222

Ba Khine, U ('Fabian'), *Political History of Burma*, 93

Balfas, M., *Tjipto Mangunkusumo*, 78

Barbosa, Duarte, 173, 175–6

Barrière, Pallu de la, 238

Barros, João de, *Décadas da Ásia*, 179–86, 188, 190, 191, 199; *Panegiricos*, 180

Barth, Auguste, and Bergaigne, Abel, *Les inscriptions sanskrites du Cambodge et du Champa*, 303

Ba Shin, U, *Myanma Thamaing*, 92

Bastin, J., *Raffles's Ideas on the Land Rent System in Java*, 233

Bayfield, G. T., *Historical Review of the Political Relations between the British Government in India and the Empire of Ava*, 262–6

Berg, C. C., 4–6, 9, 108, 136, 143–4, 154, 159–162, 164, 222–3, 318, 323–4, 326

Bernard, Fernand, *Indochine, erreurs et dangers*, 238

Bernet Kempers, A. J., 125 n. 21, 146

Bhāratayuddha, 17, 141, 168

Bhaṭṭakāvya (Sanskrit poem), 131

Bi, U (Burmese historian), 91

Bibliographical information, 3, 36; Burmese writings, 55, 58–62; writings on prehistory, 118–20; Krom's works, 125 n. 21; Sir Henry Yule's writings, 267; American writings, 299–300; Khmer MSS., 307; Vietnamese writings, 308; Buddhist, 334

Biographies of Dutch statesmen and scholars connected with Indonesia in the nineteenth century, 233–4

Bocarro, António, *Decade*, 189; *História de Maluco no tempo de Goncalo Pereira Marramaque e Sancho de Vasconcellos*, 189

Boerma, J. J. Westendorp, *Een Geestdriftig Nederlander, Johannes van den Bosch*, 232

Bogaert, A., *Historische Reizen door d'Oostersche deelen van Asia*, 214

Bontekoe, Willem Ijsbrantsz, *Journalen*, 213–214

Bor, Livinus, *Amboinse oorlogen*, 214–15

Bosch, F. D. K., 135–6, 143, 156–7, 326

Botelho, Simão, *Tombo do Estado da India*, 173, 177

Boudet, Paul, 304, 305; *Bibliographie de l'Indochine française* (with Remy Bourgeois), 307; *Iconographie historique de l'Indochine française* (with André Masson), 308

Bourgeois, Remy, 307

Braddell, Dato' Sir Roland, 'An Introduction to the Study of Ancient Times in the Malay Peninsula and the Straits of Malacca', 132, 285

Brandes, J., 123, 164–6, 170, 217, 221, 222

Bṛhatkathā, 134

Búi-quang-Tung, 304

Bukhari Jauhari (Bukhari of Johore), *Tāj al-Salātīn*, 45

Burma Historical Commission, 93

Burma Research Society, 92

Burma Translation Society, 93